The
Bookmaker's
Daughter

BOOKS BY SHIRLEY ABBOTT

Womenfolks:
Growing Up Down South

The Bookmaker's Daughter·
A Memory Unbound

The

Bookmaker's

Daughter

A MEMORY
UNBOUND

Shirley Abbott

Ticknor & Fields
New York

For information about permission to reproduce selections
from this book, write to Permissions, Ticknor & Fields,
215 Park Avenue South, New York, New York 10003.

Library of Congress Cataloging-in-Publication Data
Abbott, Shirley.
The bookmaker's daughter / by Shirley Abbott.
p.   cm.
ISBN 0-395-62944-6
1. Abbott, Shirley—Childhood and youth.   2. Abbott, Alfred
Bemont.   3. Fathers and daughters—United States.   4. Bookmakers
(Gambling)—Arkansas—Hot Springs—Family relationships.   5. Women
authors, American—New York (N.Y.)—Biography.   I. Title.
CT275.A149A3   1991   91-6619
974.7'1043'092—dc20   CIP
[B]

Printed in the United States of America

BTA 10 9 8 7 6 5 4 3 2 1

The author is grateful for permission to quote from "The Tale
of Custard the Dragon," from *Verses from 1929 On* by Ogden Nash.
Copyright © 1936 by Ogden Nash.
Reprinted by permission of Little, Brown and Company.

For June Wilson Owen, my cousin, who lived all this

in her own way and helped me understand it;

and for Katharine and Elizabeth,

the bookmaker's granddaughters

"Whether I shall turn out to be the hero of my own life or whether that station will be held by anybody else, these pages must show."

— CHARLES DICKENS, *David Copperfield*

$\mathcal{A}$CKNOWLEDGMENTS

Writers sometimes complain of the loneliness of their task, but I have had good company while writing this book, and many helping hands. I owe a great deal to the Garland County Historical Society in Hot Springs, Arkansas, especially to Inez Cline, Wendy Richter, Bobbie Jones McLane, and the late Jean Ledwidge. Heroically — and for many years without salaries or expense accounts or so much as a file cabinet to sustain them — these historians unearthed, collected, and conserved documents that would otherwise have vanished. They have shared their treasures with me generously. In 1980 they planned and carried out the Leo P. McLaughlin Oral History Project, a series of interviews with many key players in the heyday of a wide open Southern town. From this collection, now housed at the Tri-Lakes Regional Library in Hot Springs, I cite especially the testimony of Judge Vern Ledgerwood, recorded on several reels of tape. An old-line, prewar, built-to-last Southern politician, the judge was too smart to tell all, but at least he told some, hinted at the rest, and bequeathed a rich document of small-town political life. I could never have reconstructed my own memories without him.

The work of the Garland County Historical Society also

produced materials for *The American Spa* (Rose Publishing, Little Rock, 1982) by novelist Dee Brown, on which I have relied. In addition, I joyfully thank Roy Bosson for his counsel and his newspaper articles. This newsman and storyteller is a shrewd, loving observer of his hometown in the fast lane. Frankie Stroud, my father's horse book colleague, shared his recollections with me, as did Mark Palmer, another observer of criminal tendencies at the spa.

And, of course, there are my parents, who gave me gifts beyond their means, and beyond my awareness at the time.

These people are in no way responsible for my opinions or for any errors I have made.

All characters in this book are real, not imaginary. Yet any childhood memoir is to some degree fictional. As the diplomat George Kennan wrote in his own memoirs, "One moves through life like someone moving with a lantern in a dark woods. A bit of the path ahead is illuminated, and a bit of the path behind." I have tried to rekindle the lantern on my early path. My companions along that trail might have different recollections of the same events. Hoping to avoid invasions of privacy, I have changed some names in this account. The names of my family, most neighbors, local politicians, public figures, and gangsters are real.

The following gave me their time, valuable critical advice, or other forms of encouragement: Brett and Robert Averitt, Robert Cowley, Carol Edelstein, Rodney Friedman, Michael Goldman, Barbara and Spencer Klaw, Zane and Norman Kotker, Charles L. Mee, Jr., Karen Meehan, Edith Pavese, Michael Rosenthal, Alex Tomkievicz, and my agent, Lois Wallace. Katrina Kenison was the editor at the beginning, Caroline Sutton at the end. Each in her turn provided the kind of guidance every writer dreams of.

$\mathcal{C}$ONTENTS

$\mathcal{A}$ HOUSE REVISITED

THE DREAM that has inhabited my sleep for a lifetime comes in the shape of a house, the one where I was born. An odd house, a Southern house, with outsized, old-fashioned, double-sashed windows and two front doors that open to me as I sleep. I wander its cool rooms, part the fluttering organdy curtains (so white, so clean, so perfectly ironed by my mother), and look out toward the side yard. The address was 122 Alamo Street, a conjurer's formula, the one unforgettable fact of my life in a forest of forgotten addresses and phone numbers and bedroom wallpapers, the address I'll give at age ninety when they ask me my name and lead me off to some other home. Like a snail, I have carried this house on my back across the United States and Europe, which is all of the world I've seen so far. I've dreamed of it in San Diego and Seville. It will be my baggage in Shanghai and Bangkok, when I visit these cities, or the moon. I can go only so many weeks without returning to it, though the return is not always comforting.

The house was more important to me than to either my mother or my father — a gaunt and hollow-eyed house with its peaked roof and pairs of large windows designed not to insulate against the cold but to attract breezes, a respectably shabby one-story duplex that could hold two or even three families, a house that forgave much and asked little when the breadwinner wasn't winning any. If the roof leaked, the women put a pan down. If the screen sprang a hole, they patched it. In the early days there was no lawn to keep up. You could raise a garden and keep a few hens out back. If the car wouldn't run, you walked to the bus stop. If you wanted to be at your ease, the porch had a swing, shielded by trellises of American Beauty roses that bloomed red and white from March through November, fragrant, droopy-headed blossoms.

In my dreams I have paced its floors (hardwood buffed to glassiness by my mother, on her hands and knees with a soft rag and the paste wax) for a lifetime, and in my daydreams sat cross-legged on its flowered carpets (blue blossoms in my bedroom, maroon in the living room). I sometimes discover the rooms of this house cleanly stripped to the studs and roofbeams, void. Sometimes, inexplicably, they are nightmarishly choked with boxes, refuse, and debris — a state of affairs my parents would never have tolerated — so that I am unable to push my way through it all.

The king of the house, of course, is my father. I dream of him, recollect a scene: we sit together in the porch swing, and he reads to me. "This is the forest primeval. The murmuring pines and the hemlocks, bearded with moss and in garments green, indistinct in the twilight . . ." He shows me the engraving of a little girl in a kerchief and cap: "Long at her father's door Evangeline stood."

"What do you suppose *primeval* means?" he asks.

"Wicked, very wicked."

"No, untouched, uncut, in a natural state."

I wait for his eyes, neither blue nor brown, to return to the page, and then I tend to the scabs on my legs: here the track of a bramble in my flesh, there a line of chigger bites finally healed over. Fascinating. Half attending the words, the earnest meters of old fogy Longfellow, I admire my father, his handsome eyes the color of dark lakes, his smooth voice eloquent as an actor's. Nobody else's father reads poetry aloud to his child. Oh poor Evangeline of Acadie, wandering the earth to find her lover, succeeding only to have him die in her arms. How dangerous it is to love!

Or this: I am lying in bed with measles, and the new kite he has given me, blue and yellow, its tail made of satin ribbons, hangs from a nail on the wall, waiting for the day when I am well enough to go outdoors and fly it. But my father tears it from its nail, smashes it (I hear the tiny slats breaking like eggshells or icicles), stamps on it, curses me for how I drag him down. Always sick, a source of never-ending anxiety. Why don't I eat my vegetables so I don't get sick? He grabs his hat. "Where are you going?" I scream in anguish, and from behind the slamming door he replies, "Going out to make a dollar." This dream wakens me. Don't do that, Daddy, stop, you know you love me more than your very life. I know it, too, but the door slams anyway, echoing.

Other times it is snowing outdoors (it seldom snows in Arkansas), and my dreaming self is me today, a middle-aged woman smothered in blankets that I cannot throw off, with the grotesquely aged bodies of my grandparents banked around me like a pair of boulders. Occasionally I dream of love, me a grown woman in my little girl's bed with a man who loved me well, and I left him. I've dreamed of lust in that same bed, too, me and some muscular man naked together, taking each other in adultery, and I know I should feel shame, but I can't. Occasionally I dream of avarice: I inherit the house and discover that its value has increased logarithmically over these many years. All my problems are solved, I'm a lottery winner, a millionaire, no worries now, hooray.

I left that house before I turned thirteen, in fact. I have perhaps two dozen snapshots of myself as a child (taken outdoors with Mama's Kodak, as all photos then had to be taken in the sunshine). Various parts of the house show up in the background: the window to a room that I could still navigate blindfolded, the back steps with the dog dish to one side and the wringer-washer a phantom presence behind the screen door. In every picture stands the same little girl — me — skinny, not pretty but with a decidedly formed face (Roman nose, definite bones) and a head of thick curls, sometimes frizzy and disordered but more typically slicked down into glossy cylinders that bear the marks of a wet hairbrush and Mama's skillful fingers.

This girl has a way of staring into the camera. "I'm the only child, the daughter, that's my role here," she says. And something else, too, a challenging look, smart, one part arrogance to two parts uncertainty, but fiery, ready to go. For years I have said of her, "This is me," and have offered her to my two daughters, "Here's what I looked like at your age." There are other faces, too, in particular my father, who stares into the camera with that same swagger: "I am the father here." He has a thick gray crew cut, his suits are smart and tailor-made. His face gleams with impatience, with that combination of arrogance and vulnerability.

Yet just the other day, in an odd moment, I perceived a barrier between me and my past. I looked at the child, and I said to myself, "This is no longer me I am not that person." The same sense of dislocation descended on me a couple of months ago on a brief trip to Paris With an evening before me in which I might have done anything, I decided to repeat an experience rather than seek a new one — to see the Comédie-Française I walked from the Left Bank to the Right in early evening to buy a ticket (horn-rim spectacles on my soul, as always, even in Gay Paree) I'll sit in the orchestra, I thought, never mind that it costs thirty-five dollars "Certainement, madame!" In search of a café, I went around the corner and found what I sought — the line of rowdy students battling to get the cheap seats. Twenty-five years ago, almost to the day, I was one of those students, an American in Paris, speaking my ridiculous French and able to afford only the topmost balcony. *Un enfant du paradis.*

But surely I was one of them even in my silk blouse, my well-tailored traveling suit. (This may sound like nostalgia, which is merely a yearning for one's lost self. But it was something else.) Later, in my seat, among the seemly and the well-to-do, I realized that I was not myself, that I had somehow, unwittingly, crossed from the Left Bank to the Right Bank of me. And from this new vantage point I lurched up against the notion that between men and women there is no love. Only bargains, most of them carefully crafted to benefit only one side. Love is merely the scrim that hides the bargains, the delicate curtain behind which the real action takes place. Enough has been written about love. Tell me no more of love. The play I saw that night was a Molière farce — or so we call such a thing, which was in fact a savage commentary on the bartering of daughters for money.

Because the connection with the snapshot child had perversely unknotted, I discovered that I must see the house where my manners in love were taught me. Where I learned everything but the final sequence, the mystery that used to puzzle me so, that act grown-ups performed at night behind the closed door. I live far away now, in a northern city, and I travel a good deal. I often go home to visit the ailing, elderly aunt and uncle who have outlived my parents by many years. I sit in their living room (the same picture of Jesus, the same rag rug, the same platform rockers) and hold their trembly hands, mindful of how honored a guest I am, for they turn off the television set to talk with me. But this time, instead of simply kissing them goodbye and heading for the airport, I visited 122 Alamo. It had passed out of my parents' hands when I was still a child. I was ready for a reunion.

I borrowed my cousin's car — a heavy, authoritative black Lincoln, a rolling fortress well suited for a foray into the past — and sat there behind the wheel, a well-dressed lady steering toward my homeplace. I drove down Central Avenue first, past the racetrack, which was and is the engine of the town, like the mine in a mining town or the automobile factory in Flint, Michigan. The August heat in the South is murderous, splits your head and frazzles your good nature, soaks your underclothes with sweat. The temperature was certainly above one hundred, but I left the windows open and the air conditioner off. I wanted the air to hit my face, the smells to hit my nose.

I approached Alamo Street from its west end. What was the matter? The street stretched only about half a block and then ran up against a concrete slab. A parking lot with a fence. Where was the house? I must be in the wrong place; but then I saw. Leveled, gone, scathed. The very thoroughfare obliterated. I didn't even know when they had done it, had uprooted my father's carefully nurtured Bermuda grass; my mother's Amy Quinard rosebush with blossoms the color of blue blood; the cherry tree that feathered the lawn with pink blossoms in spring, and in late summer rained tiny inedible fruits that stained my feet and the soles of my sandals, so that my mother met me at the front door, barring the way toward her shining floors; the flowering peach that brought forth only flowers, not peaches, and was therefore my mother's favorite tree. Pleasure without consequences. It led its innocent, infertile life near my bedroom window, which was also gone. The giant spirea bush in whose topmost branches I spent endless summer days reading and dreaming of my future lovers — my gypsy skirt and my princess robes arranged like wings — had been replaced by concrete. I was glad not to have heard the roots ripped out of the soil, the splintering wood, the rumble of machinery.

I backed out of this cul-de-sac and went around the corner to the head of the street, and found the most extraordinary thing. The street had been shut off by a pair of enormous wrought iron gates with a central medallion bearing the inscription ROYALE VISTA HOTEL. (They still tack *e*'s on words in this town to let you know how elegant they are: Olde Shoppe.) And behind the gate, a swath of concrete. My childhood home a parking lot. A uniformed attendant played the role of the fiery-sworded cherubim, barring my path to paradise. I had to laugh. This was the American experience, and I was having it. A high-rise motel had replaced a small neighborhood of houses. Wilting in the borrowed automobile, I could reconstruct the patterns of the kitchen linoleum in four of those houses.

I drove around to the other side of the hill once more, and saw with relief that the vacant lot next door to 122 Alamo Street had been left untouched, undeveloped, unimproved, unscathed. Uncanny what survives and what doesn't: the same pines, the same underbrush, the same blackberry brambles, even the same faint smell of resin. In that primeval landscape the curly-haired child, protesting in vain that the briers scratched and poisonous snakes surely lurked underfoot, had picked the makings of berry cobblers and thrifty jars of jam. The same cardinals sang "sweet sweet cheer" in the same rich contralto. I have never believed that birds die. If they died, you'd see their bodies all around, but you never see them. They live forever. These selfsame birds had sung to the blackberry picker forty years ago, had awakened her on a summer morning, like the nightingale serenading Ruth, who stood in tears amid the alien corn.

I must relearn the logic of narrative, the syntax of dreams. To tell the story of a little world that ended. My father and I lived under the same roof less than two decades, but his history shaped me, and if you lay our lives end to end, we span almost the whole of this century. Fraudulently or not, he coolly impersonated a tall, blond gambler-adventurer. Lacking a high school diploma, he was known as a highly educated man — not too difficult a scam, I admit, in Hot Springs, Arkansas. He posed as a man of action, but his passions originated in books, not life.

Fathers are supposed to teach their daughters how to be women, that is, how to love men and serve them and use them, coexist with them, how to desire them in a seemly manner. A good father domesticates his daughter, so that when she is twenty or so he can hand her over, polished to a high gloss, to another man. But my father refused to do that. Perhaps he never intended to hand me over to another man. ("Be strong," he said. "Depend on no one.") A tutor in subversion, he taught me that words were sweet, and fairly tales superior to life, and books more valuable than love itself. I walk in his steps. Last night, reading a novel, I glanced at the clock, saw that it was only 9:30, and realized that I had many more hours to read. The house was silent. There was no one to insist I put my book away, no child calling for water or comfort from a bad dream. No man with hurt feelings turning his back to me or unceremoniously switching off the lamp. I would know, *know,* before midnight how it came out, who lived, who died. Like a drunkard about to break the seal on a bottle of whiskey, I was profoundly content and wished for nothing else. In the beginning was the Word, and the Word was God, and the Word was with God.

Even as a child, as I read what my father told me to read, I came to question the very notion of feminine identity. How are women born and shaped? Why do we require someone to deputize us? How, finally, did he persuade me to live his life for him? My father, dead so long now, looms up as unexplored landscape, the mountains of the moon, a text that has lain in a drawer, undeciphered, for which I have had no Rosetta Stone.

When he died many years ago I stood by his graveside with ill-concealed gladness, erased his name from the monuments in my head, consigned him and all his deeds to the memory hole, spoke no more of him, poured no libations at his tomb. The ultimate act of barbarity, as the Greek tragedians knew. The killing of the dead. Still, it's a lucky woman who at age thirty buries her father and is thus set free. Athena the gray-eyed goddess, known as the Contriver, with no mother to claim half her loyalties, emerged from her father's head and lived under his thumb, tidied up the messes he made, did his bidding. Perhaps I too was Athena. But the gods are dead now; my father shall spring from my head. He shall be my creature. I am the only living person who thinks of him or even knows where he lies. Come, old ghost. Perhaps we can speak to each other at last.

The
Bookmaker's
Daughter

$\mathscr{H}$OW HE BROUGHT ME
INTO THE WORLD

I DON'T KNOW where the love of stories comes from, I mean the love of them deeper than the love of life. I have always lived by stories. "Don't tell stories," said my mother, meaning lies. "Do tell them," said my father, for he dealt all day in stories. My father was a man of many trades, but for the part of his life that I knew him, he was a bookmaker. Not a crafter of fine volumes, though he allowed my mother to believe as much while they were courting. His craft was writing bets on horses and paying off the winning tickets: white-collar work behind the counter, he was quick to say.

On summer mornings he'd depart for the horse books in the costume of a gentleman bandit, three-piece ice cream suit, tailor-made shirt, two-tone shoes, the tiny gold chain across his breast swinging between his pocket watch and his pocket knife, and a straw boater shading his eyes — always something in the depths of them, love, melancholy, or anger. I would dance around him like a maenad in a pinafore, demanding attention and a kiss, and my mother might exclaim, if she felt cheerful, "Look at the two of you, and me without a bit of film in the Kodak!" He'd reply, without a touch of irony, "Just going uptown to make an honest dollar." Off he'd go to where the sun rose and set by post time for the first and eighth races.

My father filled my head with stories, so that our lives became a narrative, a mystery play, a drama of many parts. We were two dancers, bending and swaying in the blackness of a giant stage with the spotlight on us — and on my mother, when it suited our fancy or when she was indispensable to the plot. My birth was such a story, and Daddy's version was this.

You came on a cold day in the middle of November, in the middle of the 1930s, in the middle of Arkansas, in the middle of the Depression, but it was the happiest day of your daddy's life. It was the most beautiful autumn I can remember, warm, warm, we went around in shirt-sleeves until way past Halloween. But that morning the dew turned to frost, and we woke up shivering in our bed. And I got up and lit the gas stove and propped the oven door open. When your mama got up and raised the shades, she saw the dead leaves banked up against the front steps. Of course, she wasn't quite your mama yet. Yes, we lived right here, at 122 Alamo, and you were born in the bedroom — that very same one where your mama and I sleep now. It was our bedroom then, and our living room, too. Oh, we'd had a hard time, such a hard time, you don't know what the Depression was like, I hope you never know, but here we were at last in our two little rooms, our kitchen and our bedroom. At least we knew the electric bill would get paid. If I didn't have the cash, your granddaddy or your Uncle Bruce would be able to get his hands on it. There were groceries enough to go around.

After breakfast that morning, your mother took the extra quilts from the cedar chest and carried them out into the sunlight. There wasn't much of it that day, just a little pale ball that ducked in and out of the clouds and sent the wind blowing down.

Your Granny Loyd had come to wait with your mama, came all the way from her farm across the North Fork, all this way to wait for you. Your Grandma Abbott was right on the other side of the house, of course, but as you can imagine, she wasn't in any position to help. A person wants her own mother at a time like that. Your mama was only a girl, you know.

Oh, your Granny Loyd, now there was a woman, Mrs. Loyd, she was nothing but an old backwoods farm lady, but she was a queen. All her children — your aunts and uncles — had married before you were born, and when new babies were about to come, Granny Loyd showed up. If the only place to sleep was in the kitchen on a cot, the way it was at our house, that never bothered her. She'd sleep on the floor if she had to. Granny Loyd knew her trade. She'd seen a thousand creatures come into the world, two-legged and four-legged. She'd bathe the baby and clean everything up, and feed the mother plenty of cornbread, sweet milk, and butter beans. She'd wash the first rounds of diapers on a rub board. She wouldn't leave before she saw everything was okay.

And so that morning she took the quilts from your mother's hands, shook them out, and pinned them to the line. They smelled like the cedar chest, and the west wind was strong enough to blow the cedar smell away. You know how your mother is, wants things to smell clean. There was a little blanket for you, too, hanging with the quilts, and I thought, "It won't be long now."

Your daddy was out of a job, you know. The governor had sent the state police and raided all the horse books, beginning of the month. The heat was on. The usual thing, heat from the Baptists. Baptists just don't want people to have any fun or fellows like me to earn a living for their little daughters. Don't know why they feel that way, that's just how Baptists are. Heat from the governor — election debts to pay, you know. Hot Springs was always expected to cough up. Leo had to cough up, the judge had to cough up. And there was plenty of money, plenty of it always.

I didn't know what he meant about money or the right question to ask. I waited for him to get back to me, which seldom happened fast. My entrance in the world was tied by mysterious and solemn lines to the mayor, to the judge, to the governor, even to the wicked Baptists, who wanted little girls to starve.

Naturally, we knew about the raid in advance. That's only common courtesy, no more than you'd expect. But it wasn't fun. They'd bust down the door and pretend to be surprised and smash a few things up, and the newspaper reporter would stand behind 'em and write it all down. Brave officers of the law, doing their duty, oh yeah. He'd get it all down, with the names spelled right, and they'd print it, and we'd all get a laugh the next day. They pinched one or two fellows, as a rule, just to make themselves look good, but Old Man Jacobs usually spared the family men, let 'em pinch a bachelor like Johnny Strand. Johnny didn't care if his name was in the paper. We'd been shut down all month. Looked like we never would run again.

Well, that morning I put on my one suit — didn't have an overcoat in those days, but I did own a good felt hat, and I put it on, too, and walked uptown to hang around and chew the rag. To stand around the lampposts on Central Avenue, or at the door of the White Front or the Kentucky Club or the Ohio, see if I could hear anything. Something from the courthouse. Some word from on high. I had my pencil behind my ear and a couple of markers stuck in my hatband, ready to do a little sneaking, but I was scared. If they caught you sneaking, you were dead. You could rot in jail. There's no free enterprise in this racket. Everybody was there, in their checkered coats and cardboard shoes — Johnny Strand, poor old Deacon Syles, Crip Hall, Frenchie Lazotte, Snitchy Sims, Dumb Johnson, Chick Strock, Papa Fish Perrault, most with women and kids at home, waiting for that pay envelope.

But I was the only man whose little daughter was about to be born that day.

Judge Witt came by. You know, honey, he parked that Buick of his and stood in the cold wind with us, with his hands in his pants pocket, jingling the change the way he does. A powerful man, a man we all think highly of, and he thinks highly of your daddy. "Well, boys, I wouldn't *worry about this situation too much," he said.* "It's just politics, nothing *but politics. It's too soon to open up again, but boys, the governor's our* *man. We know he understands reason. He just can't give us the nod this* *week. Don't fret about it. You'll be back to work before long. It's all going* *back to normal." Then he took your daddy to one side, behind the door to* *the Ohio Club, and put his arm around my shoulders.* "My friend, don't *give it a thought. You know I'll see you're looked after. We'll take care of* *our own."*

Old Man Jake came by that morning, too, cripping along, dark and *swarthy like an old Indian brave.* "Howdy, Mr. Jacobs, how're things *coming?"* "Hang on, boys, we'll get this straightened out. Leo's working *on it right now." Of course, Leo, I mean Mayor, McLaughlin never came* *out to talk to anybody. Thinks he's such a big shot, him in his New York* *suit and his flower in his lapel. Honey, if you want to know the truth, Leo* *doesn't have much to do with it, Vern Ledgerwood, old Judge Ledgerwood,* *is the kingpin, him and Judge Witt, not that tinhorn with the carnation.* *Judge Ledgerwood never comes down to the Ohio to chew the rag, you* *wouldn't catch him near a horse book. But he sent word by Old Man Jake:* *Tell the boys to be patient. Tell the boys to tighten their belts. And that's* *what the Old Man said, and off he went, swifter than most people who* *aren't crippled.*

Ah, there was some good news. The governor had to bide his time, but *Judge Ledgerwood had invited him over to the lake, fish a little, sit in the* *duck blind, bag some ducks, figure things out. They'd get it fixed. All it* *took was patience and good will, and Judge Ledgerwood has plenty. As* *sweet a man as ever lived, my darling, we should all learn a lesson from* *him. Nobody needs to fight, we all just need to get along. Oh, he has a fine* *place out on the lake, Judge Ledgerwood, and there's nobody who won't* *soften up after a few days at the lake with him and his wife. But that* *didn't buy any groceries, of course. A terrible day, no morning line, no* *boards to mark, no pay envelope. And those two-year-olds rounded the clubhouse turn at Hialeah for nothing. They might as well have shut down the track. I thought of taking the bus back home, to save shoe leather, but decided to save the nickel instead.*

And when I trudged up the front steps, what do you think? I got there just in time to rush out again. Your mama and your granny had been finishing up the noontime plates and glasses, and you let them know this was your birthday. Your mama was a little afraid, you know. She had wanted to go to the hospital, where they knock the ladies out with ether. But your daddy couldn't manage that one. It's cash on the barrel head at the hospital. "Run call the doctor," she said before I got inside the door. I ran, honey, did I run, back to the grocery store on Central Avenue, and told the operator to get me Doc Browning. Here he came fast as lightning in his old Ford, with that little black bag. You know, I don't believe he had much in there except his stethoscope and some tongue depressors and a few aspirins. But I was glad to see him. I was scared, too. I thought Mama was going to die, and I prayed out loud to God to save her, and I couldn't help crying. The tears ran down my face. Your mama thought I had gone crazy, and she began to laugh.

Well, your Granny Loyd, she laughed, too, and said what on earth could you expect of a man and shut me in the kitchen and told me not to bother them. So I sat by myself in there and smoked two packs of Lucky Strikes and cried the whole time. I couldn't take this. It went fast, though. By 5:30, there you were. Doc Browning wanted to charge me five dollars, but I told him, "Doc, I'm out of a job. I'll get you the payday after the joint opens." And he said, "Sure, Hat." What else could he say? Everything was on the credit in those days, even babies. And he was just an old country doc, didn't work for the money.

I never saw anything so tiny and frail. And red? Red as a beet! No hair, either. But you know what? To me you were the prettiest thing I ever saw in this world. You weighed five and a half pounds. No, that's not much for a baby. Granny had fixed a big laundry basket for you, with feather pillows. You were so small she was afraid you couldn't live the night, so she took hot-water bottles and propped them all around you. And you know what? Your granny kept the bottles so hot that you screamed. And there we were, three grown-ups, scared to death about one little mite. Granny didn't know what to do. She'd never seen a baby cry like that. Finally I told them, "Take those bottles away, she's too hot. She can make it on her own. She's going to be all right." And they did, and you stopped crying right then. Next day I borrowed the money off Johnny Strand and bought your mama that beautiful heavy red sweater, you know, the one she still wears. It was a combination coat and baby carrier. She buttoned you in at the front, just like a kangaroo.

We named you Shirley, for Shirley Temple, and because your mama was praying you'd have those blond curls. And added Jean because your mama liked that, too. Oh, but you were skinny as a baby rabbit. We could have diapered you with a handkerchief. Your diapers hung all around the kitchen that winter, little clothes drying in front of the stove. We couldn't turn around without slapping ourself in the face with a wet diaper. But we didn't mind. You were sick all the time with first one thing and then another. One night we had to take you to the hospital and put you in one of those big metal baby beds, and it looked like such a cruel place. I cried worse than the day you were born, and your mama cried, too. I thought you'd die, and Doc Browning didn't think you'd make it. But by morning you were bright-eyed, fever all gone, and we took you home again. I said, "I'll never ask for anything more, O God," but of course I haven't kept my promise. That's how people are, darling — never satisfied. Always wanting more.

My luck changed that night. Old Man Jake got things going again. They sent for me the next morning and the pay envelopes started coming again. You slept in the laundry basket for eight months, until some little neighbor boy we knew outgrew his baby bed and passed it on. By then you were doing just fine, the prettiest little thing in the world. Your mother put a bonnet on your head. You looked like Daddy's baby then, instead of a poor little possum.

Soon you stood up in the crib and chattered. You were an early talker, you could say everything. And then that slick head sprouted blond fuzz, and pretty soon the fuzz turned to hair, real curls, all over your head, thick and glossy. Your mama used to spend half the morning combing and fussing with those curls. You hated that.

No, good Lord, honey, I didn't want a boy. If you'd been a boy, I'd have taken you straight down to Belding Avenue to the orphans' home. I wanted a girl. Who could want a boy when they had you? Who could want anybody else at all when they had you?

Deeply instructed, I asked for the tale a hundred times. It was my trust fund. He was the hero of the tale — tinhorn among tinhorns, hustler among hustlers, coatless on the first day of autumn, weeping among women, too broke to pay the doctor, but the protégé of powerful men. Yet I was born to some purpose; my birth was attended by portents, the wild wind, the leaves, my young mother airing the quilts, my Granny Loyd. She was a dream to me, then as now, a tall craggy presence with a dark Indian face and a snuff-stained mouth, her lap a bony meadow carpeted in a flowered apron, her voice crooning endearments. As if I had summoned her out of the gas flame, she would appear at twilight from time to time and rock me to sleep or kiss my skinned fingers to make them well, and then vanish into the countryside the next morning, across the river and into the naked red fields, the blue mountains. We sometimes went to visit her, if the river wasn't up — her house of raw pine boards with its peaked roof so simple in form and detail as to be the archetype of all houses.

I struggle to remember my father in those days, but summon up only a pair of arms that lifted me, a pair of hands that tousled my hair, paternal kisses on my cheeks. We spent a lot of time in the car, a green Chevrolet with frog eyes and a running board you could stand on. He bought it on credit, as soon as he had a steady job again and could get the loan. Baby seats had not been invented, so I rode beside him, standing up. He'd put his arm around me and drive one-handed, or hang on to my sash to brace me. One day, on one of these trips, Daddy hit the brakes hard and I bounced off the dashboard. We both arrived home screaming, me with blood running from my forehead and him drained of all blood and weeping: "I've killed my baby." He had to go to bed for a while and seemed unable to believe that I was alive, with such a tiny cut under the bandage and my mind still intact. "I didn't know which one of you to take care of first" was how the tale ended when Mother told it — the theme of her married life, forever, until death did them part. Still, I was always eager to go with him and see the world.

Sunday mornings we went to buy the papers — we usually went in search of something to read, even before I could make it through the funny papers, or in quest of trains. Daddy knew the train schedules by heart "Hurry," he'd cry as he fastened my jacket buttons cattywampus and hustled me into the Chevrolet, and the pebbles would fly from under the tires as we left Alamo. We'd park close to the Missouri Pacific depot, and the iron engine would roll down the track, hissing and clanging, pistons pumping, like some monstrous black beetle on wheels. "Make him whistle, make him whistle, Daddy," I would scream, and often the engineer would catch sight of us and cut loose with the shriek of steam and iron, no doubt drowning out prayers in the churches nearby. "Big choo-choo, all dark," I remarked at age three or four, and my father repeated the words for years afterward, like a blessing, whenever he saw a train. All along, he knew exactly what he wanted me to know

"Shirley Jean," he announced one Sunday morning — for everybody used my full name — "it's time you rode the train. I want you to know what it's like to travel, for I know you'll be a traveler. One day we'll all go. But for now, you and Mama will ride the choo-choo a little ways, and I'm going to race you in the car " In our best coats and dresses, pretending, as Daddy sug gested, that we were off to Chicago, Mother and I boarded the day coach and traveled to Malvern, the next junction, about twenty miles away, with the window open and track cinders blowing in our faces. The scrubby fields rolled swiftly past us, the locomotive sighed and screamed. I caught the fever, forgot my fear. Parallel to us on the road sped the green Chevrolet, my father laughing, waving, shouting, speeding out of sight from us, coming back into view, vanishing altogether. He got there first. As we pulled into the station, he lounged against the car hood, smiling, waiting for me to run into his arms and be carried safely home. This, too, was a story.

On another day when I was very young, the green Chevrolet pulled into the yard as I played around the front steps, and out of the back seat bounded a white puppy, so joyous to have found a home that it peed on my feet, licked my face extravagantly when I bent to greet it, and then knocked me flat in the dirt. "It's a boy dog," my father explained, dusting my hair and drying my feet with his handkerchief. The overwrought pup threw himself into my arms again and once more we tumbled over. Then he raced hysterically to the front steps, where Mother, holding a folded newspaper, was waiting to do her assigned task — take him in hand, bring him to his senses, teach him to control himself. Daddy said we'd name him Buster, after a funny man in the movies.

As long as the horse books stayed open, my father was a creature of the morning and evening meals, a man of Saturday nights and Sundays. He would toss his pay envelope on the kitchen table — crisp bills that he fanned out on the oilcloth, always with a lesson. "This is a C-note," he said, his eyes alight, one night when he actually had one. "It comes from Latin. *C* is the Roman numeral for one hundred. You don't know about the Romans, but I'll teach you." If nothing else was handy, my father would pick up pebbles in the street and expound on them for my benefit.

"Hush, Hat," my mother murmured in the weary tone that underlaid our lives. "Can't you just hush? Can't you just let her be a little girl?"

For a time, at least, I listened greedily to all my father's stories, for I was going to win the horse race, two dollars on my nose and him cheering. There would be no way to hold me back.

$\mathcal{H}$OW HE
EARNED OUR LIVING

"This book, being about work, is, by its very nature, about violence
— to the spirit as well as to the body. . . . It is, above all (or beneath
all) about daily humiliations. To survive the day is triumph enough
for the walking wounded among the great many of us."

— Studs Terkel, *Working*

MY FATHER was always the first one up in the household. For
the first few years of my life, I slept in my parents' bedroom, in
my baby crib — with my feet sticking out through the bars as I
approached school age, but there was no alternative just then. In
winter Daddy would arise in the dark and light the little gas
heaters that kept the rooms warm and gave us splitting headaches. One eye open under the quilts, I'd watch him hunched
over the stove in his gray bathrobe, striking matches, burning his
fingers, confound it! doggone it! and finally the thing would
make a bloop when the flame caught behind the grate. This was
a man's job, he said, to light the fire for his family on a winter's
morning, so I played the role of innocent, sleeping child and
never let on that I knew how many matches it took or watched
him suck his fingers. Every day but Sunday, Daddy shaved (some-

times I'd watch him cut wide trails through the beard of shaving cream, lift the tip of his nose, and apply the razor to his upper lip) and then put on proper business clothing and departed, just like a banker or a lawyer. "It'll be early today, it's Belmont," he'd say. Or "God only knows when I'll get home, it's Santa Anita." So my mother would figure supper for an hour after the last race.

He took care not to let us know exactly what he did all day, and I've pieced together some of this just lately. His first stop was Schneck's Drugstore — "Snacks," people called it, for we jingoistically resisted alien words — and there he bought a pint of whiskey. The liquor store within a drugstore, I now know, was a holdover from Prohibition, when whiskey was sold only by prescription. And his pint of rye was indeed medicinal, for he had massive, blinding headaches more days than not. By ten o'clock his migraine would have begun to pound, and he thought a drink eased it. Quickly, discreetly, he put the cash on the counter, cracked the seal and gulped, then slipped the bottle into his hip pocket. Liquor, in theory, was a pleasure only men understood. They drank alone and they drank together, whiskey neat in a glass or straight from the bottle, or beer. Decent women never drank. They had a highball once in a while, if their husbands forced them, or eggnog at Christmas. Only winos drank wine, though sherry was permissible, along with a little port, in doctors' houses after supper. Cocktails were for the upper crust; a restaurant required political protection to serve drinks by the glass. Daddy never drank at home in the evening, and he'd no more have offered liquor to guests than he'd have read the Song of Solomon aloud to them.

With the first deep swig under his belt, he proceeded up Central Avenue to the Ohio Club, where the wire service came in. This was not an elegant casino like the Southern Club but the nerve center of Hot Springs bookmaking. On the way he would greet his fellow workers, such as Deacon Syles, Frenchie Lazotte,

Snitchy Sims, and the others from my birthday story. He would shake the hand of Snipey Lockwood (a cigarette bummer), pat the backs of Birdie Fulton (like Snitchy, a stool pigeon), Stud Byrum, Diddle Searcy, and Hardpecker Rush (ladies' men, or so they said), Dog Posey, Mutt Carrigan, and Rip Kirkham, as well as On-the-Ground Brown, an ex–football tackle from the high school. Grandma Abbott had christened my father Alfred — Alfred Bemont, in fact — but his street name was Hat, and he had earned it himself, just like a college degree. As a boy on the make in Hot Springs, he had worked for a shop called the Hat-terie. This was where the gentlemen merchants and gamblers and men of substance and quality purchased their fedoras, Stetsons, and checked wool caps; my father delivered this prominent, socially significant headgear, wrapped in tissue paper and packed in round gray boxes. "Your daddy was a skinny, industrious lad," he told me. "Your daddy thought he could Horatio Alger himself into a wealthy man. But all I got from delivering hats was my name of Hat And I learned that crooks and con artists are the big tippers. Doctors are stingy. Bankers, the old skinflints, never tip at all "

No hustler went by his real name. To call a man by his Christian name was mother-talk: an insult. Would you refer to Owney Madden as Owen? Lucky Luciano as Charles? Old Creepy Karpis as Alvin? Scarface Al Capone as Alphonse? These fellows, my father confided in me early on, were gangsters but basically good fellows who minded their own business, unlike such public nuisances as the Baptists. Public Enemies, as tagged by the FBI, inhabited Hot Springs, in flesh or in spirit. Al Capone was dead now, had entered history; Lucky Luciano stayed in New York most of the year; Alvin Karpis was in the pen. But there'd been fabulous past days, Daddy said, when Old Creepy paced the streets of Hot Springs and climbed the marble stairs to play the horses at the Southern Club! Indeed, the great gangster Owney

Madden had left New York forever to settle down among us. He brought his flock of carrier pigeons, the very same birds that in the old days had carried messages between Owney and his boats offshore, loaded with fine whiskey from Scotland and waiting to make a landing so that New York City might drink — especially the patrons of the Cotton Club, which also belonged to Owney Madden; a fabulous place of entertainment, according to my father, shaking his head over the evils of Prohibition. As a child, of course, I did not comprehend that birds could work for boot-leggers or that men chased women and bragged about it or what "hard pecker" meant or why Al Capone was famous or why grown men worried so much about liquor or that nicknames carried such weight. It was all simply part of the landscape, the way igloos are part of an Eskimo childhood. Owney lived in a pretty bungalow next to St. John's Catholic Church, and would tip his hat to my mother and me if he saw us on the street.

The Ohio Club, to which my father made his way each morn-ing, consisted of a bar and poolroom in the front room and a horse book in the back. His partner, Johnny Strand, was waiting for him, and the two of them spent the next two or three hours writing sheets. Johnny Strand got paid for it; my father just needed a quiet place to drink his rye. A genial young hustler with an open Irish face and red hair, Johnny not only worked in the books but gambled, too, and chased women and drank. He really wanted to get married, he said, but his girlfriends had a habit of discarding him on the way to the altar. This may have been because he drank too much, or because he incessantly collected speeding tickets on his motorcycle and in his yellow convertible, or maybe because he owned a seaplane, which he flew as recklessly as he drove his vehicles. Mother called him "that louse Johnny," as if that were his proper name, and he certainly lacked the identifying features of a family man.

Making book is simple. The sheets my father and Johnny

wrote were just that — sheets of paper. The morning line — that is, the lists of races, horses, jockeys, and starting odds — came from the racing form, and the sheetwriters copied it in pencil, with last-minute scratches and odds arriving by wire. Then they gave the sheets to the runners, ragged apprentices, of whom the supply was endless. The runners delivered the information to the ten or eleven horse books that operated at any given moment, including the two joints operated by and for gamblers in the black ghetto on Malvern Avenue. Anybody could run a horse book. Racial and ethnic boundaries gave way to hard currency. All that was needed besides the sheets was a room, a telephone, as many clerks as could be kept busy, some customers, a bankroll, an accurate clock, and sharp wits — and, of course, the permission of the local authorities. (Since the gamblers down on Malvern were short of cash, owing to the poverty of their patrons, their operations were considered a joke by the politicians, and their taxes were adjusted accordingly.)

The gaming hall could be fitted out with cut-glass chandeliers and genuine Honduras mahogany, or it could be a sleazy hideout over a barroom. Regardless of the decor, the sheets, and the information that came in on the phone, had to be utterly reliable, and the results of each race had to reach the house before they reached the customers. The cashier had to figure the worst case on every bet: no matter how cockeyed the parlay, could the house pay off if the parlay won? If all the customers played the favorite and the favorite won, what would that do to your day's profits? The big decision was laying off bets—another reason you had to have a telephone. If the house had reached its limit, a clerk called and placed a bet with another house, locally or as far away as Memphis. There was no labor to it, just quick thinking and a head for the law of probabilities: Daddy's specialty. It was not too different from Wall Street, he said, except what they did on Wall Street was legal. No rake-off, he supposed, had to be sent periodically in a little brown package to the governor of New York. Though on the other hand, you never could tell.

Around eleven o'clock, with the pint inside him, my father would say goodbye to Johnny and start hanging around the pool table, not looking for action but showing off his muscle. Pool was his game, and his skills were legendary in this town where hustlers and sharks from all over the country got off the train and flexed their knuckles and elbows nearly every morning. Nobody ever got a shot off him. An exhibition player, he had given up hustling years ago. He was too skillful: to play for money would have broken the code. An employee of the town's premier horse book did not hustle pool any more than he played the daily double. Bartenders didn't drink, bookmakers didn't gamble, and the proprietor of the casino did not seat himself at the blackjack table. Some politicians benefiting from regular rake-offs wouldn't place a bet in the horse books they protected. "Don't look right," they said. "It just don't look right."

Moving on up the street a few more doors, Daddy would stop off at the Greek's for a ham sandwich and some coffee. Greeks ran all the restaurants in Hot Springs, and Greek food meant a ham sandwich on a fresh roll, with many layers of lean pink meat and lots of mustard. The Greeks also made good chili (plain chili, bean, or with macaroni), and everybody said that if you ate at a Greek's, you knew the food was clean and good.

As time for the first race approached, Daddy polished off his lunch and ambled up the street a few doors to the Southern Club. Known to the entire horse-playing nation, the great palace of the Southern Club was fronted with gleaming black marble trimmed in chrome—little abstractions that I later came to recognize as art deco in style. Downstairs was a restaurant, the Southern Grill, fit for Sicilian gangsters from Chicago and New York, who indeed often lunched there. But up a flight of curvaceous marble stairs was the horse book, with mahogany counters and Prussian blue carpets with white roses woven into them and a domed ceiling embellished with a mob of radiant plaster cherubs frolicking among the swags. From the center of the dome hung an immense glass chandelier, worth a fortune, people said, worth driving all the way from Little Rock just to look at.

Bathed in the brilliant light, a roomful of gentlemen studied their racing forms, chewed their cigars, and calculated their chances. Ladies seldom played the horses at the Southern; they were not exactly unwelcome, but smoke was thick, and the language not reliably genteel. Because real horse-players hate comfort or anything else that might distract them from the game, the chairs were hard and straight. A hungry man, a thirsty man, was welcome to descend to the Grill, but there was no eating or drinking in the casino, except a snort from your hip pocket on the sly. Against the far wall, a man in shirt-sleeves diligently chalked the boards — the morning line, the fluctuating odds, the scratches, and finally the payoffs. Board marker was a beginner's job, and Daddy had served his time with the chalk. He'd also been a clerk, writing bets all afternoon. But now he sat in the cashier's cage, a noble prisoner behind the silver bars, his face serious under a green eyeshade, the smoke rising from his Lucky Strike, and his pencil behind his ear. He'd count out the bills as expertly as a teller at the Arkansas National Bank, riffling through the stacks of new money, snapping the bills, dealing them out like poker cards. His thumb and forefinger were so sensitive, he said, smiling his gambling smile, that he could pick up exactly five twenties off a stack. By early afternoon the results would be coming via the Ohio from all the big tracks: Hialeah, Gulf Stream, Pimlico, Churchill Downs, Santa Anita.

No better story than a horse race has ever been written. It takes less time than the telling of it, is as irreversible as a meteor's plunge, as inevitable as death, and you can't ever know the outcome in advance. You do sometimes have history to help you. After all, you can use a tip sheet, do scientific calculations from the racing form, figure the odds for the mud, listen to your tout, slip your handicapper a fin, rub your rabbit's foot, consort with the jockeys, buy the trainer a drink, or pray. But the starting gate clangs, the horses break out and take flight with your two dollars riding. You strain to see across the giant ring, use binoculars to follow the pack as it flows like molten lead down the backstretch and around the far turn. You try to guess, you shout, or you coolly turn your back. It's already decided long before they hit the homestretch — which jockey intends to win, which one is holding back, which horse has the heart to win, which is doomed to stumble, and which one is running on dope. No system has yet been devised that can predict it, and there's no legal way to control it. One horse pulls ahead, another moves up on the outside. This is when your luck could change forever. It's only partly random, or perhaps not random at all.

The stream of horses flows onward — silently, for until they round the clubhouse turn, you cannot hear the pounding on the turf. But then the story quickens, you hear the action, like the pistons of an oncoming locomotive, and the crowd begins to roar and you cry out, too. The winner makes his bid, clinging to the rails or shooting through the pack like a comet. The jockey lays on the whip. And then the numbers flash past. Indifferently, the camera records the facts. There is never any doubt about it, even if it's a dead heat. The winner gets the roses and the purse. You throw away your ticket or you cash it, depending. The plot line is as clean as a new needle, the outcome precise. The horse that won the Preakness in 1939 won it. Quite different from history and from life.

But the gentlemen of the Southern Club breathed no dust and smelled no horseflesh. They never cried out, never cursed except silently, only stood with their papers and pencils, watching the board, scratching their ears, lighting their cigars, listening. The results came in via Western Union, a service supplied, it was said, by Owney Madden. There were no parimutuel machines as yet, not even an adding machine. Armed with nothing but a sharp number two Dixon Ticonderoga pencil, my father could pay off a three-horse parlay faster than most people could pronounce the names of the horses. Not for him the ringing up of pennies on some wheezy old cash register, or the grease of gasoline pumps, or the grime of stockrooms. He was a professional, a genius at figuring odds and paying off bets, who swore he never made a mistake, who used up grosses of sharpened pencils without ever erasing. He would bring home the stubs topped with virgin erasers for me to add to my pencil box, and since the boss knew I was a smart little girl, he often sent home a brand-new box of number twos for me, unsharpened.

When the results came over the wire, the phone men at the Ohio got on the line to all the joints, and by post time at the first race it was all business, the bettors getting their bets down, the cash changing hands, the manager on the telephone laying off bets, the stacks of bills being carried to and from the cashier's cage, the board markers scribbling, the loungers lounging, the clerks and the cashier striking up friendly conversations with the customers when the chance came. The porters (best-paying job in the city for a black man) emptied the ashtrays and cleaned the gleaming brass spittoons, pushed the carpet sweeper and the brooms, ran errands for the gentlemen. Their coats were white, their voices soft, their smiles eternally polite. In the good seasons it was over by five o'clock, but the California tracks lengthened our day unbearably. "Oh, California. I just hate that old Santa Anita," my mother often said with a sigh, and I hated California, too.

The tracks, nevertheless, were my primer of American geography, more significant to me than the Indonesian hemp and Bolivian tin in my schoolbooks. What took place in these magic circles determined what time I ate my supper, or indeed whether I had any, and their seasons marked the seasons of the year for me, like the rising and setting of the planets. Even as a small child, before I knew about schoolbooks or planets, my head was filled with visions of grandstands, excited horse-players, turf raked with military precision, the jockeys in their silks riding the sleek equine bodies like Thumbellina riding the back of a robin, the delicate Thoroughbred legs pumping like wings, the long muscles straining under the shining coats, the long necks reaching, the lovely mass of horseflesh flying, the crop judiciously applied to the flank: win, place, show. All this my father carefully described to me, not mentioning that in the Southern there was only cigar smoke and mahogany counters and men with little pieces of paper, waiting, counting, writing the finales to the stories of the afternoon.

Children were barred from the Southern, but one afternoon my mother dressed me in dotted swiss and the kind of white socks that bag quickly around your shoe tops and laboriously curled my hair into something that looked like a pile of fat woodshavings. Goaded by her from below, I clattered up the curving staircase, burst in the door, and was terrified to find myself suddenly in a forest of gentlemen's pants legs, where I couldn't even see my father. But he found me and set me on the counter beside him as he totaled up and locked the cash drawer Little Miss Marker. Having been named for Shirley Temple and dressed like her, I fell easily into the role of Sweet Innocence Beguiling Grown Men. All Daddy's friends — Deacon Syles, Cecil Barker, Johnny — patted me on the head and teased me, asked me where I got my pretty curls, and gave me nickels for ice cream cones. Even Old Man Jacobs, with his fierce, terrifying black eyes, smiled in my direction

The boss gambler at the Southern was a personage so powerful, so mysterious, as to have no first name: Mr. W. S. Jacobs, Old Man Jake, with his velvety brown skin and black eyes and a leg that had been shattered in a gunfight years ago, or maybe it was a train wreck, but nobody ever asked him about that, or called him anything but Mr. Jacobs to his face. Anybody who'd been in Arkansas more than one or two generations had Indian ancestry, though one's grandparents invariably denied it. But Old Man Jacobs was a real Cherokee, or so we thought. If his heritage had been diluted by Anglo-Saxon genes, they did not show in his face. So far as anybody knew, he had no vices. He neither smoked nor drank nor gambled. His weak spots had yet to be discovered. He knew how to stage a dinner party for a local politician, how to run a business, how to treat his employees fairly, how to train apprentices, and how easy it was to get the governor and the state police chief to lay off Hot Springs. Sometimes, waiting for my father to come down the stairs, I saw him standing out on the street, getting a breath of air. If he noticed my mother and me, as he often did, he was all courtesy, but his mind was elsewhere, far away, back upstairs, counting money, laying off bets.

He ran all the joints, peaceably and profitably, not only the Southern Club but the Belvedere, a snug little palace in a tract of lawn, forest, and golf course, a casino in the European manner. He could always find men experienced at dealing a dice table or blackjack or conducting business at a roulette wheel, men who dressed impeccably and comported themselves like gentlemen and knew how to please customers. He gave out such jobs as shill, waiter, porter. The Old Man saw to it that a hundred or more pay envelopes were distributed, and that discreet unmarked bundles were also delivered into the city and county treasuries and into the pockets of the judges and prosecuting attorneys and treasurers and county clerks and police captains and even the governor of the state, all of whom had to be paid off. These payments were different, in quality and size, from the payoffs made publicly in court, tagged as "fines." Exact in his bookkeeping, Old Man Jacobs was on friendly terms with the man from Internal Revenue, who kept tabs on gambling intake in the city and hung around the horse books, watching. The Old Man understood exactly how to keep the heat off his operation.

To Old Man Jacobs, Daddy always said, came the frazzled music teacher in need of funding for a band trip and the wife of the porter who'd been dismissed for drunkenness but deserved a second chance. He listened to the woes of the black yardman whose son had been jailed over a cutting and to the pleas of the bookie's widow, the church committee, and the ladies who made up Thanksgiving baskets to carry down to Cone's Road, where white folks went to starve. The Old Man never turned down a worthy request. We heard the same of the mayor, too, holding court each day, eager to dry the orphan's tear. All I know is that every evening, after my father descended the stairs and Johnny Strand boarded his motorcycle to search for a woman and something to drink, the Old Man locked the doors of his horse book and made his way to the drugstore of the Medical Arts Building. The counterman waited for him till he got there, an hour or more past closing time, Santa Anita or no Santa Anita, proud to be of service, and the rumor was that Old Man Jake tipped him a dollar. Sitting alone on a stool, the master of the rackets ate a vanilla ice cream soda for supper.

Winter and summer my mother and I waited at the curb in the green Chevrolet, with supper congealing in the stew pans at home and Mother drumming her fingers on the steering wheel. "My Lord, supper won't be fit to eat." Johnny Strand would amble down the stairs and stop to say hello to us, and some of the other boys would lean on the fender, feeling good about the world. Maybe it would be payday, and the brown envelopes in their breast pockets, and they would think of the raid that might have happened but didn't, and the mistakes they avoided making, and the Old Man's palpable satisfaction as Hat counted up the take. The pretty young wife and child at the curbside in a paid-for car were the very emblem of how things should be, the security of men working and coming home with pay envelopes, no matter what violence had been committed in Europe and Asia that day. You just did what the Old Man told you, and he slipped the bills into the envelope on Saturday — good folding money.

We never knew exactly when my dad would appear, or how. By evening, the pint of rye (of which we knew nothing) would have worn off. Sometimes, his straw boater on the back of his head and his necktie loosened, he bounded down the stairs like a tap dancer, the toes of shoes flashing, and I would clap my hands at the sight. Those were the good days, when there was no shortage and no migraine. Hat Abbott never, almost never, ended the day short, but if he did, it was news all up and down the avenue, and he would sit refiguring bets and recounting cash to find even half a dollar. It was the disgrace of the thing — the cashier at the Southern did not come up short.

On the rare days this happened, one of the boys would come and tell us. One evening we waited a whole hour, only to see him stagger down the wide steps, pale and ill, leaning heavily on the shoulder of Jimmy Parker. "I never found it," he groaned as Jimmy handed him into the car and closed the door, saying, "For Christ's sake, begging your pardon, Miz Abbott, it was only a dollar. Forget it. You'll find the mistake tomorrow. The Old Man didn't care." On really vicious migraine days Mother drove home. That was the headache index: Mother behind the wheel. Like any self-respecting man, my father rode in a car with his wife driving only when he felt that death was overtaking him and it wouldn't matter what people said.

The migraines, I understood, were my father's distinction. They caught him in their vise at least twice a week, sometimes oftener. He had his remedies — cold cloths on the forehead or, more often, a white handkerchief tightly tied around his temples, like an Indian's headband. There was a certain doctor not far from the Southern Club who would give him hypodermics of a pain-killer, and he took the drug in pill form as well. When the white headband appeared, that was the signal to Mother and me to go around on tiptoe, to speak in whispers.

This malady may be inherited — or perhaps it was my sense of loyalty that caused me, in those days, to suffer from migraines, too. They came with being his daughter. One of my earliest memories is of the knife in my left temple. I had migraines while I was still in high-top shoes. We searched endlessly for a cause. The strains of being a bookmaker? Of being a bookmaker's daughter? Was it something we had eaten? Failed to eat? Bad reading light? Atmospheric pressure? Gas stoves? Lack of sleep? Constipation? Getting a haircut? The curse of too much inces-sant, pointless talking? (My mother thought so.) My father blamed it on foods, and banned one thing after another from our table: chocolate, tomatoes, carrots, apples, eggs, butter. He never blamed meat and potatoes or tobacco, which he thought essential to life, and certainly not his morning pint. But later I developed my own theory: anger. Anger made our heads split. It would take me a long time to discover what the anger was about.

Mappa Mundi

AT 122 ALAMO we lived in a bedroom and kitchen on one side, and to the everlasting resentment of my mother, Grandpa and Grandma Abbott had three rooms opposite — the big apartment. In the tiny bedroom off the back porch, my father's younger brother, Bruce Abbott, and his wife, Hazel, kept house (after a fashion), sleeping together in a narrow bed. Hazel cooked in my grandparents' kitchen, or sometimes ours; sometimes all seven of us sat down in Grandma's kitchen. Bruce was a house painter — not steady work. Besides, he was a heavy drinker and not always up for breakfast.

These relations enveloped my father, much as my woodland granny enveloped my mother, except that the Abbotts, as he said so often, were grief, nothing but grief, a cursed lot, while Granny Loyd was a blessing. She appeared and vanished like rainshowers or lightning. Though she died when I was three, and I touched her gray face in the pine coffin, heard my mother weeping for her, I imagined I saw her afterward. Grandma Carrie Abbott, however, was solid flesh, and snagged Mother, Aunt Hazel, and Daddy in her net of complaints and commands, though they dodged her like game fish. Carrie was an invalid — an early word in my vocabulary. She arose only to haul her vast mass to the kitchen for meals or to ease it over the side of the bed and settle her hips on the chamber pot, a white enamel urn with a lid. It had other names (slop jar, for instance), but by whatever name, my mother had to empty and wash it, except when Aunt Hazel was around. The dirtiest work went to the youngest adult female — a protocol I hoped I'd never fall into.

No one quite knew what was wrong with Carrie. "Rheumatiz" was her diagnosis, along with a string of other words such as lumbago and shingles and dropsy. If one thing got better, another got worse. I thought she just liked staying in bed. And I could see why, for the jobs she did — working crossword puzzles, listening to the radio, crocheting, and reading fairy tales — were easy, compared to the drudgery that fell to my mother and Aunt Hazel. Grandma's bed loomed as a landmark, superior to a penny arcade. I loved to stand beside her, or be hoisted up, smothered by the bedclothes and the sickly smells. I tried to imagine her as the mother of a young son or sons but could not. I believed that like others in the household, she existed as an appendage to me.

She sat propped up against a wall of a half-dozen pillows, flat, sour-smelling, soaked with years of sweat. The pillowslips, trimmed with ragged hand-tatted lace and raveling crocheted roses, needed to be in the ragbag, Mother said, offering practical new ones she had stitched by hand. But Grandma, patting the old lace, a tear spilling into the gullies of her cheeks, would explain that the rags were part of her trousseau. ("The nice things you have in your hope chest when you get married," she explained to me. "Two dozen pairs of pillowcases, I had, all trimmed.") Everything about Carrie had once been white but now was yellow — skin, smocked nightgown, hair, bed linen. Close by her she kept a can of talcum whose label bore a dainty sprig of lilacs, and every couple of hours she'd cloud the air with powder — a sweet, artificial, lavenderish odor. It didn't quite mask the Grandma smell — sweat, urine, milk, and greasy hair. My mother hated dirt, personal dirt most of all. "I don't care if she is crippled," she would tell my father, "she don't need to be so filthy."

"Miz Abbott, don't you want a shampoo today? I'll help you" was how she spoke to my grandmother, calmly, sinuously, coaxingly.

"No, don't bother me about it. I know I'll fall and break my hip in the tub. It ain't been but two months since you had me in there washing my head."

Bathed, as I was, twice daily by my mother, manicured, groomed, and curled like a marquise, I could afford to like the way Carrie smelled.

Carrie was truly the keeper of letters — the letters she laboriously inserted in the grids of a hundred thousand crossword puzzles. She began her day with the puzzle in the *Hot Springs Sentinel Record* (flung on the porch by 7 A.M.) and ended with the one in the *Hot Springs New Era* (in the shrubs by sundown). She also had her puzzle books: double crostics, crosswords, anagrams, millions of letters painstakingly inscribed and warehoused in those tiny little squares. The letters she formed were beautiful, nothing like the block letters I had begun making, but a slanted, graceful way of writing that made me think of ladies in long dresses. "What's a seven-letter word for Greek vase?" she'd yell toward the bathroom door as Daddy shaved. "Amphora!" he'd shout. She knew all the two-letter words: Ra and Ba (*Egyptian gods*), em and en (*printer's terms*). Ten across, *They toil not, neither do they spin,* would be lilies, which would then link up with four down, Stimson (*member of Roosevelt's cabinet*), and the two would lock together in such a way that stet (*proofreader's term*) fit in. The letters tumbled off the point of her pencil, and she'd crow with joy as Ute (*American Indian*) joined sample (*a specimen*) and then Oahu (*Hawaiian Island*). It was black magic — all those letters waltzing together in curlicues, locked into patterns like stars in the firmament, governed by one another as if by the force of gravity.

"Alfred," she pleaded each time my father went out the door, "bring me a puzzle book from Kress's," and if he forgot or brought one she'd already worked, she wept.

"Women! Always sniveling! How can I keep up with all these puzzle books? You can't tell me you remember whether you worked this one or not!" And he would run his hand across his crew cut, like mown grass, or loosen his tie knot or make some other gesture of desperation. I would dodge the lightning bolt of his contempt. Women! Maybe *they* were always sniveling, but not me. Nevertheless, Grandma did indeed remember whether she'd worked the puzzle or not.

"Velma, bring me a glass of milk. Ain't there any bread and butter out there? Let a poor body starve!" This last muttered or hissed, just loud enough for the sense of it to be heard in the kitchen. My mother did Carrie's housework as well as her own, laboring several hours each day at her in-laws' stove and sink. And she would appear with whatever was wanted, her mouth hard but her face composed: "Here I am, Miz Abbott!" Old Miz Abbott had in fact commanded Alfred's wife and Bruce's wife to say "Mother," but Alfred's wife would have swallowed her tongue first ("Mother! In a pig's eye."). In this household war I learned deceit, or diplomacy, for I curried favor with all combatants.

Bruce Abbott, the house painter, was a dark, thinner version of Hat, with a grin that hung in the air like a funny odor. He and I shied away from each other, and never thought of a thing to say beyond hello. My mother's brothers always took notice of me, lifting me off my feet and rousting me around. "Hey, young 'un, where'd you buy them pretty curls at?" (Grown men made small talk by asking little girls where they got their gorgeous eyes, noses, hair.) "You get 'em at Kress's? I want some." Or "Your ma says you've been actin' up today. Do you reckon you need a good whipping?" This was not child abuse, just country manners. My mother's brothers were endlessly sweet, though their chins were plenty bristly as they hugged and kissed. Uncle Bruce paid me no mind, which was more irritating than whiskers. I strove to be the center of all worlds, including Bruce's, but he liked bourbon better.

He fell off ladders into paint cans, turning up at the back door cut and bruised, muttering and weeping, dripping enamel and in need of a bath in turpentine. My mother would bar the door and send him packing to the garage, lest he track paint into the house or get it on the bedclothes. He mixed his lead and oil paints himself, as all painters did then, and nobody thought anything of it. My father confided to me, however, that Bruce would end up with "painter's colic" and go crazy as a loon. That was part of the painter's trade. Everybody knew that work was dangerous and would eventually poison you, ruin your eyesight, drive your blood pressure up, give you a nervous tic, break your bones, riddle your lungs with disease, deafen you, cause you to have a stroke. Kill you. This, obviously, was another reason Grandma stayed in bed.

Our house had secrets if you cared to look for them. Behind the front steps, a flight of rickety planks, lived certain creatures who stared with their enormous eyes at the toes that went up and the heels that came down. If you tarried, they were ready to snatch at untied shoestrings or small bare feet. And there was the worn spot in Grandma Abbott's kitchen linoleum that would open into a cavern if you said the right words, which I hadn't yet discovered but would (you could tell it was a cavern if you squinted your eyes in a way I knew; you could see the edges of the hole, going down under the house and into the earth), and the yellow circle on the bathroom ceiling that marked the territory of the freak that watched us when we bathed (I drew pictures of him, with eyes like a fly and bells on his antennae). Because my grandma had nothing much to put in her huge bedroom closet, I kept my dolls there, four of them, two with their own little cribs and two in a baby buggy. Way in the back in a shadow lived the dolls' other mother, a girl just like me. She never came out. I tried leaving votive offerings — chewing gum when I had an extra piece, but she never chewed it. One day she ate a cookie, which proved to me that she existed.

My mother wouldn't listen to any of this, and I quickly learned not to discuss it with her. But Aunt Hazel knew I was right and also told me about the floorboard on the back porch with the face of the devil on it, which had been painted over in gray, but if you looked at just the right slant, you could see it plain as day. If you stepped on his face, the devil would kill you. I had to tell my parents, whom I needed to protect, but it only got Aunt Hazel in trouble.

She was a sallow hillbilly girl, pliant as a reed in water, flat-faced, hollow-chested, thin-tressed, watery-eyed, her print dress patched in five places, ill-clothed, ill-fed, and ill-housed, and afraid of everything, including fear itself. But like the house, she could take whatever life dished out. On some hapless day when she was seventeen, she left her hometown, Amity, a farming village about an hour's drive away, drifted to Hot Springs, encountered Bruce Abbott, and married him. If she had sisters or brothers or graves to visit in the cemetery, or complaints about her lot or ambitions for herself, she never mentioned them.

Once she shyly asked my mother to drive her to Amity for a visit — "Could you cah'y me to visit Mama?" — and we set off in the bug-eyed Chevrolet. While Mother and I waited, Hazel entered a dusty shack without a sign of light or life, not even a chicken coop, no mangy dog, no spavined mule leaning against a shed, nothing. She emerged an hour later, her face impassive, and we drove home.

"Mama's all right and so happy to hear I'm married" was all she said.

"Well, good Lord, Hazel, hasn't she ever met Bruce?" my mother replied. "I'll be glad to drive the two of you out here one Sunday." I knew my mother wouldn't be glad to drive Uncle Bruce anywhere, but she was willing to exert herself to correct a wrong being perpetrated against somebody's mama.

Hazel smiled and tried to say how much she'd appreciate such a favor, but the visit never took place. "Not a bit of gumption about her" was my mother's verdict, but she took up for Hazel as best she could against Carrie, who thought of her as a beast of burden or a scullery maid. Mother hated Bruce's drinking and when he came home besotted and violent would dispatch him to sleep in the garage. She was low in the pecking order in this house, but when she drew a line, she drew it.

Hazel was the gentlest of playmates. Kids my own age, like the Miller sisters from across the alley, demanded their rights, snatched my dolls, pulled my hair, and hogged the doll buggy, and then told my mother I had started the fight. But Hazel did not construe herself as having rights. I really believed the dolls were babies. If nobody was looking, I pulled up my shirt and nursed them against my flat nipples. I worried about their future, slapped them severely for their own good, insisted that they take afternoon naps, forced them to eat cooked carrots. Hazel needed play-pretties, not babies. She sat on the floor with me for hours, dressing and undressing my dolls, trying Betsy's bonnet on Sarah, cutting out pictures from magazines to make furniture for them. "Oh, pretty dollies, sweet babies," she crooned. If I got bored and made them die of scarlet fever, Hazel said boo-hoo, boo-hoo, covering her eyes with her apron. When I spanked them, as I often did, and viciously, she comforted them: "Oh, poor little baby, poor little baby, Mama love them." When we cut out paper dolls, Hazel would clip industriously around all the tabs, the sweetheart necklines, the ruffles, the pleats, not just chop straight across as I did, to my inevitable regret. Paper dolls came in sets of two, a dominant blonde with better clothes and a brunette with not so many; blond bride with lots of uplift, brunette bridesmaid with less. If the dolls were supposed to be high school prom queens, I got the blonde and Hazel the brunette. If mine was a doctor's secretary, Hazel's had to be my doll's younger sister. "I'm going to be a secretary when I grow up," I'd tell her. At tea parties with the baby dolls, Hazel sampled the air in the tea-set cups and agreed that babies like Jody and Mary were too little to drink tea. What she liked best was for me to run away, leaving the dolls naked and face down on the floor. Next day I'd find them propped up in their doll beds, their blank eyes open, their cupid-bow mouths smiling, their buttons buttoned, their cardboard shoes fitted to their toeless feet, their bonnet strings tenderly tied in bows.

My grandfather Abbott, the patriarch of 122 Alamo, Samuel Bemont Abbott — Bemont, as he wished to be called — was both a powerful and a weak force in this system. Under a white-cliffs-of-Dover forehead, he had a specter's face with an overhanging brush of eyebrow and both nose and eyes keen as a razor. Grandpa's bed was in the kitchen behind his wife's bedroom. His smiles were only for me, though his rage was terrible when he stumbled over my abandoned tricycle or found I'd carried off his only sharpened pencil. I liked to sit on his army blanket and examine the objects littering the tabletop by his bed, a collection of rocks, bottles, scraps of paper, newspaper clippings, pencil stubs, and books. Crystals encrusted with red clay. Pebbles gleaming with mica. Small chunky stones with veins of white or silver running through them. His books, I discovered much later, bore the stamps of public libraries in Michigan, Illinois, Ohio, Indiana. Amid the clutter of stones was another clutter of 'bottles, tiny dark brown ones, some of which contained heart medicine and eyedrops and eczema cream, some filled with vitriolic liquids that could cause the stones to fizz and bubble, as Grandpa watched through his eyeslits and calculated where he had picked the rocks up in the first place. He cautioned me never, never to touch those bottles. "They're deadly acid," he explained. "They'd burn your fingers and put out your eyes. Only Granddaddy knows how to use them. They're not for little children."

Grandpa had once been a respectable businessman, my father explained, his voice tense with anger, but now was only a minerals prospector, an occupation that used money rather than brought it in — a distinction Grandpa thought vulgar. Bemont would let me take the rocks in my hands, or would hold them up to the light and trace the path of riches along their surfaces with his jagged, dirty nail. "Look. Silver. Vanadium. Bauxite," he would whisper, his eyes gleaming. Every rock he possessed was laced with precious metals, some so rare that only he recognized their value, some utterly common, except that people hadn't discovered proper uses for them.

Grandpa owned a Model T, an artifact of the Dark Ages, a comic object that broke down every two blocks and needed full-time tinkering and coddling. But whenever he could afford to fill the gas tank, he would crank up and head out for a day on the open road, chortling and sputtering and backfiring like a Chicago gun battle. With him he carried his chemical kit, plus a stack of papers — deeds to mineral rights in contorted legal language and a hand-drawn dotted line for the suckers' signatures. He walked the woods, picking up rocks, and then, when he was sure he'd found a mother lode, tracked down the property owner and thrust the grimy document under the man's nose. "Ten dollars for rights to your vanadium," he'd offer guilefully, though guile was hardly necessary, since the cash spoke. When he had unloaded his last ten-spot, he'd walk some more, improving his rock collection.

By suppertime, the Model T would clank triumphantly into the yard or be pushed over the hill by some good-natured motorist, and Bemont would leap from the contraption, straighten his lapels, and resettle his black fedora above his bushy brows. If supper proceeded without a war breaking out, he often took me on his knee and showed me his collection of documents — and pictures in his books of gashes in the earth and piles of gray slag, railroads leading underground to caverns of silver, bauxite, and vanadium. Such mines would belong to us, him and me. I'd never want for anything — jewels, strawberries in winter, dancing lessons, a pony in the vacant lot, trips to France and England, boarding school in Chicago. Of course, I must avoid sharing these secrets, especially, God forbid, with my mother, who thought only of such trifles as the grocery bill.

But the next morning, when we were breakfasting in our own kitchen, Carrie might insist on knowing what he'd done with the rent money, and Bemont would rev up his engines and careen off the runway, for his tantrums were as precisely staged as an air raid. From our side of the house we could hear doors slamming or pans ricocheting off the walls, along with explosions of goddamns and Carrie sobbing, *obligato*. Mother would cover my ears or even seize me and run out of the house, and my father would have to mount the counterattack.

The old man would deny everything: "I never had any money this week. Nobody gave me any money." Or "I did pay the rent, there's been some mistake." Or "Mind your own business, and give that girl a good tanning next time she leaves the goddamn tricycle on the walk."

"Oh blessed Lord, help me," Carrie would cry. "We're bound for the poorhouse. Just send for the drayman now, I might as well go."

"Mother, shut up about the poorhouse. I'm sick of hearing poorhouse."

"And when I'm dead, I want to be buried in Goshen. You must promise me that much, Alfred. We own our lots right there in the burying ground. Paid up. And a good thing, too. That's all I've got now, all the land we'll ever own. And with you and Bemont at each other day and night, I'll soon be dead and gone." The words rang in my head like churchbells, dead and gone, dead and gone.

My father would burst into our side of the house again, and his migraine would strike, hitting him in the left temple like a bullet. He would set off to work with a white handkerchief knotted so tightly around his head that his forehead turned purple. If I tried to stop him for a kiss, I didn't get it. "Let me out of here. It's enough to drive a man insane, it's a living hell." The tears would splash down my cheeks as I watched him go, but none of this seemed like hell to me. It was home, it was family. This was what grown-ups did. I waited for what would happen next.

Absent, off in the gambling dens, he left some essence behind him in the house nevertheless, especially in the parlor — a silent place, behind locked doors, Carrie's front parlor, transported intact from her home in Indiana, battered in a dozen moves, the musty furnishings covered with sheets like grave garments. The stiff settee and the hard chairs with their elaborately carved backs and arms and horsehair upholstery embodied some heavy, ominous authority that I'd better pay attention to, better not turn my back on, ambassadors of a foreign power that hated children in general and me in particular. Grandma forbade me to sit on these chairs in dirty clothes or get Crayola on them or bang on the upright piano. I was to take lessons someday. Nice little girls played the piano, and Mother was saving money in a jar to pay Miss Pauline, the music teacher, when I was old enough to begin. I wasn't sure I wanted to be a nice little girl.

But despite the settee and chairs, I looked at the wedding

photograph on the claw-footed table — Grandma and Grandpa at twenty-five, he seated in his cutaway coat, she beside him anxiously displaying her plump white satin skirt, her hair in limp, elderly ringlets, and her nosegay in a death grip. This was not my idea of a bride, nothing like my luscious bride paper doll. The claw-footed table also wore a skirt, which I used to lift to see whether the little box on the lower shelf was still there. It always was — an empty chocolate tin with a lovely girl painted on the lid, tendrils of brown hair escaping from her topknot and curling around her high Gibson collar. She was my sister, and I gave her a glamour name, Jeanine. The box held a secret I revealed to no one: five or six curls, pale and fragile as gold leaf as I wound them around my fingers. A little boy's curls, for under them lay his photograph, a lovely child about my age, with these very same curls framing his face and a smile illuminating his dark sweet eyes. I loved him. I wanted him beside me. Surely, I thought, a little dead boy, not my father, who had an iron-gray crew cut and smoked Luckys. A little dead brother or uncle who might have been my playmate. And yet, penciled on the back of the cardboard frame were symbols I recognized: Alfie, age five. There were other pictures, too. A tall youth in knickers with a violin in his hands and the same dark eyes, now sardonic. And finally a tall, handsome young man with such a wild, brilliant look that I fell in love with him at once, without connecting him to the man he had become.

And the bookcase, ten tiers high and stuffed with volumes — a law-office bookcase, with hinged glass doors on the tiers and a little keyhole in each door frame, as if books were dangerous, or infinitely precious, and needed to be locked away. I was forbidden to open the bookcase (I assumed it contained some powerful magic, though the reason Grandma gave was that I might smash the doors somehow and cut my little fingers). Of course I opened it constantly, when nobody was looking, unlocking the little locks and flipping the doors open as quietly as I could, though hinges creaked and the panes of glass rattled.

Some of the books were in sets, done up in red or navy blue, some with gold letters. The first book I opened was entitled *Casanova's Memoirs,* which was meaningless to me at the time, since I was unable to read. The pages of this book were heavy and rough-edged, so that they didn't riffle but had to be handled methodically, one at a time. Toiling along, I found delicate drawings of men and women (quite different from the fat little creatures in my own books), which caused an inexplicable physical shock in me. In one a long-limbed man and woman, naked except for their hats, strolled arm in arm in some vast and fancy room. One of his hands casually rested on her hip, while the other held a black mask at his crotch. Her breasts, with nipples like eyes, looked outward toward her elbows. I had seen breasts before, but these were challenging and provocative in some way. Behind the happy couple stood an enormous black man, also naked and smiling, flourishing a mantle as though he intended to wrap them up. In the background a pipe-and-drum trio played.

Further on in the volume, a lady, naked except for her stockings, was seated at her dressing table, smiling contemptuously over her shoulder while an evil-looking male servant brushed her hair. And in a chair nearby was an elaborately dressed gentleman, a sword between his legs and his severed head upon his knees. I'd no idea what all this meant, but it was forbidden fruit, and now I had tasted it. Aware of some odd throbbing within myself, I put the volume back and shut the glass door. Later, using my ABC book for scratch paper, I tried to make similar drawings. I knew what was behind the willowy gentleman's black crotch mask and I earnestly tried to unmask it, but I couldn't achieve the easy, graceful line that so pleased me in the book. All I could make were wretched stick figures with no convenient place to attach the fascinating accessories. So I drew, erased, crossed out, scribbled, made holes in the pages, grew desperate with fear of getting caught. Finally I heaved the tortured ABCs into the trash. I owned only a dozen or so books, and now I should have to lie and play dumb when my mother asked me where the ABCs were. A small price, I decided, for the pleasure all this gave me.

Between Grandma's apartment and ours was the bathroom — with two doors — where all three families met, usually shouting. Whatever Grandfather Abbott did in the bathroom, it took a lot of time, and he hated to be hurried. He also hated any breach of procedure. I, or any other occupant, had to latch both doors upon entering and unlatch them when exiting. If I failed to latch, someone was sure to burst in — usually Bemont or Bruce — and catch me half-naked, to our intense mutual distress. (The blame always fell on me.) If I left without unlatching or stayed too long on the pull-chain toilet, a fearful pounding and shouting from the other side shook the framework. "Goddammit, are you parked in there forever? Let me in." We were an extended family, and no one who has ever lived in an extended family can harbor any romantic illusions about it, especially when the toilet has to be shared.

"Goddamn," now drained of its voltage, was to my ears a thunderbolt, a terrifying curse. I came rather to like it. I was an insignificant little girl — "we are weak but He is strong," as I caroled dutifully in Sunday school — yet my slightest action (taking too long on the toilet or standing in the sink to inspect my chest in the medicine cabinet mirror) could cause the very heavens to open. I could and sometimes did defy the household, lock the doors, and force Bemont to shout goddamn. After all, nobody could get at me, except by crawling precariously through the high window that opened onto the back porch.

"I'll snatch that kid bald-headed when I get my hands on her" was a standard threat of retribution — pure verbiage, of course.

Nobody could lay a finger on me except my mother, who administered spankings with her broad palm or with what she called "a little keen switch" plucked from the spirea bush in the front yard. But angry as these whippings made me, and determined as I was to even the score with her, I knew her heart wasn't in them. Three or four licks were all she could muster, even for the most outrageous sassiness, and she never hit very hard. My father disdained physical punishment. I was too smart for that, he stated, and he was too smart for that. My mother could switch my legs if she liked. He would use words.

$\mathscr{A}$BOVE THE VOLCANO

ALAMO STREET FORMED a crazy L whose long arm ran over a steep hill and whose short one angled off into another street. Our house was at the crook, more or less, and the vacant lots to the north and south were forest — thick enough to get lost in, pick blackberries in, hide from your mother in, meet snakes and stray dogs in. Across an apple orchard to the east stood a row of substantial houses, showing us their back doors only, "real nice homes," my parents always said, belonging to a doctor, a lawyer, and to the judge who protected my father's bookmaking interests. Once in a while, I saw a black woman in a white uniform hanging out wet clothes And in summer, through the apple trees, I glimpsed the doctor's daughters sunbathing and yearned to play with them, but they failed to respond to my shouts. Further on was a real mansion, where a lumber magnate called Mr. Brown lived in splendor with his two unmarried sisters — and we never saw hide nor hair of them, only their chauffeured Packard pulling into the drive and pausing under the stone carriage port to discharge the three of them in their black clothes. Oscar, the chauffeur, brought my mother tulip bulbs and told her how to plant them, and sometimes gave us excess gardenias and irises from his greenhouse.

I planned that Mr. Brown would see me skipping charmingly in my weedy yard one day and decide to raise me in the mansion. I'd visit 122 Alamo as often as I liked, but Mr. Brown would give me a bed with ruffles on top. "A can-o-pee," Aunt Hazel said you called it. "The rich man keeps the can-o-pee on top of the bed, and the poor man keeps it under." We'd giggle until we almost peed ourselves.

To the west of our house, across an overgrown alleyway where Grandpa's Model T sometimes broke down and sat, for days at a time, like a rusting tractor, stood another line of houses, turning their back doors to ours just the way the rich houses did — plain frame houses one room wide, inhabited (as I recall) by a mechanic, a shoe salesman, a dry goods clerk, a teacher. In the best of these houses, because it was newly painted and had the biggest yard, lived my playmates, the Miller sisters, Janny Louise and Mary Jane. Mr. Miller had the best job of all the neighborhood men, after my father (not counting the doctor and the lawyer and Judge Witt and the millionaire, of course): he drove an enormous red Texaco oil truck and went around to all the filling stations. The Miller house, as I was later to discover, harbored a secret better than the secrets at 122 Alamo Street.

At each kitchen sink and over each ironing board in these houses, a woman labored, and even in these hard times, the neighborhood was well populated with children. Every back yard was crazily wired with clotheslines. The linen that flapped in the sun and wind was often ragged. With clothespins in their mouths and crammed into their apron pockets, which looked like kangaroo pouches, the women hollered across their fences to one another, and to my mother across the alley, keeping their weather eye cocked skyward lest clouds gather and darken.

"I'm ashamed to hang these out Ort to put 'em in the ragbag "

"Oh, Lordy, don't worry we'll be talkin' behind your back. I need to do some patchin', but these old things aren't worth a patch."

"They may be raggy, but nobody can say I'm not particklar how I hang 'em up. Hems downward on my sheets, and I don't skimp on the clothespins."

"If I don't get me some better clothespins, aye God, I'll have to quit warshin'."

To and fro they went between washtub and line, toting soggy baskets, lost to view among the billowing sheets and fluttering towels, their hands above their heads, pinning dozens of sock toes to the wires. Meticulous souls mated the socks before hanging them out, while the slaphappy pinned them up any which way (there being a kind of pride in that, too).

"Oh, thunderation, if a bird hasn't squatted on this towel!"

"Old bird dukey's the hardest thing to warsh!"

"Aye crackey, if I ain't hung out ninety-eight pieces this time, and I reckon they'll all be to iron."

"Well, I don't know whuther that makes you the cleanest or the dirtiest" — a ritual remark that always got a laugh

When the last washrag and brassiere had been fastened to the line, they would stop, lean across their fences, and dry their reddening hands in the clean air. They counted their laundry. They enumerated floors mopped, floors that must be mopped, quarts of tomato juice and jars of pickles put up, mattresses turned out, hems whipped, rugs beaten: a census of cleanliness, which they claimed was next to godliness or (laughter) just a sign of a strong back and a weak mind.

Women rested on the seventh day, for God took it as a personal affront if He saw clothes on the line Sundays. On weekdays they quit just before dishing up the supper — husbands wanted the meal on the table at five o'clock and a wife with her hair combed. Alerted by the kitchen clock, my mother applied Maybelline to her lashes and Pongee to her lips and buttoned herself into a clean housedress, thus rendering herself fit to drive to the Southern Club and wait for my father so life could begin — the decent supper of meat and vegetables, the shared evening, the night skies with North Star and Big Dipper and Orion, the sheets that smelled of wind and sunshine. I was thus far exempted from this women's business: the clothesline traffic, the swabbing and wiping, the rinse water lugged thriftily to the tomato plants, the wrinkles and creases and monkey faces that needed to be pressed out of the heavily starched clothes.

One other house stood on Alamo Street itself, a dark green cottage trimmed in gingerbread scrolls, where time was not measured by a kitchen clock, or the eighth race at Pimlico, or closing time at the dry goods store, or indeed at all. Long ago, in the front yard, someone had planted pear and apple trees that still blossomed in spring and bore wormy fruit in the fall. Someone had planted roses, which now crept among the apple trees and hedges, stubborn, fragrant things, chewed by insects, thorny with neglect. The path from the broken gate to the front door had long ago been obliterated; milk trucks and mail trucks passed without stopping. This was the residence of Jewel Blossom, a madwoman

Nobody knew her age, or why she lived all alone in her dark cottage Every few weeks, a black Cadillac like the ones that took people to funerals pulled up in front of Miss Blossom's house, and a well-dressed man got out and went inside while the driver waited, and then carried boxes from the trunk to the house. Her father, we assumed. The tiny Viennese lady on the other side of the hill said he drove all the way from Memphis and spent the night at the Arlington Hotel at his own expense just so he could deliver cans of soup and take the empties away.

Miss Blossom was afraid of us, of everybody; yet many times I glimpsed a slender presence behind the fruit trees — a body clad in a print dress, the head ducked, the fingers covering the eyes, the hair an uncombed frazzle. Now and then, devising some game for myself and Buster in our front yard, I would suddenly know she was there, a disheveled phantom behind a tree, watching me from a distance. I didn't want to be watched. I played intensely private games, using the porch and the steps and the spirea bush in front of the house for a stage and draping myself in old dresses or curtains or anything long and filmy I could beg from my mother or grandmother. I played both prince and princess, leaping from tree branch to tree branch, courting danger (princess) and then rescuing myself (prince). A lot of fainting and kissing and exchanging of vows went on, which had to be concealed from all eyes I always made sure no one was watching from the house. But then Buster would bristle and growl, and I would freeze, gazing toward Miss Blossom's cottage, Miss Blossom's tree, too frightened to move, unable to call for help. More than once she came all the way to her front gate and opened it, as though she were ready to wrap herself in my finery and leap from branch to branch, but I screeched each time this happened, causing her to take flight as I did, and both of us to be swallowed up by screen doors, bang

Though she showed herself to no one but me, everyone heard her. When no lights shone through our windows and we were all in bed, she would scream in the darkness — not every night but unpredictably, so that dogs replied in similar howls, and men got out of bed in their pajama bottoms and peered through their bedroom windows And that wasn't all, for as children walked past her gate in the daytime, she would shout, "Damn kid," or if Mother and I were driving past, she would yell, "Damned old kid woman" or "Damned old grocery woman," so loud, so clear, that her voice seemed to come from the very rose brambles. It knocked the breath out of me, although I was snug among the grocery bags, my mother carefully downshifting to save the gearbox as we climbed the hill toward home.

"Poor Miss Blossom," my father said at breakfast one chilly morning. "Nobody to get up and light the stove for her. Nobody to put her breakfast on the table." I stopped in the middle of my bacon and toast. "Why do you suppose you're lucky and Miss Blossom is not?" Seeing how this comment affected me, he said it every chance he got. He even said it on Christmas Day, when Miss Blossom had been the last thing in my mind and I was testing out my Betsy Wetsy (you poured a little water through the hole in her lips, which duly dampened the diaper) and counting my lovely new books. My mother offered to deliver a plate of Christmas dinner to Miss Blossom's door, but didn't.

Men, emissaries from another world, entered this housebound community, men with dirty clothes, unshaven cheeks, and a beaten-dog look, usually white men, since Negroes sought help from their own. "Could you spare me something to eat, ma'am? I'll chop wood, draw water, weed the garden patch." We had little such work. Maneuvering me by my shirt-sleeve away from the back door and into the safety of the kitchen, Mother heated up the food, even on washday, piling the old tin pie plate high with meat and vegetables and two slices of bread. (Surely sometimes she refused, or skimped, since we hadn't very much ourselves. But I only recall the heaping, steaming plates.) What sort of man would go from house to house, looking for a back door to knock on? Did these men have mothers, wives, children? Where did they go to the bathroom? Why didn't they have jobs?

Silenced by my mother's transparent fear of an untethered male, I never asked questions, but now and then one of the men would notice me, or ask the way my uncles did, "Where'dja get the curls, little miss? Fine girl you got there, ma'am," as I cringed against her leg. Then he would disappear into the uncharted space he came from, a place that lacked streets and numbers and bedrooms. As Mother scalded the pie tin to rid it of tuberculosis germs or whatever microbes he might have deposited on it, she would explain why she fed these shamefaced men. "Your daddy told me I must never turn anybody away. It's not right for men to have to be without work in a country so rich. Imagine having to beg for your dinner! But President Roosevelt will change this."

I was happy to hear it. I loved him. He and Jesus and my father took an interest in such people. Maybe the president could get interested in Miss Jewel Blossom. Or maybe, as my father seemed to imply, setting all this to rights would be up to me

If I understood my town at all as a child, it seemed normal to me, as predictable as my grandfather shouting goddamn or my father nursing migraines. With all the surface markings of a dusty Southern county seat — the courthouse square that on Saturday filled up with farmers, the men chewing tobacco and snapping their galluses and spitting, the women with a flock of children at their skirts and snuff in their lower lip, the wagons later transformed into a flock of pickups parked around the feed stores — it was a town of homeplaces, cottages, and bungalows, where most women baked biscuits and fried ham seven mornings a week and set a meal on the table as the noon whistle blew. Except of course for Sunday, which was fried chicken at two o'clock after church, with salty, crusty flecks from the pan in the white cream gravy, mashed potatoes, and turnip greens or beans swimming in nourishing brown grease. Perhaps a cherry pie, so sweet it made your teeth hurt and gave you a sort of choked feeling. Sunday nights only heathens and backsliders went to the picture show or skipped the BYPU meeting (Baptist Young People's Union), for the churches opened their doors twice on the Sabbath and once on Wednesdays, and the deacons and Missionary Circle ladies scurried in and out the side doors seven days a week. At least one synagogue and two Catholic churches also served large congregations.

People never locked their doors. You could leave your car on Central Avenue with the keys dangling from the ignition and the windows rolled down and a pile of packages on the front seat, and nobody would touch a thing. A schoolgirl could wander the streets without hearing a rude comment. The streetlamps glowed respectably at twilight. To discourage free-will male expectorations, retail establishments supplied spittoons. Men tipped their hats to women and refrained from smoking without permission and saying damn and mentioning the word *bull* in mixed company even when they meant male cow, because if they did say it, eyes would be averted and lips pressed shut, and lacy hankies would fan the air, as if to dissipate a bad odor. Schoolboys who uttered the name of God or spoke of hell except in prayer were dispatched summarily to the principal, who might be a man or might be a woman but either way had muscle and gumption enough to turn a boy into a Christian gentleman on the spot. Even parricides no doubt said ma'am and sir.

When I was still in high-top shoes, Daddy taught me what a Democrat was, but I had never seen a Republican. You could throw a rock five hundred miles in any direction without hitting one. Everybody was Smith or Wilson or Bradley or Jones or some name you could write down without having to ask the spelling. Nobody spoke standard English, or made any apologies about it. (Rather, you needed to apologize if you talked like a professor — "perfesser," a verbal slight.) Though I could not have said so or explained why at the time, this was a white man's society, as genteel and clean, on its surface, as marble. Black men ran elevators and swept floors and did a little yard work if they got lucky. Black women worked as maids or, occasionally, in laundries and restaurant kitchens. White men ran the law offices, the banks, the retail stores, and the utility companies, always at the same measured pace. Nobody ever seemed to hurry. Occasionally my father would take me into city hall or the county courthouse, where the ceiling fans turned at a speed that matched our political processes and the papers piled up under dusty paperweights or on spindles atop the solid oak desks and stayed there undisturbed from one generation to the next.

To this extent Hot Springs was no different, as I later realized, from Pine Bluff or Fort Smith or Arkadelphia or Itabena, Mississippi, or the whole gazetteer of sweaty, godbegotten, segregated, cursed little towns strung out across Alabama, Georgia, Louisiana, eastern Texas, and the other Southern states lying somnolent in the grip of poverty. We were proud, amazed, when President Roosevelt spoke to us: "My friends." Us? The radio linked us to the continental United States, but our receiving sets, electronic and intellectual, were none too good, and Franklin D. Roosevelt's clear voice was often drowned in the static of "Ma Perkins" and "Just Plain Bill," medicine salesmen lecturing on the importance of regular visits to the toilet, or Russ Morgan's orchestra from the Claremont Hotel, "high atop the Oakland-Berkeley hills," wherever that was. We barely conceded that other places actually did exist. We sang "O say can you see by the dawn's early light," but many remained unconvinced. Could "God Bless America" really apply to us? Had anybody remembered to rejoin the Union back in 1865? Who had signed the papers? The only anthem I sang with all my heart was "Arkansas, Arkansas, 'tis a name dear, 'tis the place I call home sweet home."

We (the white Protestant majority) had our attitudes about Catholics and Jews. Our mayor was a Catholic, which showed our easygoing tolerance. Live and let live, we said. Nevertheless, when the nuns went down the street in their long dresses, dangling crucifixes on chains, we felt as embarrassed as if they had been Arab ladies from a harem. Still, the nuns ran an excellent school and a hospital everybody preferred, and nobody was a better nurse than a nun, we all agreed. As for the Jews, they were more prominent than the Catholics, though simultaneously less visible. Most of the bankers and many of the doctors and a few merchants were Jewish — German Jews, we called them, and they had been in the South forever, in Arkansas forever, had been rich and educated forever, so far as anyone recalled. They, too, ran a hospital, the only hospital (out of four) that took charity patients. Large numbers of visitors were Jewish; yet we had never heard of a yarmulke or a seder and didn't know bagels from lox. In spite of their wealth and influence, Jews were never asked to join the country club, nor did their daughters make debuts like other rich girls. We Christians could not afford to be openly anti-Semitic, just as they could not afford to emphasize their Jewishness. No doubt they called us unpleasant names in the privacy of their homes, and most of us reciprocated (though decent people disapproved of epithets like "yid"). Real animosity was rare.

To be sure, we were racist, though in our own peculiar way. Black people in our county were a small minority descended mainly from free immigrants who'd come as servants or artisans or laborers. It took courage for a black person to settle in Arkansas, whose whites could exhibit not only the paternalistic racism of the Deep South but the more brutal, roughshod attitudes of the frontier, as well as indifference or friendship, or unpredictable mixtures of all these attitudes, toward their black neighbors. As in all other matters, however, Arkansas was not as bad as Mississippi, a fact people literally gave thanks for when they said grace. In Hot Springs, the races now lived in peace. Local memories of the Civil War were different from those in Georgia and South Carolina. Our part of Arkansas (unlike the rice country along the Delta to the east) had stood on the outskirts of the slave South and during the Civil War had suffered far more from marauding bands of free-lance killers like the Kansas Jayhawkers than from federal troops. Sour grudges about the "lost cause" did not complicate our relations. By 1940, twenty years had actually passed since the last lynching. I heard elderly eyewitnesses recount that one in graphic detail — a young man accused of rape was hustled into the courthouse square in a horse and buggy, hanged alive from a streetlamp, and shot to bits. But after assuring you that the Negro was guilty, the old fellows would piously add that the white mob had been composed of riffraff.

That's what my father claimed, too, swearing his loyalty to due process. Black votes were useful, and black support vital to Leo McLaughlin's machine. "The niggers love him," the riffraff said. "He couldn't get elected without 'em." However, there were no wealthy, influential black people in Hot Springs, and if white people thought of it at all, we assumed this condition to be the will of God rather than any doing of ours. Black people made their homes in certain sections of town and went to a certain school and sat at the back of the bus and in the top balcony of the picture show (in the one theater that admitted them), and if they were clean and sober were hired as maids and porters and cooks and janitors. They drank from separate drinking fountains and used separate toilets, or did without drinking fountains and toilets, for all the ruling classes cared. Nevertheless, most of us were as hard up as they were, and thus a profound and genuine civility existed between us, which we deliberately, self-deludingly, mistook for contentment on their part. Nice folks like us never said "nigger." We were content, after all. Why not they?

But none of this was precisely the heart of the matter. As we were all too proudly aware, Hot Springs was nothing like Fort Smith or Itabena. We had glamour, and depth, and a wicked soul that few outsiders understood.

Our true character as a place must have begun with the landscape, a most seductive landscape, a thousand blue-green weathered hills that have nurtured forests and forest creatures since the continent lifted itself from the sea. The town lies in a valley within a valley, set like a jewel between two mountains in a clearing at the heart of a woods that stretched (and still stretches) two hundred and fifty miles or more from east to west in central Arkansas. This deep and fragrant forest of shortleaf pine clothes the ridges and valleys of a mountain range rounded and softened by geologic eons of rain and wind and the dropping of pine cones, and only within this century touched by rough and grasping human hands and cruel machinery. It is one of the grandest forests east of the Rockies, and the very last to be lumbered. In other ages, our hills must have been fierce peaks, but on the horizon at twilight in my childhood, they were the bodies of plump old women, prone, asleep on a daybed in housedresses; you could almost lay your cheek against their gentle gray-green curves and partake of their mountainous sleep.

The lonesome pine outside my bedroom window had belonged to this forest; the tangled, wooded lots on either side of our house were remnants of it. Both mountains and woods are called Ouachita (*Wash*-i-taw), perhaps the name of some Indian people who've left no other trace or record, or perhaps the Choctaw word for hunting ground. The forest stood at the edge of every clearing, promising a swift reinvasion via pine cone and flying seed and creeping vine, if ever you gave it the chance. It was not a threatening woods, though, but a secret sort of place, thick with weeds and wildflowers, wild fruits, grapes, and berries, swarming with mosquitoes, ticks, chiggers, and other bloodsuckers as well as bears, wildcats, foxes, groundhogs, razorback hogs, turkeys, uncountable varieties of songbirds, and snakes said to be capable of strangling humans with their tails and other unspeakable aggressions; a welcoming woods, singing and moaning in the wind by night, beckoning to fishermen and hunters and their dogs, and peopled for centuries by as numerous a company as ever inhabited any Shakespearean landscape — the Ouachita people, if they existed, and such tribes as the Caddo, whose arrowheads and painted pottery turn up in the forest to this day, and finally newcomers from the forests of the British Isles as well as Africa.

These people liked living among the trees, feared the plains and the deltas, and shrank from the very notion of beaches and seas, the inhumanity of deserts. The underbrush was tangled with briers and a thousand hardy, nameless flowers. Mockingbirds mocked, and cardinals sang coloratura. Jays contended and screeched, doves burbled, and at dusk the whippoorwills called back and forth from horizon to horizon like Caddos signaling. It was an ocean surrounding the islands of habitation, tossing restlessly as water, hiding the forest dwellers from one another. Laced with pathways, copses, hollows, fierce little creeks and wide rivers, and all manner of passageways, the forest concealed its inhabitants, protected them from one another, from the rest of the South, from the rest of everything. This sheltering arm defined a world, and somehow those who lived within dreaded the outward. When I heard of Sherwood Forest, and encountered the Forest of Arden in ninth-grade English, I felt at home and understood why storytellers loved the woods.

Contrary to the habits of most mountains (the Appalachians, for example, and the Ozarks up toward Missouri, which are oriented north to south), the Ouachita hills run east to west after their own manner. Indeed, though we were often said to be an Ozark people, we were not. On our mental maps, the Ozarks were far away, and those who lived in them were Northerners. Among my earliest emotional baggage was the notion that I was a Southerner, not kin to any of those northern folks. This valley belonged to the United States, for it was a national park, my father bragged, just like Yosemite or Yellowstone, and the park rangers were always around, suited up like Western Union messengers or doughboys from World War I, with their strange flat-brimmed felt hats and the Great Seal of the

USA on the sides of their Ford pickups. Thus we felt singled out, admired.

Our character was also formed by the hot springs. One of the two round-shouldered mountains forming our valley abundantly and dependably produces a U.S. government—certified miracle: waters pouring forth, boiling hot and clear, rich with a score of minerals. Buried deep in the earth is a fiery furnace, a geologic heating system that sends waters to the surface bubbling and seething, cascading out over your bare hands at 140 degrees Fahrenheit. In some epoch when the trilobites were supreme on earth, the volcano began burning under our mountain, causing the rocks to spurt hot waters, fusing the elements into brilliant blocks of quartz crystal all around this landscape, and creating every manner of hard and soft stone, including, besides the quartz, zircon nuggets that could be polished to shine like diamonds — all of these beautiful hard goods fated to prove worthless in the economy of the modern world. (Why, my father sometimes wondered, couldn't the fires have forged rubies for us, or tin?)

Water was our element: besides the springs we had lakes, two large and lovely ponds in the palm of a giant's hand, from whose depths the rich and poor alike caught fish — always the common denominator, the South's great unifier, cutting across gender, race, and class. Just as a successful horse-player can be a fool or a king, a fisherman can be of either sex, can fish with a line and a worm or the most expensive bait and tackle. Education and privilege and a white skin and a Y chromosome give you no edge when it comes to fishing. Boats are another matter, and the wealthy plied the smooth surfaces of the lakes in sleek, noisy craft, dodging rowboats and drowning them in their wake, and evoking pangs of awe and envy in the hearts of the poor, watching from the banks, or of the tourists, rounding the bridge abutments in overcrowded, lumbering pleasure craft that charged five dollars a head.

Down deep the furnace burned, reliable as the embers of Hades. As I shut my eyes at night, I would try to envision the core of fire that made the water bubble and steam, half expecting it to blow us all into archaeology, dusty corpses, fallen columns, paralyzed by lava like Pompeii (another loose-living resort town). Or perhaps it might envelop us in fire, as it did the native South Sea islanders in Maria Montez movies, which in my childhood struck me as terrifying masterpieces. But no eruption has ever occurred. Chilled, aching humanity began bathing here long ago, wallowing gratefully in the warm mud. The Caddo, the Quapaw, the Natchez, the Arkansas, the Natchitoches, and the Cherokee, sibling tribes within the Mississippian culture, discovered a merciful god in the springs, and believed the first man and woman had emerged from the steaming waters on the stones. These springs, some say, were what Ponce de León sought in Florida centuries ago, the fountain of youth, the magic waters that washed away the years and stopped the flow of time. It was not our fault they didn't live up to Spanish expectations.

The hot water sealed our fate. Our settlers had come not with Bibles and plows and sacks of seeds but with swollen knees, cricks in their necks, and charley horses. According to a government report of 1885, pilgrims came to the springs for rheumatism, sore eyes, malaria, catarrh, kidney disease, sciatica, nervousness, locomotor ataxia, lupus, measles, ulcers and dyspepsia, eczema, blood poisoning, stricture, enlarged glands, gout, boils, tumors, and womb disease. Although my father told me many a tale about Hot Springs, he did not mention that after arthritis the commonest ailments "cured" at the spa were syphilis and gonorrhea, treated in those days with sitz baths (useless) and mercury injections (lethal). Syphilis was listed on the books as neuralgia, pronounced as two words, new ralgia, and if you had a long-term case of it, old ralgia, for a joke. One spring was even known by that name, Old Ral for short, and I've lately seen accounts, even drawings, of blacks and whites, males and females, sitting companionably together in the warm pond, bathing their sores. Though the whites never exactly thought of black people as social equals, there was less to-do about race in the days before Southern politicians passed the Jim Crow laws in the 1880s, deconstructed Reconstruction, and repossessed the South. At first the springs, not the people, were segregated: springs for the kidneys, the liver, the feet, the stomach, and for the skin and warding off old age. If the waters didn't heal you, an army of doctors, chiropractors, homeopaths, this-paths, and that-paths offered miracles in offices and hotel rooms. Indeed, the medical men sent out drummers, press gangs who hauled sick people bodily from incoming trains or stagecoaches and carried them off to be doctored, drugged, pounded, and boiled, willy-nilly.

The run-off from the springs in the early days turned the main street into an open sewer, and a journalist from New York reported that pigs ran free, thousands of them, beside the warm creek that rolled down the valley with only footbridges over it. Laundresses used the creek to wash in and hung the clothes on the bridges to dry. In 1876, one woman bather found a water moccasin in her bathtub, but managed to beat it off. The incident made the papers and caused no end of bad publicity. Management began to look out for the snakes.

Up and down the avenue, in side streets and shabby boarding houses, in rocking chairs on the porches of the bathhouses, people complained at length of stiff backs, hitches in their get-alongs, trick knees, shooting pains, sick headaches, scrofulous symptoms, heartburn, female complaints, lumps, bumps, bloody fluxes, burning sensations, skin eruptions, constipation, swollen passages, growths, pinkeye, frozen joints, insomnia, and a string of other agonies. Lamentation was a civic industry. But lamentation gets old, and eventually a man needs a shot of whiskey and an hour or two at the craps table to relieve his mind, or an afternoon in the life-giving sunshine to watch the ponies race. Perpetual bad health, unfortunately, gave rise to frippery and con games — for what were these souls to do once they had bathed in the waters? The answer was that they should game, gamble, wager, and swindle. From the first, we attracted a high proportion of bandits.

After the Civil War, Hot Springs became a haven for Mississippi riverboat gamblers and Confederate veterans and scoundrels disguised as such and rough trade of one kind and another. It was a spot known to everybody in the United States who was either sick or on the make or both, anybody who had given up on the sweat of his brow except as a source of skin irritation. By 1884, seven gambling houses were operating along the main street alone. "The more a man laid down, the less he had to pick up," one sportsman observed. The police were always in cahoots and on the take — they were openly subsidized to serve the gamblers, a system so convenient that it continued well into modern times.

The boss gambler in the 1880s was a black-haired Irishman named Frank Flynn, who in his surviving tintype wears a top hat and cutaway coat and the expression of a man who could watch his best friend die on the rack and never whimper. His jet-black eyes, people said, would "remain still for an instant, but wander all around the room as if in search of something." One day a Texas cardsharp arose from the poker table with too large a portion of the house bankroll in his pocket. "Young man," Frank Flynn said, "you haven't won enough to pay your fine for gambling." The fellow just laughed, and a few minutes later, out on the street, an officer of the law arrested him and imposed a fine exactly equivalent to his winnings. (Don't try to beat the house, my father advised, repeating this old tale and laughing.)

But Flynn helped engineer an event that altered the course of history. (My father said that if you didn't know about the Flynn-Doran war, you couldn't understand Hot Springs.) About the mid-1880s, a Confederate veteran and high roller named Major S. A. Doran showed up in town and opened a bigger saloon than Flynn's. Getting ready for the showdown, both men began hiring private armies of gunfighters, quick-draw artists, mixed-bloods in Stetson hats, killers, and drifters, the flotsam and jetsam of those harsh times, men known from Dodge City to Tombstone. As the rivalry deepened, Major Doran opened his casino, the Palace, about where the Southern Club is now. According to the newspaper account of the day, the place was "thronged with lawyers, doctors, bankers, the most respectable citizens of the place, crowded around faro or stud-horse poker games, or at the supper tables groaning under gigantic pyramids of chicken-salad and sandwitches; whisky and champagne flowed like water. The rough element was there, too, but on its best behavior, for scattered about the rooms were the Major and his satellites, well-heeled and ready for action."

The next days were tense. The dealers kept their rifles by their tables and one eye on the door. Suddenly, Frank Flynn sent Major Doran a challenge to come out on the street and shoot it out. Cigar in teeth, six-gun drawn and cocked (an eyewitness reported), the major came down the stairs and shot Flynn in the chest, lightly wounding him: "I know I hit him once over the heart. I saw the dust fly off his coat. Next time I hit him I'll plug him in the eye." But the wounded Flynn mustered his gunfighters and rented a hotel room looking out on the Palace, intending to turn the room into a snipers' nest. (True to form, local gamblers, perched on a balcony nearby, were laying odds and taking bets.) Major Doran meant to kill Flynn, however, and he didn't intend to amble into sniping range. The next morning he posted his hired guns up and down the street in doorways and behind tree trunks and waited until Flynn and two of his brothers, heavily armed, made their way along Bathhouse Row in a horse-drawn cab. At the major's signal, the troops opened fire as if they had been at Antietam. The cab driver was shot right off his box and died before he hit the street. One man died inside the hack; Frank and his other brother leaped out into a shower of gunfire, attempting to take cover, but both were wounded. Two passers-by, including the driver of a little dray and a man waiting for the barbershop to open, were gunned down. When the bullets stopped flying, the chief of police finally showed his face and the town's fire bell began a wild, hysterical clanging, while on the plank sidewalk and the street, wet with blood and brains and flesh, people wept in horror at the wages of sin. That was the end of it. Flynn and Doran and any other rascal who could walk were run out of town.

The town fathers covered up the old bathing holes and tore down the footbridges and slaughtered the pigs and passed a law against doctors' shanghaiing trade. They covered up and rerouted the filthy, warm creek running down the floor of the valley, paved it over so that it became a thoroughfare of pride, Central Avenue, curving southward in the cleft between the two mountains. They built bathhouses of tile and marble and steel, with fine porcelain tubs and copper pipes and even music rooms, so sternly segregated as to race and gender that no woman bather could ever catch a glimpse of a man or he of her, and no white person, swathed in towels, would ever lay eyes on a Negro except in an attendant's uniform. They built the racetrack — a great track, Oaklawn Park — and the best horses began to winter there. And around 1926, my father said, along came the present rule of enlightenment: Mayor Leo P. McLaughlin, who enticed the gangsters from New York and Chicago within our city limits to practice the Beatitudes and observe the Ten Commandments. The mayor and his colleagues also crafted the arrangements that kept money flowing into the proper pockets — their own, chiefly.

Central Avenue began to be lined with palaces, including a tile-and-marble hall where they sold bottled mineral water, and you could get free samples to estimate what good it would do you. The Medical Arts Building, our skyscraper, was completed just by a gnat's bristle, the day before the Great Depression struck in 1929. A sixteen-story art deco structure like a lonesome pine, it was where the best doctors and dentists had their offices, because everybody knew that good medical care could only be dispensed from a building with elevators. People would come from fifty miles or more just to get their teeth fixed. And in the shadow of the Medical Arts, another art deco marvel rose up, the Southern Club, major bookmaking establishment, its broad facade decorated in chrome and black mirrors with a sort of theater canopy to shelter the well-to-do from the rain as they extricated themselves from their Cadillacs. On the upper windows were striped awnings, just like at Monte Carlo.

The best part of all was the Arlington Hotel, yellow sandstone and set right on the face of the mountain, in a hollowed-out place with one of the hot springs directly under it. It towered over the municipality like a tiara, a Bavarian castle, turreted and verandahed and striped awninged, with stately stairs that only ladies and gentlemen might mount — an architecture of wealth, comfort, and ease. Inside the flapping revolving doors, uniformed attendants would bow to you, ceiling fans would solemnly turn, and the orchestra would play foxtrots until two in the morning — and all that would come only after you'd dined off a white tablecloth, with the black waiters bobbing all around you and carrying things under silver domes, and the domes would start arriving only after you had played the horses all day in the Southern Club across the way and then returned to your room for a bath and a massage.

You couldn't look at the Arlington without remembering Alphonse and Ralph Capone, who had lodged here, in this very hotel, whenever they needed a vacation from murder. That was back in the 1920s, of course, a long time before I ever came on the scene and before Al went to the penitentiary and died of syphilis. They'd commandeer the entire fourth floor for themselves and their girlfriends and their bodyguards, and would leave all the doors open while they caroused, and of course Al could get plenty of women to make love to him whether he had syphilis or not.

Downstairs, in those days, the mayor and the judges and the lords of the casinos and the doctors and all the other powers of the town could reserve their tables right next to gangsters, and the clarinets and saxophones would be singing in the ballroom, and the lovely, innocent Hot Springs women would be filing up and down the long staircase coifed in little pompadours carefully secured with bobby pins, and wearing fluttering, slim dresses that came all the way to their shoe tops, blue chiffon, or peach, with hems in handkerchief points and white gloves and the wristwatch clipped on top. Each lady would be wearing an orchid on her shoulder strap ("Oh, Hubert, can you fasten this on me, I can never get it straight"), and they'd all eat fried chicken with mashed potatoes and drink highballs and step-close-step around the dance floor, wedded wives and dental surgeons and possessors of the Buick franchise and Honorable Judges and Prominent People rubbing haunches with Al and Ralph and their goons and doxies, and it was Mount Olympus, better than the Rainbow Room or the Palmer House or the Cotton Club, better than anything, better than New York or Chicago where soot, grit, and bullets flew like dandelion floss. This was what money really could buy, and it was here, right here: what else in the world could matter?

As you strolled down Central Avenue on a summer afternoon, in those days when only the picture show had air conditioning, the doors and windows would be open in all the horse books and the floor fans roaring, and you could hear the results of the sixth race at Saratoga broadcast over the loudspeakers in the joints, and what the daily double paid at Santa Anita. The whole operation was completely illegal, and everybody involved in it could and should have gone to the pen. However, the whole operation could not have existed at all if it hadn't been illegal. The bulky, pig-eyed men who stood guard for the gamblers, polite as pie but ready to get tough with any troublemakers, were the same men who at other times of day thundered around the streets on motor-cycles in policemen's uniforms.

Across from the old hotel lay an expanse of park so green and neat, so decorous and shady under the long-tendriled willows, delicately brushing the grass, and the thick, gleaming magnolia trees, that people used to drive by on an August day just to gaze upon it. At the foot of the park, lining Central Avenue as it moved southward, stood Bathhouse Row, a string of eight stately mansions in stucco and brick, each one distinct from its sisters, some with tiers of awnings, others with turrets and gables, one with a mosquelike dome paved with mosaics. Some of the houses were named for their builders (Fordyce, Buckstaff, Lamar, Maurice, and Hale), others called merely Superior or Ozark, or Quapaw (a token for the Indians). "Can you name them, can you name them?" children chanted in the back of the car, for these names meant more than the seven seas or the Great Lakes or even the continents.

Inside their welcoming doors, fearful and amazing things awaited: people who took all your clothing away from you and ruthlessly wrapped you in a sheet; steam tubs where only your head stuck out; bathtubs so huge you feared drowning; water so hot that some people cried; tile floors that only briefly cooled your roasted feet; a bath mitt with a surface like coarse sandpaper, and rough Turkish towels that the attendant mercilessly applied; hard

metal cots on which you lay motionless; hot packs slapped on
your body like poultices; cups of hot water poured down your
throat; huge steel tubs into which paralyzed people could be
lowered like stacks of brick on a fork lift; large-armed women,
their hair wet with sweat and their white uniforms soaked, who
massaged and pounded and slapped you until every cell in every
muscle had relaxed and you lay naked on the table, your brain
shorted out and your circuit breakers tripped, a blob of uncaring,
overheated flesh, lacking the energy ever to rise again, forgetting
the ordeal you had just come through and with no recollection of
what clothing you'd worn into this place and no desire ever to get
up and be gone. But leave you did, without ceremony, as soon as
they were sure you were past fainting on the street. There was no
law, of course, against collapsing in a rocking chair on the veran-
dah, if you chose, where bathers compared notes and watched the
passing scene.

You learned in your cradle that you could never know the
truth, or perhaps that there wasn't any such thing. Criminality,
I thought, meant wiring a dice table, skipping out on your
marker, or, worst of all, past-posting: a shocking act, inexpressi-
bly loathsome, in which a man places a bet on a horse race after
post time with foreknowledge of the results. The punishment for
such conduct was loss of honor, loss of job, consignment to the
terrible realm where men earned their bread by cutting down
trees and hoisting the logs onto truck beds or digging ditches or
teaching school or leading songs in church or cutting flannel from
bolts and fitting oxfords to the feet of nasty little boys and yes-
ma'aming their cranky, demanding mothers. Banishment to a
life beyond the games. Maybe even starvation. A man's life,
I heard it whispered, might be forfeit for cheating at gambling. Breaking the law, compared with breaking the code, was
negligible.

Finally, the vocabulary of the place boiled down to a few

simple definitions, and kids who had never heard of the Bill of Rights knew this much:

Liberal: a person in favor of the status quo, i.e., a person who voted for Leo.

Reformer: anybody else, but reformers were scarce and easily frightened on election day.

Politics: you scratch my back, I'll scratch yours.

WOMEN'S STUDIES

WANTING TO UNDERSTAND what women were and what they must do, I looked into books. Even before I could read, I studied the empty, puzzling hieroglyphs on the pages. Most houses I knew were vacant of books — some people didn't even take the newspaper — but 122 Alamo Street was full of what we called reading material. Daddy kept magazines in a wooden stand by the head of his bed: *Life* (tall and noble), *Look*, and the *Saturday Evening Post* (also noble), *Liberty*, *True Detective*, *True Police*, *Argosy*, *Field & Stream*. You never knew what you might find in the magazine rack, and I leafed through everything, looking for interesting pictures and cartoons. Daddy took magazines seriously: if you bought one, you read it cover to cover, squeezed all the good out of it, and then offered it to the neighbors. (Later, he would require me to read *Life* and the *Saturday Evening Post* and would quiz me on the contents.) And of course Grandpa had his stolen library books, as well as others, for Hot Springs had a small library, filled mostly with detective stories. Besides her puzzle books, Grandma had magazines with crochet instructions, endless pages of abbreviations, as gray as granite. My own books were stacked on a little shelf in the big closet on our side of the house.

Only Hazel would play dolls with me, but everybody felt obliged to read to me. I went everywhere with a book in hand. "Here she comes again," my mother would say, "wagging that book."

"Mama, read me. Please read me."

"I'm too busy." And she'd glance at me from the sink or the washtub, her elbows pumping in the suds, her large young hands twisting the pillowcases or the shirts into double coils, mercilessly, so that the seams almost burst and every drop of water popped out. In thrall to my grandmother's endless demands, she believed she could conquer both Carrie and the housework if she only kept at it. She searched the calico curtains for specks of dirt and ruthlessly snatched them off the rods. Never mind that ironing the ruffles took three hours. She scrubbed the kitchen floor each morning with a brush and rag. She laid down not one but two coats of wax. She ironed the towels and washcloths. At four o'clock she'd often be at the sink, desperately peeling potatoes for supper, her housedress soiled, her frizzled curls clamped down with a bobby pin — for she deemed herself the only thing or creature not entitled to meticulous, continual grooming. On the Old Dutch Cleanser can ("Chases dirt") was a ferocious housewife rolling up her sleeves, her face hidden by her bonnet. "That's your mother," Daddy would say to me, and Mother would sputter, "Yeah, who'd do it if I didn't?" or "Well, you like your clean bed and shirts in the drawer," so that my father and I would smile knowingly behind her back. "Brings it on herself" was what the smile meant.

But I had the power to make her call a truce with the house, for when I showed up with my book, she often turned off the iron or dried her hands and sat down at the kitchen table with me in her lap. She had got her education in a one-room Arkansas schoolhouse where books had been scarce, indeed sacred. "Taking up books" was country language for starting school, and that was how she envisioned the act of learning — you went into a room, took a book in your hands, and inspected the open pages. Every volume to her was the Bible. She had deep respect for the bones and bodies of books, their backs, their leaves. If she had caught me defacing my ABCs, I don't know what would have shocked her more: the dirty pictures or the idea that I could put marks in a book. Not for nothing had she married a bookmaker, though he proved to make a different kind.

"What should Mama read you?" she said once she settled down, searching expertly for the shortest items so she could get back to her hellish tasks. She liked my books of poems. They went quickly, had even meters and dependable rhymes, and she understood them. We didn't know one poet from another. Anonymous or Shakespeare, it was all the same to us. Though we didn't pay attention to the author, we usually began with one by a person called Ogden Nash.

> Belinda lived in a little white house,
> With a little black kitten and a little gray mouse,
> And a little yellow dog and a little red wagon,
> And a realio, trulio, little pet dragon.

Why, I wondered, had they not named me Belinda?

> Custard the dragon had big sharp teeth,
> And spikes on top of him and scales underneath,
> Mouth like a fireplace, chimney for a nose,
> And realio, trulio daggers on his toes.

The poem went on to say that a pirate had invaded Belinda's house and brave Custard had chased him away, though the dragon ended the verse "crying for a nice safe cage." I loved him, since he seemed exactly like my dog, Buster. It seemed proper to me that a girl child would have a dragon to protect her, even if he was timid.

Mama liked the animal poems:

> A hush had fallen on the birds
> And it was almost night
> When I came round a turn and saw
> A whole year's loveliest sight.
> Two calves that thought their month of life
> Meant May through all the year
> Were coming down the grassy road
> As slender as young deer.

Little Orphant Annie, who washed the cups and saucers up and brushed the crumbs away, told her cautionary tale:

> You better mind yer parents an' yer teachers fond and dear,
> An' churish them 'at loves you, an' dry the orphant's tear
> An' h'ep the pore an' needy ones 'at cluster all about,
> Er the Gobble-uns 'll git you
>   Ef you
>   Don't
>   Watch
>   Out.

I didn't like this one so much, for I thought it impossible that an orphan child should be sent out to work in a kitchen. She would go, of course, to the orphans' home, and stand behind the fence waiting for my worn-out clothing to be donated. (I had absorbed some nasty upper-class attitudes.)

I loved all the other poems in this book, for each had its special delicious thing, I thought. There was even one that Mother wouldn't read, "Where the bee sucks, there suck I, in the cowslip's bell I lie." She didn't know it was a famous line, and thought it must have some hidden indecent meaning. "Read that one," I always asked, but she hushed me up. Just before going back to her soapsuds, she recited,

> Time, you old gipsy man,
> Will you not stay,
> Put up your caravan,
> Just for one day?
> . . .
> Goldsmiths shall beat you
> A great golden ring,
> Peacocks shall bow to you,
> Little boys sing.
> Oh, and sweet girls will
> Festoon you with may.
> Time, you old gipsy,
> Why hasten away?

I pictured a real gypsy, not the crazily whirling globe that gives us a day and eats it up savagely in one gulp — for a child knows nothing of time but eternities between Christmases, birthdays, snowfalls. If time was a gypsy, he certainly wasn't in a hurry, and I imagined him dark and enticing, like Bemont in a turban.

But I went to Grandma more often than to my mother, always bringing books. Before we read them, however, we listened to the radio. She opened her arms and helped me shimmy up the side of the bed, and then boosted me over her vast belly to the open space on the other side. The extent of her spare flesh amazed me: flabs of it, flaps of it, rolling waves of it, decorated here and there with odd hairs and pale little moles and spots of one sort or another. I would settle down in the crook of her arm, next to the undulating breast that threatened, like a giant amoeba, to engulf me. Her damp armpit fit neatly over my shoulder; the arm with its wattles of flesh enclosed me in blissful warmth. "Ahhh," she'd say, capturing my small body and positioning it, just so, in the bedclothes.

Before she could read to me, the radio read to both of us. A switch of the dial, and a deep male voice declaimed, "The Guiding Light!" or "The Right to Happiness!" and sweet, keen pipe organ notes, just like in church, swelled from behind the radio cloth. Did Evelyn or Rosemary or Vickie have the right to happiness? Grandma and I exchanged glances: oh yes. As the music faded, worlds rich beyond my imaginings emerged. "I never knew what it meant to be happy," said Evelyn to Rosemary, whenever she had fallen in love or a baby was on the way or George was getting out of the hospital, and then the man with the deep voice returned to sell us Oxydol. Then the song of the pipe organ transported us to "The Romance of Helen Trent." "Because a woman is thirty-five, or even more, romance in life need not be over," the man would state. And there were questions: "When life mocks a woman, breaks her hopes, dashes her against the rocks of despair, can she fight back bravely to prove what so many women long to prove?" "Can a poor girl find happiness married to a rich man?" "Can a plain girl from a small town find happiness married to the most sought-after matinee idol in America?" "Will Robert live long enough to see his child?" The answers never came, but the questions multiplied, punctuated by chilling music. One thing was sure, they were stingy with their information — it took weeks for anything to occur. We fished around — fifteen minutes here with Carter's Little Liver Pills, ten minutes there with Ivory Snow. "Ma Per-

kins," "Amanda of Honeymoon Hill," "Young Widder Brown,"
"Just Plain Bill," "Young Doctor Malone," and "Backstage
Wife" made a crossword puzzle of their own, with interlocking
heartaches and ethics. Grandma often wept, and I soaked up
information.

Women's lives on the radio were mostly agony. Having babies
was important, but only possible for married women. Widows
often earned the living, as did women whose husbands got
crippled in car wrecks. Men didn't matter as much as they themselves thought. Some of them were pretty exciting, though they
always kissed the wrong girl.

Grandma kept the volume low because my mother disapproved of the babies and divorces. Daddy wasn't around while we
were listening, but every evening he scolded Grandma for per-
mitting me to listen to such stupid stuff, such trash, such idiocy:
the first point on which I recall utterly disagreeing with him. "It's
not trash, Daddy," I said. "If you'd listen, you'd like it." And
Grandma would begin to whimper about not wanting to miss her
stories, and he'd simply look grim and go away. I dreaded Saturdays and Sundays, when the airwaves were devoid of passion.

But the books were ours days, nights, Sundays. Grandma
savored the Brothers Grimm and Hans Christian Andersen, always picked the longest stories, and never had enough. She read
to my pleasure, read until the rain stopped or until it started, read
until my mother commanded me to depart. "Why don't you play
outdoors with the other kids? You need some fresh air. Buster is
whining for you to come out. It's not good for you to sit up in that
bed reading all day."

"I'll only finish 'Heart of Ice'" was Carrie's malicious comeback, referring to fifty pages of fine print in the Hans Christian
Andersen that we hadn't even tackled yet. Mother's favored poems
were brief, sweet, and intelligible; Grandma's fairy tales were
long, bloody, and mysterious. Snow White's doomed mother cut

her finger and bled on the palace windowsill, and then died, leaving her baby daughter to a wicked queen. The huntsman sent into the woods to murder Snow White was supposed to cut her innards out but carried out the sentence on a deer instead, bringing back the dripping heart and intestines to the palace. When it was time for the queen to be punished, they heated the cruel iron shoes red hot and put them on her feet — such a satisfying demonstration that people who abuse little girls are going to get it in spades eventually. Yet when I told my father about it — for I shared these stories with him — he said, infuriatingly, "What about the poor queen? How could she ever walk again?"

"There was once a woman who had three daughters," my grandmother read, "of whom the eldest was called Little One-eye, because she had only one eye in the middle of her forehead; and the second, Little Two-eyes, because she had two eyes like other people; and the youngest, Little Three-eyes, because she had three eyes, and her third eye was also in the middle of her forehead. But because Little Two-eyes did not look any different from other children, her sisters and mother could not bear her. They beat and starved her." My father informed me that the story was crazy, that things went the other way around, with the normal people beating up the freaks.

Twenty times a week I asked for the tale of Snow White and Rose Red, the mysterious sisters, one blond and shy as an angel, the other a sensible brunette. I always played Rose Red, joyous and unafraid when the fierce old bear tapped at my door on a winter's eve. I would stroke his coat and roll around with him, catching a glimpse of a golden doublet beneath the fur. Aha, a handsome prince whose treasure had been stolen by a wicked dwarf. I would carry a pair of sharp little scissors in my apron pocket, and when I came upon the dwarf, caught by his beard on a tree limb, I'd smartly clip the dwarfish whiskers. But the gleaming prince shook off his bear suit and married Goody-two-shoes, the blonde.

"Why didn't Rose Red get the prince?"

"Honey catches more flies than vinegar," my grandmother pointed out.

So we'd turn to the twelve dancing princesses. These wicked girls slept in the same room, sneaking out each night and dancing their pretty slippers to rags, so that the king, their father, had to buy a dozen new pairs every day. He announced that any man who solved the mystery might choose his wife from among them and inherit the kingdom; unsuccessful candidates, of course, would die. Grandma showed me the girls, in ball gowns, on a spiral staircase I was all for them, though I did wonder why the king didn't just ask them straight out what they were up to. Five or six princes died before the old soldier arrived, with a cloak that rendered him invisible The princesses slipped out their secret exit into a woods where all the trees were silver and gold and the flowers were jewels. Each girl was rowed across a lake by a prince to a castle where the dancing took place The youngest was frightened, as she sensed the presence of the spy, but the eldest scoffed at her. To my astonishment, the eldest was the bride he chose (They always went for the dumbest or the shyest.) Anyhow, the party was over "When a girl marries," my father joked, speaking of the soap operas, "love flies out the window." And maybe it was so

In Grandma's nest of flesh and flab and ancient sweat, I learned to read for myself, I now believe, or at least I imagine it as the locale where the black hieroglyphs on the page, meaningless scribbles until the mind's dimensions expand, finally opened like a flower, and the frivolous, seductive illustrations shrank into the background. One afternoon I made the startling discovery that a person reading aloud can skip around, sweeten things up, lie.

"Grandma, it doesn't say the wolf ran away, it says the little pigs burnt him to death." Between the printed page and the spoken word lay an empty space, apparently. Those words on the page were the key to power. To be illiterate was to be a child forever, at the mercy of those who read, at the mercy of the words themselves. I couldn't have expressed this notion at the time, but in the prison of my grandmother's bed, I loved the words, saw them as my pathway of escape. From what I didn't know — from whatever made slaves of my mother and my aunt and an invalid of my grandmother.

But other stories, other words, led in more ominous directions. Grandma loved Hans Christian Andersen, his idea that within each flower there lived a tiny man or woman or that the girl who "trod on a loaf" to keep her shoes from getting muddy would be punished for her vanity and wastefulness. One of the stories we read a hundred times. (I still read it.) It, too, featured an old soldier. It, too, was about dancing shoes. But it seemed to have been written especially for me.

An orphan girl named Karen went to her mother's funeral wearing a pair of ragged red shoes. She might have starved by the roadside, but a blind old lady took pity on her and adopted her. Soon after, the princess of the land passed by, wearing a pair of wonderful red morocco slippers, and Karen wanted them. So she tricked the old lady into buying her a pair, and wore them to her confirmation. The town was shocked. Red shoes in church! But Karen could not resist wearing them to church a second time, and this time an old soldier with a long red beard and a crutch was waiting for her.

"See what beautiful dancing shoes!" said the soldier. The shoes began to dance, and Karen danced with them. She could scarcely wrench them off her feet, and she promised the blind lady never to wear them again. But the old lady fell ill and was dying, so Karen buckled the shoes on her feet once more and danced all over the world. Then the red shoes, as willful as

Karen herself, carried her into the dark forest. Something shone up above the trees. She thought it was the moon, for it was a face, but it was the old soldier with the red beard. He nodded and said, "See what pretty dancing shoes!"

"Who's that old soldier, Grandma?" The bearded face shining through the trees terrified me. I can see it still.

And Grandma answered, "I suppose it's God. Yes, it must be God."

"No, it isn't God."

Karen danced onward, never even stopping for food. And as she danced, an angel came and cursed her, tired and frightened and hungry as she was. She tried to enter a church to pray, but the priest saw how wicked she was and stopped her at the church door. He said she would go to hell. Next she danced up to the executioner's house. He was waiting for her; his ax was already trembling in anticipation. Karen pleaded with him to cut her feet off so she could save her soul.

"Cut her feet off? Grandma!"

He did cut them off, and Karen was reconciled and died in church, her heart so overfilled with sunshine, with peace, and with joy that it broke.

Why did they always go for the feet? I thought, clutching my bare toes. Sometimes I dreamed of the soldier, with his red beard hanging down like Spanish moss, his face aglow as he muttered a spell over my shoes, which then carried me across the world. No, I would never go against God, never do the forbidden thing, never beg to have my feet chopped off. Imagine the executioner's blade trembling! I would be a good girl. And yet, if I found red shoes in the roadway one day, and the old soldier appeared in a tree, his face shining like the moon, and I wanted to dance so very much, what would I do?

Since this was one story I never shared with my father, he had no comment.

Books were not everything. My mother and my grandma thought my hands needed training — sewing, quilting, embroidery, crochet. My mother gave me scraps of cloth and buttons to sew in place, showed me how to knot the threads with a little spit and a quick motion of thumb and forefinger. "Now you're not going to cry over a little thing like that," she said when I stuck myself. She drew flowers on a cloth, and I stitched daisies and asters with petals like spokes and clusters of yellow French knots in the middle.

Some afternoons, when the housework was finished early, out would come the scrap box, full of cuttings and pieces of old shirts and little outgrown dresses of mine. Mother laid the tiny pieces together and joined them with miraculously fine stitches in perfect rows. Every stitch the same length, the same number to every inch, so that when the laborious little squares were finally sewn together, they were all exactly the same, ready for the quilting frame, ready for hard use, ready for the critical eyes of other women. I slept under such a quilt, one that she had made. Now, inspecting the millions of tiny stitches and knowing how difficult it was merely to sew a button to a cloth, I could not imagine creating such a thing.

My grandmother's art was also bedcovers: not pieced but crocheted. Ladies — her only visitors — came and commissioned crocheted spreads for their newly decorated bedrooms. This, too, was an art of squares: worked laboriously, repetitively, relentlessly, according to a stern, unvarying template (described endlessly in crochet books). Carrie held the hook in her bent right fingers, which had stiffened into just the right position to hold it, and the thread was in her left, feeding past the hook, inch by inexorable inch. She put the hook into my fingers and wound the string around my left hand, and I set about making a useless chain. She herself turned out lacy, identical rococo squares, some dead white and some ecru (the color of her pillowcases, her hair). She kept several dusty-lidded boxes under her bed, some filled with thread and others with squares. One day she told me that for every square she made to sell, she made another for me. I too would possess a thing made up of millions of twitches of my grandmother's painful hands, miles and miles of thin cotton thread, knotted precisely, over and over, unendingly until death.

"I don't want a crocheted bedspread."

"It's only for when you get married; of course you can't use it now. It's much too fancy for a little girl "

"I'm not going to get married. It's too much trouble On the radio, all they do is cry."

"Well, listen to this talk. What else would you do? Do you want to be like Miss Blossom, and never comb your hair and yell at folks all night? That's what happens to girls who don't get married. You'll see " And she would laugh as she chained onward, the steel tip of her crochet hook flashing like a surgical instrument

My father was aware of all this. He willingly admired the tacked-down buttons, the crooked piecework, and the lopsided doilies I displayed for him in the evening. "All very good," he would say. "An accomplished little seamstress." But I knew he hadn't given me over to the women. He was waiting until I crossed some bridge. One day — I don't remember how old I was — he caught me with the doors to his bookshelf propped open, looking at the dirty pictures in the Casanova book. *In flagrante delicto.* He had come so swiftly that I hadn't been able to replace the book and close the doors. I thought I was done for, but he sat down companionably on the floor with me and said, "You'll be able to read that book one of these days. And I want you to know one thing. This bookcase is yours. You can turn the keys. You can open these doors. You don't have to have anybody's permission. You can read anything in here. In ten years perhaps you will tell me you've read every book on these shelves. If something seems too hard for you, try it anyway. Bring it to me. I'll help you. If you want other books, I'll take you to the bookstore. I'll take you to the library. I want you to read."

He took volumes out of the shelf one by one and said the names aloud. I understood none of it, had nothing whatever in my head to compare it with. I might not remember one title, except that I have carried these books with me, my legacy, my impedimenta, sometimes my dead weight, lugging them in liquor cartons from Arkansas, into and out of apartments and houses. The set of Dickens, bound in red (his method with Dickens was to read the first fifty pages aloud and strand me as soon as the plot had caught me). Half a shelf of memoirs of eighteenth-century court life in Austria and France. Book-of-the-Month Club novels (he was a charter member). Rows of Pocket Books — paperbacks were a novelty in 1940, and Hat Abbott was their most enthusiastic purchaser. Their pages would turn to crumbs in my hands one day. Blue-and-gilt volumes by Edward Gibbon ("A great man, the greatest of all historians. We'll save him for when you're older"). Henry Wadsworth Longfellow in a stately brown binding. Ralph Waldo Emerson. Oscar Wilde. Sir Walter Scott. W. Somerset Maugham. Casanova. Erasmus. Rabelais. *The World's Greatest Stories. The World's Greatest Essays. Ben-Hur*, by Lew Wallace. Sir Edward Bulwer-Lytton's *The Last Days of Pompeii. The Decameron. The Heptameron.* A road map toward all writing. There was hardly a woman's name on any spine, except for Margaret Mitchell and Kathleen Windsor and Marguerite of Navarre, but I'd no idea this mattered. I hefted the volumes as my father passed them to me, learned how a real book felt, knowing at once that they were superior to radio stories and fairy tales and sweet poems and children's books. Here was the world of ideas, and I knew it was identical to the world of men.

My father had his private motives as he took the crochet hook and the needle out of my hand. Perhaps I am only imagining that this happened all in the same hour, on the same day when he discovered me and Casanova. In the battle that we came to wage against one another, at least he equipped me with equal weapons.

ℒESSONS

WHEN I WAS SIX, I was sent to Oaklawn School, which was only a block from the racetrack. The horses arrived in winter, and beginning in late January, as we burst out-of-doors at the end of a school day, we could hear the hooves hitting the turf and smell the manure on the air (the excrement of Thoroughbreds is fragrant and clean, like hay). In the month of March, when the race meet was actually on, passionate roars from the grandstand interrupted our lessons every half-hour in the afternoons. Hearing the bugle for post time, I would imagine myself grown up, at the track in nylon stockings and a silky dress; would picture my mother in the grandstand, wearing a pretty new hat and screaming for her horse to come in, for sometimes she did leave her housework behind and go to the track; and would imagine my father uptown in his green eyeshade, shuffling the crisp fins and sawbucks like playing cards. Thus, temporarily jailed in our classrooms, we were deliciously close to the heart of things.

The school, a ramshackle old pile of red brick, had the dimensions of a palace and enormous double doors in front and back that on warm days, when they were propped open, made a breezeway of the main floor. On either side were smaller entries marked

BOYS and GIRLS, already quaint and in disuse by the 1940s. There were eight classrooms, an auditorium that doubled as a storeroom, the boys' and the girls' toilets in the basement, and on the main floor the principal's office, which we all feared to enter.

Even for Mayor McLaughlin and his cronies, who were ashamed of very little, Oaklawn School was a disgrace. Its timbers groaned in the wind like a ship under sail, its broad wooden staircases creaked, and the banisters wobbled as we marched up and down. The wood floors throughout the school were saturated with decades of heavily applied oil, so that a few electric sparks or a dropped match would have sautéed us. The fire escape from the top floor clung to the facade by a few screws and bolts and lacked a step or two. Indeed, the fire chief had condemned the building years before, but first the Depression and then the looming European war made it unthinkable to break ground for a new school. Nevertheless, the classrooms were of lavish dimensions, each with forty scarred desks nailed down in rows and dark green windowshades folded out of the way to admit the sunshine, which poured in copiously even in winter. Each room had a cloakroom, with cubbies for lunchboxes, hooks for coats. It also served as the punishment cell, where bad girls were sent to cool off and make up their minds to "act like ladies." Bad boys, who vastly outnumbered bad girls, were taken there and thrashed with wooden paddles.

The teachers were eight tough veterans with rollbooks and rulers — all women, of course. The three married teachers, who were holding down jobs to "help out," as working women described it, came to school in new dresses occasionally; the single teachers wore the same thing every day. Ill-paid and lacking all forms of employment benefits, they nevertheless ran Oaklawn School like the Royal Navy: you defied authority at your peril. Miss Pettigrew, who taught third grade, exemplified the rewards of forty years of devotion in an Arkansas classroom. A skeleton with transparent skin thickly knotted with blue blood vessels, she had never been seen to smile. She snapped her right thumb and middle finger continually, in and out of class; after school, making her way home on flamingo legs, she chattered angrily aloud, and she no doubt scolded the walls of her furnished room. We called her "old witch" and scorned her thick stockings, her lace-up shoes, the long print dress she wore in all seasons, in winter adding a threadbare cardigan. We hated her not for being crazy or ragged but for being old and out-of-date. Why couldn't she make progress like the rest of us?

The first-grade teacher was Doris Love, a brisk, entirely lovable young woman. Her green eyes saw everything, her black hair was smoothed back under a little bow, her smile shone like a knife blade. Well scrubbed and perfectly buttoned in her perpetual checked suit and red blouse, she wore granny oxfords that increased her age by half and brought her almost to the shoulder height of the sixth-grade boys. She lived many miles from school with her elderly, dependent father, whose ancient auto she drove back and forth when it would run. When it wouldn't, she hitchhiked: people thought it an honor to stop for Miss Love. Only the married teachers had nice cars. Even then I knew that women's automobiles showed what kind of men they had, and it seemed no stranger than anything else I knew.

Miss Love seated the boys and girls in separate rows, but she had no prejudices about smart and dumb. Although there was a desk and chair at the front of the room, she never seemed to sit down. "Now, boys and girls," she said almost at once, "we're going to study penmanship."

Because my mother had visited school in August to find out what I would need, I arrived at first grade with a Blue Horse tablet of pulpy, wide-lined paper, six new pencils, a pencil box, and a dozen crayons, all of which I stowed in the desk except for the tablet and one pencil. (I also brought a Thermos of milk and a sandwich, crusts trimmed.) Miss Love turned and chalked the letters across the blackboard, great plump capital A's like bosomy queen mothers, little a's, "their daughters," she explained. And giant, bulbous capital B's, with majestic curlicues in front, more suggestive even than A's, which made the little b's look like orphans. Miss Love took me first, bending over me, her small hand covering mine while I formed the letters with a blunt pencil. "One big loop-the-loop, no sirree, don't hold that pencil tight, keep that elbow loose, loop, loop." Only half-a-dozen children had shown up with school supplies on the very first day, five of them girls with trimmed crusts as well. For the rest, Miss Love had to tear up a tablet of her own and give out paper and pencils. A boy named Benjamin, too thin for his overalls, never did get the cash together for a tablet and pencil and lived off Miss Love all year

Robert Seaver, across the aisle from me, shot me a handsome grin of disbelief when he saw my tablet and realized he had to conjure fifteen cents from someplace. He was way too large to be in first grade. Indeed, he was taller than Miss Love, and he shone like copper and had blacker eyes than even my Uncle Bruce. Clearly his mother was not the sort who visited school in August to find out what her son might need. I gave him one of my pencils and offered him some crayons, too, which Miss Love forced him to return. (Charity came from the front desk, not across the aisle.) By the second week he turned up with his tablet "My dad give me the money," he said when I inquired. "I ain't got no mother "

Miss Love announced that same day that Robert Seaver was an Indian. Not only that but a Cherokee, which she said was the best kind of Indian, a very superior Southern kind of Indian, and we should all be proud to know one. During the coming winter we were going to study Indians, and Robert would be able to help us. We were going to set up a model of an Indian town on the worktable. Yes, Indians did have towns, didn't they, Robert? She didn't tell us that Robert was already ten years old and this was the first year he had made it to first grade. She did mention that he had an interesting condition called epilepsy. This meant, she said, that on a rare occasion Robert might lose his awareness of us, might look strange, might even fall down and twitch, and if this happened, we were to come and get a teacher right away, any teacher. We mustn't touch Robert or try to help him, but we mustn't be afraid that anything much was wrong with him. Actually it was a kind of distinction.

Meantime, while we waited to build the Indian town, our main job was learning to read and write. We had to learn to make our letters, Miss Love said, not just any old letters but letters that would make us proud of ourselves. Illegibility was not to be tolerated, nor inkblots. Only perfection would induce her to cover our tablets with purple elephants from her stamp pad. The more elephants, the better she loved us. And she'd write it on the last page of the tablet — "You are a dear pupil, and I love you. Miss Love" — so that you could read it for the rest of your life, could spread it before your parents. (My father valued my high marks as much as I did, and saw to it that they carried material rewards at home.)

Thus throughout that whole first year we learned a fine italic hand. The children of bookmakers, carpenters, and grocery clerks, the orphan, the epileptic Indian, yes, even Benjamin, who walked six miles to school wearing overalls with no shirt underneath: each would grip his pencil, chew the eraser, and work against his will and the laws of social rank until he achieved the handwriting of a gentleman. "Loop, loop, loop," Miss Love cried, her stub of chalk inscribing the lovely letters in thin air as she skipped from window to wall. Straining, almost weeping, we formed the lavish capital *P*'s, the ornamented *E*'s that began like the slope of a schoolground slide and ended with a half-moon, the *S*'s with double curlicues like elves' shoes, and the *X*'s transformed from crude crosses into billowy helixes more like wisteria tendrils than letters. Soon the whole first grade, or at least the feminine half of it, possessed the flowery script of the penmanship book — the cultivated hand of the ruling classes. We did ovals. We did push-pulls. And sometimes while we did them, Miss Love would read aloud or sing little songs.

> Higgledy piggledy, my black hen,
> She lays eggs for gentlemen.
> Gentlemen come every day
> To see what my black hen doth lay.

Although the eggs were for gentlemen rather than ladies, the boys fell behind almost immediately. Miss Love would bring them gently up to her desk one by one, grasping their paws in her small hand, loosening their elbows, poking at their shoulders. "Loosen up those fingers. Don't be afraid to take up space. Write with your whole arm, loop, loop, loop." Only one time did I have to be taken to the desk. Robert stood there daily.

I loved the letters. I loved Robert Seaver, even as I waited for him to fall down and twitch. I asked him when he thought he might do it, but he told me that it hadn't happened in a long time. It must be like fainting, I decided, which I thought exciting and romantic and yearned to do myself. It seemed more logical for girls to faint.

More amazing was that Robert Seaver didn't care if he learned anything or not. But when Miss Love had her back turned, he would lean cozily over my shoulder to watch what I did. I noticed a wonderful smell about him — smoky, leafy, musty; entirely unlike the starched-and-ironed, soaped-and-curled fragrance I gave off. He said he lived in a trailer with his daddy way out on Ferry Road. (I thought this meant Fairy Road, and imagined Robert's trailer deep in the forest, with winged creatures perched on mushrooms.) Sometimes he would sit back and try to form the letters, but halfway through he'd mutter and laugh and begin looking out the window.

At recess I played with Robert, because he loved to play girl games and didn't care who won. I never wondered why certain games belonged to girls — house, for instance. Robert was the only boy who'd sit under the oak tree and play house, sweeping out each little compartment among the roots, making furniture out of acorns and leaves and bits of glass and people out of twigs, who would then have twig children. His twig children were unpredictable, sometimes rampaging through the neighborhood, upending beds and tables, mocking other twigs. Sometimes he broke rank entirely and threatened the whole enterprise with crawdads captured in the creek, just to hear us scream.

He played jacks, too, the very essence of a girl game — an immobile, sit-down-right-on-the-sidewalk game, so that you got your panties and skirt dirty and the imprint of the concrete on your legs, a game of eye and fingertip rather than of muscle and lungs, scoreless, devoid of all physical contact, but intensely competitive nevertheless. You needed a tiny rubber ball and a bag of metal jacks — at least a dozen, though two dozen was better, because then you could never be done. You needed to be obsessed with precision, to delight in repetition and in the neat stowing-away of small objects, you needed to hate small errors, you needed a hawk's eye to spot the errors, and you needed doggedness — almost the same equipment as for Grandma's crocheted squares. First you did the onesies, twosies, threesies, allsies — one bounce. Eggs in a basket — no bounce. Double bounce (for babies). Hens in the henhouse (one jack at a time, shoved into the hollow of your hand), cow over the moon, pigs at the trough, horses in the stable (between your fingers), shooting stars — the jacks tossed up and caught, which became improbable when you reached twosies and impossible with allsies. But then you went back to onesies again. (Here in this game housewives, seam-stresses, librarians, and secretaries were made.) Robert, with his big square fingers, seldom got past the plain one-bounce onesies, and would roll on the sidewalk laughing and trying to jar our arms as we worked our way to shooting stars while he was still on twosies in a six-jack game.

Though he never jumped rope himself, he'd turn the rope or stand on the sidelines chanting, "Vote, vote, vote for Charlotte, here comes Lola at the door," or "Teddy bear, teddy bear, turn around, teddy bear, teddy bear, touch the ground. Teddy bear, teddy bear, that will do." Sometimes as one of us touched her shoe and ran out like a dancer, he'd catch her in his arms and pretend to kiss her, and one day I kissed him back and the whole playground began to screech, "Shirley Jean loves Robert, Shirley Jean loves Robert." And I did love him. He didn't know how to read any better than he could write, and he couldn't play jacks, but he seemed dazzled that I could do all those things. My perfect lunchbox, my neat clothing, my apparently endless supply of sharp pencils and nickels for candy had already drawn some hurtful lines between me and my less affluent classmates. But Robert didn't hate me for my trimmed crusts and my mittens.

At supper, my father's first question was what I had done at school, and he wouldn't take "Nothing" for an answer. Robert's name must have appeared once too often in my accounts, for he asked my mother about him and was told he was "that Indian boy." "Wouldn't you just know she'd take up with him, when she's got so many nice little girls to play with? He looks just like a colored boy. I don't know what he's doing at Oaklawn School. But he seems like a good little fellow, I have to say." My father warned me to keep away from Robert, and began a relentless litany about boys, a catalogue of evils that he repeated whenever the subject came into my conversation: boys played rough, lied, couldn't be trusted. I had plenty of time to get to know them, plenty of time.

Why didn't the playground monitor do her job at recess? Indeed, there was a boys' side and a girls' side to the playground, and the two sexes were technically forbidden to play together. But I adored Robert anyway, for how was my father to know?

I soon learned that boys did amazing things: for example, they smoked. Some sixth-grade boys smoked Luckys just like my father, and though Robert was a first-grader, they let him smoke too. "Stunt your growth," the teachers warned, but the smokers were always the tallest. Boys kept up with the ponies, too. "Arabian Knight in the second, and the daily double paid twenty-six dollars," Robert would whisper if the race meet was on, somehow having gotten his hands on the racing results. Some of the older boys made book for nickels and hung around the stables after school, hoping to become handicappers.

Boys also got beatings, and I soon heard a wooden paddle applied to human flesh. Sometimes it took two teachers to do it, and Miss Love often served as part of the team. One wild, outsized third-grader named Tom Ransom was beaten regularly — he said goddamn and shit right out where Miss Pettigrew could hear him, not to mention smoking and refusing to get his lessons. Some said he even drank. One afternoon Mrs. Tomkins, the fourth-grade teacher, called Miss Love out of class to help her beat Tom. (Miss Pettigrew could only watch, grimly.) Wood lashing a backside echoed through the school, and Tom Ransom's screams could be heard on the last two licks. Mr. Ransom appeared at the school the day after the beating and demanded that Miss Love come into the hallway with him. We heard his curses and shouts echoing up the stairs, but Miss Love stood her ground. "You have to whip those big old boys," she said to us, her face hardening, her eyes sharp. "They don't understand anything else. I'm certain none of you will ever earn a licking." But the sounds had made us first-graders big-eyed and sick, and kept us very quiet for a few days.

"Naw, don't worry," Robert Seaver told me. "They never whup the girls. I ain't going to yell like that if they whup me. And I don't care if I do get a beatin'. My daddy beats me ever day, nearly." I had by this time become a rescuer, at least in my fantasies. I hated the sound of the blows, and imagined throwing myself between Miss Love and Tom should the occasion arise again. "Don't touch him anymore," I'd cry. "Leave him to me. I can save him." Astounded, she would do exactly as I said, and I would lead Tom away, outdoors to the crawdad creek or home to the little pasture where he kept his pony (which I walked past every day on the way to school). I'd help him with his homework and teach him to write a beautiful hand the way I could, and he'd be grateful. No more beatings for him, lots of pony rides for me. It didn't work out. If I became his friend, I feared, the teachers might start beating me. Anyway, Tom scorned me and refused even to learn my name.

In November, when the heat went on, I also learned that boys peed on the radiators — on purpose, for fun. The whole basement smelled of scorched urine from the first chill day until February, when the heat went off. First and second grade met in the basement, and sometimes we were gagged by the stench, which merged in my mind with chapped faces and freezing temperatures. One of Miss Love's duties was to catch the boys peeing, and it made me sick to imagine a woman bursting into the boys' room, discovering them peeing horizontally.

As the winter wore on, Benjamin and Robert and other children arrived at school hungry, in the thin jackets they had worn all fall, with their bare hands split from the cold. Robert only laughed, but one morning Benjamin couldn't stop sobbing. Miss Love took up a collection. The PTA ladies came and set up hot plates and tables in the basement on cold mornings, so that three burnt fragrances floated on the air — oatmeal, toast, and urine. We girls who came to school with pimiento cheese sandwiches and red apples, and an extra Thermos for hot soup, watched in embarrassment as our classmates lined up and wolfed the free food.

One day as school let out, the father of one of the other children was waiting outside the door for Miss Love. Having nothing against eavesdropping, I heard him say that Robert Seaver was a nigger and had no business in our class. "He ought to be in nigger school. I don't want him around my boy. And he has fits, they tell me. Fits, falling down, where he foams at the mouth. I saw him down by the courthouse with his old man two Saturdays ago, and he fell down foaming. Old man was nearly too drunk to notice. He has no business in this school." At that moment, Miss Love shut the classroom door. I went outdoors to wait for my mother, who'd promised to meet me in the car. Foaming at the mouth? Not Robert. I said nothing to my parents but cried in my pillow that night, expecting Robert to be gone the next day. Who would tell us how to make the Indian town, who would tie the tops of the teepees and show us how to find arrowheads in the school-yard? Nevertheless the next morning he was there, across the aisle, unaware that his life had been in jeopardy. The school year wore on, and turned to summer. The last day came and all the schoolmates vanished. First grade was over as surely as if we had all died.

That summer, just before the United States entered World War II, the Depression ended at 122 Alamo. The gambling business looked solid; Old Man Jake gave my father a raise just when he and my mother had saved enough to make a down payment. Within a few weeks, we not only had the house to ourselves, we owned it. The accumulation of rent receipts in the miniature cedar chest atop his bureau had lacerated my father's heart, and now he had the wherewithal to take out a mortgage and buy 122 Alamo from the landlord. He then turned the tables on his relations and told them to move out. Grandma was hardly surprised — she knew quite well that the world revolved on infidelity and treachery, and that far across the waters Hitler and Mussolini goose-stepped into other people's countries, turning many a grandmother like herself into a refugee. I was an indignant but inconstant advocate of her cause, for my mother had sworn she would move out if my grandparents didn't. Besides, Mother told me, if they went elsewhere, I could have my own bedroom, with ruffles on the bedspread and a dressing table all to myself. We'd have a proper living room, where I'd be proud to bring my playmates. We'd be rid of that musty old-timey parlor. We wouldn't have to share the bathroom anymore. We'd have birthday parties, cakes, balloons. There'd be a place for Mother to set up her sewing machine, and she would turn out dozens of beautiful little dresses. From that moment on, I was a traitor, a double agent: accompanying my mother to pick out wallpaper, wavering between the blue daisies and the yellow tea roses, then returning to enshroud myself in Carrie's bedsheets and piously pat her hand as she read stories to me and wept.

The truck arrived on schedule, and the men quickly emptied out my grandma's parlor, dismantled respectability and family pride, upended the horsehair settee, the fierce old chairs, the claw-footed table, the whatnots, antimacassars, and all. I had no regrets for the ugly chairs and settee, but darted in and rescued the box with the curls and the little boys inside it, and the picture of my sister. Grandma refused to let me keep it, though. Two things were left behind for us: the upright piano, since now we had enough money for lessons, and the bookcase, which had belonged to my father all along. The space was stripped, and the stains on the walls were revealed as pictures were ripped off their hooks. Carrie's bedroom went next, and then Carrie, weeping in her coat and hat, was somehow wedged into the Model T, which erupted like firecrackers as Grandpa drove them away to the first of a series of apartments where they would live out their lives.

Hazel and Bruce required no truck. They left, the pair of them, clinging to each other like Adam and Eve expelled from the garden. Hazel kissed me and then opened the door to the big closet. "Must kiss my dollies bye-bye. Reckon I need to find me some new play-pretties." She smiled and waved goodbye as she and her husband set off on foot like gypsies with their things in a laundry bag. They had rented a house nearby, I understood. "Reckon you and that little dog will do okay," Bruce said to me — the only time I remember him addressing me at all.

"Having a child makes a person merciless," I'd overheard my father say that morning at breakfast, as though all this were my fault. As my mother swept up after the movers and surveyed the rooms that were hers to possess, she looked mean. The first thing she did was open the doors between the two apartments, and Buster and I ran crazily through the spaces. "Let's leave it like this," I shouted. That afternoon workmen arrived with lumber and paint cans, paste buckets, rolls of wallpaper. They took away the sink and stove in our kitchen and turned it into a bedroom for me, with blue-and-pink-flowered wallpaper, a white chenille spread to cover my new bed (a double with two fat pillows), a dressing table with a hand mirror and a brush and comb in a matching set. Oh, I loved them! In Grandma's kitchen, about where Grandpa's cot had been, they installed a new sink and a new metal cupboard. Our purchases often ended in "ette": a dinette set with yellow leatherette chairs, and for the living room a dark red, prickly "divanette." New linoleum for the kitchen and the laundry porch covered up the spots where the cavern had opened into infinity and the devil's face had leered in secret, visible only to Hazel and me. We turned Grandma's bedroom into a sewing room, against the day when we'd be able to afford a dining table. However, we never got beyond the dinette set.

The closet where my ghostly sister had lived was aired out, repapered, and fitted with shelves for a linen closet, so that one never needed to dodge the shadows in there or leave offerings of food for the phantom to eat. The workmen painted the bathroom ceiling, so that it was slick and goblin-free. Most astonishing of all, Grandma's parlor became my mother's up-to-date living room, with the divanette, two matching chairs, and a blue platform rocker, and a new carpet, and the dark blue draperies she coveted, lined with what she called panels, lovely straight strips of sheer white that shimmered in the wind. And on every other window in the house, yards and yards of white organdy, lavished with ruffles. (These curtains replaced my grandmother as a slave driver, for they had to be washed and ironed every two or three months, a task that required days and always ended in exhaustion.) Without a thought for my grandparents, I whirled through the redecorated rooms when the neighbor ladies came to see the new furniture. "I'm thrilled for you, Velma, honestly," they said, though it was clear they were sick with envy and we had damaged communal life by setting ourselves above them.

Behind the new couch, my father hung a picture of an all-purpose seaside village ringed by bare mountains and boats anchored in the blue water, and not a soul in sight. My parents had got it in the furniture store where they bought the double bed for me and a wringer-washer with three separate galvanized rinse tubs standing on their own legs, so Mama could just roll them around to the sink and drain them with a hose instead of lifting them. My parents hadn't intended to buy a picture, but the salesman threw it in free with the furniture. Daddy believed it was a famous painting, but he didn't know of what or by whom or where. As soon as he got it tacked to the wall, he stationed himself in the platform rocker and gazed at it, saying he wished he lived in that village, because it looked trouble-free. Nobody had migraine headaches there or wondered where their next dollar was coming from or made payoffs to the state police. And soon, in the living room, he added his heart's desire — a 1940s RCA with arches and columns, a monument on the floor. "Short wave," my father explained. "You can hear England, China, Australia on here," and in fact we did hear voices, crackling like wads of cellophane.

Outdoors changed, too. The nursery truck arrived with bushes and shrubs, including the flowering peach tree that bloomed but did not bear, as well as snowball bushes, spirea, variegated evergreens, and roses with delicious names: Amy Quinard, talisman. Workmen plowed up the weedy yard and scattered grass seed for a lawn. They tore down the henhouse and carried the planks away — we were not to harbor chickens anymore. We would gather bouquets rather than baskets of eggs. A carpenter came and ripped out the old front steps where the creatures lived that watched the heels and toes going up and down, and I saw that there'd been nothing behind the steps all along. The new steps were solid concrete.

The mortgage now assumed a role of its own, along with our other acquisitions. At breakfast Daddy would congratulate himself on being a homeowner, and at suppertime he would curse the mortgage as well as the bank, which he viewed as a hurricane boiling permanently offshore, certain to wash us out into the street. Nevertheless, as the expenses of remodeling were gradually paid off, he added one more amenity — a chicken-wire fence that ran completely around the huge yard on six-foot posts and could be entered only by latched gates at the front and back of the house. Daddy said it was to protect Buster and me from the traffic. But the only traffic on Alamo Street was our green Chevrolet. You could hear the motor and the crunch of rocks long before any car ever nosed over the hill. Buster hated the fence and desperately dug under it, escaping to the thorny vacant lots around us in search of companionship, regardless of how often I scolded him for running away. My mother believed in swift justice for dogs, and she would flail him with the newspaper if she caught him. Daddy methodically plugged up all the holes and anchored the fence to the ground, but the dog never gave up. After staying inside for a month, he would tunnel out in the dark of night through a massive hole that astounded us.

I perceived the fence as a bargain of some kind: "Be content within these boundaries, little girl, and we'll make it so pleasant inside that you'll find it hard to go out those gates." I began to like being inside my own estate, where no one could bother me unless I let them in. I could leave the yard easily, but the high wire had its effect. I often played alone in my grassy compound, listening to the shouts and tough talk of the mechanic's sons across the alleyway. Sometimes I was glad to be excluded; sometimes I yearned to be part of the bicycle gang. Of course, I wasn't allowed a bicycle. It was a question of traffic again, but I sensed that boys had more to do with it than cars. An only daughter being purposefully groomed should not risk her bones with nor learn dirty words from boys who ate onion sandwiches for breakfast and rode on one wheel and never combed their hair and perhaps had lice. And there was Miss Blossom to think of, too. Beyond this fence, she could never get at me. She could curse us as we passed her door, perhaps, observe me from behind her drawn shades, shriek in the night until the dogs howled, but nevermore would she creep up on me. As I grew older, I sometimes dared myself to go up on her porch and make her tell me what was wrong with her. But I never did: for what if she told me things too terrible to bear, what if madness was catching and I began screaming in the night myself?

Briefly that year my father's job was shaken by the death of Old Man Jacobs in a car crash. It was just an accident, could have happened to anybody, but whispers of murder ran around the town. Any change in the fragile pattern of unwritten law that held the town together constituted a threat. If it had been murder, would the murder be avenged? No event occurred without our wondering who the beneficiary might be. My father contracted a marathon headache and tightened his head rag around his purple forehead for days, while Mother looked grim and anxious. But Leo and the other powers quickly put a new man in place, and Daddy's job went on. Thus our heyday as proper middle-class people began. What my father brought home in his pay envelope on Saturday was a special kind of money, not dirty and wilted — aces and fins and ten-spots so clean they rattled, and he taught me to talk about money in this hustler's vocabulary, warning me that it was inside information I must not share. Once I even saw, and held, a five-hundred-dollar bill. No matter how fat the pay envelope, the money was gone by next week. But so what? Up those stairs in paradise the wealthy sportsmen mingled, and all around America the great Thoroughbreds raced, chronicled by Western Union, and on Saturday our horse always ran in the money.

I scorned the daughters of grocers and bankers and doctors. What did they know of the world? They were dull offspring of dull men who never wore their hats back on their heads, or talked about the fix being in, or joked about the laws of God and man (or got away with breaking them), or talked about how to lay off bets, or flashed the sweet bills in the brown envelope and spent them so quickly on dresses and ripe plums in the middle of winter. My dolls were the prettiest and my curls the blondest, just as my fingernails were always the cleanest when the school nurse came. Daddy wore tailor-made shirts, and soon my mother was sporting a real fur coat (mink-dyed muskrat, the label said) and I wore a little white rabbit jacket with matching tam and muff.

Oh, the raids still came: the state police periodically broke down the bookmakers' doors and made arrests, so that the governor by whose connivance the horse books existed might publicly voice his shock, his astonishment at the unrepentant wickedness of Hot Springs. Sometimes, to our shame, my father got pinched, as he called it, and his name was printed in the paper: "A. B. Abbott, charged with gaming." But his boss always posted bail, and Judge Ledgerwood instantly and apologetically set all the bookmakers free the minute the case was called. "Chicken one day and feathers the next," Daddy would joke when times got hard. "Remember the eleventh commandment — thou shalt not go broke." He and I would have our worldly little laugh together, but when I repeated these aphorisms to the children of grocery clerks, they failed to see the humor and told me I didn't have the sense God gave a goat.

In the fall, I went back to Oaklawn School. Miss Love had been promoted to principal, and Tom Ransom to fourth grade. By October he got his first beating. Miss Pettigrew looked even more cadaverous, but in fact she was doomed to ten more years at Oaklawn. Robert came back but was in the other second grade. My teacher, Miss Woodward, was a bird of passage sporting an engagement ring. She disliked earnest little girls on sight, and thus I had a miserable, tearful year. My grades fell slightly, on one report card. My father blamed this vociferously on Miss Woodward, and my mother went to school and conferred with Miss Love. I saw Robert on the playground, as always, but his love for me was less intense. Benjamin still walked his six miles to school with no coat and gloves, but without crying. In November, when the winds began to blow, the boys began peeing on the radiators again, and the stench enveloped us.

By third grade, Robert seldom played with girls. That winter I had a series of diseases, beginning with an abscessed tooth and progressing to whooping cough, and was absent so long that the whole school was required to write me letters, not only to comfort

me but to provide training for them. Robert sent a notebook page
that said in huge block letters, with no flourishes,

COME BAKE, I LOVE YOU.
SCOOL TARBLE WEN YOU
NOT HERE.

I wept with love, and scorn. He veered off shyly when I did return.

One day — in fourth grade — Robert stopped coming to
school. A week passed, and Miss Love sent the truant officer out
to Ferry Road to find the trailer. Nothing remained but the
charred outdoor fireplace where the family had cooked. The
Seavers, father and son, had moved on. Gone to Oklahoma,
pulled up stakes, and I never found another boy as sweet as
Robert, who sometimes played house or jacks and had that wonderful smell about him and beautiful coppery brown skin. All the
other boys had light hair and freckles. We'd never yet studied the
Indians or the Cherokees or made our miniature teepees or found
the arrowheads. Miss Love just never got around to it.

Later that year, Miss Love stopped me in the hall and asked if I
remembered Robert Seaver. "I know he was your playfellow. It's
very sad," she said, "but I'd like you to know what happened to
him. His dad took him to Oklahoma, and the school out there
sent for his records. I didn't have much to send them. I guess they
could hardly believe a big boy like Robert had completed so little
school. He was fourteen, you know. When they lived out on
Ferry Road, it was the longest time they stayed in one place.
Anyway, I was glad to know where Robert was and that his daddy
had put him in another school. Today I got a letter from his
teacher. She said Robert used to talk about me a lot. He told her
how I had taught him his letters. He told her he never wanted to
leave Oaklawn School. Well, now the poor child is dead."

"How did he die?" I asked, but she refused to provide details.

One afternoon as we lined up for recess (we left the building in lines, class by class), I happened to be standing at her elbow as she told the story to Miss Pettigrew, who was hall monitor that day. "His father was a drinking man, a bad drinking man, and nobody else at home to look after the boy. Robert fell down in an epileptic fit while his father was drunk. They had a cooking fire going, and Robert fell too near it. His clothes caught fire and burned the poor child alive. They say his daddy never knew it till next morning."

I reeled with the horror of it, sat down on the steps outside, began to cry, and eventually was hauled into Miss Love's office to have my head felt and my throat inspected. Burned, burned, burned. For many years afterward I dreamed of Robert's face, his wide smile, his dark eyes, consumed in flames. I reached toward him but could not stop the burning as he went down, still smiling.

Though my grandparents had been thrust out of our house, they stayed with us. They darkened our supper table and took the luster off the shining floors, the comfort out of the freshly turned-down beds. "They're moving again today," my father might announce as he left the house, suggesting but not requesting that Mother offer them a hand in getting to the next cramped apartment. I heard my mother talk of government checks, of old-age assistance, of long lines that Grandpa must be persuaded to stand in, of complicated forms that had to be filled out. But I also knew that when my father failed to pay their rent, they usually got evicted. Sometimes Grandpa got them ejected by shouting goddamn at the neighbors. Still other moves were Grandpa's own idea — "Goddamn landlady won't repair the faucet" — and he would vacate without notice. A rickety truck would pull up to the curb and a drayman would load Grandma's bed and Grandpa's cot, his bedside table with the rocks and the bottles, the claw-footed table, the settee, the chairs. As a rule, the drayman would knock at our back door next day, demanding his wages.

We hauled Bemont and Carrie to Sunday dinner regularly, then less regularly. The war broke out just before Christmas, making it hard to get gas and tires for the car. You couldn't just joy ride, Mother said. Grandpa had to scrap his Model T. When they did come, they drove my father to distraction with their constant pleas for money. "You couldn't spare five dollars this week? Rent's coming due. Carrie's got to see the doctor, and he said not to come without something on account." Visiting them was torment. I had given up the afternoon radio shows and put away my crochet hook. I no longer needed this ailing old woman, whose bed I had once so eagerly shared. I watched unappreciatively, indifferently, as the box of little ecru squares under her bed filled up: thousands and thousands of them, destined to cover my marriage bed. The greasy, dirty smells, heavier now that my mother no longer served as Grandma's personal maid, disgusted me. So did the evil little bottles on Bemont's bedside table, the piles of rocks, and his wild projections of wealth, which my father had convinced me were a lunatic's ravings. I dreaded his bony hand clutching my upper arm as he poured nitric acid on the tiny stones to make them fizz.

My father taunted his parents about their pretensions. "Why lug all that parlor furniture around the way you do? What good is it to you or anybody else? Anyhow, you've got so much junk in here we can hardly step over it," he told Carrie one afternoon. He and I had brought our offering of puzzle books and a sweet roll from the bakery, which she devoured straight from the white paper bag in one gulp. I realized, unhappily, that he wanted to make her weep, to twist her arm behind her back, verbally if not literally. I saw that he knew just how to do it.

Hazel and Bruce lived for a while in a two-room house they'd rented about a mile from us. Once a month or so, Mother and I would stop in. Hazel never changed — thin, sallow, amazed to be noticed, full of shy smiles. Now there was nobody to scold Bruce and no garage to send him to when he came home drunk. My mother would sigh as we drove away, wondering if Bruce beat Hazel. More than once he appeared at our back door, begging my father for money. I would hear the angry voices, and my mother would forbid me to go out there, would shut the doors to our new living room and turn the radio louder. "Just don't listen to them, just don't listen." Then one day Bruce and Hazel were gone. Moved to Texas, my father announced in a manner so evasive that I deduced he had given them bus fare. Hazel and I exchanged letters for a year, hers in an inconsistent, babyish hand that I can see on the paper yet, the lines slanting perilously and many words misspelled. And then the letters stopped, and our Christmas card was returned, "addressee unknown." We never heard from them again.

$\mathcal{P}$OLITY

IN OUR TOWN, you needed pull. The time would come when you had to get hold of somebody — if not the mayor, then the county clerk or the city attorney, the dogcatcher, the truant officer, or at least a copper who'd tear up the ticket some other copper gave you. (To pay a fine for gaming in city court, the way the bookmakers did, was honorable, because that's how the government fixed potholes, cleaned the streets, and met its payroll. To pay a traffic ticket meant you were friendless or a hick.) Our family was positioned far above petty officialdom, however, for we were the friends, the proud vassals, of Judge Earl Witt, the circuit judge, higher than Judge Ledgerwood, higher even than Mayor McLaughlin, for Judge Witt was the only public official with the power to call a grand jury or send people to the penitentiary — a word children learned early, a concept that, along with the daily double, figured in schoolyard conversations. Truly, the thought of Tucker Farm with its fields of rocks needing to be split and its cruel guards with blacksnake whips made grown men as well as schoolboys shudder. The man who sent people there was taken seriously; not as seriously as God, perhaps, but nearly.

Across Alamo Street through the broad apple orchard we saw

the back of the Witt home, sitting snug to the ground. Coming to visit us, as he frequently did, the judge could have made his way through the apple trees and across the fence, but he always arrived by car, as though the distance between us were too great to be breached on foot. I would be languishing at the supper table, refusing to touch my stewed okra and meat loaf and thin lettuce with orange goo on top, or whatever the bill of fare happened to be, when I would hear a sudden crunch of rocks on Alamo Street. Only a Buick made this massive, authoritative crunch, and only the judge drove a Buick. (Fords, like the ones my uncles drove, kicked the rocks around and had something like fits of asthma when starting. Our Chevy rattled and squeaked as though made of tin.) You could hardly hear if a Buick engine was on or off, it was so dignified, and when Earl Witt got out and shut the door, it went *hershunk*, decisively, like the door of an Electrolux refrigerator. I'd rush out, banging the screen door and not getting yelled at about it for once, because my father would be racing alongside me, calling, "Come in, come in," and my mother following me, smiling and drying her hands on her apron.

The judge's handsome face broke into a smile as he caught sight of me. This tall, muscled man in gabardine trousers, a leather jacket (in winter), and boots that he seemed to have been born in had white hair, a nose cut of patrician marble, the glint of a diamond on his finger. He also had the voice of a country lawyer, a perfect Southern gentleman, soft on the consonants, sharp on the vowels, and with an aura of civility, as befitted the liege lord who stood between us and the poorhouse, who put in the word for Hat. Oh, I was glad we had him instead of Judge Ledgerwood, who could only send people to the jail, or Mayor McLaughlin, who everybody knew was a figurehead, a popinjay in Jimmy Walker clothing.

But it wasn't gratitude or fear that led me into his arms,

made me wish to kiss his cheek and be swept up momentarily to smell the leathery smell. I loved him. Nobody knew I loved him, I figured, or how much. Sometimes he smelled like whiskey as well as leather — a highly literary combination, as I now knew from the stacks of romantic novels I read. Rhett Butler kissing his daughter, Bonnie Blue, smelled like whiskey and leather. And Bonnie asked him to stop drinking, so as not to smell whiskeyish, and he stopped; but I didn't want Earl Witt to change his ways, particularly not parking his Buick beside our house and sitting with us in the twilight.

Mrs. Witt existed, but in name only. No doubt she shopped and cooked the way married women did. But we never saw her admiring the banks of spring blossoms or picking apples in her orchard or hanging wash out to dry or buying a hat on Central Avenue. In fact, we never mentioned her, never even asked in fake surprise, "Well why didn't you bring Miz Witt with you this evening, judge?" Apparently she didn't make calls with her husband. There were no Witt children, happily for me. The judge was mine, except I sensed my mother was crazy about him, too. He had business with Daddy, the horse books or politics, private stuff, urgent stuff, little envelopes that must be exchanged. But after they were done, Earl Witt would smile, and the two men would settle in rocking chairs and Mother and I in the swing.

They talked the price of cattle, the crops ripening in the fields to the north of us, where my Grandma Loyd had lived and Judge Witt's landholdings lay. Cattle and corn were uninteresting, at least to me, but I developed an appetite for politics, mysterious and scandalous, better than gossip. Elections were simple, since nobody ran against us. Why should they, when poll taxes were sold in blocks and the votes counted in advance? Nevertheless, heat was an unending problem: heat from the governor, heat from the G-men, heat from the Ministerial Alliance (the Baptists again) and the Arkansas Better Government League (a parliament of do-gooders, Daddy said, financed by the churches), and heat from vendettas between politicians, none of whom were friends but who blackmailed one another as a way of life. All this and more was regularly chronicled on our front porch, and I was sent inside to prepare pitchers of ice water when they wanted to tell the steamy parts.

"Life is not led according to the civics books," Daddy liked to say. "Life is not Sunday school. Life is two-thirds con." And Judge Witt would add, "You'd be surprised what a little money can do." They stuck to the standard definitions of *liberal* (wise and sophisticated and merciful toward human failings) and *reformer* (tight-fisted, sour, and punishing). Jesus Christ, according to Daddy, was a liberal. He befriended prostitutes, turned water into wine, and reminded folks not to cast the first stone Judge Witt always added that if Jesus Christ were in our midst, He would want the people of Hot Springs to make a good living and would turn those narrow-minded, pursed-lipped hypocrites who complained about local morals out into the streets

We laughed as my father read such items as the following aloud from the evening paper

BOOKMAKERS UNDER FIRE

Hot Springs, October 19 — Circuit Judge Earl Witt met with a group of 20 citizens, including officials of the Arkansas Better Government League and ministers this afternoon for what was termed "a frank discussion" of the alleged gambling in Hot Springs

The Rev. Claude L. Jones, pastor of the First Christian Church, said the meeting was the beginning of a movement to stop gambling in Hot Springs. Handbooks came in for considerable discussion. Judge Witt replied that he had charged every grand jury to investigate gambling, and that bookmaking as now operated was preferable to conditions as formerly obtained, since the city and county derive revenue from it. Furthermore, he added, if the committee opposing the handbooks wished to get results, it should have the legislature amend the law and make the operating of handbooks a felony instead of a misdemeanor.

Indeed, such stuff made everybody laugh, which was why they put it in the paper. Well, it made the preachers look pretty silly, but so what? I listened silently to the two male voices while the night thickened and the roses lost their color in the darkness so that you could no longer tell the red American Beauties from the white. The branches of the cherry tree, heavy with fruit toward summer's end, swayed in the night breeze. Buster prowled the lawn, pausing to gnaw a flea in his hindquarters or nip at flying night creatures, patrolling the fence for the hole or the weak place that might become a tunnel to freedom. The lightning bugs would emerge, and sometimes I would get a Kerr Mason jar and chase them, clap the lid on them, watch them flash and search for their freedom (for I at least had the power of life and death over bugs). Anyway, I knew the grown-ups would say more if they thought I was not listening, would speak of love, murder, and getting sent to the pen.

One evening Earl Witt told the story of Irene, the most beautiful of the McLaughlin girls, a pretty thing, as he recalled, in a yellow dress with flounces at the hem, different from her sisters, who were all funny-turned and touched in the head; Irene knew how to have a good time. She fell in love with a boy and began keeping company with him. But Old Lady McLaughlin was determined to break the romance up, for the boy was not a Catholic. Oh, she threatened to disown the girl, and none of them could stand up to the old lady. Well, Irene told her young man to go away, and he refused. Their last night together, he drove her out near the lake in his little roadster and they parked in the moonlight, and no one knows to this day what their last words were. It's all guesswork from there on. But perhaps the boy insisted that they run away and get married, because he was so crazy for Irene, had talked all over town, said he would marry her in spite of the old lady. But she must have refused him, because he shot her and then himself. Some people thought it was a double suicide.

The judge sometimes told tales of a more distant past, for his family had a long pedigree in Arkansas, with a memory that went back to the frontier — not a very long reach, he assured me — back to the years when the South had just been beaten by the Yankees and law was made by gunfire or the sharp edge of a Bowie knife. Gamblers and sick people wanting to take the baths flocked to Hot Springs, but they had to travel by stagecoach in those days, since there wasn't any railroad yet. And no banks, either, so the travelers often carried large amounts of cash. Malvern was the nearest train junction, and naturally the road from Malvern was thick with outlaws — not just any old outlaws, but Jesse and Frank James.

"One day," he began, "the stage was rolling along, and five fellows dressed in blue army jackets bore down on it. Blue, you understand, not gray. And who do you think it was in those Yankee jackets? Jesse and Frank James, with Cole and Bob Younger and some other desperadoes, all packing pistols and shotguns, armed to the teeth, and dressed up to look like General Grant. Old Jesse James was a good fellow, you understand, and he always asked if any of the men had served in the Confederate Army before he robbed 'em. He always did that, he was a man of principle. If he felt sorry for anybody he was robbing, he often would leave him enough money to telegraph home when he got to Hot Springs. And he always rode away hollering, 'Better pick up your guns. You might meet robbers on this road.' Ol' Jesse was quite a joker, all right You don't meet many like him anymore. Posses from Hot Springs lit out after the Jameses and the

Youngers more than once but never caught up to them. Years
later, Cole Younger came to Hot Springs on a lecture tour. Yes
ma'am, a lecture tour. Used to be that reformed drunks picked up
a lot of money preaching on the evils of drink, you know, they
would preach and preach and then hold up a glass of whiskey and
drop an earthworm in it, and the worm would die. They never
told you the worm would die just as quick in a glass of water. Cole
Younger was doing more or less the same thing preaching against
lawbreaking, only he didn't use any earthworms. By the time he
took to preaching, Frank James was running a tourist trap on the
outskirts of town. I saw them both myself as a boy."

From the James and the Younger brothers, it was a short jump
to the Capone brothers — a yarn of my father's. "Al and Ralph
were out on the Hot Springs golf course one day, minding their
own business. They knew they had to act like gentlemen in Hot
Springs. But they had their bodyguards with them, and a local
boy for caddy. Well, the bodyguards and the caddy took to
horsing around, trading insults — dumb galoot, pipsqueak,
things of that nature — and finally the caddy took a swing at
these bruisers. The goons knocked him down, and all of a sudden
the police chief showed up, threw the cuffs on Capone's gorillas,
and took them off to jail. Well, Al went first to Owney Madden
and said, 'Do something.' And Owney said, 'What in the hell can
I do?' And Al said, 'My boys aren't serving no time in some
Arkansas jail.' And Owney came over to Judge Ledgerwood and
said, 'What in the hell can you do?' And the judge said, 'If they
haven't got sense enough to obey our laws, let 'em rot in jail. We
let those boys come in here and go out on our golf course. Lots of
places won't let 'em light. But they have to act like gentlemen.
Anyhow, how long do you think the gambling in Hot Springs
could run if I got caught doing favors for Al Capone?' So Owney
thought it over, and a solution occurred to him. When the case

came to court and the caddy took the stand, Judge Ledgerwood said, 'Young man, please tell the court what these gorillas did to you.' 'Judge,' he said, 'I got smart with these fellows and jumped on them. I didn't know who they were. I got just what I deserved.'"

We'd laugh again, for even I understood exactly what Owney Madden's solution had been.

Some evenings, however, my father and Earl Witt spoke of dangerous matters, tremors that threatened to split the ground in this peaceful valley, mischief erupting along with hot waters, steaming over the cold stones of civic order. Sent in for the water pitcher, I thought I heard them say that government agents had chased outlaws through our quiet streets. I heard them whisper that one of our very own policemen had committed — and been convicted of — a murder at the city jail. He and the chief of police had been sent to the penitentiary, and were laboring at this very moment under the blacksnake whips. It was unfair, my father said. They had been railroaded, others should be there instead, with the whips breaking on their shoulders. I hated hearing such things, tried not to believe them. And yet they said that the mayor's own brother had actually shot and killed a man in a dispute over the take from a slot machine. Such a crime could not be ignored, no matter how many blocks of poll tax receipts the mayor controlled. The grand jury had to be called and the man indicted, and yet the brother of so powerful a man as the mayor could hardly be sentenced to split rocks at Tucker Farm. Things were arranged: the jury returned a verdict of self-defense.

Earl Witt himself had family problems, less pernicious but agonizing. Whenever this subject came up, ice water wasn't sufficient: Mother sent me in to bed. But I overheard them anyhow. The brother of the circuit judge not only got arrested for drunken driving, but he and his woman companion were driving down the road stark naked. Since nobody had actually died of gunshot wounds in the process, however, the case was shelved and transformed into a local joke.

Many nights, if the judge didn't come to call, we toured the city in the green Chevrolet. Even when the migraine was pounding in his head, my father would push back from the supper table and pat himself approvingly on the stomach.

"Want to take a little spin?"

After doing the dishes, Mother and I would take our posts as passengers in the bug-eyed car — a family unit so tight you could have founded civilization upon it. Daddy would shift into first, do his hand-over-hand wheel turn, and hoist us over the hill and out into the world at fifteen miles per hour, slowly so that he could lecture us on history, politics, and art without running up a telephone pole. As we drove off, Buster would yowl at the front gate like an abandoned lover, unable to focus his doggy thoughts on our inevitable return.

Mayor Leo P. McLaughlin's mansion, dazzling white, amply verandahed, with a porte-cochère broad enough to receive a coach and six, dominated one end of town, the Malvern Avenue end, in fact, where the black ghetto began. We were drawn to his house like blood pumped back to the ventricle, compelled to drive past it, to marvel at the greensward, at the wrought iron fence, at the stables out back where he kept his high-stepping, nervous little horses. Looking at that house, you thought of tea dances with orchestras in the drawing room, but it was a dark and hollow place ruled by old Bridget McLaughlin, Leo's mother, and Daddy said she was so tight they did without furniture and window curtains. Nobody ever got away from her: Irene dead, the other sisters single and living at home, working in the kitchen, growing older Besides being a killer (in self-defense, to be sure), Leo's brother was a drunk. And when Leo had married, years ago, and brought home his bride, Bridget made them set up housekeeping in a hotel, and Leo soon went back to Mother. People said the walls were stuffed with money, because Leo had to be the richest man in town, and yet the house was never lighted up. No Cadillacs or Packards ever pulled up to the porte-cochère and discharged pretty women in party dresses, men in dinner jackets with champagne bottles under their arms.

"There's Owney Madden's home," Daddy would say after we turned around and headed away from Leo's. "Nobody can accuse him of showing off." Our resident gangster, our Grade A year-round criminal, had gone straight, or anyway had married our postmaster's daughter and lived in a cottage shielded by rose trellises, right next to St. John's Catholic Church, an institution the town mistrusted more than they did Owney because the nuns were said to lead wild lives and flirt, or worse, with the priest. Daddy said that was an outright lie, and added that only rednecks accused the Catholics of such carryings-on. He would switch the subject back to Owney, who was so mean that New York had just run him off, in spite of him owning the Cotton Club, the most famous nightclub in the world, where Duke Ellington played. But somehow Owney hadn't minded leaving. He'd brought his flock of carrier pigeons with him, the ones that flew with messages to the rumrunners offshore, their boats lying low in the water so they could bring the good Scotch whisky to New York for people to drink out of teacups in places known as speakeasies.

"Do the pigeons live in his house?" I asked, for the cottage was almost aggressively tidy behind the roses, and I knew pigeons were a mess. But they were in there someplace, and Daddy would tell how, one moonlit evening, Owney had driven his speedboat right up to Judge Ledgerwood's house on the lake and offered to hand over the pigeons, flock, stock, and barrel, if the judge would only give them a good home, because Owney loved them so much, they had been good pigeons for him, and maybe they could carry messages for the judge — birds being superior to Western Union, which was a matter of record and could be traced by any investigator — but Judge Ledgerwood just shouted back, friendly as anything, "Owney, you know I can't take anything from you, not so much as a dime, not pigeons, not anything, because if I did they'd be down on me like a duck on a June bug." Owney didn't get mad, because the judge smiled and waved.

Not far from Owney's cottage was Judge Ledgerwood's mansion, comfortable, dignified, sedate amidst its neighbors and its venerable magnolia trees — a sociable, approachable house, like the judge himself, a house with a proper Mrs. Ledgerwood, eggnog and balsam wreaths at Christmas, a maid in the kitchen, and a dining room where the silver always gleamed. The judge would nod and tip his Panama hat to my mother and me whenever he saw us on Central Avenue, and he called my father Hat, after seeing him in his courtroom so many Mondays, paying off the gaming fine. But he did not exactly count as our friend. He was too rich, too prominent Oddly enough, there were no Ledgerwood children Neither the Ledgerwoods nor the Witts, nor Leo P., had produced any heir to the throne — an ill omen, my father thought, and counted himself luckier than they, for all their pomp. And so we'd roll on past, and maybe take a turn up Central Avenue.

Every night when the horse books closed, the auction houses opened: sucker traps, my father called them, and he wouldn't allow me or Mother to go in one. Once in a while, though, we'd park the green Chevrolet and stroll the avenue at night. Their whole fronts would be thrown open, like carnival midways, glass doors folded to the sides, and from the sidewalk you could see the silver coffee sets and tea sets, cases of diamond necklaces, rings set with emeralds and rubies, radios, rolled-up oriental carpets, hanging tapestries, gigantic Chinese pots, ebony sphinxes, and gilded French bronzes of naked ladies showing off their dainty fingers and their uptilted bare metallic breasts and the clocks in their slender abdomens. This gleaming mountain of treasures was the ultimate of man's desiring, things that no one in my family had ever possessed or knew the names of or even had sense enough to want or would know where to put if they had them.

"Works of art," the auctioneer would shout, and then, as though possessed of unknown tongues, like the Holy Rollers, he would utter such words as *ormolu* and *compote* and *sconces*, and his melodious, garbled yodel would curl out into the night: "Odeeodeeodeeodee yah yah yah, goin' once goin' twice. Merely walk inside and seat yourself in one of our very comfortable chairs and feast your eyes upon these fabulous works of art." In the auctioneer's mouth was the first time I ever heard the phrase, and each time we strolled past I would beg to go in and see the works of art. "Look," I would plead, pulling my father's sleeve until he swatted at me, "it says you're eligible for a hundred-dollar prize, Daddy, just for walking in. Oh, please, we might win it."

"Piffle. They're just out to pick your pocket. It's all knick-knacks, gewgaws. Glorified doorstoppers. Cheap imitations. Your mother wouldn't have that junk in the house if you won it. Gyp joints, that's all those places are. Gyp joints."

"But everything's a gyp joint," I'd say, crushed, "if you want to look at it that way." And indeed, though I didn't yet grasp to what extent, everything was a gyp joint — the municipal and county courts, the casinos, the churches, the public schools, and perhaps least of all the auction houses. I wondered what these objects were inside the gallery, clearly useless and many down-right ugly, these works of art that anybody could live without but that people feverishly bid for. I wanted to own the bronze lady with the delicate hands and the clock in her abdomen. She could stand by my dressing table and tell me her secrets, as well as keep track of the hours. She would be my doll, and I could dress her, cover her curls with a bonnet and her provocative breasts with one of my mother's brassieres. But my parents wouldn't even let me get near this enticing creature. The only work of art at home was the Italian village over the divanette, which was valuable, my father said, but I couldn't imagine it in an auction house.

Oh, how we loved it, here at the heart of the cosmos. Few of us had any reason or desire to go to Memphis, which was the nearest big town. We'd all heard of the Peabody Hotel, of course, but "good Lord, the Arlington's a better hotel than that. Hell, honey, even the Majestic's a better hotel than the Peabody. No hotel, south or north either, can touch the Arlington."

St. Louis? "Well, Aunt Lilymae and Uncle Ned lived there for six months, and she said the soot was so bad she had to wash her kitchen curtains every week. Couldn't wait to get back here. Filthiest place."

California? "That's where Cousin Lester's boys went. Made good money, they say. But they'll be coming back here to retire. People aren't the same out there. They just call you an Arkie, don't matter what kind of trash they are themselves."

Chicago? "Big old dirty city. You couldn't pay me to set foot in the place." Al Capone and his cronies came to Hot Springs for vacations, which said enough about Chicago to us. Why go to what even Al Capone longed to escape?

New York? Horrible, a city of dark canyons, the wild East, where hardly anybody even spoke English.

The state capital, Little Rock, sixty miles away over a winding two-laner, was a day's journey there and back. (We had to do it, if at all, on some holiday.) People went only for business transactions, such as buying goods wholesale or getting an audience with the governor (just to say they'd done it) or seeing some pal of their uncle's who was on the state payroll and could do them some sly favor, or to see the new fall clothes (costing twice what they should) displayed in a really large department store, and the kids went along in order to see an elephant. Among its eight exhibits, the Little Rock zoo boasted Jumbo, fastened by a foot to a stump. Day in and day out, it rattled its chain, swinging its trunk and its poor lacerated leg in the same restless rhythm and accepting peanuts in the orifice of its black proboscis and transferring them to its mouth. Ever experimental when it came to a gullible creature, the public fed it candy, cigarette butts, pieces of glass, and wads of bubble gum, and the elephant swallowed these items with the sublime contempt of a holy man on a mountaintop, oblivious to evil and good. Jumbo's companions were a monkey with huge, desperate eyes, a bear in love with easeful death, its eyes void of all hostility to its visitors, a fox with bald spots, a razorback hog, a moribund alligator, and two parrots, poor addled prisoners of human curiosity.

But once your parents had done their errands and taken you to the zoo and shown you the state capitol and the woolly winter coats in the windows at Blass's Department Store, you'd be hot and weary, and your cousins in the back seat would be whining and hitting you and even vomiting or sneezing, and your daddy would lose his way trying to get back to Highway 70, and your mother would tell you that the thing she'd liked best all day had been eating the vegetable plate and the custard pie in Franke's cafeteria, which she could get just as well at home because there was just as good a Franke's in Hot Springs, with better custard pie, if you wanted to know the truth — and you did, you did want to know it, for your homesickness was by then a knot in your belly — and everybody was dying to start for Hot Springs, if Daddy could just find the dad-burned highway, and after he finally found it, he'd swear he wasn't coming to Little Rock again for at least a year or two, maybe not then. Nobody went to Little Rock for his health. Nobody went there to find the best hotel or the most beautiful main street. Nobody went to Little Rock for fun. Who needed Little Rock?

When you finally got back to Central Avenue, feeling better now that people had stopped throwing up, you never knew what might be trotting briskly past the bathhouses. Usually it was an open vehicle advertising something: the mayor's snappy horse-drawn gig skimming along, carrying His immaculately tailored, red-carnationed Honor and his maiden-lady sister — the one who went out; the other only did housework — the pair of McLaughlins and the pair of horses, called Scotch and Soda, tossing their handsome heads, preening themselves. The mayor's enterprise not only enriched himself and Owney Madden but also provided the bread and meat over which pious women said the blessing each evening in a hundred houses. He felt he had earned the adulation. His job, however, was display: to dress nicely, tell jokes, and shake the hands of visiting politicians, which tasks he faithfully executed, according to his oath. And behind him and his sister and Scotch and Soda might come a cart from the ostrich farm, pulled by one of the huge, bewildered birds, its keeper switching its gnarled legs smartly and bellowing, "Come see the smartest animals in the world." From time to time, it was said, the proprietor of the leading whorehouse and her most beautiful employees cruised the street in a topless Cadillac, their white gloves up to the elbow, the pink and yellow ribbons on their picture hats fluttering in the wind. Everybody understood the value of an airing. The smart money, of course, stayed off the streets, drove inconspicuous old Packards, and tried, above all else, to keep its name out of the paper.

Mixed in among the usual inhabitants of any small town in the South were the gamblers and the touts and the foreigners, Jewish ladies from the East Coast in housedresses and hairnets, rocking in their rocking chairs on the front porches of bathhouses and rooming houses, warming their dinners over a hot plate, held in thrall, fated to rock forever, never to return to Brooklyn or Boston. There were the owners and operators and employees of the massage parlors and the specialists in high colonic irrigation, who practiced their craft in private houses, not always well kept, with signs hung out front proclaiming the miracles they could bring about if only you believed. Out on the streets you'd see shady characters of all kinds, maybe crooks taking a little holiday to play some golf and do a little business, who knew? It was nothing unusual, at night, at Western Union, to see a small, slick, George Raft ish sort of man inside at the counter, penciling a message in block letters while the clerk quavered behind the counter and a beefy bodyguard blocked the doorway, his check-ered jacket bulging with some unspecified object and his eyes harder than cold lead. The real George Raft had a vacation house on our lake at one time, a point of pride with us, not because he was a handsome movie star but because of his gangland connec-tions. "He's really a gangster, not just an actor," ladies said happily to one another at bridge tables. "He's a pal of Owney Madden's. His money comes from the mob."

The gangster glamour was intensified by the whorehouses, those addresses no decent person was supposed to know, the enterprise no woman or child was allowed to mention, the lure that brought in bevies of males, like guppies, from nearby high schools as well as the cities of the North. "Can't have a resort town without the houses," I heard Earl Witt say to my father one night when I wasn't supposed to be listening. I'd no idea what people did in those houses, and stared into the curtained windows as we drove past, striving to get a glimpse.

Sometimes, as we neared home again, I fell asleep in the back seat, to be pleasantly awakened by my dog yelping, crying, leaping, as though his broken heart were suddenly mended. Musing about Owney Madden and the prostitutes and killers and George Raft's dark eyes, I readied myself for bed, brushing my hair one hundred strokes and applying a ribbon of Ipana to my toothbrush.

THE SENTIMENTAL EDUCATION

I COULD NOT get enough of love. As a child, of course, I'd no idea what love consisted of, whether it came from the brain or the body or the printed page. When I first began to think of love, and to observe what others said and did about it, my own small body was so plain, smooth, hairless, and lean, I never thought that it could interest anyone but me. Between your legs was what Mother kept telling me to wash carefully and to hide carefully. "Stop sitting spraddle-legged," she hissed at every opportunity, and of course it wasn't the spraddled legs she objected to but those nameless parts that folded between the thighs. Parts to be hidden, not to be shared. She and my father certainly hid whatever they had, at least they hid it from me. I didn't stop to think they might show it to each other, or might touch each other in those places that were too secret to be seen in daylight, too private even to be mentioned. I doubted my father even knew about such things.

You washed those parts quickly, without looking at them. They had no names. Good people were required to refer to them with prepositions, rather than straightforwardly with nouns, as with decent things like tables and chairs. "Down there." "In between." "Behind." The closest one could get to a downright noun was "your bottom." It was a bottom, more or less, when you sat down, but not otherwise. Only your feet really had bottoms. What feet certainly did not have was any of those little quick places that felt so delightful when properly touched. But that was my own private knowledge, I felt, a childish thing that probably vanished when you became an adult.

Of course, I knew that if you ventured into the bushes with a boy or even another girl, these little quick places were likely to be the object of interest. I had played games behind bushes. I wasn't the only kid who had such places or an interest in touching them. But how trivial they seemed, these sensations that came and went so fleetingly that you could easily pretend such things had never happened. Surely grown-ups had no time for such nonsense. Such rushing, keen sensations surely had nothing to do with love — great, noble love.

Love was what you felt for your mother and father — that mix of need, fear, anxiety, trust, anger, and ease. They might be angry with you, too, but they were stuck with you, more or less. One morning when I was about five, a man arrived early and painted the front porch, and though I had been warned, I skipped out the front door into the gray, wet expanse and fell down, splat, three different ways before Mother rescued me with a broom handle. I had to be dipped in turpentine and thoroughly scolded and the man had to paint the porch again, and then an hour later I walked out there again, a repeat performance that spoiled another little dotted swiss dress forever, but after my mother got the paint and turpentine out of my hair the second time, she patted me on the back, laughed, and called me "Goosy!" That, I realized, was love. When I came down with chills and fever on Christmas Eve, as I did for several years running, or started vomiting and breaking out with something the first day of Daddy's two-week vacation, or my permanent teeth rotted, or I fainted when they took me to the freak show at the circus and had to go home, they always stood by me. Love was what you felt for your aunts and uncles: that same thing you had for Mother and Dad, but a simpler mix with more fun to it, less anxiety, need, anger.

Love was what I reckoned my parents felt for each other. I guessed they did. I figured they must. They felt something, anyway, and it always expressed itself in *things*. The orderly house, the meticulously ironed shirts in the drawer, the mended socks and underpants, the quiet of their nighttime breathing, the parsnips and carrots because they were good for you, the flower beds planted with cosmos and nasturtiums and roses, the pay envelope with crisp bills in it: those constituted adult love.

Sometimes in my fantasies I casually broke the bond between my parents just to see what that felt like. Earl Witt, I had come to believe, was in love with my mother. But I also fancied him in love with me. I was a constant invalid, down with whooping cough, scarlet fever, strep throat, toothaches, tonsillectomy, measles, colds, and stomach upsets so numerous as to be routine. If my mother had had a job in those days, I would have caused her to be fired. She nursed me endlessly, and with unfailing tenderness, but Judge Witt nursed me too. By some mysterious network he always learned about my illnesses, and as I lay sniffling and moaning, the Western Union man would knock at the front door with armloads of flowers or boxed candies from the Aunt Jemima Candy Shoppe. Nor was I required to fall ill to receive his presents. On most of his visits, he arrived with a gift in his hand — candies or a locket or charm bracelet, usually the sort sold at jewelry stores rather than the dime-store merchandise little girls like me were accustomed to. Was this what love meant?

Feeling that we owed Judge Witt, that he must at all costs be loved because of his generosity toward us, I nurtured the idea that my mother was seeing him in secret. Indeed, she did go out alone sometimes, and seemed once in a while to turn away from the soapsuds and exist separately from her family. I loved to watch her beautify herself, apply the purple eye shadow and the dark lipstick she kept in her dresser for special occasions, pull on the prized stockings she stored in a soft handkerchief, zip herself into the black dress with the lace collar, the one that smelled enticingly of her perfume as it hung on the hanger in the back of the closet. I wanted to see her leave the house in the high-heeled sling pumps with bows, the ones I teetered across the carpet in when she wasn't looking.

And on the rare evening when she left the house alone, I would watch her dress and put on her makeup and plead, "Tell me where you're going. Where are you going?"

She would laugh. "Oh, never you mind. I'll be back when you're sound asleep. Be a good girl now. Mind your daddy."

"Your mama deserves to get out of the house once in a while," Daddy would remark from behind *Life* magazine.

She would pat her hair, squirt herself with her atomizer, and depart. Next morning she'd be frying bacon in her old housecoat. The pumps would be hanging in the shoe bag, the dress in the closet, as if they'd never been worn.

"Mama, where'd you go?"

"Oh, just to see the new Gary Cooper. Mmm. Wish he'd run his fingers through my hair like he did Ingrid Bergman."

She couldn't fool me. She'd been out dancing with Judge Witt. Marriage already seemed so constricting, so boring to me that I had to imagine a love affair for her, a man courting her and kissing her. Love couldn't happen to you in an old housecoat.

Settling in the back of the closet in the laundry basket (my old baby bed), where I could count on privacy, I went through my father's books, looking for the secrets of love.

The restraint he had shown thus far now vanished swiftly, giving way to a passion that was savage, violent, ruthlessly selfish. Amber, inexperienced but not innocent, returned his kisses eagerly. Spurred by the caressing of his mouth and hands, her desire mounted apace with his, and though at first she had heard, somewhere far back in her mind, Sarah calling out to her, warning her, the sound and the image grew fainter, dissolved, and was gone. . . . She saw his face above her, and his eyes had become pure glittering green.

One day, going through several such passages by flashlight, I heard a shriek of laughter and emerged hastily, blinking in the daylight, to find my father in full pursuit of my mother, who fled like Daphne from Apollo. I don't believe I had ever seen him run before, let alone after my mother. Now that the house was ours, they could go round and round in it, since the doors between the two apartments were all open. She dashed crazily through the kitchen, out onto the back porch, into my bedroom, into their bedroom, and then he caught her as she paused to try to shut the door on him, grabbing her in his arms, pinning her arms behind her, and kissing her. By then I was doing jumping jacks and applauding. It was the only time I can recall them playing. Was he experiencing a violent and savage passion? Did his eyes glitter green?

"Hat, stop it, Shirley's right here," Mother kept saying, as though in my presence they ought instantly to furrow their brows over mortgage payments or whether the tires were showing signs of wear.

It was over in an instant, and she patted her hair back into shape and straightened her blouse, and everything went back to normal: the potatoes stewing, the sheets pinned to the clothesline by their small hems, the towels folded longways, the beds meticulously made right after breakfast and not rumpled again until 10 P.M. exactly. Oh, the despair of orderliness, the tyranny of neatness, the pristine doilies stiff with starch, the scent of furniture polish hanging over the house like death, the dishes inexorably washed and dried and put away right after supper, which ought to have made us happy but merely used up the last half-hour of twilight and reduced the day to nighttime and consumed the last spark of my mother's energy so that she fell asleep listening to "One Man's Family" and the "Longines Symphony Hour."

Once my parents offered a definition of love. At supper one night, Mother said she just couldn't believe the way her brother Delmar's wife labored over his khaki pants and shirts. Delmar was a logger, drove a huge, roaring, unmuffled truck many miles into the woods every day to where he and his partner cut down pine trees. Before he even left the house, his clothes would be wet with sweat, and when he came home at night, they would be soiled with the grime of the truck and the forest, motor oil, dirt, and resin, but Aunt Olive would take these garments and wash them, scrubbing until every inch came clean, carefully starching and ironing the heavy fabric. She would stand under a bare electric light bulb, until late at night if necessary, long after Delmar and the children were asleep, forcing the wrinkles out of the khaki with hard downward thrusts of the hot iron, so that six mornings a week perfect shirts and trousers were ready for him to put on. My mother said this was her idea of love, and her eyes filled with tears as though she spoke of a sacrament.

My father agreed. "That's love, that's really love. Only a woman who really loved a man would do that for him when no one can tell the difference. Most women would let him go in wrinkled clothes."

"I wouldn't do what she does. I'd wash work clothes for you, but I'll be darned if I'd do that starching and ironing if all you did was work a log truck and everything was sweated through before you even got out of the house."

The words, when I thought of them later that day, wounded me. Of course Mother ironed Daddy's shirts and handkerchiefs, but in a different spirit, with rancor in the starch, as an act not of love but of propriety, because it was her duty and because a bookmaker must look slick. And yet, I stubbornly told myself, what my aunt did, the starched pants and all, surely wasn't what they sang about on the radio, not what made those mariachis shake and your blood pound in "Begin the Beguine." When even the palms seemed to be swaying, a man surely wasn't interested in ironing.

The Millers across the alley, parents of my playmates Janny Louise and Mary Jane, lacked all the elements of tidiness but conspicuously exhibited another quality as nameless to me as the little secret parts. Whatever it was, it made Thelma look suddenly happy when she heard the sound of the Texaco truck Owen drove. Owen never noticed that the bed wasn't made and here it was noontime. It was nothing unusual in this house to see the grown-ups chasing each other around, dodging behind closet doors, laughing and grabbing and shrieking and kissing. They kissed a lot — usually just big smacks, joke kisses, but you figured there were other kisses, too. Thelma told kind, funny stories about Owen over the clothesline, how he did without a Sunday suit in favor of new spring coats for the girls, which gave him an excuse to sleep late while they went off to church.

They had married when she was only sixteen, and both girls had been born before their mother was twenty-one. When I was a kid, hanging around her house for companionship, she wouldn't have been thirty yet, with thick, curly brown hair and a mouth and eyes too large for her face. She wore print housedresses or broomstick skirts and shirtwaists, with an old cardigan sweater for warmth in winter, so that she always looked the same, just Thelma, with some kind of light in her eyes perpetually, and a quick laugh. Owen, three or four years older than Thelma, was as slight as she, with a shock of auburn hair that wouldn't lie down and acne-pocked skin. He wore his Texaco clothes all the time, dark green, with his sleeves rolled up and his wide belt and Texaco buckle holding pants and shirt and body and soul together all at once. When I first knew the Millers, I didn't know what lovers were, and they seemed very mundane; yet I knew there was something between them, a mysterious thing, invisible in the day but glowing in the dark, I imagined, like radium on a watch dial.

Thelma loved the garden better than the house, because, as she said, the house needed cleaning every day whether you cleaned it or not, but the vegetables and flowers grew and changed and gave things back to you. She was a potent gardener. Rosebushes sprang out of the ground at her command and bloomed yellow and pink and red all summer, supplying bouquets for houses all around. She kept everything weeded and turned and watered and pruned and pinched back and deloused. Her ironing might pile up for weeks and dust balls grow peaceably under her beds, but there was no disorder in her garden. Hollyhocks grew to the size of pine saplings, the tulips and daffodils of spring were superseded by snapdragons and sweet peas, gardenias and camellias and peonies. Masses of blooms appeared in Thelma's yard in March and cycled miraculously on through until the last aster and mum died in mid-November. Garden club ladies in their big sedans stopped to marvel at the diameter of the dahlias, sunbursts of magenta and pink and yellow. Always in need of cash, Thelma sometimes sold her blossoms to local florists. With their arms linked, she and Owen would stand beside her flower beds. He would praise her flowers and her genius for growing them, untroubled by the thought that there wasn't a clean sock or ironed shirt in the bureau.

One fall Thelma rescued a forlorn, injured mockingbird and installed it in the back room of the house, where it flew about, perching on the rickety chairs, shedding feathers and milky turds. This had been Thelma's ironing room, where the clothes

piled up and she quickly pressed dresses for the girls to wear to
school each morning. With Chipper there, the ironing board had
to be moved to the dining room, where it became a rack for coats
or school bags or an occasional dirty dish. Entering through the
back door, as I always did, I spoke to Chipper as if to a person and
took care not to step in the droppings. It filled me with high
glee — the bird, the droppings, the whole glorious mess, which
my own parents wouldn't have tolerated for one moment. It
thrilled me to see the principles of housekeeping violated in this
manner, and I knew that Owen's adoration of Thelma had something to do with this heresy. When he married her, he somehow
allowed her to keep her license to play. He permitted her to
play for him, instead of insisting that she become a solemn
housekeeper.

In the spring, in a ceremony to which I was invited, Thelma,
Janny Louise, Mary Jane, and I fed Chipper his last meal and set
him free, a sleek fat creature who flew to the nearest tree branch
and seemed hesitant to depart. "Come back, come back," the four
of us pleaded. "We'll wait for you, Chipper." Thelma watched for
him every day and swore that every mockingbird she saw was
Chipper, coming to visit us. The back room had to be scoured
and repapered, and the windowsills scraped down. The neighborhood laughed about it, over the clotheslines, with Thelma joining right in. But Owen never complained, the way some fathers
would have done, even when he had to buy paint and Thelma
never quite got round to applying it. I'd pound at the back door
to be let in, and she'd appear, always smiling, and I'd step over
the paint cans to get into the kitchen. They became part of the
decor. You expected to step over them.

In spite of her contempt for housework, Thelma was a devoted, ingenious cook. She could put a blackberry cobbler together in five minutes and wash up a few bowls while it baked and
get the cornbread going, delicious crusty stuff that came steam-

ing out of the oven just as the cobbler was done. We girls would come and quickly wash and dry enough dishes to set the table with, and Thelma would laugh and sing. She had a repertory of old songs from her childhood —

> There was a girl named Madelene,
> Fell from a cloud and bumped her bean.
> Catalina Madelena
> Hoofenstyla Wallendyna
> Hogan Logan Bogan was her name.

or

> The Deacon went down in the cellar to pray,
> He fell asleep and he stayed all day,

and a score of rounds,

> Whither shall I follow, follow thee?

— and the four of us would sing them out, plugging our ears and swearing that this time we'd get it right and then getting off-key and laughing until we cried.

Thelma would take the broom for her partner and dance, chanting, "Go left, go right, go left, go right, go left, go right, go le-uffft," rolling her eyes and tapping her feet and stirring up dust with wild motions of the broom, which she'd then chase across the room in perfect parody of an efficient housewife. I'd shriek insanely, crazy with delight, not knowing what I was laughing at, and we'd all have to race to the bathroom to keep from wetting our pants. When, in the midst of all this gaiety, we heard the roar of the Texaco truck, it only heightened the frenzy.

When Owen Miller came in the front door, female laughter did not have to fly out the window. We kids would rush to the front porch to wave, as though a general had come home from the battlefield, and Thelma would forget about the okra frying and the crowder peas simmering and dash through her house, apron sashes untied, to throw her arms around her husband's neck and kiss him. We'd all be giddy with happiness, and I would yearn to throw myself into their embrace, to sample that heat and light, but was too shy.

In the quiet of our porch swing, behind the rose trellises, I used to tell my father about these scenes, and his eyes would darken. "You see," he would murmur, "they're poorer than we are, but they're better off. He only drives a Texaco truck, and yet his wife loves him." If I told my mother, she would stare thoughtfully at a spot just over my head. "Yes, Owen's really crazy about her. It's a sweet thing to see. I guess it wouldn't matter how you kept house, if that's how it was." And she'd go on working.

"Why don't you two have that?" I wanted to ask. "If you don't have it, why don't you get it?" But I never dared inquire. And since none of my relations appeared to have it, either, unless you counted Aunt Olive's ironing, I concluded it didn't run very strongly in our bloodlines.

Not even what passed between the Millers was good enough for me. They spent long, boring evenings like everybody else. They ran out of money, had fights. Like an addict looking for ever more thrilling highs, I concluded that grown-up love was stupid, even if an undignified act was required of you. Grown-up love also meant you had to sit through long meals and listen to interminable dull conversations. It was all so open and ordinary. Married love didn't seem so different from sisterly love, aunt-to-niece love, cousinly love, uncle-to-nephew love. All very proper and mentionable, the sort of love the minister referred to in church. Sanctioned by God and Uncle Sam. Approved of by Jesus.

I didn't wonder in those days about the peculiar biological accident that put me here on earth in just this time and place. Obviously I *was* here and was meant to be here. My parents had been provided to take care of me. If I wasn't here, I reasoned, they wouldn't be here either. Or else I'd have been an orphan and have lived in the orphans' home down on Belding Avenue. I saw those orphans behind the fence sometimes, when Mother would park the car at the curb and donate bundles of clothing. Mostly, though, they were kept inside — scrubbing the floors and toilets, Mother said. I would be in the front seat as she told me this, my dress perfect, every curl coaxed into a perfect blond sausage. ("If only I could get your hair trained," Mother would say with a sigh, for the gloss turned to frizz at the first raindrop, and she believed that every part of me, from hair to bowels to cuticles, would respond eventually to her discipline and patience.) I'd never be an orphan. Why not? Because somebody loved me enough to enforce this propriety on me, and to polish all the furniture with Johnson's Wax. Yet the love I wanted was a different kind.

I'd first heard about it from Hans Christian Andersen, reading with Grandma. Once upon a time a little mermaid (Walt Disney hadn't fooled around with this story yet — it came straight from the printed page like a belt of brandy) kept a garden at the bottom of the sea, with a statue of a beautiful boy — flotsam from a shipwreck — and she fell in love with it. One night, on her fifteenth birthday, she swam to the surface and witnessed a shipboard party, the birthday celebration for — who else? — the handsome prince whose statue she loved. A storm promptly sank the ship, and the mermaid rescued the prince, carrying him, unconscious, to the shore.

Now she was truly in love with him She hid in the foam,

being unable to walk on sand, and watched as a two-legged princess came and pretended to have saved the prince. The mermaid fled. (I saw myself in the romantic, seaweedy drawing that accompanied the story, a creature with tiny white breasts and a fishtail cradling the prince in my arms, kissing him. How thrilling to have nice little breasts like that and a lovely masculine head to hold against them.)

So the mermaid went to the wicked sea witch, begging for legs. "You come in the nick of time," said the witch. "After sunrise tomorrow I should not be able to help you until another year had run its course. I will make you a potion, and before sunrise you must swim ashore with it, seat yourself on the beach, and drink it; then your tail will divide and shrivel up to what men call beautiful legs. But it hurts; it is as if a sharp sword were running through you. All who see you will say that you are the most beautiful child of man they have ever seen. You will keep your gliding gait, no dancer will rival you, but every step you take will be as if you were treading upon sharp knives." The mermaid had to persuade the prince to marry her, or else she'd turn to sea foam the instant he married another woman.

And the price for these privileges? "You have the most beautiful voice of any at the bottom of the sea, and I dare say that you think you will fascinate him with it; but you must give me that voice — I will have the best you possess in return for my precious potion! I have to mingle my own blood with it so as to make it as sharp as a two-edged sword . . . Put out your little tongue, and I will cut it off in payment for the powerful draft."

The mermaid traded her tongue for the beautiful legs, swam ashore, and completely captivated the prince. But when it came to a wedding, no dice. "We'll always be friends," he told the mermaid just before he married the princess. On the night of the wedding, the sea witch sent my mermaid a knife, which she was to plunge into the prince's heart to save her own life. But standing over him in his bedroom, she couldn't do it. (I wept.) She kissed him, threw the dagger far out to sea, and died herself, becoming sea foam.

Mr. Andersen scraped up a happy ending: poor sea-foam ladies, it turns out, have a chance at immortality, too. After they hang around for three hundred years, foaming about in the sunshine, they might get into heaven. A bitter sham, I thought, and was angry at God for inventing such things. I hated the filthy sea witch. I wasn't advanced enough to hate the prince. I'd absorbed the lesson: you must love a man so much you are willing to die for him and to forgive him anything. Often on a summer night, the moon would shine so brightly that I would wake at three or four in the morning, and staring out my window, half asleep, breathing the fume of roses, I would gaze at the dark grass, like a sea in the moonlight, and wish for a marble prince to be there, and think about the man I would hold in my arms in only a few short years. I hoped I needn't cut out my tongue to get him, or walk on knives. Lesser sacrifices, of course, I would be ready and eager to make.

Then there were Romeo and Juliet. I made up jokes about Julio and Romiette, and sometimes climbed a tree to declaim, in silly crescendos that pulled my mouth out of shape, "Romeo, Romeo, wherefore art thou, Romeo?" I had found a copy of the play in my father's bookcase and had read it, or at least read through it in my manner, looking for the sexy parts. So far as I could see, there weren't any sexy parts, but somewhere in my father's collection I found a summary of the play, and one Sunday morning on the radio I heard a piece of rapturous music entitled *Romeo and Juliet*, which expressed the notion perfectly.

Ah, yes, this was it. This had something to do with the little quick places, I knew it instantly. For here were lovers defying parents, church, and state, and doing whatever you did to make the music rise and fall that way, and dying for each other. And then parents, church, and state arrived and found them and were sorry, though I knew already that such people never are sorry. But how did she manage to stab herself that way? When nobody was around, I used to take the butcher knife in hand and try to make a start at slipping it between my own ribs. I could never have begun to push that hard. If I even started to bleed, I'd have dropped the knife, even with Romeo dead at my feet. But somehow I would have done it. It was so satisfying to think of your lover dead at your feet.

Tristan and Isolde were more proof. Again it was the radio that corrupted me. Needless to say, I listened to the opera on Saturday afternoons, all alone, with my ear up against the speaker cloth. (No kid that I know of ever listened to the Metropolitan Opera broadcasts with a friend, at least not in Hot Springs, Arkansas.) The mere idea of it drove my mother almost to tears, and I never knew whether it was the rasp of the soprano voices and the chatter of the recitatives or the spectacle of her daughter indulging in deviant behavior. "Let her alone," my father said. "It's highbrow." He bought me a book with all the opera stories in it. I loved Wagner best, not because I understood the music but because I instantly sensed the powerful sexuality of it. I loved Tristan and Isolde better than all possible Wagners. That was the way to do it, in ecstasy on shipboard. Drink the potion, fall into his arms, defy God, and then everybody die under the windy sky with the sea raging all about.

Some books tried to warn me that female bookworms can expect hard times in love. I read *Little Women* compulsively, twenty times over, falling in love with Jo because she was independent and a writer, rejecting her sisters — for who would wish to be nothing but a pretty homebody (Meg) or a beautiful twit (Amy) or dead (Beth)? But I went crazy every time Jo rejected

Laurie, Theodore Laurence, her Teddy as she called him, her handy, handsome lover from next door. Why did Louisa May Alcott allow her to do such a stupid thing? Nobody told me that Jo was Miss Alcott's alter ego except that Miss Alcott spent her life single, writing books she hated, and never even had a Professor Bhaer, let alone a Laurie.

I took a page in my notebook and began:

JO AND LAURIE
by Louisa May Abbott

I copied out the part where Jo and her lover meet on the riverbank, the scene where at last he declares his passion for her, where "something in his resolute tone made Jo look up quickly to find him looking down at her with an expression that assured her the dreaded moment had come, and made her put out her hand with an imploring: 'No, Teddy, please don't!'" And I kept the part in which he announces, "I've loved you ever since I've known you, Jo; couldn't help it, you've been so good to me. I've tried to show it, but you wouldn't let me; now I'm going to make you hear, and give me an answer, for I can't go on so any longer." But then, instead of allowing my heroine to send her lover away, I began to cut and edit ruthlessly, for after all, Miss Alcott was dead.

In my version, Jo did say, "Oh, Teddy, you can't mean what you're saying. You know we are not suited to each other, because our quick tempers and strong wills would probably make us very miserable, if we were to marry." I even allowed her to utter the famous speech that broke my heart: "I'm homely and awkward and odd, and I don't like elegant society, and you'd hate my scribbling all the time and I couldn't get on without it, and we should be unhappy! I don't believe I shall ever marry. I love my liberty too well to be in any hurry to give it up for any mortal man."

But when Laurie swung despairingly away, down to the riverbank, I abandoned Miss Alcott completely and brought Jo to her senses. "Teddy," she called. "Teddy, stop! It isn't true. I do love you with all my heart. It's only that I'm afraid of making you unhappy. It's only that I can't believe you love a girl like me, tall and thin and cranky, always reading, always writing in notebooks! But I will marry you, my dear! Don't run away." And then I had them clinching passionately, just like in the movies, and wrote them into bed, and dispensed with the dreadful German professor and his boring boys' school.

I was unsure what Jo and Laurie would do in bed. Obviously, breathe hard and have a lot of fun, although women were scared at first and usually got pregnant. Back in my laundry basket, I ransacked Casanova. I had gradually come to love the old boy, picturing him as Errol Flynn or Cornel Wilde or any of the 1940s movie stars who flourished their rapiers with an engaging smile and wore knee breeches and ruffled shirts. Callously skipping the master's descriptions of Venice and similar passages, I followed the prince of dalliance from chapter to chapter ("I fall in love with the two sisters, I forget Angela") through a score of trysts with Giuliettas, Lucias, Bettinas, and Teresas, some of whom were married, some underage, but whose bosoms were always delectable, whose legs curved prettily under their petticoats, and whose charms rendered the poor rake "inflammable as straw." Many an endless page ran between the good spots, but Casanova taught me speed reading.

What he and his lovers did was never too clear, but at least in Casanova's world the woman was always as eager as the man and enjoyed herself as fully as he did. I dimly grasped that it wasn't Casanova's eyes turning hard, or if they did, he didn't mention it. The women were really in charge of this passion that drove him. They always had the upper hand. The men were the ones who suffered, and they only suffered a little. It all seemed rather like playing in the bushes: great fun and no penalties, unless your mother caught you, though of course we pretended we did it as medical and scientific research.

When Janny Louise Miller told me, giggling breathlessly, what really took place between a man and a woman, I was dumbfounded, as children of my epoch tended to be. In spite of all the buttons, belts, and zippers I had seen undone in print, I thought the fires were in the mind, not between the legs. Could my elegant Casanova really have spent his life obsessed with that? "Some people may get in bed at night and do crazy, stupid things like that, but not your parents and not mine either," I replied heatedly, but she only laughed at me. After a moment I thought, Great God, she must be right. No wonder grown-ups were so eager to keep the thing a mystery. They must look awfully silly doing it. What did they do with their legs? It sounded about as thrilling as boiled parsnips. I wanted to marry Laurie. I wanted the marble prince.

$\mathcal{D}$REAM LINES

THE NATIVE AUSTRALIANS write no books, I'm told, but instead tell one another stories of primordial wanderers, inventors of the universe who shaped themselves from clay (at a moment or continuum they call the Dreaming Time) and made shining paths across the continent, singing these paths into existence as they went. Unless they chose to walk in a certain direction, the path could never exist. Everything worth knowing, or possible to know, was created then, lies there in the Dreaming Time to be discovered. And thus it was with my father. There were paths in his past, in the stories he told and half told and refused to tell; other paths he sang a hundred times, as though making certain that these lines were forever incised in my head. He wanted me to know, among other things, why he hated his mother and father

"I was born in 1903," he began one day, "the year Orville and Wilbur Wright launched their contraption on the beach at Kitty Hawk Like Icarus, they were, but Orville and Wilbur's wings didn't come unglued." That same year, some trailblazer drove a Packard clear across the continent But though the twentieth century had begun, people lived in the previous one Queen

Victoria was barely in her grave. In Goshen, Indiana, in 1903, women wore corsets and long dresses and said "Mr." to their husbands; little children said "Papa"; every person had a boss and did as he was bidden.

Samuel Bemont and Carrie Abbott lived in a gaunt, tall, green house, which to their son was a place of darkness. Like a prison matron's lace cap, the scrolls and scallops of the front porch trim only made the outlook grimmer. A front porch is meant to be a cooling room, indeed the stage where summer life is lived, where children play and the daughter of the house is courted and lemonade is served. Carrie never put a wicker settee on the porch. "Too hot in the summer. Too cold in the winter. And I'm always in the family way." She sat indoors. Often when Alfie came in with his schoolbooks, he discovered Mama still in her dressing gown in her unmade bed. She had miscarriages — too dreadful to be spoken of, too terrible for a young boy even to know about. Mama was ill, Mama was always poorly. What sapped her energy, he dimly realized, was Papa, for Papa sapped his energy, too. Made him feel like an animal, caged and wary, waiting only for the door to be unlocked half a minute so that he could escape.

Sam Abbott, the millwright, a high-paid technocrat, traveled a lot, driving his buggy or journeying by train from one factory to another, lumber mills, steel mills, any vast barn where wheels turned and circle saws screamed and furnaces glowed and men labored to feed them. Like a computer expert today, he understood the mechanisms, advised the owner on business matters and the foreman on the maddening complexities of gears and motors, kept the equipment in working trim, taught the paid labor how to use it.

Carrie was the daughter of Danish immigrants to Michigan. Bemont had purchased the house in Goshen and fully furnished it, and she told her son how he had brought her there as a bride, to the very house they now lived in, and she had gone from room to room in breathless disbelief, admiring her husband's possessions. The parlor was the greatest marvel, so many things all at once — the horsehair settee, the tea table, two armchairs, a carpet, and an upright piano, its ivory keys gleaming and ready to be played. She was spared the years of yearning for respectability: here it was. Everything was in place, except antimacassars, which she immediately set about crocheting, and whatnots, which she set about collecting. The first thing she unpacked was her wedding photograph, which she placed in its stand-up frame on the claw-footed end table. Within a year, she framed Alfie's first baby picture. But it would be twelve years until a picture of another baby appeared. Besides the miscarriages, three baby girls left the house in miniature coffins, dead too young even to have received names.

To his son, Bemont was more terrifying than Jehovah. His boots required a daily blacking (Alfie's job); his first act on entering the house was to check whether the coal scuttle was filled and the ashcan emptied (Alfie's responsibilities); he thought all children potential criminals who must be tamed by God and by their fathers: he was a papa of his times, with the rectitude of a Gothic revival armchair. To the world at large, Papa was a gentle man, an observer of proprieties, a good provider who absented himself from home out of a sense of duty. Ulysses, off to the wars. But as with other papas of this era, one chamber of his fine Anglo-Saxon brain housed a madman, who emerged at intervals trembling with rage, cursing small boys, and brandishing a leather belt

How heavenly it was when Papa was away and the picture postcards came

Hello, Alfie boy. Papa and Mr. Hardy went to the circus in Chicago. We saw the lions and tigers and elephants and giraffes and a lady who turned somersaults on a wire. There were clowns and ponies, too. With love, Papa.

Or

Hello, Alfie, I am bringing you a toy when I come home. Your loving Papa.

Or

I thought you would love this picture of puppies. Would you like me to bring you a puppy when I come home?

(An empty query, since no puppy ever appeared.) These cards Alfred treasured, and Carrie saved each one of them. When my father saw them in my hands and I commented on Grandpa's sweet paternal ways, he said, "Oh, sure. He talked a good game."

What happened to the postcard papa who took time off from business to go to the circus or buy a toy? Why didn't he come home instead of Bemont, the iron duke whose decisions knew no court of appeal?

Because mothers were briefly allowed to shield their sons from paternal harshness, Carrie dressed her boy in skirts — pleated and sashed little dresses, lace-up shoes — and kept his hair in long golden ringlets until he was six. Then, to his relief, Papa took him to the barber shop and had the curls cut off. He was at last allowed to wear trousers, to comb his own hair. His father told him it was time to learn arithmetic, time to think of becoming a moneymaker like Papa. Now thoroughly masculine, he posed for his portrait in knickers and sturdy boots and a jacket — not quite out of Mama's jurisdiction, though, for during these years he also fingered the violin she so anxiously wished him to play, brandishing the bow with his long fingers. Having learned his sums and made his way through several books before he ever started school, he began his academic career in third grade: smaller than all his classmates, but smarter. Nevertheless, he became the hero of the toboggan slide. He was loved by a pretty child called Bernice, whose school picture and lacy valentines his mother carefully preserved. Oh yes, here was my father, the fellow with the gift of gab, brightest scholar in the class, the captive and the captain of words.

In those days boys were required to master the classics, if only in translation, so Carrie procured copies of the *Iliad* and the *Odyssey* and began to read aloud.

Now when the young Dawn showed again with her rosy fingers,
the dear son of Odysseus stirred from where he was sleeping
and put on his clothes, and slung a sharp sword over his shoulder.
Underneath his shining feet, he bound the fair sandals
and went on his way from the chamber, like a god in presence.

These same words, too, were read to me, and I saw the books, from his childhood, in which my father had inscribed his name as Telemachus rather than Alfred. Telemachus, who was led on his pathway like a child by gray-eyed Athena. The boy who wanted to occupy his father's estate, and yet yearned for Odysseus to come home. No bands of suitors besieged the house in Goshen, tempting Penelope while Odysseus rode the high seas and Telemachus searched the dark places of his imagination, hoping to find a father.

Carrie had much else to teach him, and because she spent most of her time on the horsehair sofa or in bed, there was time. She wanted an aristocratic lineage for her son, and why not? There was a schoolbook at hand, *The History of England*, and out of this she began to construct the family ancestors. "Your father has

French blood, my son; Bemont means 'beautiful mountain.' His people probably came to England with the Conqueror. They're in the Doomsday Book, you know. That's where William of Normandy wrote down all his friends' names. One of these days, we'll go to England and have them look it up for us. You'll see, it will be right there: Bemont Abbott. We'll have our coat of arms done. And you are also named for the first great English monarch, King Alfred. So you have noble bloodlines."

Alfred did not see how bearing King Alfred's name gave him the bloodlines of English kings, but he didn't care. Old Alfred was okay, hiding in the marshes while everybody else was out raping and pillaging. "The preserver of the Wessex dialect," it said in the book; hence the defender of the English tongue. Saving his hide, avoiding the barbarians, and emerging with a whole language as his gift to posterity — not bad. In the history book my father also saw the engraved portrait of William the Conqueror, known as the Bastard: tall, angular, and bushy-browed, with eyes that pierced castle walls and children's skulls, nose like a hawk's bill, black hair as shiny as a raven's. It was Samuel Bemont Abbott in person. Bemont could even have handled the chain mail and the prancing steed.

As Alfie weeded the garden and split kindling, peeled potatoes, shoveled the snow, followed his paper route, and blacked his papa's boots, he tried to believe what his father told him, that he was a privileged child. More than any of his chores, he hated Sunday in the parlor, where Carrie insisted that the family spend the afternoon in their stiff clothes. Whether he was sitting on the settee beside Mama or in one of the pierced-back parlor chairs, Alfred's feet did not quite reach the floor. Would they ever? Putting one's feet on the footstool was forbidden, except for Papa. Piano playing was forbidden, too, on Sunday. Only serious reading was permitted. Bacon's *Essays*, perhaps, or *Pilgrim's Progress*. Alfie loathed the dank green walls and the starched doilies on the tables, the scratchy antimacassars hiding the even scratchier upholstery. He hated the furniture and the parlor and the whole prison of propriety his parents had created. If he squirmed, as who could have helped doing, Papa would threaten to whack him with the cane.

Besides the miscarriages and the stillbirths, Carrie was beginning to be ill in some other way. The summer the third baby daughter was buried, she kept more and more to her bed. To Alfie's horror, something happened to his mother's fingers: the knuckles contorted into permanent angles and her joints grew stiff and her legs refused to support her weight. "Invalid," she called herself, the first time he had heard such a word. To pass the time in bed, she crocheted, and her hands stiffened around the crochet hook and thread until she could handle nothing else. But these developments were not utterly tragic: the piano remained closed, and Carrie called a halt to his violin lessons. Papa stayed out of the house more than ever. Best of all, Sunday afternoons in the parlor were abolished. Carrie could not endure being moved downstairs, even for a few hours. Besides, she grew so stout that Bemont could not carry her, or even give her the support she needed to get back up the stairs. On Sundays the couple sat in their bedroom together in the heat and fanned. To his relief, Alfie was not required to attend

Each morning Alfie went into Mama and Papa's bedroom, to say good morning in the early heat of the day. She would be lying against the pillows, perspiring in her summer nightgown, her bare feet uncovered, a paper fan in her hand. The window was always open, and the white lace curtains stirred in the breeze. He had been stricken at first to see her in only a nightgown, to see her bare feet. The room gradually took on an unpleasant, sick aroma, and he found it harder and harder to make his daily visit.

"Good morning, Mama." And she would grasp his hands and begin her lament "Your mama never can sleep in this heat.

When is the doctor going to be here? Bemont only brought me bread and fruit for breakfast. I couldn't eat it. I want some porridge. Come and sit with Mama and fan her." (Oh, this voice, the endless pleading! It would echo forever in the hollows of our lives. I heard it in my childhood, as my father heard it. Take pity on your grandma, don't let her lie here all alone.) For a while he would comply with her wishes, fanning the dead air uselessly, allowing her to stroke his hair, fetching the wet cloths that gave the pillows their sour smell, listening to her read aloud from the pile of books that she kept by her bedside. But before long, he would find his courage. "I can't stay with you today."

As he bolted down the staircase, her voice echoed after him, curled pleadingly around the banisters. "Alfie, come and sit with me. Read to me, my lamb. Alfie, fetch me my crochet hook. You mustn't leave me alone so long. The doctor wouldn't like it." He quickly learned that if he ran far enough fast enough, he would stop hearing her voice and could stay gone all day. If she complained to Papa, he'd get a beating. Yet since she knew he'd get the beating, she probably wouldn't tell. And so he ran free in the streets of Goshen, choosing his companions where he found them, swimming in the pond on the outskirts of town. He spent hours reading in the public library, and the librarian grew so accustomed to his presence that she stopped noticing what he read. (Chiefly sagas of noble canines — *Lad: A Dog*; *Beautiful Joe*, a tearful screed about animal abuse with a mutilated terrier for a hero — books that he now unearthed in the library and insisted I read as well. I must weep as he had wept over worked-to-death cart horses, starved cows, and mangled dogs.) He went to work as a paper boy, delivering house to house on his bicycle. And, to his surprise, Papa allowed him to play outdoors after supper on weekdays, once the dishes were cleared away and the leftovers covered up. Only one string was attached — he had to be inside the front door before the parlor clock struck eight

Motherlessness, he discovered, was a happy state. In addition to days spent outdoors and evenings that were over only at dusk and a disused piano and a forgotten violin, the circus was coming to Goshen that summer. Posters had been up for three weeks, and everybody in town was planning to attend. Not Mama, of course, but Papa. Alfred washed windows around the neighborhood to earn the price of a seat, and Papa took the money and bought a pair of excellent tickets, which he tucked under the sugar bowl on the kitchen shelf. The performance was on a Saturday night, and on Friday the circus train arrived and the whole company paraded into town and pitched their tent. Having finished his paper route, young Alfred rode his bicycle to the campgrounds and joined a few older boys who were teasing the elephant and talking to the bareback riders. (After thirty years, he recalled every detail.) As boys did in those times, he considered becoming a roustabout, running away.

By the time he started home, the shadows were falling all around him. His father's image in his head, he raced in terror through the streets and dumped his bike in the arborvitae by the porch. As he reached the front door, the parlor clock began to chime. But he couldn't get the door open. One, two. Thank God I'm here. I'll get the door open. Three, four. Somebody has thrown the bolt. Papa must be waiting for me. Five, six, seven. It seems very dark tonight, sure sign that winter is coming. Eight. Nine.

Nine. An hour late. Not possible, not possible. The town clock had only struck seven when he passed by on his way to the circus grounds. It couldn't be nine. He stopped rattling the door. After a time he heard the bolt slide and saw the handle rotate downward. Papa was waiting for him, one hand behind his back. His face was black with fury. The good papa, the millwright, the breadwinner, had vanished. The madman had emerged, like a murderer from a dark London alley.

"Papa, I'm home. I know it's only eight o'clock."

"Get in here, you lying scoundrel. You think I don't know how you've been running wild around the town? You think I don't know what you've been reading? You think I don't care how you treat your mother, and how she lies for you? You are badly in need of a lesson, little lad, and you won't forget this one so soon."

"Bemont," Carrie shrieked from upstairs. "You mustn't beat him. Don't hurt our little son. Have mercy on him." But Bemont slammed the kitchen door against her screams. Alfred could hear her crying through all that followed.

"It's only eight, Papa," he said. But he knew there was no escape, and since he was well trained to his beatings, he unbuttoned his pants and let them down to the floor. Alas, he had stopped wearing drawers that summer, since there was no one to notice whether he wore them or not. Held roughly by the left arm and bent across the kitchen table, he took twelve hard blows with Papa's leather belt, and the eleventh cut the skin of his haunches and raised a raw blister. After the ninth lash, Alfie stopped screaming that it was only eight. After the tenth, he simply screamed, though he had resolved not to give his father such satisfaction.

"Go straight to bed. You'll be catching up on some of your chores tomorrow. Wait just one minute." And from under the sugar bowl, Papa took the two circus tickets and tore them neatly in half. "Tomorrow you can begin the day reading to your mother. The garden wants weeding. We'll see how well you do scouring the floor in here."

Alfie had no trouble stifling his tears that night. He was a burned man, in shock. He scarcely slept, since his blistered buttocks woke him each time he moved. He did not weep the next day, as he knelt in the garden pulling weeds. Nor as he scoured the floors or stood by his mother's bed. He could hear the distant beating of a drum, the sound of a trumpet. Carrie read aloud to him from *Ivanhoe*, and then he did weep, angrily, over the wounded knight, unable to do battle for half the length of the novel, and the torments of Rebecca, who loved him, and of her father, Isaac the Jew, whom the Normans threatened to fry on a grill. That evening he stood by the open window, watching as the neighbors departed for the circus, straw hats in hand. But his father never relented. The madman had gone back in his chamber. Here was the good father once more, taking his opportunity to Teach the Boy a Lesson.

This story had several versions, all of which I simultaneously believed. In one, he peered through the parlor window and saw Papa resetting the clock. In another, he returned home late as an act of defiance. In another version, he wept all night. In another, he never cried at all. I came to accept this as a mythic event in my own life as much as in his. He surely knew I was aware of the discrepancies, as I knew he was aware of them, but as if we were collaborators in a screenplay, he never explained them and I never asked. Each time he told the story, it was to remind me that he himself had never beaten me, had never approached me in anger, with fists raised, as fathers for a thousand years had approached their children. The aggrieved child in the old photographs, blistered by his father's rage and perfidy, climbed into my arms in my dreams. "Injustice, injustice," he cried. "Will you right my wrongs?"

My father never knew where they heard it, the rumor that was to transform their lives, but Bemont began to talk of a cure, a spa in the middle of Arkansas, where women with illnesses like Carrie's were hauled off the train on stretchers and restored after six weeks of taking the waters, healthy women again, bringing children into the world, cooking, keeping house. "Papa will have to give up his profession and close up the house, and Alfie, of course, must stay on in Goshen," Bemont said, while Carrie wept and protested. Alfie was eleven and, according to his father, old enough to get along for a few weeks or even months, old enough to begin earning his own way. So one morning, as Bemont prepared to depart with his wife on the train, he packed a suitcase for his son and led him to his new quarters, a tiny room only big enough for a bed, at the top of a ramshackle house, and his new livelihood, as milk-cart driver for a small dairy farm on the outskirts of town. He was required to arise at 3 A.M., hitch up the horse, load his cart, and make his rounds. He'd be finished by seven, in time for the family cook to give him bread and cheese for breakfast and a lunch pail for school, and then he'd be off to walk three miles to the room where he'd always been a hero, Alfred the Great, king of every spelling bee, sharpest mathematician, the boy who could recite half the *Odyssey* by heart and whose attitude to all schoolwork was "veni, vidi, vici." His mother wept helplessly when she kissed him goodbye that morning, but all she said was "Be a good boy." Those were Bemont's words, too, as he turned away — as though goodness had anything to do with it.

Unlike the circus story, this was not a tale my father often told. I heard it only after dark, on the front porch swing perhaps, as the moon rose over the cherry tree in our front yard, and there were shadows over his eyes, his cheeks. He did try being a good boy, as there was no other way to earn the breakfast and the contents of the lunch pail. He did try to hold on to his brilliant record at school, though when he arrived in the morning, often late, he sometimes fell asleep at his desk. He did try parsing the Latin in the evening, but the lamplight in the dairyman's kitchen was dim, and nine o'clock was bedtime. The cook woke him at three, long before the rosy-fingered dawn summoned Telemachus to follow Athena, and he would stand dazed by his bedside, unsure of who he was or what his next action should be. His teacher, a stern young man who'd so eagerly heretofore brought the star pupil to the head of the class, took to rapping his knuckles with a ruler. Finally, one afternoon when Alfred slept so soundly on his desktop that he failed to hear his name called sharply for the third time, he found himself seized by the ear and dragged to the high stool. There he was crowned with the dunce cap and forced to sit until the dismissal bell.

In time a postcard arrived at the farmhouse. Carrie was cured. They had bought their tickets to Goshen. Alfie was to meet them at the station, was to see his mother walk off the train, unaided. Indeed, she did walk off the train and take him in her arms, and Papa praised him right there on the platform for having survived his ordeal. He was a young hero who'd been sent out to prove his manhood and had won the laurel. But Carrie was not cured, nor had Alfie survived his ordeal. Next year, Carrie gave birth to another son, whom they called Bruce after the Scottish king. Royalty or not, his older brother greeted him with anger and contempt. On the way to the bakery to fetch a loaf of bread for his mother, Alfred went instead to the depot and rode out on the top of the next freight. "I came home three or four days later," he told me. "But I had a taste of it. I even spent the night in a hobo jungle and drank coffee out of a tin can."

Overwhelmed with the care of a new baby, crushed by Alfred's fury, Carrie took to her bed once more. Now the only solution was to go and live forever where the healing waters flowed. This time Bemont purchased tickets for them all, one way. But by the time the dray backed up to the green house with its gingerbread trim and loaded the parlor furniture, Telemachus had decided to become an outlaw. He quietly, dutifully rode the train with them from Goshen, Indiana, which he was never to see again, to Hot Springs, Arkansas. He walked his baby brother up and down the aisle of the coach to relieve his mother. He stood on the platform with his family when they arrived at their destination, and then fetched a horse-drawn cab as his father directed. But he was only counting the days until he left from that same station, bound for San Francisco and the China trade, for Wyoming, for any locale that did not choke and bind him, where he did not have to hear his father's shouts or his mother's complaints. He returned sporadically, to attend high school (but never to graduate, for he'd lost his early love of school) and to earn his street name as a delivery boy for the Hatterie. Finally another boxcar took him to Chicago, where he began his life as a wage-earner and found a woman for the first time.

As I created a love life for my mother, I did the same for my father, fabricating it from what he told and did not tell. His first wife, red-haired Imogene, suited my purposes nicely. She had known him when he looked like the boy in the photograph, tall, blond, angry, fresh off the freight train, a youth in Prohibition Chicago, ready for anything, a pair of arms and a strong back, good for any work that came along. How had he met Imogene? My father only laughed when I asked him, so I had to work it out. Not when he was the floorwalker at Marshall Field's or the spinner at the candy factory or the laborer at the steel mill or the door-to-door salesman of Eureka vacuum cleaners. Maybe they met at the Chicago Public Library, where he spent every moment he could find. But he never spoke of Imogene as a reader, a person of the book. It must have been in his cab-driver days, as he drove the streets, carrying well-dressed people from one speakeasy to another, possibly with a load of bootleg whiskey in the trunk.

I would conjure Imogene hailing his cab. She's dressed in a pretty brown coat with fur around the collar, and silk stockings and slender shoes with thick heels, the kind the flappers wore to show off their ankles. Her hair is done up in a French knot (he told me she had long hair). He picks her up in the Loop (I knew all about Chicago). She's been shopping and now she must get home to her three children. She's older than my father (fourteen years, he says, a mature woman of thirty-two) and has been married quite a while. In my fantasies, these children are a nuisance, an encumbrance, but I can't simply banish them, since my father himself could not banish them from his romance and subsequent marriage. The oldest, a boy, is only five years younger than the young taxi driver his mother is now eyeing. She stares, according to me, at the back of my father's blond head. She leans slightly forward to check the profile, talks softly to him (What would she talk about? The icy wind off Lake Michigan, of course). She says it's been the coldest winter she's ever seen. Then he says that he went to hear Al Jolson at the Palladium last week and intends to take in Jeanette MacDonald next week, and he stopped in at the Art Institute that afternoon to get warm. Has she ever gone in there to look at the paintings? Or just to get warm? She is amused by this, but moved by his good looks. Taxi drivers aren't supposed to be good-looking or go to shows or art museums.

She asks him what his name is, and then laughs when he says, "Hat Abbott." "Hap? Did you say Hap? Hat? Where'd you get such a crazy name as that?" As they reach the building where she lives, she invites him to come to her apartment for a little coffee and some cake, just to warm up. They both know she's being brazen. Neither of them cares. At the top of the stairs, he suddenly remembers that a woman this pretty certainly has a husband. A large burly husband. "Don't worry," she says, reading his mind. "I'm divorced, so you needn't worry about my husband bursting in and throwing you down the stairs. But I do have three children. They'll be home from school in an hour." He resolves to be safely out of the way by then, but somehow they've hardly begun to talk, hardly drunk their coffee when the door opens and three kids troop in. They like my father right away. They are lonely for a father. (Imogene doesn't make me jealous, but her children do. I don't want them looking suspiciously at my father, thinking he's not good enough for Imogene. And yet sometimes I yearn to have them as part of my own family.) Gray, a grown-up boy of thirteen, says hello, though he's startled to find his mother with a man. Abigail, ten, with red hair like her mother, is friendlier. Henry, six, says nothing.

I have trouble getting the story past the cake and coffee, allowing my father to unwind Imogene's long tresses out of the French knot. I have difficulty staging their first kiss. I want a time machine, to show me precisely how it was with them, how he looked at her when he said he loved her, to allow me to hear exactly what they said when they agreed to get married. How did they rid themselves of the three children long enough to go before the justice of the peace, which is what they soon did? Did they marry with Imogene's children looking on? Gray, Abigail, Henry, if only I'd been able to find you! How did the bride and bridegroom dress that day? What did they eat for dinner that first night, where did they sleep? Though I knew such things were forbidden, shameful to imagine, I longed for just one glimpse of them making love. Was it in the morning before the children woke up?

The marriage itself requires no crystal ball. Having sworn to support the five of them, he often comes home empty-handed when the rent is due. He takes a second job (that part is true). But Imogene still buys groceries with her own money, and her young husband rages. The children, now rapidly turning into adults, tiptoe around the apartment when he has migraines, but they don't really care if he gets his sleep or not. Gray grows angry, bitter, rebellious. He had planned to study medicine. Now he threatens to quit school (that part is true). My father is overwhelmed to find himself, not yet twenty-five, the father of three children who fill up every cranny of his living space and are never out of earshot. All he wanted was to share the bed of this beautiful woman, this serene and wise adult who did not have to be lifted out of her chair and carried to the kitchen table and whose tears never needed to be dried. But tears fall regularly now. He weeps, the children weep, she begs him to be calm. In the evenings, the few evenings Hat is home, he and Imogene scream at each other, tear at each other. Gray slams out, adding to the angry noise. He, too, will find a freight train, he shouts. He'll be a hobo instead of a doctor. Abigail and Henry cover their ears behind the thin walls. All this I can easily envision — the screenplay writes itself.

But elsewhere in Chicago, this golden city (as Daddy tells me endlessly each night on our front porch) where a poor young man can stand before a Rembrandt or warm his bones in a library that contains every book in the world, there lives another character: Mike, whose name appeared inside a dozen of my father's books, always the fine editions, always the books that I recognized as being philosophical in nature or meant only for connoisseurs or filled with sexual references or all of that. As a young girl, my mother had made a friendship quilt, each block bearing a signature meticulously embroidered in black, so that all her life she could go over the names, and when I lay under the quilt suffering from my continual colds, she told me what had become of each of the signers. My father's friend Mike had made a patchwork of a rather different sort — words laid down like pieces of mosaic in a destroyed Pompeiian villa, tantalizing half-clues to my father's biography. Mike is a stranger, but I'd know his hand anywhere, and I long ago committed to memory the score of words he wrote on the flyleaves of books he gave my father. Like the books he chose, his inscriptions were self-consciously learned; indeed, it took me years to decipher the references. In some odd, almost supernatural way, he became responsible for my education, for my inclinations in reading — me, whom he never saw or dreamed of.

Inside the *Satyricon of Petronius*, in his mellifluous script, Mike wrote, "Dear Hat, Read on to the bitter end, and especially savor the delicate beauty of the thousand and one nights." Mike was the donor also of *Casanova's Memoirs*, my childhood sourcebook, and of an edition of the *Decameron* with lovely engravings. Inside the

Collected Poems of Oscar Wilde, Mike signed himself "Panurge."
What or who was a Panurge? Laboriously, I tracked Panurge to a
book my father said was the raciest ever published, *Gargantua
and Pantagruel*, by a Frenchman called Rabelais. And on the
flyleaf of the Rabelais, where Panurge dwelled, Mike addressed
my father as Charmides, which was the name of a poem back in
the Oscar Wilde book. What kind of puzzle was this? Inside
Sesame and Lilies and The Queen of the Air, by John Ruskin, he
scribbled elegantly, "To the Mad Hatter, from Telemachus."
Another Telemachus. Inside Erasmus's *In Praise of Folly*, he wrote
"To Hat on Christmas Day, a token of everlasting friendship."
Everlasting friendship? But Mike was gone. No letters ever came
from him. We signed no Christmas card for him. My father
refused to answer my inquiries about him, looked at some distant
object, became even more reticent than when I asked for details
about his first marriage. "Mike was my dearest friend, the best I
ever had" was the most he would say. Or "He was a great reader.
A learned man, a scholar. We used to walk the streets together,
talking of books. We used to walk the city parks together,
reading aloud. We used to memorize great poems and say them to
each other, him one stanza, me the next." He told me this at
supper one night, which caused my mother to roll her eyes and
mutter, "Lordy mercy. Thank God I wasn't there."

I went through the volumes like a rodent, collecting string and
fuzz. Mike's inscriptions all by themselves were an introduction
to literature. I was determined to find out what they meant.
I knew Telemachus already, the alter ego of my father's boyhood,
son of Odysseus and Penelope. *Gargantua and Pantagruel*, so filthy
that decent libraries wouldn't have it on the shelf, proved less
entrancing than Casanova. "Charmides," the poem by Wilde, my
father always referred to as a masterpiece. He and Mike had
shared it, he said. He urged me to read it, but would not read it
aloud. Charmides, according to the opening stanza, "was a Gre-

cian lad, who coming home with pulpy figs and wine from Sicily stood at his galley's prow, and let the foam blow through his crisp brown curls unconsciously." Aha! Plodding through it searching for the good parts, I came across several:

> And all his hoarded sweets were hers to kiss,
> And all her maidenhood was his to slay,
> And limb to limb in long and rapturous bliss
> Their passion waxed and waned, — O why essay
> To pipe again of love, too venturous reed!
> Enough, enough that Eros laughed upon that flowerless mead.

Limb to limb in long and rapturous bliss! Not so good as Casanova, but better than Rabelais, I found.

Out of all this I concocted Mike the teacher, Mike the connoisseur, Mike the companion, and finally, in a fit of perverse, perhaps perverted, imagination, Mike the lover. I didn't know what homosexuality was, had no idea that such things had ever been thought of, much less practiced, or any notion that my father ever loved anyone besides Imogene and my mother. And of course me, which, as I've said, was in its own category. But one afternoon he told me why, more or less, Oscar Wilde had been committed to Reading Gaol. He had loved a rich young nobleman, my father said, a silly youth unworthy of a great poet's attentions, but the boy's father had had Wilde arrested and brought to trial. Somehow, when my father said "loved," I could just picture the whole thing. I was profoundly shocked. Everybody in England was shocked, Daddy said, though half of them were doing just as much themselves, or had done so. But the hypocrites threw the poor poet into prison.

"Of course, it was a terrible vice Wilde had. I'm not recommending it. But men have such feelings sometimes. The Greeks, you know, liked men better than women. You'll find this all through literature if you look. You have to be tolerant. You'll discover that love is a strange thing. Jesus said, judge not, that ye be not judged."

As I realized even then, this was not standard paternal advice in central Arkansas in the 1940s, even with a Christian commandment thrown in. I noticed that he kept his voice very low as he confided this to me, behind the rose trellises. He took care to say that I ought not mention it to Mother. I did not ask — and he did not say — whether women could be similarly inclined. But for sure, love was a strange thing. I kept this knowledge scrupulously to myself, applying it only in an occasional fantasy. I have speculated for years that Mike played the lovestruck poet to my father's faithless, unworthy young nobleman. Or was it the reverse? Or simply two lonely, bookish, half-educated young men strolling the streets of Chicago, pretending to be devotees of an academic literature whose high priests would have scorned them, calling one another by such names as Panurge and Telemachus, declaiming overdecorated Victorian verse, and imagining themselves aesthetes of the highest order?

But of all my father's myths and half-visible mysteries, the wanderer was what I loved best, and the defiant young man of fifteen or sixteen clung to my imagination more strongly even than the abused boy, beaten and deprived. The wanderer crouching in the tall grass, slipping through the open door of a boxcar, riding the rails, the wind howling around his ears as he leaped like a cat from one car to another on a fast freight. In the quiet of our conversations, when my mother could not hear, Daddy pictured himself to me on a street in St. Louis, just off the eastbound freight, knocking at a back door the way our hoboes knocked, those vagabonds he had forbidden my mother to turn away. "Any odd jobs, ma'am?" he said to the housewife. "I'm hungry." And the woman, whoever she was, gave him a plate of food, clean clothes, permission to pump water from the well and wash, lent him a razor for a shave. In Laramie, Wyoming, he came in from the hobo jungle looking for work. They made him the foreman of a chicken ranch, he said, but he didn't stay long. Next month, with an adolescent's beard sprouting on his cheeks, he arose out of the tall weeds in Oakland, California, to join the throng boarding the ferry to San Francisco — without the bother of paying his fare. He got caught the first time, but succeeded the next. Then he signed on as deckhand on a China-bound merchant ship, only to be dismissed from the crew when the captain discovered he was fifteen. (I always held my breath at that part. What if he had shipped out to China? Would he ever have returned? Would there have been such a person as me?) He went home then, or at least back to his parents in Hot Springs, Arkansas, and enrolled in high school once more, and also apprenticed himself to the local bootleggers, who taught him to drive a car at top speed and round the corners on two wheels, in case the law was on his tail. In hushed but gleeful tones, he told me how he'd brought a shipment of Canadian whiskey to Hot Springs from Memphis one night — ordinarily an easy job, but this time the sheriff of the next county pursued him, then gave up as Daddy sped out of his jurisdiction with the bottles rattling.

His life as he constructed it was a tangle of close calls, near misses, contingencies, and accidents. One half-second's difference, and he might have joined the merchant marine, or become a chicken farmer in Wyoming, or spent his adult life in jail. Yet all the contingencies had nevertheless crisscrossed, connected, placing us in our swing on a porch in Hot Springs, Arkansas, where Telemachus could recount his adventures. It might all have been pure legend, like the *Odyssey*, except for the books signed "Mike."

And except for the troublesome letters that arrived occasionally from Imogene. Sometimes, sick with dread and curiosity, I found one of the missives in the mailbox myself and carried it up Alamo Street to the house, debating whether to open it and read it or simply rip it up and throw it in the bushes. I knew we were in for a stormy day or two. She always wrote from the same Chicago address, using her best penmanship, Miss Love style, with flourishes and curlicues, so that "Mr. Alfred Bemont 'Hat' Abbott," as she always addressed the envelope, using every name he had, as if to show she knew him inside out, looked like a creeping vine. Mother refused to say anything about Imogene in my presence, but by adroit positioning, I managed to eavesdrop on my parents' fights about the letters.

"She writes to me because she wants me back, of course," my father would shout in answer to my mother's angry questions. "She's a rich woman now, you know. Her old man died and left her a lot of money. Gray's a doctor now, married, with two little kids, and Henry's in medical school. Abigail married a banker last month. Big wedding. Imogene says any time the going gets too tough around here, I should hop the next train and my worries will be over. She says she'll never love anyone but me."

"Well, as far as I'm concerned, you can go to the depot right now. Can I drive you?" (No, Mama! What if he said yes? Later that night I heard her sobbing.)

After the atmosphere had returned to normal, I would excavate his dresser drawers and his closet shelves for the letters, but he must have burned them. I never got my wish — to read her spidery handwriting, to decipher these strange, unsettling messages from a woman over fifty by now (old enough to be my grandmother, older than I could imagine), whose hair had surely turned from red to gray.

How They Stayed Married

MY PARENTS' LIVES did not demonstrate that man and wife should be one but rather that the gap between two bodies can never be permanently bridged. Oh, they had a very close relationship: I never quite imagined them separating, though there were the shaky moments over Imogene, of course.

"Do you love him?" I would ask my mother.

And she would laugh. Or frown. Or twist her mouth. "I reckon."

"Do you love her?" I would ask my father.

"Well, what a question. I guess I do. You don't understand about love. It isn't like the storybooks."

Couldn't either of them simply say yes?

"How I came to marry your mother" was another story my father told, not so comforting as some.

My mother, Velma Loyd, grew up on an Arkansas farm and knew nothing about books, bookmaking, gambling, or any form of literature. An honor graduate at age seventeen of a one-room school, she chose not to marry any of her suitors, who were as numerous and hardy as ragweed, and instead moved to town, where she roomed with her older half-sister and looked for work:

maid in a tourist court was the work she found. She changed the sheets and cleaned the toilets, dusted the little wooden tables, swept the pine floors. The next-to-youngest of a large family, she was used to doing beds. She could make a bed tight as a drum, and knew how to boil the sheets and soap and air them until they smelled like a pine forest in spring. (Washing was not part of her job in the city, of course. Bed linen went to a laundry.) They'd never had flush toilets at home, so her first encounter with one was when she had to clean it. How could anything so obviously useful create so much work on its own? Now that she was a working girl, Mother could pay a dollar a week for her room and board. She had entered the modern world, the cash world of labor and labor-saving devices. (How odd she would have thought it, this slender, pretty, black-haired girl, lugging her mop pail and rags and her supply of clean sheets, that so many years later, after she was dead, someone would describe her labors and refer to her as Mother. Or that anyone would set down an account of her labors — women's work, long hours, low pay.)

One day, as Velma stood on the front porch, here came this city fellow in a red Pontiac coupe, just the man she dreamed of, rolling easily up to her door. He introduced himself as Hat Abbott.

"Hat?" She was gently disbelieving. She herself carried the nickname Sook, had a brother Jake, knew boys called Skeet and Raz, Vel and Dude, but Hat was new to her.

"Yes" (with a slow smile, I can just see it), "that's what they call me. When I was a kid I had a job delivering hats from a hat shop. On a bicycle. Men's hats. I'd balance the hatbox on the handlebars and off I'd go down Central Avenue. So everybody called me Hat. And it stuck."

The next thing he told her was also true, except that for her it was a story. He said he earned his living — and the cash to pay for sharp-looking red cars — as a bookmaker. And she imagined

that he sat in a room somewhere all day, stitching up book bind-
ings with a thread and needle. Besides the Bible and her schoolbooks, she had hardly seen ten books in her life, but she revered
them, treasured them not only for what they contained but as
material objects. She was overjoyed to meet a person who actually
made them.

She was a creature of the brier patch, meadow, and spring, the
kitchen and the smokehouse. She could can beans and drive a
mule. She could take cloth and a needle and thread and stitch up a
man's fancy shirt in a day and make a skirt for herself in two hours.
She knew how to preserve seed corn and how to sow the pasture in
vetch. He did not know sweet clover from dog fennel and had
only recently worked his way up to bookmaker from bootlegger.
He had had other jobs that he failed to mention — steel mill
hand, floorwalker at Marshall Field's (nothing but the best for
Daddy), and door-to-door salesman of Eureka vacuum cleaners
(which were far superior, he told her, to Hoovers. It was an honor
to work for the Eureka company, which made a vacuum cleaner
he was proud to sell). The world was full of jobs for a man like
him, he said, but why brag about it? Nor did he make haste to
tell the farmer's daughter he had been married once already, at age
eighteen, to that beautiful Chicago redhead.

When he finally chose to tell her what the story really was, it
was too late. They already had the marriage license, and Velma
had grown accustomed to the Pontiac, cruising along at lan-
guorous low speeds in it, the moon shining on the lake where
they parked. Oh, there were moments, moments that brought
tears to his eyes as he alluded to them. My father hadn't the
money to take her out for a chicken dinner and a movie — who
did, in 1933? — but in his Pontiac he was a wealthy man. She
loved the car. Did she love the bookmaker? The joke was on her,
she felt — how could she have been so silly as to imagine him
stitching pages? Gambling — well, was that any way to support

a family? If she had thought of gambling at all, Velma had classified it with worshiping graven images and coveting thy neighbor's ox and his ass and his maidservant. But he told her that farmers were the biggest gamblers of all. ("Why yes, Hat, I suppose they are.") She did not pause to think that farming was legal while making book wasn't. She did not know that when the governor turned the heat on, a man might have to put a pencil behind his ear and do business from a telephone booth. Nor that men in my father's business sometimes went to jail.

Then there was the matter of the divorce. How could she tell her Baptist father about that? (Answer: not tell him. Anyway, Papa had had two wives himself. Just so happened the first one died.) Velma had never so much as spoken to a divorced person before now.

"Why did you marry that woman in the first place?" Velma was sitting on the fender, dangling her new pumps, pleased with her silk stockings. He was smoking a cigarette and gazing toward the lake.

"She fell for me, I was a good-looking boy, only eighteen. Didn't know any better. She was thirty-two at the time."

That must have been it, she thought — a grasping woman, an innocent boy. She had heard that some women went after young boys. It happened in cities like Chicago.

Daddy had had the dollar for the marriage license, but when they went a day later to the justice of the peace and got married, Daddy had to owe him the two dollars. "The best classroom," my father always said, "is the school of life." My mother had an education in store for her.

The next week the governor closed down the gambling, and the month after that the Pontiac dealer repossessed the Pontiac. They worked at what they could find — anything, everything — and after a few months got jobs in a laundry, Daddy washing clothes, Mother handling a big mangle. By then my mother was pregnant. One afternoon she burned her arm on the mangle, and seeing that she was unfit to work, her boss fired her. In a rage, Daddy quit, and the two of them walked home together. (That same laundry stayed in business for many years afterward, and each time we drove past the place, Daddy would say "Killers!" and direct me to pity the women who worked there and to scorn their exploiters.)

He couldn't get a job anywhere. He and Mother would walk past the grocery store windows and look at the canned goods. (Three days was the longest they had to do without, said Daddy, unable ever to tell the tale without weeping. By the time he got to this part, I would be sobbing out of control, watching this film of my young parents staring at soup cans.) It was thirty miles to the Loyd farm, where they knew that they'd have a bed and enough to eat. Grandma and Grandpa Loyd did not believe in currency and trafficked chiefly in edibles. Hence the Depression meant nothing to them. So now the story turned into Mary and Joseph walking toward Bethlehem, without even a donkey. My sobs would recommence. I could imagine how Mother must have missed the Pontiac that day. After ten miles, she sat down by the road and said she could go no further. But a man came along in a car and rescued them, found them some water and food, drove them onward. Daddy, like most authors, was fond of the deus ex machina. They lived on the farm awhile, but then the horse books opened up again and a man drove up to the farmhouse one morning to fetch my father to work, which is why I was born on Alamo Street instead of in Granny Loyd's bedroom.

My mother and father slept in the same bed, drove the same car, made deposits into the same bank account, yet were always estranged. I sensed this otherness, the refusal to be yin and yang, most vividly in the kitchen and the grocery store. Marriage counselors rely on sex, or lack of it, as their barometer of misery.

They almost never mention food. Mother was a country cook and a country eater — six or seven dishes of turnip greens, beans, tomatoes, crowder peas, okra, corn, and raw onions, plus fried meat, cornbread, butter, a pitcher of molasses, a variety of home-made relishes, and either buttermilk or sweetened tea made up a dinner table. And dinner was at midday. Then for supper you ate buttermilk and cold cornbread or a biscuit and a piece of leftover bacon. Mother could have eaten this way all her life. Sometimes in the summer she would cook meals like that. Daddy grumbled, but I noticed that he ate them.

He, in contrast, was a scarred, embittered veteran of main-stream Yankee cooking. Even before his mama got sick, her food had been a form of vengeance, the ultimate in female passive aggression, the punishment males had so richly earned for de-manding three meals a day but never peeling a potato or washing a plate. Carrie Abbott sloshed together just enough food to keep body and soul intact, never caring if it suited anyone or looked fit to eat. Never washed the pudding bag, and served up starchy, soggy messes from it that made her little boy want to run away from home. Dished the soup up lukewarm, so that the grease rose like scum to the top of a pond. Boiled spaghetti for two hours, so that it turned to mush in the unseasoned tomato sauce. Sliced the pork chops paper thin and fried them until they looked and tasted like tanned leather. Never wiped the oilcloth. Kneaded the pie crusts until you couldn't cut them with a cleaver. "Alfie, would you return the blessing? Eat what's on your plate. You'll never grow into a man if you don't eat your soup. You finish your dinner." And of course the starving of the earth were ushered to the Abbott table to turn their hollow, angry eyes on Alfred because he could neither eat his pork chop nor send it to Armenia parcel post — the act generations of guilt-ridden American chil-dren have yearned to commit.

Vigorously rejecting the foods of his maternal line, my father invented his own repertory of culinary preferences, his own manner of eating. Preferences were all he invented, of course — he never dreamed of cooking. What he wanted to eat was very different from what my mother knew how to cook. She was willing to change her ways to please her man. Her only problem was that she didn't know how to cook his way, and though she said it didn't matter, his wants at table impressed her family as perverted.

What Daddy wanted was a high roller's diet. He had learned to eat in Chicago, where he saw if not always shared what smart operators ate. He insisted on beef, lots of it, particularly porterhouse steaks and standing rib roasts, and it all had to be cooked bloody rare. T-bone steak was Daddy's ideal supper, and lunch, and sometimes we had it for breakfast on Sundays. "It's good for you," he said. "Rare meat makes you tall, strong, and brainy." Mother came from a pork-eating culture. Her younger brother, who was down on his luck, sometimes dropped by at mealtime; he would cry "Eeeooo" at the sight of the bleeding joint and fill his plate with vegetables and light bread.

Daddy also wanted lamb. Not chops, which wouldn't have been so blatant, but legs of it. Our relatives would not even come near our house when this pungent, gamy fragrance was in the air. Muttering "Godamighty, that shore does stink," the neighbor kids who might have come to play in my yard would climb the fence and go home. If my aunt happened to arrive when we were making lamb sandwiches out of the leftovers, she too would exclaim "Eeeooo," backing off warily from the object on the platter, and add, "I can just taste that old sheep wool in my mouth."

Daddy also wanted yeast breads, oysters, and shrimp, and chocolate in every possible form. He went to expensive greengrocers uptown that catered to the tourist trade and purchased such delicacies as greengage plums and ripe Bing cherries. He wanted his pies made with a proper puff pastry, and he sent my mother to a cooking class to learn the technique. "Had to educate her before I could eat a thing she cooked," he liked to remark to guests when we had any — or merely to me if no one else was at hand. "Those first bride's biscuits like to have broke my teeth." Now instructed in the higher arts, Mother would turn out three or four pies a week, apple and egg custard and cherry and coconut creams in their delectable layered crusts. There was no such thing as a meatless meal, or one without dessert.

Ignorant about cholesterol, sodium, and saturated fats, we consumed them by the kilogram. In the summertime we even took salt tablets. That wasn't all, of course. To get more fat into a meal, Daddy would zigzag between standard American and down-home cooking. The prime steaks were combined with vegetables cooked Southern style, with lots of fat pork, and we also ate pork in thick chops, stuffed and breaded, or lovely fatty loin roasts with brown gravy. When it came to turkey, he wanted the stuffing cooked inside the body, not in a roasting pan, and he wanted it made from white bread and chestnuts; but Mother always made an extra pan with cornbread and sausage. Chicken had to be done à la Maryland, which meant dipped in flour and baked, or à la king, served over rice. The only "à la" anybody else ate was pie à la mode, which we ate, too. On this diet my father grew plump and then enormous. My mother, picking sparingly at the kingpin's table, stayed slender somehow. I ate only the sweets and grew gaunt.

There were two dishes Daddy recalled from childhood — only two that made it through the grid he applied to his past. One was a Danish specialty called elflesk — apples fried with bacon. The apples were always soaked with grease, but since I liked bacon and had no objection to grease, generally I would sample the elflesk. The heavy, sweet, dirty flavor exactly called up the picture of Grandma Abbott's upbringing on the Mickelsen farm in

Michigan. I could imagine that the cows stayed indoors with the people all winter, the way they did in *Heidi*. Maybe Grandma drank warm milk from a bowl. The other maternal specialty that had somehow survived was fried green tomatoes. Mother never could quite make them come out right, but she tried, hoping someday to win her gold star. I would no more have eaten fried green tomatoes than fried green caterpillars, and used to watch in disgust as Mother dipped the firm slabs laced with whorls of shining seeds in egg batter and cracker meal, then laid them in a bubbling pool of grease in the frying pan. Elflesk and green tomatoes were royal dishes, seldom served. On the days that Mother made either one, Daddy would announce its imminent arrival, and we would gather in the kitchen to watch the preparation. Like the ogre in "Jack and the Beanstalk," he would seat himself ceremonially at table, his napkin under his chin, his knife and fork at the ready, and then, when Mother set the dish before him, would eat while we watched. Daddy was being served.

Another element imposed itself on these queasy combinations arising from my parents' separate histories, for America had just embarked on the Age of Jell-O, based on the notion that anything that saved time was good (whether it actually saved any time or not). Jell-O was not the only thing, of course, merely the epitome. Preparing it was the essence of fake cooking. You had to put the colored powder into a bowl, and you had to measure and heat a cup of water to the boil. You had to wait for the Jell-O to set. Maybe you wanted to put canned Bartlett pears in it, so you had to wait until it had set just enough. You felt you had cooked, but the process was clean, aseptic, foolproof. And somehow the manufacturer had convinced people that Jell-O was nutritious, that it contained protein, that it made one's fingernails as long as a Chinese emperor's and improved one's muscle tone and digestion. "It's good for you."

This was the dawn of plastic eating in America. The things we had always eaten suddenly looked unappetizing. We yearned for miracles. Canned vegetables had already replaced fresh, and Birds Eye peas were just appearing in the frozen cases. We doted on Velveeta. Spam. Canned ravioli. Instant puddings. Instant anything. The further a thing was from the texture, flavor, and terrifying unpredictability of real food, the better. As a modernist, my father looked with favor on all this, and my mother dutifully followed what the advertisers told her. Any aspersion cast on her ancestral habits was richly deserved, she felt. "Now new" was everybody's rallying cry. And she knew that in this cooking style lay another route to revenge, should she need it one day: plastic, sterile, instant revenge that dirtied no dishes, left no spills on the counter, disfigured no fingernails with stains. So all these culinary forces converged at our supper table like a symphony orchestra gone bats, with every instrument screaming and two conductors grappling.

The yellow leatherette and chrome dinette set, so prized by Mother, was the scene of pitched battles. Somehow, in my eyes, when we all sat down, our sizes seemed to change as we girded up for the fracas. My father loomed opposite me at his end, his face set in hard lines, his presence somehow overbearing. The Man Who Would Be Pleased. In the middle, beside my rapidly shrinking self, my mother, suddenly nervous. The Woman Whose Fault It Is. My role, of course, was the Ingrate Who Will Not Eat. One set piece was as follows: Mother would place supper on the table, and my father would discover something amiss. What might it be? Lumps in the gravy? Grit in the lettuce? The meat overdone? The standard line would be exhumed and uttered.

"Velma, what's the matter with you?"

She would stiffen.

"What do you mean, what's the matter with me?"

"You call this a meal?" Eyes would flash fire.

"Oh, Hat, don't start in."

Fist might at this point be brought to table. The flatwear would jump. Slightly.

"I work my fingers to the bone. I stand up blind with migraine in a horse book, and you can't make a decent pan of chicken gravy for me." Or whatever it was. "If you don't care about your husband, don't you care about your child?"

"Hat, please." She'd still be trying to eat, but by then I'd have dropped all pretence.

"What do you do all day, scrub the floor? Iron the curtains? Don't you give a damn what your family eats?" To say *damn* in our house was as much an act of violence as when Grandpa said it, and *goddamn* was the moral equivalent of setting the roof on fire. My father hardly ever got mad enough to say *goddamn* at table. I would hunker down, terrified by what might be coming next. I would want urgently to interrupt and say that I was not offended by the supper, I even fantasized shouting that he could damn well leave me out of it, but I could never get a word out of my throat

"Hat, shut up. There's nothing wrong with the gravy." Mother would take the lashing, as I crouched at my end of the table in silence, aware that my silence made me a collaborator with a madman but unable to find the secret passageway out of the room. I knew they were not talking about food, but I couldn't decode the text or figure out what drove my father to badger my mother in this way, as though it were expected of him, part of his masculine role

One evening, after he had run out of one-liners, she hid her face in her hands. She made no sound, but her tears dropped onto her white plate through her fingers I thought instantly of Snow White's mother, sweet queen weeping at her casement, and then the wicked stepmother takes over, and I wanted to put my arms around her so she wouldn't die When my father saw the tears, he shouted even louder

"Just like a woman. Shield yourself with tears. Why do women always snivel?"

"Henry the Eighth! Bluebeard!" I shouted. "Why do you do this to my mother?"

"Keep a civil tongue in your head or leave this dinner table," he answered, and then ate his dinner.

Without being asked, I helped Mother clear up. Always ashamed of letting me see her cry, she would not speak to me. She did not always act the part of long-suffering royalty when attacked; sometimes the drama included her shouting from center stage or rushing from the room to find her handbag, and then we'd hear the front door slamming and the car engine choking to life and the gravel flying in the driveway. My stomach knotting, I thought of the Millers, only a few hundred feet away, with the mother and father kissing before they sat down to eat, and everybody laughing, no matter how many lumps were in the gravy, if indeed Thelma had had time to make any.

Sometimes the battle raged around my head: I was dinner. My crime was not lumpy gravy but the fact that I ate nothing. Or at least, I always ate as little as I could manage. I remember a June evening, one of thousands of evenings. Supper was on the table that day at five. Belmont must have been running. Out playing red rover in the Miller kids' yard, I had smelled the nauseating smells floating from every kitchen — the crowder peas, the cornbread, the fried pork, the squashes simmering with onion slices. You couldn't smell the tomatoes and the lettuce and the radishes, but I knew the mothers were standing at the sinks, peeling and washing the hated salads, heaping them up in chipped bowls like so much garbage. The gardens along the alley were already abundantly yielding. You couldn't give the stuff away. Why did grown-ups like it?

Red rover, red rover, let Shirley come over. There were about eight kids in each line, on a weedy slope between the Miller house and the next, some big kids and some little ones. The idea was to break the barrier of arms when your name was called. I would rear back like a baseball pitcher and then streak across no man's land, hurling my skeletal ninety pounds against the linked arms. I never broke through unless Janny Miller was in the lineup. Her bones were made of sticks, the same as mine, and I would aim as viciously for her as everyone aimed for me. They never put Janny and me on the same side, unless the game was fixed, in which case they would shout our names repeatedly, and we would hurl ourselves and be tossed back, gasping and bruised and furious

I knew I ought to get home and set the table, and had been dreading the paternal bellow "You get in here and help your mother," but Mother's voice from the back door sang out sweetly: "Supper's ready." The game broke up, sixteen sweating children vanishing to their own kitchens, their own five- or ten-minute confrontations with their disapproving fathers, glaring over a plateful of vegetables and fried meat

The steak was on the table when I sat down. Unlike lots of kids, I had to wash my hands and face before coming to table. My mother served my plate, huge portions "Finish your supper and you can sit out in the lawn chairs with us afterward," my father said by way of an opening. He might as well have told me that if I ate my spinach, I could have cooked onions for dessert

"No, I want to play red rover with the kids."

No reply. They began to eat. The T-bone on my plate, outlined with suet, was a continent of meat. I cut a corner off it and inserted it in my mouth. It seemed to turn to cartilage as I chewed. I thought I'd wash the morsel down with milk, but the milk tasted sour in the summer heat. I thought I'd not complain of this yet, however. They served themselves iced tea in summer. Why was I stuck with loathsome milk? I pulled a wad from the middle of my slice of Wonder Bread and balled it

"Stop that," my father said "Eat your supper "

I set the bread ball under my plate rim. Our dishes came from several sets, and you never knew what would turn up under your T-bone. This evening it was the purple and yellow morning-glories, little flowers on black trellises. I don't know why I hated it. My mother had put a bowl of salad before me, the lettuce and tomatoes all neatly diced against a pattern of bluebells. She knew I wouldn't want the salad dressing to get all over the mashed potatoes. I hated both dishes — the designs as well as the food. I couldn't cut another bite of steak.

"Pass the dressing," I said, and the bottle of orange goo was quickly handed down the table to me.

"She wants the dressing." My father shot a look at my mother. He was cheered up. There was hope. I had asked for something.

"Not so much of that," he cautioned as I poured. "Don't you know that stuff costs money? You waste too much food as it is. When you have to stand on your feet to earn it, you'll be more careful."

"Hush, Hat, let her eat."

I knew more speeches were coming, and I knew which ones. Maybe, I thought, there was some way I could maneuver the garbage can close to my place and drop little bits of food into it when no one was looking. I had once used the dog for this purpose, but of course they had caught me on the spot, and Buster had to stay outdoors at mealtimes now.

I took a forkful of mashed potato. I often escaped eating the potato by pointing out that it had soaked up the steak juice and looked disgusting, but Mother was now trained to segregate the various piles carefully on my plate. She and Daddy exchanged relieved glances as I placed the potato in my mouth. How enormously my little acts mattered to them. The potato tasted like eraser dust. I gagged.

"Drink some milk," Daddy commanded.

"I can't It's gone blinky."

"It's not blinky," my mother said, her temper rising. "I just bought it. This afternoon." Stern as a prison matron, she lifted my glass and tasted, smacking three times to show that she was really sampling the stuff. "It's not blinky. It's good milk." She handed the glass on down to Daddy. He tasted.

"Not blinky." Now the glass, certified pure, came back to me. Oh Father, remove from me this cup. I set it down and did not drink.

"It's blinky."

"I stand on my poor feet in that cashier's cage to try and keep food on this table. But you won't eat. You're skin and bones. You're always sick. Mother slaves over the stove and then has to spend hours sitting in a doctor's office with you. I spend a fortune on cod liver oil, the expensive kind that you take with an eye-dropper. You don't care what happens to your father. You don't care what happens to your health. Are you trying to kill yourself? Why won't you eat? Young lady, if you don't care enough to cooperate with me, why should I cooperate with you?" The way my father said *young lady* would have turned the Virgin Mary into an ax murderer. The worst thing on earth, *young lady*, worse than *old lady*, worse than *old maid*, worse than *goddamn*.

"Hat," my mother said, "stop it. She can't eat with you yelling like that." They had finished their first helpings and were thinking of seconds. Or should they now go on to the fresh apple pie with a slice of cheese on top?

"Can I go out and play?"

"You'll sit there till you've finished every bite on your plate, if that takes till bedtime."

They had their seconds. They then ate their pie. Mother's pies were so good that when she cut through the crust you could hear it flaking, and when she removed the two slices, pools of thick apple syrup sluiced over into the pie tin. But as I watched them fork the delicious thing into their mouths, I lost all desire for any

This is what adults did. They stuffed their mouths, and they fought. I hated everything they stood for. I'd rather be hungry. Mother cleared their end of the table, wiping every crumb and grease spot from the oilcloth.

"No, don't you move an inch from there, young lady." Now she took up the insult. How much sweeter to my ears were her other epithets for me: hunyok, little twerp, smartypants, Miss Priss, or simply the good old "Be ashamed!" She stacked the dishes and reminded me that I could depart once I had finished my dinner, whereupon they went to the living room and turned on the RCA. It was 5:30 and they had just missed the news. Though there was one whole room between us, they could see me at table — my chair was close to the open door — and could check on whether I was chucking things into the garbage or not. Far away in the Miller yard, I heard voices. The kids were choosing up sides again. They had no doubt eaten all their salad.

I took another slice of bread and folded it over. Maybe I could make a sandwich out of some salad. The orange goo soaked nicely into the bread, and I managed to swallow some lettuce and tomato sheathed in the wet package without actually putting my teeth through the tomato. But there was still a lot of it to go. I took most of what was left in the bowl and shoved it tightly under the plate rim. That left the pile of cooked carrots, the most disgusting of all vegetables, except possibly parsnips. Who had hatched the idea of eating carrots, hideous roots? Worm food. Maybe some sugar would help. I poured it on. The taste was even more sickening. I took another slice of white bread and packaged three pieces of carrot, swallowing it as I had the tomato. The steak was cold now, the suet turning white.

Buster sat whining at the back door, and a plan occurred to me. My shorts had pockets, and in one pocket was a handkerchief. I sliced most of the steak from the bone, then leaned forward against the table edge so my parents could see only my avid back and wadded the meat up in the hanky. No good. It was instantly blood-soaked. One slice of bread remained. I carefully made it into a basket for the steak hanky, adding a dollop of potato. My plate was beginning to look empty. Almost vacant. You could count the morning-glories. I took the five remaining carrot pieces and shoved them under the rim. That was about all the underside of one plate could hold. I stood up, thrusting the steak-and-hanky sandwich into my shorts pocket. I felt it squish.

"I'm done, can I go out?" It was now 5:45. One evening last week I had been forced to sit until six and had sprung myself only by a fit of bitter, noisy weeping, but now perhaps I had beat the game. My hope was that my mother would come to inspect my plate and excuse me. She'd tell me, of course, to clear my place, and once she turned her back to return to the radio, I'd pick up the plate, sweep the garbage into it, and with a lightning hand dump it in the trash can. Then, on my way out the back door, I'd give Buster the steak and potatoes, rescue the handkerchief, and bolt toward the Millers'. It would require the precision of Paul Henreid stashing his crystal set while the Nazis broke the door down. I could do it.

But as she approached the table, I felt the warm red steak juice begin to trickle down my thigh, and as I glanced downward, terrified, I saw that my whole pocket had taken on the color of blood and grease.

"I ate it, Mama." I grinned, hoping to keep her eyes off my shorts. She inspected the plate. I had cunningly left little bits of everything so she wouldn't suspect cheating. I had forgotten the glass of milk. Before she could say anything, I snatched it from under her eyes and took it like a shot of whiskey. It was disgustingly warm now, but I was too near freedom to argue, or to gag. Then, to my horror, she lifted the plate, exposing salad, carrots, bread pellets, and all

Her face a study of sadness, she swept it all into the plate, as I had planned to do. "And what did you do with the steak and potatoes?"

"I ate them" — but by then the trickle had reached my knobby knee and was dripping onto the floor.

"You hunyok." (An ambivalent term of endearment, similar to *lummox* or *Wild Indian*. But at least she wasn't angry.) "I ought to paddle you till you can't sit down," she hissed, but with tact and discretion. Swiftly she dragged me by my shoulder seam into the middle of the kitchen, out of Daddy's sight and hearing. "Get that mess out of your pocket. This minute. Get that handkerchief out of the mess, you're not throwing away a good handkerchief." She put the steak into a dog dish. "Now go put those shorts in the washing machine and get your dirty clothes from yesterday. And get out of this house. Don't come back till bedtime."

I knew that she had done this to gain a star in my book, and that if Daddy had come into the kitchen alone he would probably have done the same. If they had come into the kitchen together, they would have locked me in my room. They worked well separately, badly together. And the gap between them widened, and the war went on. The love that I saw passing between men and women (the small private touching of fingers, the casual kiss, the meeting of the eyes) passed less and less often under my own roof Love was a game played in other people's bedrooms. My parents, I knew without really knowing it, lay separately and alone

$\mathscr{P}$AX ROMANA

ON DECEMBER 7, 1941, standing beside a radio bigger than I was, I heard Franklin D. Roosevelt's voice, and frightened by the fear in my parents' faces, I pooh-poohed the whole thing. Why be scared by something coming out of the radio? I asked, "What's Pearl Harbor? A place way across the ocean? Why does President Roosevelt care whether those Japs bombed it or not?" At least for a time I was protected by my own ignorance. I didn't yet know that when bombs fell out of planes they splintered bones and crushed parents' bodies in front of their children's eyes, or that soldiers set farmers' huts on fire and bashed heads with rifle butts and ambushed one another in deep jungles with sharp knives.

As the war went on, I began to have some hint of what people were capable of inflicting and enduring, courtesy of *Life*, the Movietone news, and the movies. I understood that the Germans and the Japs, even the Italians, would like to smash me personally, if only they could cross the oceans. I woke screaming from many a bad dream; I realized that with every breath I drew, someone somewhere else, maybe even thousands of people, were dying, probably in horrible ways. "Don't talk about it," I pleaded, as World War II replaced the Great Depression as standard adult talk. "I don't want to hear it! Don't tell me that!" I shrieked to boys at school who described Nazi tortures in detail. The Japs, they said, were worse. "Shut up! I won't listen."

But in fact, as humanity blasted, burned, tortured, suffered, murdered, and died on a monstrous new scale, my life went on in the most satisfactory way. My father earned more money than ever before; I had a lawn, a swing with long ropes, a dog that yowled with grief when I left for school and went crazy with joy when I came home. Of course, Mother had to give up nylons, which she'd only been able to afford for a couple of years anyway. Once, as we giggled, I drew lines on the back of her legs with an eyebrow pencil, to look like stocking seams. She tried leg makeup, but it soiled her dresses and the car seat. "I'll just have to go bare-legged," she decided. At times we were short of sugar and shoe leather and gasoline and rubber tires and butter. Occasionally Mother had to mix yellow coloring into a greasy mound of pale oleomargarine.

But here in paradise the rationing board was amenable to suggestion. If my father whispered a word to Judge Witt, Judge Witt would whisper another word into another ear. Next time Mother appeared at the rationing board, she'd be issued an extra stamp book or two, and thus I'd wear real leather as usual, or even have an extra pair of Mary Janes. On a moonless night, a man would deliver a hundred-pound bag of sugar to the back door, along with butter and fresh beef — commodities that ought to have been shipped to some army depot. "Don't you dare tell a soul about this," my mother warned me. We felt sorry for our boys, of course, but Daddy often pointed out that they were provisioned better than any army in history: they were the first soldiers ever to eat white bread. "Most of those fellows," he said, as I slathered my toast with butter, "get better food in the mess hall than they did at home." So why worry?

"Our boys" were conveniently somebody else's boys. We knew a few people with flags in the window. Our neighbor Mr. Miller, who drove the red Texaco truck, had volunteered for the navy and been shipped to California for training almost the next day. My father was too old to fight, and anyway had flat feet: 4-F. Like the rationing board, the draft board listened when Judge Witt talked. One afternoon soon after Pearl Harbor my mother and my aunt wept for hours at our kitchen table because their younger brother, the baby of the family, had been classified 1-A. Why must he go to Europe to die, or be bayoneted in some jungle in the South Pacific? That evening the judge dropped in for one brief moment to tell us not to worry: he saw no reason why our family should be singled out for sacrifice. After all, the boy was very young. Thus our 1-A quietly became 4-F.

World War II, for us, became the Trojan War: a source of entertainment. War was Spencer Tracy and John Wayne in their battle jackets on a screen; Gary Cooper and Ingrid Bergman in each other's arms outside Madrid somewhere, and him cradling his rifle in his arms at the end, with that look on his face. Or Gary Cooper in medical whites, falling in love with Jennifer Jones, a nurse, as the Japanese captured Singapore. "Isn't he precious," I said with a sigh. Chiefly, World War II was *The March of Time*, fifteen minutes of propaganda courtesy of some gentlemen in New York, the same folks, my father said, who gave us *Life*, but *March of Time* was excruciating, whereas I rather liked the magazine. *March of Time* said we must love the Germans who lived in America but hate the Germans across the water. We must hate all Japanese without exception, because they worshiped their ridiculous emperor instead of God and were treacherous by nature. Thanks to President Roosevelt we were turning out thousands of warships every day — and the camera would switch to Mrs. Roosevelt, smiling and baptizing a destroyer, which slid down the ramp and plopped into the water like a turd while sturdy tunes were piped in the background. I avoided most of this by long visits to the ladies' room or by fits of indecision at the candy counter.

I did like seeing Princess Elizabeth and Princess Margaret Rose in their uniforms, hearing their sweet courageous voices. I'd gladly have stood beside them in the war effort. Imagine going to bomb shelters at night, imagine being sent away from your parents to safe locales in the north of England! Why didn't the British children come here? We were so perfectly protected, so remote. But they didn't. We didn't even have scrap metal drives in Arkansas. Meatless Tuesday we observed with bacon for breakfast, ham for lunch, and beef or chicken for supper. It was hard to believe that anything we did here could alter the death rate in other places. Loose lips might sink ships out where Humphrey Bogart plied the seven seas, but not here. My only piece of classified information was the bag of sugar coming through the back door and the extra ration books.

As instructed, I self-righteously loathed Hitler, Mussolini, and Hirohito and cleaned my plate to kill a Jap. I learned all the words of the marine hymn and the army air corps song and sang them day and night, making flyers' goggles out of thumb and index finger as I yelled the words from a perch in the white-blossomed spirea bush. Each evening, courtesy of the Mutual Broadcasting System, I pulled a long face as Gabriel Heater intoned, "There's bad news tonight." In short, I turned into a patriot. Yet it all seemed too terrible and too far away. I told Jesus not to let the Japanese win, pointing out that they tortured our boys at Bataan and were heathens, and implored him not to let the Germans win either, but if somebody had to take us over, let it be the Germans, who at least weren't yellow. I didn't hear of Dachau, Auschwitz, and Treblinka until I was ten or eleven years old, and didn't grasp what happened in these places until many years after that.

My mother was determined that I should be like other girls, while my father was determined to make me different. He shared his passions with me, heaped my plate with them as if they were T-bone steaks and mashed potatoes. Romans (with Greeks lurking around the edges) were the roast prime rib au jus of history and literature. Any Romans would do, though he preferred those of British manufacture. He searched the library and the bookstore and newsstand racks of paperbacks for Romans, who were intelligent and skilled at practical things, such as staving off barbarians. They built roads, roads that had lasted two thousand years. They bathed. They were cynical and wise. "What is truth?" the Roman procurator demanded as the mob voted to crucify Jesus. "And indeed, what is truth?" my father would demand, wafting his Lucky Strike in the evening air.

Yet the Romans were doomed. They declined, they fell. The barbarians howled at the gates. Daddy's Romans answered the howls in English. They were Englishmen. They were Southerners. They were us. Somehow, civilization had leaped from ancient Rome to Hot Springs, Arkansas, and now was ours to defend. The barbarians were upon us, and they might be anybody: the Japs whining around in the skies in their nasty little papiermâché Zeroes, the Huns buzz-bombing England. But he and I both knew that the true barbarians were the Ministerial Alliance of Hot Springs, crusading to shut down the gambling, as well as the bigots who hated to see anybody have a good time, not to mention greedy governors who hijacked Hot Springs for heavy campaign contributions, or reformers (however short-lived) who threatened to rock the municipal boat.

This was the moment in my childhood when our life seemed

perfect, happy beyond all possibility of improvement. I understood what *civilization* meant. It was what we had inside our fence at 122 Alamo. But it was also Hot Springs: our mayor, Leo P. McLaughlin, in his little gig with the matched horses and wearing a red carnation in his lapel; Judge Ledgerwood presiding over his court and forgiving Johnny Strand's traffic tickets; Judge Witt liberating my uncle from his draft card and dispatching the Western Union boy with boxes of chocolate for me if I so much as sneezed; the results from Saratoga floating like a vapor on the soft summer air; my father in court the first Monday of every month paying the Southern Club's fine for gaming; Fat Earnest, the cop who protected little children by day and shook down prostitutes by night, working as a bouncer at the Southern Club; Owney Madden making huge contributions to the Boys' Club; the candidates in uncontested elections nevertheless stuffing the ballot boxes and hauling the black laborers to the polls to vote, and if anybody voted the wrong way, they tracked you down and told you that life would be rough from now on: all that. Cosa Nostra.

In those days my father read *The Decline and Fall of the Roman Empire* aloud to me — an unlikely choice for a child, but I took to it without complaint, swimming gamely along in Gibbon's deep rhetorical sea. "When you can read this for your own pleasure," Daddy would say, "you'll be master of your craft." Like a surfer on a thin, swift board, I rode the crest of the majestic, rolling sentences, powerful and relentless breakers that threatened to drown me and simultaneously offered an exhilarating and addictive test of my survival skills. If my father saw that I was going down for the third time, he would interrupt and parse the great periodic strophes for my benefit.

The Empire was above two thousand miles in breadth, from the wall of Antoninus and the northern limits of Dacia, to Mount Atlas and the tropic of Cancer; . . . it extended, in

length, more than three thousand miles in breadth from the
Western Ocean to the Euphrates; . . . it was situated in the
finest part of the Temperate Zone . . . [and] it was supposed to
contain above sixteen hundred thousand square miles, for the
most part of fertile and well-cultivated land.

This is how the great historian described the map of the world
in that period of peace from Nerva's reign through Hadrian's,
Trajan's, and the Antonines', a hundred years of human happiness, a golden age when "the Empire of Rome comprehended
the fairest part of the earth and the most civilised portion of
mankind." I absorbed about half of this information, and didn't
trouble about the rest. I heard it as "Once upon a time, when the
world was happier than it has been since," as fairy tales so often
began. I heard it as a world remote from and yet exactly like our
own, where great men were merciful to the poor, where the lords
of the earth spent their lives "enjoying and abusing the advan-
tages of wealth and luxury," and I felt like one of them — the
crisp bills on the kitchen table, my rabbit coat with the matching
tam and muff, my lunch box with the butter and sliced steak on
the bread and the crusts trimmed. I too was a Roman, the
privileged of the earth.

My father would sit in the blue-upholstered platform rocker
with me folded up in various bony attitudes on the woolly
maroon sofa ("Get your feet off the divanette, Shirley Jean,"
Mother would call from the kitchen, a shout in the perpetual
battle for my soul, for it drove her crazy to see him ruining me
so). As the sumptuous prose rolled off his tongue, I did get one
thing straight: vague though I may have been about the boundaries of Dacia or the credentials of Nerva and the Antonines, my
father was introducing me to mysteries that only he and I could
share. A figure looming in the background with mop and broom,
my mother wearily shook her head when she heard us reading

Gibbon. What craziness was this for a girl? Why didn't I tell him to go and jump in the lake with his history? Why didn't I run out and play in the sunshine, or dress my dolls, like a normal human being?

"How do you put up with that?" she demanded, openly hostile one day as she wound my hair into precise spit curls all over my head and clamped each one down with a bobby pin.

"I like it," I said with a supercilious smile. Here was another dark secret, like the sugar and butter: I read Roman history with my father.

There were other meals to be eaten besides the Romans. These novels will be good for you, Daddy seemed to say. Take three helpings. *Ben-Hur, The Last Days of Pompeii, Lorna Doone, The Bride of Lammermoor.* Nothing was too silly, too old-fashioned for me, so long as it had men and women in it and a villain and love. Ah, love! I'd no idea I was being educated in the vernacular of another epoch, my mind fattened and my arteries clogged with nineteenth-century puddings. Always the exotic, the remote: the Holy Land under Roman rule, the corridors where Cleopatra ruled. (Why, why didn't she and Mark Anthony win that war? The noblest Roman of them all, my father said, brought low by love!) Always the curious interplay between Christianity and the old gods — or the godless, such as Pontius Pilate and various other Romans who sent Christians to be eaten by lions. I never knew which side my father would root for. He loved to read the passage from Gibbon in which an exasperated Roman official confronts some Christians who, according to the historian, wanted to leave this wicked world and begged for admission to the Coliseum. Get out of here, the Roman says. You must be suicidal. Are there no cliffs to hurl yourselves from? Daddy admired the way the Romans kept clean, by washing their hands and issuing disclaimers. He also liked the Scots, who were merely Romans in plaid togas, wilder than their counterparts along the

Tiber but equally noble. Besides reading *Ivanhoe*, we wallowed in the romance of Mary of Scotland, put to death by another woman. "The female of the species," Daddy was fond of saying, "is more deadly than the male."

If our lives had been a newsreel, my father would have been the narrator — the soothsayer, the bard, the scop. I was born, he thought, to listen, and I understood that listening was the essential votive act. Friends, Romans, countrymen, lend me your ears. Attention was what he needed, and I had the power to bestow it.

> Lars Porsena of Clusium,
> by the Nine Gods he swore
> that the great house of Tarquin
> should suffer wrong no more.
> By the Nine Gods he swore it,
> and named a trysting-day,
> and bade his messengers ride forth,
> east and west and south and north,
> to summon his array,

he would declaim, brandishing the poem book like a broadsword. From Lord Macaulay and Romans triumphing over Etruscans we went to Alfred Noyes and "The Highwayman," a poem that cluttered my head like a whatnot on a shelf.

> He'd a French cocked-hat on his forehead, a bunch of lace
>   at his chin,
> A coat of the claret velvet, and breeches of brown doe-skin;
> They fitted with never a wrinkle: his boots were up to
>   the thigh!
> And he rode with jeweled twinkle,
>   His pistol butts a-twinkle,
> His rapier hilt a-twinkle, under the jeweled sky.

As he intended, I took this highway robber to be my father, and wept over the next-to-last stanza: "They shot him down on the highway, down like a dog on the highway, and he lay in his blood on the highway, with the bunch of lace at his throat."

He read Oscar Wilde:

> Yet each man kills the thing he loves,
> By each let this be heard,
> . . .
> The coward does it with a kiss,
> The brave man with a sword!

Like a creature from the ocean floor, with gills instead of lungs, my father was never at ease in life's punishing air. Reading supplied his oxygen. He stretched out in the four-poster bed, fully shod and dressed, propped against two fat pillows but on top of the white chenille bedspread, book in hand and a pile by the bedside: the land of counterpane. As he read he would stroke the chenille of his crew cut, laughing theatrically from time to time. When the laugh rang out, my number was up. Unless I had already fled noiselessly out into the yard, where I pretended not to hear, I was obliged to ask what was funny and freeze into attentiveness as he read aloud. Then I'd laugh, and he'd laugh some more, squinting his eyes shut, until the laughter turned to coughing.

As a nod to my mother's notions about propriety, he would fold yesterday's newspaper neatly under his two-tone shoes. Her position was this: "You make a bed first thing of a morning and you expect it to *stay* made, unless a person gets too sick to stand on their feet, and then you take the bedspread *off*." To lie atop the bedspread in daylight was the equivalent of allowing the dog to pee on the rug or a cat to take up residence indoors. (In my mother's ethic, a cat did not live in the house, any more than a pig or a goat would. But a dog was smart enough to learn some manners and thus could come inside.) Muttering about the trouble men caused women, my mother washed the bedspread weekly. Worse than anything, Daddy kept a Lucky burning in the ashtray by the bed. Mother was ahead of her time. She hated cigarettes and told Daddy repeatedly they would make him sick: coffin nails. "Get that old cigarette away from me," she would cry, frantically fanning the air, when he smoked in her presence. His response was patient: "My only pleasure, my sole indulgence." To control the tobacco stench, Mother asked him to dump all butts and ashes down the toilet, but he left them unflushed or undumped — another marital burden. The web of life they wove, with their contrary warp and woof, had the texture of a brier patch.

Determined as he was that I would experience what he had experienced, that the meat and bread of his childhood would be my own, my father led me into Homer and the classical Greeks, always working by fits and starts, never systematically, picking up a tale here, a story there, sometimes reading from his old copies of the *Iliad* and *Odyssey*, sometimes from schoolbooks that retold the stories of the gods. Having been recruited into the Methodist church at an early age, having read the entire New Testament in order to win a prize at Sunday school, I asked my father how people could believe in such cranky, dangerous gods as these unpredictable, all-too-human Greek ones, and he replied that they were as good as any, better perhaps. Take Venus, the woman with no parents who'd been born from the spume of the sea, such a lovely lady. Nobody like Venus in the Bible. Maybe Delilah, but she wasn't beautiful.

Take Athena, who had no mother and had sprung from the head of Zeus fully armed, after giving her poor father a migraine.

Yet what a good daughter she was. It was true that she played a role in starting the Trojan War, but Athena was a grand lady, doing far more good than harm. "I am Athena," she said, "and I give wisdom to men." Zeus loved her best of all, Athena, queen of the air, weaver of webs so fine that everyone on Olympus gasped, the gray-eyed goddess who guided Telemachus as he searched for his father, Odysseus, but also Athena the Contriver, the queen of the hearth and home, a woman not to be trifled with. She was always in the picture, where the gods were concerned, but she never crossed her daddy.

After the war in Troy, for example, King Agamemnon came home to Argos, bringing his girlfriend with him. But his wife, Clytemnestra, had several grudges against him, including the fact that he had cold-bloodedly murdered their daughter Iphigenia, just to persuade the gods to make the wind blow. When he showed up with a Trojan girlfriend ten years later, Clytemnestra up and knifed him. However, Agamemnon had another daughter, Electra, a devoted girl. Electra had been so fond of her father that now she refused to eat and sleep, and stood by his tomb moping and crying all day, in spite of how angry this made the mother, who had a boyfriend herself, a trashy neighborhood fellow. Well, finally Electra's brother, Orestes, showed up, and he in turn knifed the mother, Clytemnestra, and the boyfriend. But then the Furies (the Greek equivalent of a guilty conscience) came and buzzed all around Orestes' ears, following him across the land and giving him no peace. In the end he begged the sun god, Apollo, to take the buzzing Furies away, and they said they would never, never go, since it was not proper to stab your mother. But Athena came right in and told Apollo it was worse to stab your father than your mother. She proposed that the two of them join forces and send the Furies packing. Actually, she offered the Furies a little underground job, supervising domestic happiness and so forth for all time to come. And the next thing Athena did was to found Athens. Civilization.

"What happened to Electra?" I asked.

"Doesn't say."

I took vacations from Romans and Greeks whenever I could. If Daddy could build a world of his own choosing out of the bricks of history, why not I? I recognized the movies as prime sources of knowledge. Here, as in the fairy tales, it was clear what men and women were up to. Men fought but seldom died. Women wore high heels and lots of lipstick and believed firmly in the men; devotion was always rewarded, and the reward was always to get the man. A somewhat circular system, and I wasn't sure how I'd get in on the game. One afternoon, however, as I lounged deep in my seat in the air-cooled dark, a woman I'd never seen before stepped into a Humphrey Bogart picture and said, after some preliminaries, "If you need me, just whistle. You know how to whistle, don't you? Just pucker up and blow." The role Lauren Bacall played in the film was merely another exercise in woman-gets-man. The message she brought, however, was not in her deeds but in the angles of her face, her lank hair, her velvety voice, her bony figure, her cigarette and the way she smoked it, just like a man, just as if women were supposed to smoke and it didn't matter. (My mother said no lady ever smoked.) Here, finally, was a heroine who wasn't cutely helpless (June Allyson), saintly (Ingrid Bergman), imperially gorgeous (Rita Hayworth). After Lauren Bacall got her man, they didn't go to My Blue Heaven but to some bar for a drink. No crocheted bedspreads for Lauren Bacall. There was room for me, I concluded, in this man-getting game.

At the same time, I cultivated a taste for sensitive masculine faces. Not Cary Grant (too hard-edged, too comic) or Clark

Gable (not quite convincing), and certainly not Van Johnson or John Wayne (burly). I went for Gary Cooper, Paul Henreid, Humphrey Bogart, and Cornel Wilde, not the men at all but the faces. For a week after seeing Cornel Wilde play Chopin opposite Merle Oberon as George Sand, I was disabled, reduced to a state resembling postcoital languor, so overwhelmed by my own fantasies that I could scarcely read Nancy Drew or Hans Christian Andersen or pay decent attention to my dog. Oh, Frederic and Franz and George and Alfred! At the end, with his muscles rippling, Cornel Wilde coughed some blood onto the piano keys and died of tuberculosis. I had never heard of Frederic Chopin or George Sand. Franz Liszt and Alfred de Musset were perfect blanks, but Cornel Wilde's face was a master drawing of the romantic ideal, and his deep brown eyes made my hands shake and my breath come fast as he flexed his elbows, pretending to play the Polonaise. And the kisses — the music suddenly dispensed with as the hands left the piano and mouths merged. In magazines I saw a perfume ad that showed the same thing, only in this one the violinist (male) seized his female accompanist, clad in a hoop skirt. Her hands dangled helplessly above the piano keys in that same sort of gesture: art crushed by passion. But I was eager to believe that for a woman, music must yield to kisses. I wasn't allowed to wear perfume, but I promised to buy myself Tabu first chance I got.

To my father's disgust — how could a daughter of his tolerate such trash? — I began squandering my allowance on movie magazines, clipping out photographs of Paul Henreid, Gary Cooper, Humphrey Bogart, and most of all Cornel Wilde, pinning them over the demure posies on my bedroom walls, these splendid faces, princes royal, until the clippings obliterated the wallpaper. These faces held secret, hopeful, dangerous narratives for me, tales I heeded as I heeded my father's: how intelligence could triumph, even in war; how love was an adventure, and you'd never end up with a scrub bucket or working for wages until you were numb and sick; how Betty Grable's legs and big breasts were precisely what a man did *not* feel seduced by — a sultry glance and a cigarette would do the trick even for the flat-chested. O world with no angry parents or sullen children or dishes to wash or bills to pay. O beautiful men whom warfare only grazed lightly in the shoulder, elegant sleek birds soaring into the wild blue yonder!

But my father always wooed me away from Cornel Wilde, back to Oscar. The bookcase was a bottomless caldron, holding more stories than Scheherazade could tell. We pressed on to the French: Jean Valjean chained to the bench of his galley, the Three Musketeers. We worked our way through the unconquerable youths of Charles Dickens — David Copperfield, Barnaby Rudge, Nicholas Nickleby, Oliver Twist — who like Hercules and Perseus went through trials enough to warp and disable a real person but never lost their good nature, courage, or good sense. Cowards, or bad boys unwilling to work, might fall dead from starvation or abuse in the streets of London, but not David Copperfield or Oliver Twist. Not all endings were happy, of course. Night after night, we read "Evangeline": "Gabriel, O my beloved! Vainly he strove to whisper her name, Vainly he strove to rise!" My father shed real tears as Evangeline found her lover, too late for anything but the funeral.

I drew no conclusions about the triumphs of men and the grief of women and children. All in the same fantasy, I could be David Copperfield, Evangeline, Mary Queen of Scots, Athena, and Lauren Bacall. I made no distinctions. Whatever my father and Hollywood and Great Literature peddled, I bought. My life went pleasantly onward behind the rose trellises and the chicken-wire fence, our skies sealed off from enemy planes, the tally of our ballot boxes a foregone conclusion, and my childhood, as I believed, ordained to last forever.

$\mathcal{D}$ECLINE AND FALL

"We had an airtight machine, honey. You had to have. We just had the votes to put in those ballot boxes. But, hell, we could all have gone to the penitentiary."

— Judge Vern Ledgerwood in old age, assessing his accomplishments for a local historian

NO ONE KNEW where they came from: thrown into the streets by misfortune or human cruelty, eight, ten, a dozen half-breed dogs, a black hound and a brown one with mange-eaten flanks, a silky dog with crazy yellow eyes and the marking of a spotted pony, two shaggy curs that might have been white if anyone had bathed them, a mastiff look-alike to whom the whole pack deferred and who had first rights to the garbage can. They appeared the summer after I finished sixth grade, awoke the neighborhood with their clatter in the moonlight, and then began to attack by day. Nervous as hoboes, they would congregate in the space between our house and the woods, moiling, circling, chasing, a tornado of canine fur, tails, jaws, and panting tongues, and then at some signal from the commander would vanish into the underbrush and the trees.

It had been a year now since America had won the war, had

manufactured and delivered not one but two atomic bombs, just in case the Japanese hadn't gotten the point at Hiroshima. The Japs, whom so recently it was patriotic to hate — yellow devils bayoneting babies — became the Japanese. The explosions had melted their children's eyeballs and burned off the skin of their faces, and people had died just the way Robert Seaver died. A book called *Hiroshima* told the whole story, and my father insisted that I read it, an antidote to patriotism.

Still, *Life* magazine said we had saved countless lives by not invading Japan. It was certainly true that the only person I knew who'd gone to war, Mr. Miller, had come home right after V-J Day, out of his navy uniform and back into his Texaco greens. The United States had joined the United Nations — a step I approved of but my father did not. "Won't work. You can't run the world by reason. Remember what Uncle Joe Stalin said? 'How many divisions has the pope?'" Old Uncle Joe wasn't our pal anymore, which worried my father but not me. Our green Chevrolet had recently gone to the scrap heap, and we'd been afoot for months. Now, however, we'd be able to buy a new car. "Now things can get back to normal," my mother said, and Miss Love said "normal," and the grocer said "normal," and Thelma Miller said "normal."

My father refused to stop worrying about the Russians, whom he likened uneasily to the Goths. We'd licked the Hun, now we'd have to lick the Russians. Why wait until they were beating down the city gates? He read me the story of Alaric, who handily deployed his forces around the Roman wall, took charge of the twelve main gates, and cut off supply and communication lines between the city and the country, including traffic on the river Tiber. The luxury-loving Romans were reduced to cannibalism. When they threatened to mount a counterattack and pointed to their superior numbers, Alaric replied contemptuously, "The thicker the hay, the easier it is mowed."

But only my father, quoting Gibbon and egged on by *Life*, theorized about such things. Everybody else talked of the dogs roaming our neighborhood like outlaws or evil spirits turned loose.

"Woke us up at midnight again."

"Ran at Johnny and knocked him off his wheel."

"Filthy, mangy things!"

"I'm sick to death of sweeping up that mess, they strew everything from one end to the other."

So said the women at their clotheslines and the men at night, calling over the fences. Jewel Blossom had been quiet the past year, sometimes failing to shout "damn kid" or "damned old grocery woman" as we passed. But now she began shrieking every midnight, and the animals answered her like a chorus in hell. The crisis traveled back and forth across the fences. We no longer felt easy in our beds, hearing the human and animal baying.

"Poor old body. Sounds like a soul in torment. Do you reckon Miss Blossom ever accepted Christ as her savior?"

"Well, aye God, Christian or heathen, we can't stand much more of this. I said to Mac, I can't warsh and arn and cook all day and listen to that woman holler ever' night. I never did get back to sleep last night, I'm wore out. I'm fixin' to take to bellerin' myself."

"She'd be better off over at Benton. What if she comes out of that house and lays ahold of some of these kids? I wouldn't put it past her, no indeedy. I b'lieve she's crazier than she used to be."

"Well, I reckon those boys of mine could handle her."

"Lordy mercy, can you feature what the inside of that house is like? Take a shovel to clear it out, I bet."

At the supper table, I argued earnestly against dropping an A-bomb on Moscow, which Daddy said was the only solution. Stalin didn't scare me, but the screams at night were getting me down. When November came I intended to have a bunking party (known elsewhere as a slumber party), a custom that had recently swept the social scene. What if Miss Blossom screamed in the middle of my party? I thought someone should take her to the lunatic asylum. As to the dogs, I theorized about amnesty, mercy, adoption, and a Christian attitude. But I went outside my fence in terror now, skimming along the tops of rocks, racing for the security of the Millers' back door, desperate to lift the latch on our back gate. Buster kept a low profile, scratched feverishly at the front door, and then hid under my bed whenever the dog pack appeared.

Miss Blossom and the dogs aside, my happiness was intense. I wished to be a perpetual celebrant in what Gibbon called "the long festival of peace." The red and white rose trellises decked the front porch like bunting; the complex yellow Talismans put forth buds at the side of the house; the Amy Quinard, with its mysterious velvet blossoms under my bedroom window, still perfumed the night air so heavily that sometimes I awoke and savored the fragrance as the moon set toward dawn. I had forty-seven pictures of Cornel Wilde on the wall, paper dolls I cherished like the brides and belles that Aunt Hazel and I had played with. I had been the academic queen of Oaklawn School, and I felt I was going to be quite popular in junior high school, as well as smart. Already I had been asked to pledge a junior high sorority, Lambda Lambda Delta, known as Lama Lama Delta or the LLD. It didn't stand for anything, it was just Greek.

The whole world was improving: every package you bought was labeled "New, Better." Near our house we had a thing called a shopping center, containing our first supermarket. Instead of ordering at the counter and having things toted up by a grocer in a white apron, you pushed a basket around the store, chose whatever you liked, and stood in line. The milkman stopped bringing bottles to the front step; we bought milk in paper cartons at the supermarket instead. My mother bought instant everything — Jell-O, puddings, cookies in packages rather than homemade. Rubber tires, gasoline, nylon stockings, sugar, butter, were plentiful — we'd forgotten that they'd ever been scarce.

Nevertheless, there were some bad signs. Leo McLaughlin always seemed to be in some kind of trouble now. Whereas once we had hailed him as he rolled down Central Avenue in his horse cart, flaunting his red carnation, tapping Scotch and Soda's flanks with a coachman's crop, people began to call him an old fool and a tyrant. Moreover, there was a scandal. A woman had sued him in open court, claiming he had promised to marry her and then brutally cast her aside. She had been a milliner, just like the little milliners in French novels. Leo had kept company with her, she said, but then backed out. Not only that, he had sent his boys around to the hat shop and told her to get out of the state within twenty-four hours. This, my father said, was known as "breach of promise." My parents made light of it.

"Silly girl," they said at the supper table.

"It's quite a joke."

"Only a perfect fool would sue for breach of promise."

"Fool around with a fellow like that and what do you expect?"

Leo won the case, of course, so that the woman became a laughingstock and was obliged to pay court costs and return to Tulsa, where she had taken refuge months before. It made me uneasy to hear this kind of talk. I was loyal to Leo, as all of us were required to be, but I wondered, timidly, what it really was like to be ordered out of town, taken and dumped on the state line with only a suitcase, as this woman claimed to have been. One evening Judge Witt said to my father, "I wonder if anybody put her up to it. It's a nuisance, you know. Made Leo look like a bully, a damn playboy. He ought to be more careful about his private life." Who would have put her up to it? Why? What did he have to be careful about? Then, shockingly, an article about our town appeared in the *Saturday Evening Post*. National publicity! (This

didn't happen to you if you lived in Arkadelphia or Texarkana.)
The *Post* called us a "town without a lid" and fingered Leo
McLaughlin as a chiseler, a crook, and a manipulator of the ballot
box. It even said our hot mineral water was all humbug.

"That reporter spent one night here, talking to some barfly.
Shameful! Taking bread out of the mouths of innocent people!
Ruining the economy of a whole area." My father was furious.
"How'd he like it if I put an end to his paycheck, that S.O.B.?"
He sent off a letter denouncing the reporter to the editors and
canceling his subscription. I agreed with him: why didn't they
pick on somebody else's hometown? Anyhow, on the positive
side, at least I no longer had to read the *Saturday Evening Post*.

One afternoon, I watched from the window as the dogs descended on our garbage can, which contained mostly carpet
sweepings. They tore the contents apart, scattering house dust
and trash all along the driveway, ignoring my mother's shouts
from the kitchen window. Buster stood between my arms, his
paws on the windowsill, watching with me, emitting phony
growls, cocking his ears behind the window screen. But then,
over where the woods began, one dog located something — a
hunk of meat — and the pack descended. Suddenly an engine
roared, a large vehicle crested the hill, and amid flying pebbles
and dust, a pickup truck came to a halt. Three men with rifles hit
the ground and the killing began, the rifle reports loud enough to
shatter eardrums. Blood and brains and dogflesh splattered. A leg
tore away from a body, and its owner screamed, a horrifyingly
human sound. Bullets winged off rocks and tree trunks and
concrete, so that my mother ran out of the kitchen, screaming
above the uproar, and dragged me away from the window. At the
first shot Buster had fled, without so much as a whine.

The battle was over in moments, and the dogs lay dead right
under our window. Somehow, not one of the pack had escaped.
Clad in the light brown of deputy sheriffs, the trio of riflemen

surveyed their kill, wiping their faces on their shirt-sleeves. They looked like good country fellows, but they never tipped their hats toward Mother and me, never stopped to make small talk or to bow to our "favored citizen" status. They seized the bodies by the tails and flung them into the truck bed, took down shovels, scooped up the worst of the blood and innards and fur. But slick dark-red patches remained on the dirt and gravel, and white stringy-looking stuff that I hadn't known bodies contained. The men hung their shovels up, stowed their rifles, and vanished over the hill.

"Well," said my mother. "I guess that does it. I guess they're gone. Deppities and dogs both."

I located Buster at the bottom of my laundry basket in the closet. He had no further use for two-legged creatures. When stroking and patting and honeyed words failed to bring him out of his hole, I offered food. But in the end I had to carry him, and when I set him on the floor, he crept under my bed, still trembling. Not until late afternoon did he forget the crack of rifles. I didn't mind being rid of the dog pack. But I did mind the arrogance of those men, who started firing without even warning us to take cover.

Almost every evening now, the crunch of pebbles and the magisterial slamming of the Buick door announced Judge Witt. I accepted his little gifts gladly — a bouquet, chocolates, a bag of peppermints — but he was preoccupied, charier of his attentions to me, less interested in what movies I had seen, more eager to talk to my father in private. What he said had something to do with poll taxes, the next election. Something that caused my father's face to go white. "They won't get anywhere with this," I heard the judge say. "It has to pass through my hands first. Where are they going to go, which court can they turn to? Ridiculous. They've not got a chance. This will all blow over. But we may have a few rough times."

My mother began to pay serious attention, too, to these twilight conversations. I felt I was old enough to hear what they said now. I stopped rolling in the grass with Buster or swinging so high that the ropes went slack, flirting with the idea of hurtling through the branches of the wild cherry and landing somewhere outside the fence. "There's going to be a challenge," Judge Witt said one evening. "They've got a slate. All veterans. Local boys. But let's be reasonable. Let's not get upset. This time next year, we'll not recall their names, I trust."

"You mean somebody is going to run against you?"

He laughed at my surprise. "Why, yes. But I wouldn't worry my pretty head about it if I were you." He retrieved his handkerchief from his hip pocket, patted the sweat from his face ever so gently. I was afraid.

They came for Miss Blossom on a sunny, insect-infested summer day, cool in the early hours but deadly hot by ten o'clock, with June bugs and bumblebees diving like Zeroes in the rapidly warming wind. I was on the front porch when the long black Cadillac, a white ambulance, and a police car crunched to a halt in front of the little green house. My mother came out the door in her apron and the two of us walked halfway up the hill, close enough to see through the thickets of weeds and wild roses, past the honeysuckle on the porch, up to the old screen door. The ambulance and the Cadillac were empty, with the doors left wide open, as though the wait would not be long. Only the police car was occupied, by a man I recognized as Fat Earnest, the bouncer at the Southern Club, now clad in policeman's blue.

"You folks stay back," he called, as though he didn't know us, though of course he recognized Hat Abbott's wife and daughter. "They're roundin' up this crazy lady. She's livin' in thar like a filthy hawg." Getting out of his squad car, his sidearm riding in its holster on his bulging hip, he grinned and twirled his index finger at his temple. "Nutty as a fruitcake. But ain't nothing to this, ladies. They got her under control in thar. You might just as well go tend to yer beeswax." He laughed appreciatively. But surely, I thought, she would come out kicking and screaming, damning kids and women, cursing the bags of groceries on the car seats, shrieking contempt for shoppers, for mothers, for all things regular and neat.

"Shame on them," my mother said. "They ought to let her be." We stood our ground, determined to see the end. The waiting began to remind me of the doctor's office. You sat and squirmed and read the *National Geographic*, dreading the opening of the door but wanting it to open, too, so he could lance your boil or poke your stomach or put the instrument down your infected ear or cut out your ingrown toenail and the torment would be over and you could go downstairs to the Medical Arts Drugstore and have your limeade. But this took longer. What were they doing to her in there? Had she hidden under the bed? Had she thrown stones at them?

Finally Miss Blossom's front door opened. Two men emerged, dressed in ties and dark suits on this tropical day. Doctors, we supposed, or maybe one of them was her father. Then came the madwoman, her brown curls matted, her face toward the ground, her torso bound in what seemed to be a large white bandage. A woman in a nurse's uniform was clutching Miss Blossom by the strings of it, leading her, pulling her. Behind them, in another kind of uniform, was the chauffeur who drove the Cadillac, carrying a small suitcase, and at the rear, as the group hurried through the briers and brambles toward the automobiles, walked another uniformed man, the ambulance driver.

"That's a straitjacket they've got her in," Mother said. "They tie you up in it so you can't move your arms at all, and you'd have to be Houdini to get out of one."

Before Miss Blossom was put into the ambulance, she lifted her head and looked in my direction, just once. Her face was calm and unwrinkled, as young as my mother's, and she walked obediently. Except for her ratty hair, she might have stood among the washermothers with their ragged towels in baskets and their bulging clothespin aprons, citizens in the commonwealth of the back fence.

My mother and I retreated. "Well," she said, "I guess she'll be better off where they're taking her. Maybe she'll get good meals, and nobody will mind if she bellers a little, not in that place. Although, if you want to know the truth, she wasn't doing harm to a soul on this earth. We could have done better by the poor thing if we'd tried harder. Shamey, shamey."

But when my father heard the story that night, he shook his head. "She should have been locked up years ago. Maybe now we can get some sleep." And yet the authorities had breached Alamo Street twice now, armed first with rifles, then with a straitjacket Whom would they come after next?

LLD meetings began in July. The idea of a sorority for barely pubescent girls had trickled down somehow from colleges. Sisters! I had always wanted a sister. My mother delivered me to the home of the club president, Ellen O'Grady, a stately triple-storied brick place on a magnolia-lined street where black maids wore white uniforms and lived in. Sure enough, the maid admitted me and seven other pledges at the back door, where we had been told to report, and showed us to the laundry room, where we sat on a bench and waited for our future sisters to be done with their business meeting. "They want us to think they're planning parties and things like that, and collecting dues and counting up the money, but they're only talking about what to do to us," one pledge whispered the first day. "This is the most exciting thing they get to do. You'll see how mean they are, just wait." She made a pistol of her thumb and index finger and put it to her temple.

After a long wait the maid took us to what she called the den, a word I had never heard applied to a room. Ellen O'Grady herself and about a dozen other girls were waiting for us. I'd never seen so many couches — the whole room was furnished with plump, undulating couches and huge pillows that some girls had put right on the floor. Ellen directed us to line up, eyes forward.

"Now listen to me. I'll tell you the rules for proper pledge conduct, and I don't want to say it twice." Snickers ran around the room. I looked for a friendly face but saw none. "Stand up straight, keep your hands behind your back, and don't move. Don't move anything. Don't even blink. Keep your eyes on the far wall, except when one of us speaks to you. Then lower your eyes to the floor As long as you're in the pledge line, you may not look any member in the eye." In my confusion, I was staring Ellen O'Grady right in her cruel brown eyes She could have watched with pleasure while I was roasted alive She was heavy but beautiful — I'd never seen anyone so beautiful before, or quite so sleek. Her clothes clearly came from Little Rock, or maybe someplace I'd never heard of. Her thick black hair and long red fingernails obviously had a beautician's attention every couple of days. She glowed with money.

"What's your name, dummy?" She was speaking to me. I replied, quickly switching my eyes to the floor, but not before I saw her put a mark in a notebook. She continued, "Anybody who doesn't obey the rules, she'll get it And from now until initiation — if any of you make it to initiation, and don't count on it — you call us ma'am Anybody speaks to you, you say yes ma'am and no ma'am You are nothing. You don't deserve to be in LLD. Maybe we'll be able to make something of you "

We were to expect "orders" at the end of each meeting —

goods and services we had to provide by the next week. Anyone
who missed a meeting without an excuse from her doctor could
expect double orders. Two cuts, and we'd be dropped. If we saw a
member on the street, we were to go down on one knee and greet
her formally, for example, "How do you do, Miss O'Grady?"
(Not in school, of course, since the principal had forbidden
kneeling, and not on Sundays, since that would be a sacrilege.)
Demerits earned in meetings (which piled up on a hundred
pretexts) were to be worked out by various punishments. Merits,
which came via orders you had fulfilled or other favors, canceled
demerits.

Before I absorbed the rulebook I failed to say ma'am and had to
roll a peanut across the floor with my nose, to screams of laughter.
The O'Grady carpet was velvety and thick, not amenable to
peanut rolling, but I finally reached the hearth, which was my
destination. By the end of the meeting, I had looked two members in the eye and had been made to kneel on a prickly doormat
until told to rise. The combination of physical pain and humiliation produced my first breakdown in tears, though it seemed as
though someone else were crying. Another pledge cracked at the
same moment and was made to kneel on the doormat herself.
Ellen O'Grady gave me ten demerits and ordered me to bring her
a stuffed toy — a pig, she specified. A stuffed animal was considered the most punishing request, because it was time-consuming
if you made it yourself and expensive if you bought it, and if Ellen
didn't like it, she'd give you more demerits than you could work
off The second-worst favor was a toss pillow, almost as hard to
make as the animals. The easiest was a lace-trimmed powder
puff. There were smaller orders for cakes or fudge, or to find out
what a certain boy's middle name was. One pledge who admitted
to keeping a diary was ordered to bring it for reading aloud

"Ellen O'Greedy, I'd call her," my father raved at the supper
table when I told him about the LLDs. "If that's the road to

popularity, they can have it. You don't need to be popular." But my mother told him I had to do these things, because this was what girls did, and she stitched a fine large pig out of blue gingham, with pink satin ear linings, hoof pads, and snout. "Your mother sure can sew," said Ellen, but I saw an odd gleam in her brown eyes — disappointment? Had she really wanted me to arrive with nothing, or with some horrid thing I had made myself? She gave me only five merits, whereas the fudge-bringers earned a dozen each. Worse than that, everybody now wanted a pig. Ellen elbowed them out, however, and ordered a sheep, specifying white with blue trim. My mother turned into an indentured servant along with me, for my demerits accumulated, each trespass of mine translating into hours for her at the sewing machine. The more beautiful her pigs and sheep and cushions and lace-trimmed powder puffs, the more of them she was obliged to make

"Lama Lama my rear end," she said one afternoon. "Lama Lama my foot. Don't those little twerps' mothers ever ask where all these things are coming from? Don't rich people ever expect to pay for anything? I wouldn't let you treat a dog this way. If you get into this thing, you aren't going to order anybody's mama to make stuffed animals." But she never refused to make them.

Waiting in the laundry room, I prayed that Ellen would be stricken with hives or mumps, but she never missed a meeting.

"You saw me on Prospect Avenue yesterday, and you didn't bow. Why?"

"But I didn't see you, Miss O'Grady. I wasn't on Prospect Avenue yesterday. I mean, I don't think I was." Snickers, giggles.

"Are you calling me a liar, stupid bitch?" More snickers.

Or, "You know no pledge is allowed to wear shorts in public. But I saw you in the Piggly Wiggly in shorts with your mother. Are you trying to get so many demerits we have to throw you out? That would really be a pleasure, dummy."

"But I didn't wear shorts to the Piggly Wiggly. I wore a skirt. I'm sure I wore a skirt."

"Are you calling me a liar? What is the matter with you? What do you use for a brain?"

I had hoped to get accustomed to suffering, but it only made me more awkward. I stumbled over my feet, couldn't recall or invent any gossip to tell them, twitched uncontrollably in line. I learned to snicker and giggle when another pledge broke into tears — if you cried yourself, the sisters punished you. I yearned to quit, grew ashamed to ask my mother to make one more lace-trimmed powder puff. Lama Lama made you popular; without it, you were done for in seventh grade. After you got to be an LLD, you could go to the banquet in the fall, wearing a formal gown, skirt right down to the floor, and you had to bring a boy. You asked him, and his mother made him do it, because she knew your mother, and he had to send you a corsage. This made the mothers feel wonderful, because they knew they had properly launched you. Only a few more peanuts to roll across the rug, and then I'd get the boy and the gardenia and the long dress.

I began to have migraines more savage than my father's, head-aches that overtook me sometimes in the afternoon, sometimes in the middle of the night, announced by flashes of red before my eyes and nausea, and accompanied by near hallucinatory visions involving black blood, dark caverns, torment. I expected the left side of my head or my eyeball to explode, could feel the artery throbbing as if tied in a double knot. They lasted for days now, not hours. My mother lived with not one but two invalids to whom the slightest footfall was a pistol shot; two of us examining every mouthful we ate, asking, "Is this what's doing it? The last time I ate a pork chop I got sick"; two of us pronouncing ourselves allergic to feather pillows or the laundry soap or fried potatoes or lettuce salads or ice cream or haircuts or her perfume or a thousand other things in her domain and under her control. She never simply gave up and left home but appeared at my bedside with milk and cinnamon toast when I finally woke up without the headache.

As the Democratic primary approached that month, my father's thinking took a disquieting turn. City life, he said, was getting him down. He longed for the joys of nature. He began reading *Progressive Farmer* magazine and ordered books about agriculture through the mail. "This may just be my year to get out of the rackets," he announced. "Not that I'm worried about the election." Cornering Mother and me in the living room after supper, or following us out to the lawn chairs under the lonesome pine where we sat on hot evenings, he read aloud as usual, but instead of the forest primeval or the *Odyssey*, it was raising strawberries. Boysenberries ("Bet you never heard of a boysenberry"). Luther Burbank and grafting apple trees onto pears, lemons onto oranges. Luther Burbank creating seedless watermelons. Green beans with no strings. Cherries with no pits. Freestone peaches with no fuzz. Perfect apples. Daddy had a book about apple and peach orchards — simply gold mines, it said, if properly managed. Chickens, too, could be gold mines. The broiler business. The egg business ("Bet you never heard of candling eggs"). Truck farming was another way to get rich. *How to Make a Handsome Living from Beef Cattle* was another title. The man who never felt completely dressed unless every stitch was tailor-made and his watch fob was precisely placed in his vest pocket now envisioned life as a gentleman farmer. *Agricola, agricolae, agricolarum.*

"Hat, I married you to get off the farm, and I don't have any *idea* of moving back to one."

"But you don't understand. You came from an old-style farm. Your mama and daddy farmed the hard way. No equipment. No electricity. No running water. Outdoor toilets. Hoeing cotton. Slaughtering hogs. All due respect to your papa and mama, but they had no education, no understanding of agriculture as a science. This will be a modern farm, with home-churned butter in the refrigerator, a food freezer full of boysenberries and peaches in heavy syrup that we put up ourselves, T-bone steaks in packages, dozens of eggs in the cellar. We'll never have to go to the grocery store. We'll live off the fat of the land. Six hours' work a day, maximum, and we'll sit in our house by the side of the road and watch the world go by. Listen to what this fellow says here in this book."

"I never saw a farm like that. You won't see one either. Besides, you don't know one end of a cow from the other. You don't know a hen from a rooster "

I stayed out of the argument, though I began to fear he meant business, and I prayed my mother would win I was happy being a bookmaker's daughter I wasn't cut out for a farmer's daughter. Oh well, the strawberries might be nice Boysenberries, too. He promised I could have a horse whereupon Mother lost her patience

"A horse! What will we need a horse for? Do you know what it costs to keep a saddle horse? You're not talking about a horse with two dollars on his nose. That kind just costs two dollars. You're talking about a *horse!*"

"Your mother always throws cold water on me. All I have to do is come up with a plan and your mother nixes it."

"Where will I go to school?" I asked one evening, forgetting the horse but remembering my mother's tales of one room with one schoolmaster and a wood stove and one McGuffey's reader to be shared by all

"Oh, well, you know country schools have changed a lot since your mother's day All modern now Look here " He waved a copy of *Progressive Farmer* under my nose, with an article on the new postwar country school, and another on 4-H clubs. "You won't be a city slicker anymore You'll find wholesome companionship and learn womanly skills, like it says here. Canning, for instance. Jelly-making. Sewing."

"I don't want to do any of that stuff. I hate canning. I thought you wanted me to study Latin, the way you did. They don't teach Latin in the country. Besides, I want to join the LLD."

"Well, what an attitude. How would you like it if your daddy was out of a job?" Nobody had uttered the words until now.

"But that can't happen. Judge Witt says we're sure to win the election. You said yourself that Hot Springs would die without the horse books." But my chest tightened up, as I imagined the three of us at somebody's back door, eating supper from a pie tin.

One evening in early July, when my father came down the Southern Club stairs, his forehead was purple under the knotted handkerchief — a migraine visible at fifty paces. "Oh, my Lord," said Mother as he staggered to the passenger's side of the car and got in

"I think I'm going to die," he said, groaning. "Have you heard what happened? Those sons of bitches dropped ten thousand leaflets yesterday from an airplane. And Johnny Strand, that lousy traitor — he flew the plane. He did it for Sid McMath and his boys, over where they opened the campaign."

"Leaflets?" Sidney S. McMath was the leader of the opposition, an ex-marine, a veteran of Okinawa, with ribbons on his chest, handsome enough to get votes just on his looks.

"A phony, a fraud, a Romeo," my father moaned. "Fellow like that's got no more idea how to run the county than a jackrabbit. Dropping leaflets from a plane!"

McMath was running for county prosecutor, a key post, and he was bringing his friends with him. What if they won? Who would take care of us? According to the evening paper, which we found in the shrubbery at home, a crowd had met the young hero as he kicked off his campaign just outside town. His picture was on page one Another veteran, young but not so good-looking,

was running against Judge Witt. McMath had said, "The returning soldier is zealous of his heritage, perhaps because he has so
recently fought for it. When he returns to his own community
and finds his own people deprived of their right to vote, when he
discovers that their lives and liberties are not secure, when he is
told that he cannot exercise the right of citizenship and run for
public office without the consent of the political boss . . . what is
his reaction?" And the leaflets had fluttered from the sky.

At the supper table, nursing his migraine, Daddy told us that
Leo's boys (in plainclothes rather than policeman's uniforms) had
scattered several pounds of tacks in the parking lot close to the
rally. He managed a grin as he said it. McMath was a thug; he and
his henchmen packed guns. The worst news was about Daddy's
sidekick, Johnny Strand. "Lousy Johnny quit his job at the
Southern. Leo will fix him. He'll never work in this town again.
Damnable traitor! What are things coming to?"

But a few weeks later, our hearts grew light. In the Democratic primary, held in July, Sid McMath was the only winner on
the reform slate. Judge Witt was safe; his opponent had scarcely
touched him. The whole machine looked safe. As city officials,
Leo McLaughlin and Judge Ledgerwood were safe, because they
were not due to stand for election until the spring. Things *would*
go back to normal. Life *would* continue to improve in every way.
Earl Witt and my father looked less pale and anxious and began to
tell tales about the old days once more. I went back to my swing
in the cherry tree. Then, like a surgeon's verdict that turns from
hope to doom with the arrival of the lab report, McMath announced he had proof of stolen elections, of poll tax receipts
purchased by the dozen. This being the solid South, the Democratic primary of the summer was supposed to settle the election.
But now the reformers bolted the party and began campaigning
as independents against the machine. The November election,
for once, might mean something.

In September LLD pledges spent a Saturday in front of Schneck's Drugstore dressed in baby bonnets and sunsuits, scrubbing the sidewalk with toothbrushes. Ellen O'Grady watched us most of the day, making sure we had no food or water, which was part of the trial. At the initiation that night, the sisters gave us plastic compacts with LLD in raised letters on the top. For the banquet soon after my mother created a long dress for me out of yellow taffeta and net, trimmed with purple velvet ribbons. The boy I invited agreed to come, and his mother saw to it that I got a corsage. I still have the photograph of us at our table, me just a month short of twelve years, grave and tense as a society matron, him baring his upper teeth, opening his nostrils, and snorting like a pig (a thing boys were doing to be humorous that year, and we'd all collapse in giggles when they did it). On the shoulder of my gown is pinned the corsage, mostly ribbon — and I can't be certain now whether it was carnations or a gardenia.

Leo McLaughlin, Earl Witt, and Vern Ledgerwood expected to prevail by the usual methods: issuing poll tax receipts to people whose names had long since been engraved on tombstones, coercing black laborers out of the field and carting them to the polls, paying farmers in cash or half-pints, threatening their opponents with bankruptcy, recruiting taxi drivers to haul the old folks, and exhorting the bookmakers to round up their voters and get them to the polls. When Sidney McMath challenged the whole procedure, Earl Witt threw the case out of court, but the reformers went to federal court, which handed down the first ruling against the ancient political system. When the votes were counted in November, the McLaughlin machine was finished. Furthermore, its members knew the indictments would not be long in coming.

Still, my father had his job until the new year. Never had Christmas approached so fast. By means that he never fully explained to my mother or me but that included a second mortgage on our house, Daddy raised the money to buy his farm. My mother helped him shop for the place, halfheartedly. I was offered no choices — and wanted none, since no house could compare in my affections with what I already had. A farm, of course, required a truck. One Sunday morning in December, when the trees were bare, Daddy pulled up to 122 Alamo Street behind the wheel of an old Dodge flatbed rig, a strange and forlorn figure in a rough blue workshirt and khaki pants but grinning like a boy. Bouncing on the hard seat, swerving to miss the potholes, shouting cheerfully over the grinding gears, he drove us the twenty miles or so for our first look at the forty acres he'd already christened Glen Springs Farm. The house was set on cinder blocks at the edge of the spread of rocky, unpromising land, nothing like the pictures in *Progressive Farmer* — a new house, cramped and graceless, with low ceilings and thin walls, linoleum on the floors, a treeless yard lacking flowers or even a flower bed. We warmed ourselves at the wood stove, and Daddy outlined his plans. On New Year's Day, he would come and live on the farm alone, to plant his orchards and prepare the ground for his boysenberries. Mother and I were to stay on in town until I finished the school year.

On December 25, I found the customary pile of books under the Christmas tree, but we ate our turkey and dressing in silence. On December 31, the Southern Club and the rest of the horse books locked their doors, as illegal gambling in Hot Springs quietly closed down. Chicken one day and feathers the next. The feathers piled up between January 1, 1947, and the next paycheck.

Like a faithful draft animal, no stranger to hard times, 122 Alamo stood ready to help out. We shut the doors once more between the two apartments. A man came and rescued the old refrigerator and stove and sink from the garage and quickly converted my bedroom into a kitchen, removing the rug and covering the gleaming hardwood with linoleum. We made sure the hooks on the bathroom doors were in good working order. I took down all forty-seven of the Cornel Wilde photos and tried to glue them in a scrapbook, but they were faded and fragile, too keen a memento of babyish crushes now that I had worn a long dress and gone to a party with a date. We rented one side of the house to a pleasant middle-aged soul who worked as a typist at the bank. My grandmother's old bedroom, where I had learned to read, became my mother's bedroom. The living room and the kitchen retained their old identity, and yet the radio and the maroon plush furnishings suddenly began to look like historical relics. I moved into the tiny back room that Bruce and Hazel had abandoned seven years earlier.

To comfort me for the loss of my real bedroom, Mother made new white dimity curtains and a lavish, ruffled, blue-and-white-striped spread for the single bed, along with a flounced pillow sham, a skirt for the vanity table, and another for the vanity stool, thus crowding the tiny space with crisply striped skirts like a ballroom. I arranged my comb and brush and hand mirror set on the vanity and lay down among the ruffles, waiting to see what would overtake us next.

$\mathcal{J}$HE END OF ORDER

THE INDICTMENTS FELL thick and fast, now that the grand juries were chosen by Leo's enemies, and they fell chiefly on the mayor. Both Judge Witt and Judge Ledgerwood went untouched. The reformers need a show trial, and easily got Mayor McLaughlin indicted for two decades of election fraud and other counts of corruption. They brought similar charges against the city attorney, a minor servitor of the McLaughlin machine named Jay Rowland, whose job had been to redistribute the small sums collected in municipal court — the "fines" for gaming that such men as my father delivered as agents of the gambling houses or houses of prostitution they worked for. Amounting to a few thousand dollars a month, these sums were undoubtedly spent on civic purposes such as uniforms for Fat Earnest and other city cops, odds and ends for the schools, and pruning the magnolia trees on Central Avenue. The rake-off from the gambling businesses themselves had clearly amounted to unrecorded millions each year (a fortune notoriously underestimated by federal agents charged with keeping the screws on Hot Springs), dollars that had not passed through city court or any public channels but had gone directly from the cashboxes of the casinos into the pockets of interested parties — to the top local official, no doubt, as well as to Owney Madden and his gangland connections, though nothing was ever precisely proved. Despite Sidney McMath's rhetoric about democracy, he was interested chiefly in revenge, and also in publicity, so that he could mount a campaign for governor two years hence.

Because both Leo and Vern Ledgerwood had to stand for re-election in April, it was important for McLaughlin's trial to take place in March. Of course, he could not be tried on his home ground, so the drama moved to the tiny crossroads of Mount Ida, in nearby Montgomery County, to a dusty old courthouse shaded by black walnut trees and with a cow pasture right under its windows. The courtroom was heated by a wood stove, which roared and crackled comfortingly, with the cold rain outside in the bare trees and the cows bawling in the raw chill of a fading Arkansas winter. We got our reports from the local papers and from Earl Witt, who attended every session. Sid McMath was the prosecutor, and because he was so young and handsome, because he claimed to have broken the deadly grip of an old-line political machine, because he claimed to represent a new era, *Life* magazine covered the trial. Reporters and photographers arrived from New York, as though covering a liberation movement in a backward Asian or African protectorate. Mount Ida hadn't toilets enough, or any hotel rooms at all, and only one public telephone, which wasn't even in the courthouse but in a nearby gas station, and Judge Witt observed that crack reporters from all over had to race across courthouse square, line up, and wait their turn. What they apparently never heard, or investigated, was the rumor that the jury — nine earnest, white, middle-aged Arkansas farmers from the immediate vicinity — was fixed.

Enraging his opponent, who had a marine colonel's sense of propriety, Leo took the stand in his own behalf, wearing an old sweater and an open-necked shirt. It was the first time he had ever appeared in public without the Jimmy Walker outfit and the red carnation. His sister, who had been accustomed to parading on Central Avenue with Leo behind the prancing Scotch and Soda, brought lunch in a paper bag every day, and the two of them shared it in the corridor. Nevertheless, in a worn-out cardigan or a tuxedo, Leo was still a shrewd country lawyer, while the prosecutor lacked courtroom experience and any idea how to cross-examine a witness. The jury brought in a verdict of not guilty on all counts. The city attorney, as he might have expected, was less fortunate. He was convicted of taking bribes.

The crunch of Judge Witt's Buick sounded in our driveway oftener than usual that winter and spring, sometimes even before supper was on the table. In the peculiar, half-comprehended protocol we observed with him, we never invited him to sit with us at the kitchen table. I noticed an odd nervousness in my mother that I never saw when my father was there. Yet we received him as we always had, his lordship, and I hardly thought that so powerful a man might be downcast or unoccupied, might be seeking something from us.

One April afternoon, after Leo's trial was finished and the weather had turned pleasant, he took his place in the rocking chair while Mother and I settled in the swing. The grass was just beginning to need mowing, the cherry tree was magnificently white, and the blossoming spirea bush had attracted a swarm of yellow jackets. I experienced a rush of lovesickness for my home, even though my bedroom had been turned into a kitchen and rented out. Spring arrived most particularly in this yard, nowhere else, certainly not on the bald hillsides my father was preparing for us.

"I never had the slightest doubt Leo would go free," Judge Witt told us. "The indictments were absurd to begin with. That grand jury would have indicted Leo for murder if McMath had told them to. He had hand-picked them, so why not? He was out to hang Leo. He still wants to see him dead. But he won't get his wish. He didn't have a chance at his so-called trial. I can't imagine he didn't know what he was up against."

He smiled, as if hesitating to say more. "I was personally acquainted with many of the trial jurors. They were my friends, you know. My father's friends. I'd known most of them since boyhood." I experienced a small shock, the shock of comprehension, the shock of cynicism. To cover my confusion, I put on a blank expression. My mother, too, looked innocent, blank, as though she had experienced the same shock. He smiled again, and repeated the old catchphrase he loved: "You'd be surprised at what a little money can do." In fact he had turned the trick with cows rather than hard currency or crude bribes. Once the jury was chosen, he sent some fellows to each farm on a cattle-buying expedition. They had offered surprising prices, two or three times market, and cash on the barrel head. No promises were extracted and no contracts signed. But the farmers knew where the money was coming from. Sid McMath might have had the skills of Clarence Darrow, for all the jury cared.

"But what about poor Mr. Rowland?" I asked. "Couldn't they have bought some cows for him, too?" Alas for him, his jury had not been so exquisitely rigged, and he might face a stretch in prison, under those cruel whips. Naturally, explained the judge, McMath had to have a bone thrown to him. He wouldn't have let his opponents go unbloodied. Still, the judge thought the ancient powers had prevailed. The Romans were still in Rome. "Normal," he said. "Things will go back to normal — only wait and see. The horse books will be running again in six months. This is only a flash in the pan." We weren't personally acquainted with Jay Rowland, and knew nothing of the sufferings of his family. (Hot Springs was not so small that you knew everybody: it had its strangers.) Yet I was struck by the bitter injustice. And as for Judge Witt, at ease in his rocker, so very skilled at determining every man's price, he was out of work as surely as my father. For him, for poor Mr. Rowland, who took the rap, and for my father, the Goths had passed the city limits and beaten down the door.

In the spring of 1947, a Frenchman, Christian Dior, managed finally to make "normal" obsolete. I was twelve when photographs labeled "the New Look" suddenly appeared in *Life*: an outfit so different from anything my paper dolls, let alone my mother, had ever worn, that the eye could hardly take it in at all. No shoulder pads. A waist so breathlessly trim that even my slender mother could only aspire to such measurements, never achieve them. The hat, the gloves, were comforting and familiar. What was alarming was the huge skirt that swirled almost to the ankles and totally hid the knees. The week before this happened, my mother had bought four knee-length, 1940s-looking dresses and a coat. "Better get yourself some pretty things while there's still a little money left," Daddy had said. "Who knows about next year? You may need clothes. You may be out pounding the streets for a job." Now all these pretty new things were obsolete, rendered instantly dowdy by this one photograph.

"I won't wear that," she announced. "I don't want to go around in a skirt that drags the floor. What good are nylon stockings if you have to go around in that rig?"

Indignantly, Mother passed *Life* around the neighborhood. Thelma Miller said she wouldn't wear the New Look either. The other women said they wouldn't wear it. The men all laughed at it. The little girls all said that when they grew up they wouldn't wear it. But when Mother put on one of her new dresses with the normal hem and the straight skirt and the bodice with a tucked yoke and the slightly puffed sleeves, it looked old-fashioned. Why did her new dresses look that way in April when they'd been perfectly nice in February? She began tugging at her skirts when she wore them, trying to make them longer. She inspected the hems of everything we owned.

"Reckon there'd be enough allowance to let this out?"

"Reckon I could let it out and sew a facing on it?"

Mother was known as an expert seamstress, and people flocked to her for advice. Thelma Miller appeared at the back door with a dress she had altered, wanting to know how in tarnation you could press out the crease of the old hem. Another neighbor came with a short black dress and a piece of new green fabric, ten inches wide. "Velma, do you reckon if I just cut off the bottom and set this green stuff in, it would look like it was made that way?" My mother gamely said yes, but I knew she meant no.

The New Look moved in two weeks from Paris and the pages of *Life* magazine to the store windows in downtown Hot Springs, Arkansas. Let-down hems (for the line showed no matter how strenuously you applied the iron) became the mark of poverty, or pigheadedness, that year. Some women covered the telltale line with rickrack or a cheery strip of bias tape. In ready-to-wear as in politics, the old order was gone.

It took a while to find a buyer for 122 Alamo. I heard what the prospects said: looks awfully old, lacks a proper dining room, the kitchen and bath need remodeling, just an old duplex, we can do better than this. These comments cheered me. Maybe no one would buy. But an elderly couple suddenly decided it would suit them fine. The money that came into our hands went directly into Daddy's farm. We moved from Alamo Street that summer.

Determined as I was to relish none of it, I have no recollection of the move or of rearranging my possessions in a new home. After my furniture was fitted in my new bedroom, there were four square feet of standing room left. A quarter mile from the main house stood an ancient log cabin of generous dimensions, with a grandiose fireplace and chimney. The man who had claimed this land and cleared it had built the cabin himself; now it served as a barn. Its wide board floors were dusty with chicken feed and dairy mash; mice and half-tamed cats patroled it in equal numbers. I liked it better than the main house and thought of using the place as a hideout, somehow befriending the cats and getting rid of the mice, but our neighbor told me that the original settler had been murdered in front of that very fireplace years ago. Not so long ago that she didn't remember him, she said — a funny old man and a bachelor. People thought he kept a fortune in the house. One night robbers broke in, some mean fellows from around these parts. They turned the poor old man's cornshuck mattress inside out, looking for the money. Finally they tortured him to death with hot pokers on his own hearth. They never found a cent, however. The ringleader died in the electric chair. I left the barn as it was.

In spite of much coaxing, Buster showed no talent as a herd dog or as a creature of the outdoors. Like me, he was afraid of large animals — and small ones, for that matter. On his first visit to the barnyard, a rooster flew in his face and pecked him, so he could not be induced to go there again. Snakes abounded, even very near the house — king and garter snakes, copperheads, the occasional stray moccasin — and we both went everywhere with our eyes on the ground. The neighbors said rattlesnakes were nothing uncommon, and showed me a huge rattle they had taken as a trophy. Buster soon developed rheumatism and spent most of his time under my bed or the kitchen stove.

I had planned to roam the woods alone, discovering patches of wildflowers and taking notes, like William Wordsworth, whose lyrics I had encountered in literature class. But Wordsworth didn't know about Arkansas farms. There were no hosts of golden daffodils. Walks in the woods were unthinkable without hip boots and a rifle, long sleeves to guard against the brambles, and a hat to ward off sunstroke. Even then you came home covered with chiggers and with a dog tick or two attached to your private parts.

Besides the snakes, there were insects, hateful in their number and variety, their thirst for blood. I was most keenly aware of them at night, in the house. The tiniest ones came in through the screens, and the big ones battered their heads and buzzed, desperate to get to the light, moths, gnats, flies, displaying ferocious phototropisms and as hungry for the human epidermis as tigers for meat. Some nights, instead of reading, I doused the light to discourage the bugs and listened to late-night radio dramas, covering my head and my new table radio with the sheet.

My characteristic act as a farmer's daughter was a kamikaze dive into my father's bookcase. He had said years ago that I must read every volume in it and I almost made it — memoirs of the court of Louis XVI and of Maria Theresa, more of Dickens, Erasmus's great essay *In Praise of Folly*, which bewildered me, but I plodded onward. My father had recently bought a one-volume encyclopedia, not too thick. I read that, too, all in the spirit of a prisoner splitting large rocks into small ones, throwing myself against the stony paragraphs, tearing at them tooth and claw, castigating myself like a schoolmaster when I caught myself skimming hypocritically along, reading words but not sentences. "Start it over, damn you, read it again," I commanded again and again, murderously angry with my own brain. My father had painted a sign and hung it on the gate, GLEN SPRINGS FARM, but it might as well have said TUCKER FARM. Like Leo's unfortunate clerk, I had been sent to the pen.

I malingered when asked to hoe potatoes or do any other kind of garden work, developing diarrhea and knots in the muscles of my neck. I suffered weekly from migraines. Shortly after we moved I began to menstruate, which was not a romantic experience, not precisely what the future wife of Cornel Wilde or Humphrey Bogart (or their equivalent) hoped for, an event belonging more in the category of scrub buckets and crocheted bedspreads than that of free spirits. Nevertheless, menstrual cramps had their uses — they were as good an excuse from farm work as they proved to be from physical education classes in school.

I didn't mind feeding the chickens and would set off dutifully toward the barn at five o'clock, but each time I went into the feed room, I remembered the torture, the missing money. The woods, only a hundred feet away, seemed darkly inhabited by outlaws. Indeed, a couple of miles or so back in the woods, far from any passable road and in a cabin no better than our barn, lived a family that associated with no one. The neighbors said the old man in that cabin had fathered a baby on his own daughter, and I was more shocked by this news than by the torture and murder in the barn. Indeed, once every two or three months the young mother, whose name was Florabelle, walked the miles to the roadside and hitched a ride to town, to take her sickly baby to the doctor. She didn't look any too healthy herself, blue eyes watering and wispy blond locks clamped down with bobby pins, but she had a kind of wan beauty. If my mother was a passenger rather than the driver, she would cradle the baby in her arms and talk to him; he had the face of an old man and neither smiled nor cried. He and his mother looked and smelled dirty, and I was too repelled by his paternity to offer to hold him. Yet, like my parents, I was overwhelmed with pity for this doomed girl and her feeble little son. She can't have been more than sixteen.

I burned with rage and sorrow on my own account as well. What was I doing here, cast backward into medieval squalor, when so lately I had worn ribbons and a long dress, had been launched into nice-girl society? The incestuous family became characters in the drama that played at night in my dreams. In the moonlight of my sleeping landscape, Florabelle and her father emerged from the woods as both the perpetrators and the victims of violent acts. By day I began wavering among various strong, unpleasant emotions toward my father: pity, because even I could see that his dream of farming like a gentleman was self-deluding; anger, because I was trapped, unable to escape (except via books) unless he granted permission; and a kind of indignant, almost tearful adoration that made me ashamed of the other feelings. After all, it wasn't his fault, exactly, that he was out of a job.

Tight-lipped but resigned, my mother, the farmer's daughter, slipped right into the harness as a farmer's wife. I got used to the sight of her churning butter, boiling cottage cheese, digging potatoes, murdering chinch bugs in the garden, milking the cows, separating fertile from infertile eggs, wringing a chicken's neck, scalding the feathers in order to pluck them, slitting the carcass open and disposing of the intestines, and then dismembering the body and frying it for lunch. To the best of my ability, I helped her with these tasks. She was familiar with the difficulties of cattle breeding and calving. She knew when it was time to wean the bull calf and call the man to "cut" or castrate it, so that it could be raised for beef. She could tell when the heifers were about to go in heat. She knew when to turn the garden over and plant seed, where the grapevines should be set out in order to bear, and how to rid the pasture of bitterweed. My father's opinions on all these subjects were worthless. "You can't learn to farm from a book," my mother told him. For once, she triumphed over his books, over his legions of Romans, his set of Dickens, his rare edition of Casanova, over Imogene, over Mike. Poetry was no use here. She went about her labors with a practiced eye.

One afternoon, as she ran a circle saw to cut wood for the stove, she caught her right hand in a moving belt and almost severed her fingers. (I can still recall her screams, which tore me away from my book, still see my father racing toward her from the barn, the second time in my life I had seen him run.) After a wild ride from the farm to the hospital in Hot Springs, with her hand bleeding into a thick towel and my father weeping aloud as he drove, the doctor sewed the mangled fingers up and bandaged them. Of course I remember such details as my father and I clumsily doing the cooking and the washing up. In a few weeks, however, my mother was slaughtering chickens again and setting the golden pieces, complete with cream gravy, on the table. With tears in his eyes, my father pronounced her "a great lady," a use of the term I could never have imagined. Somehow, it made my mother laugh.

Sid McMath was serving what proved to be his only term as prosecuting attorney and openly campaigning for the governorship simultaneously. So long as he had his reputation as a reformer to maintain, there would be no gambling in Hot Springs. My father dared not show his face on Central Avenue. He considered doing a bit of free-lance bookmaking, using a pay phone and keeping the scratch sheets in his pocket, but that would surely have landed him in jail. He never put on a suit or placed the pocket watch in his vest pocket. He gave up his morning pint of whiskey as easily as if he had never been habituated to it. Like a proper farmer, he rose at dawn and fell asleep, exhausted, in his chair after supper. He had little time for reading now but seemed to want my company more than ever. Some days I got up at sunrise too, amazed by the early morning darkness and the mists clearing from the treetops far away, the hens scratching cheerfully and the roosters crowing, and the cattle already cropping in the fields, before they had been watered and fed. Mostly I went with him at night, for the chores of morning were the chores of evening as well. Farm animals know no Sunday, as I saw to my regret, and don't take two weeks off in the summer or celebrate Christmas.

I tried to learn milking, but had not dreamed how hard and unromantic the job was, how hairy the udder, how uncooperative the cow, how short and dry and ungraspable the teat, how easily the milkmaid could kick manure into the milk bucket and spoil forty-five minutes' labor. Why did the beast turn and eye me so angrily as I seated myself beneath her hind leg? What kept her from lowing gently and standing still? Even when I succeeded in doing a proper job, a full bucket of milk was a backbreaking load, almost more than I could lug from barn to house. And then the stuff had to be strained through a fine sieve, transferred to sterilized jars in the refrigerator, and every utensil scrupulously washed with soapy water and scalded. The cow soon put an end to my career as a dairymaid, delivering a swift kick that knocked me off the stool and put a black bruise on my arm.

Since I was ashamed not to contribute some kind of labor (scattering corn for the chickens didn't qualify), I drew heavy buckets from the well to water the livestock and reluctantly took on the chore of gathering eggs, until one day I encountered a monster black snake in a nest, its eyes glinting and yellow egg yolks running out of its maw. Like a child who'd been mistreated by her playmates, I ran all the way to the house, weeping and clutching my wire basket, smashing the eggs I had gathered. My father came and shot the snake and relieved me of the task of egg gathering, at least for a few months, until I could enter the barnyard again without becoming paralyzed outside the chicken-house door.

During the day, often under a hot sun, my father performed such tasks as plowing, setting fence posts in concrete, and clearing the land of sassafras bushes. His fingernails were broken and dirty, and his hands became callused. The boysenberry and strawberry plants promptly died, without yielding a berry. After considerable labor and investment, my father realized that he had planted the apple and peach orchard on the north side of our hillside, so that it could never thrive, even though the summers were hot. The trees lived, but that was all. The promised saddle horse never was bought — it was, of course, beyond our means — and thus another of my mother's predictions materialized, while not a one of Daddy's ever did. He began to grow thinner from the hard labor. Suddenly he needed reading glasses. Suddenly no C-notes appeared in stacks on the kitchen table. In fact, money was so scarce that needing glasses or getting a toothache or finding a hole in your shoe or losing your best sweater turned swiftly into tragedy, while such events as leaking roofs or a well running dry or car trouble were full-scale disasters. Even a dollar or two for the movies was not a foregone conclusion. A petted child whose parents bought her the occasional expensive dress and nonessential new patent leather shoes, I now learned that if I broke, misplaced, or outgrew my possessions, I had to do without.

I became isolated. We drove to Hot Springs, where my friends were, only when necessary. We were many miles past the nearest phone connection. The kids my own age who lived in the area looked rugged and dirty to me, and I knew that to them I seemed overeducated and citified. Once, on a Saturday, a teenage boy stopped his pickup truck at our gate, sized me up, and invited me to go out with him. He was rawboned and loud, no sort of person to be courting me, I thought, so I sent him away, in spite of his promise to teach me how to dance. He must have told the others I was a stuck-up bitch, because nobody ever stopped in again.

Like the majority of Arkansas schools, the nearest high school lacked accreditation. Its graduates could not even be admitted to most colleges. "You might as well let me quit school as send me there," I pointed out angrily to my father. Though the road was bad and the journey long and expensive, I continued to go to school in town, and thus at least was spared the 4-H Club. But every time the car failed to start, I saw my schooling going out the exhaust pipe. I went in last year's clothes and then in my cousin's hand-me-downs, and then in skirts and dresses my mother created by cutting up her own things.

The children of other bookmakers had similar problems — the fate of all families when the plant closes down or the wage-earner gets fired — and we eyed one another's makeshift clothes and worn-out shoes. I threw out my LLD compact and refused to attend meetings, partly because my wardrobe was deficient and partly because I had no interest in tormenting pledges and forcing their mothers to sew lace ruffles on powder puffs for me, but also because I was growing lean and bitter. I despised LLD girls, and I didn't want them to approve of me. Anyway, it was a lie that they were popular. Popularity meant dating football players, and what football players looked for was long shiny hair and a C-cup bra. C's on your report card, I began to notice, didn't do you any damage, either.

More than ever I became my father's friend. Besides the farm work I did (or failed to do) in his company, there were the long drives to and from Hot Springs, about forty-five minutes each way, which made a captive audience of me and allowed him, as he put it, to lecture me. But the communion we had known when I was a child now began to lose some of its power for me. Perhaps one day I'd have ideas he disapproved of. The 1950s were dawning, and though the concept was frightening and unmanageable, I had begun imagining a future for myself, one that might not unroll in Arkansas. My girlfriends, once we were past puberty and began to look like women, started dating and soon were going steady. At age fourteen they spoke — jokingly and in whispers, of course — of pins and engagements, of the wedding dresses they would choose, and would the bridesmaids wear pink or yellow? Didn't they see, I wondered, what was at the end of the aisle? Where they had once made A's, they began to be happier with B's. They took typing, home economics, bookkeeping. Yet I was as hungry for love as they were, with less idea how to get it and no notion what to do if I found it. My father preached relentlessly against all forms of love: stay away from those bad boys, keep to your books. I suspected his motives. The rage I had briefly felt, as when he made scathing comments to my mother at supper, began to inhabit my mind like a familiar. Bad boys, indeed. Who did he think he was kidding? Yet I was determined never to land in a marriage like my parents'.

As my father drove me to town one morning, I began complaining that I was sick and tired of Latin — didn't want to parse the damn stuff anymore, had had enough of Cicero, didn't care if I made a D. He turned on me in fury. "How dare you say such nonsense? Your studies are your only hope. You think you're tired of Cicero — how tired do you think Mama and I are of what we go through for you? You'd better not bring any D's home. You'll see what happens if you bring home any D's." He was white with anger, and oblivious to my tears, by the time he finished elaborating on this theme.

Instead of a green Chevrolet, my classroom now was the black Dodge he had bought with part of the Alamo Street money, or occasionally the cab of his flatbed truck, which had to be driven to town on farm errands: we needed feed and fertilizer, we crated and sold eggs. More than most teenagers, I grew up in the society of my parents, under their thumb, listening to their voices. My mother became a regular driver, too. Understanding from her first day as a farm wife that we could never earn a living here, she found work as a saleslady in a Hot Springs department store, though this scarcely lightened her workload at home. I no longer built romantic fantasies about her secret love affairs. Her closet now contained only work dresses and low-heeled shoes, and she left the house only to meet her obligations. When my mother was behind the wheel, she never used this interlude to preach. "I'm too pooped to pop," she'd joke when five o'clock came and we headed home, usually in silence.

Earl Witt still called on us; indeed, I yearned to see him more than ever. He talked of making a comeback — this evil new regime couldn't last. The town was dying, he said, bank deposits were shrinking, merchants boarding up their shops, lifelong residents moving away — all to support the ambitions of a gang of ex-marines. This was true; the judge and my father pounced on these signs as indicators that the old imperium would be restored. I listened to their speculations about what might happen in the next election, drove miles over back-country roads with them to hear favored new candidates make stump speeches. But privately I had no more hope of seeing Earl Witt's reign restored than of waking up to find that pinched waists, pointed bras, and circle skirts had vanished and we were once more welcoming the spring at 122 Alamo Street.

One afternoon Judge Witt arrived, as he so often did, with a gift for me. I must have been fourteen at the time, and I tore into the tiny package expecting a locket. Instead I found a diamond in a gold setting, not too large a diamond for my years but large enough to dumbfound my parents and me. "I thought you should have a pretty ring," he said, as shyly as a boy. "Don't think I haven't noticed how you've tried to help your parents here. And of course, we're all so proud of your record in school. I feel somehow as if I've brought hardship on your shoulders." For the first time I saw him not as our liege lord, not as the leading man in any romance of my mother's, but simply as a childless old gentleman of sixty-odd, unhappily married, with a drunken brother who went from one calamitous scrape to another; and now he was deprived of the questionable dignity his office had brought him. Indeed, he must thank God daily that the laws of the state and the nation were still not carefully enforced in this county. Embittered as I was against the reformers, I had come to realize that Earl Witt and his colleagues had stains on their consciences.

I put my arms around his neck and kissed him, laughing, thanking him, dancing in delight. I wore the ring gladly as an emblem of the old regime and the final gift of love from Earl Witt. This was almost the last glimpse I had of him; he came again once or twice, I believe, and then his visits ceased. Perhaps a few months had gone by when my mother, arriving home from work one Saturday evening, alighted from the car and burst into tears. Judge Witt was dead — of throat cancer, according to the rumor that had gone around town. But there had been no sign of throat cancer on his last visit, or of any other illness. What had killed him? More than most, we felt, we had cause to mourn him. They buried him on Monday, and because it rained heavily that day, my father refused to let me attend the funeral. Afterward, seeing that we were utterly without a protector and advocate, he abandoned his belief in a liberal restoration. "Damage is damage," he said. "It can never be undone. I must learn to live with failure."

My diamond ring brought me a very transient joy; it was stolen only a year later from a change purse I had temporarily and foolishly stored it in. I received another gift about this time, however, one that became an heirloom. Carrie and Bemont had continued to move from one lodging to the next, and my father dutifully visited them, though nowadays I used every possible excuse to avoid going with him. Mother had announced that they were Hat's responsibility rather than hers, and that it did no good for her to go. One day, however, my grandmother sent an urgent message. Mother and I must come and collect her masterwork, the crocheted bedspread. She had looped and tied the very last picot, sewn the last block in place. We hadn't seen Carrie and Bemont for over six months, so Mother and I went somewhat shamefacedly to claim my prize. They were living in half a two-family house behind the racetrack, in one of the poorest sections of town. But the parlor furniture was still more or less intact, and we settled ourselves in the hateful straight-backed chairs while Bemont took the crochet box from under the bed and placed it on the settee. I opened the lid on the heavy yards of fancywork, hundreds of lacy squares, each one precisely like the others, a web of toil, a knotted document of female dexterity and of upward striving and of respectability proclaimed. I scarcely had the will to lift it, unfold it.

"You must wash it, Velma," my grandmother commanded. "It got soiled with me working on it all these years." Indeed, the squares were marked with sweat and dirt. But they would all come clean in the water and the sunshine, white as a new ball of cotton thread.

"This is something you'll have all your life," Mother said, in awe of the thing. "You'll be using this bedspread when your own children are your age. Just think of that."

Because there was no avoiding it, I leaned over my grandmother and put my arms around her, smelled her peculiar, dirty fragrance masked by the dusting powder, kissed her cheeks, and thanked her. She was almost seventy now. In her arms, not very long ago, I had listened to a tale of princesses dancing out their slippers. In this bed, as the radio blared, I had tasted the ups and downs of modern romance, had learned the price of craving the red shoes. I hardly knew whether to embrace her or denounce her and all her works. I promised to treasure her handiwork forever — a promise I have kept, for the bedspread lies to this day, pristine and unused, inside a linen chest. As it traveled with my grandmother from dwelling to dwelling, so it has traveled with me.

A year or two later, my grandparents' penultimate tragedy occurred — predictably, given Bemont's habits and the clutter of his bedside table. Though the Model T had been turned in as scrap metal soon after Pearl Harbor, he had never given up prospecting. On the streets of Hot Springs he could always find a gambler, a down-and-outer, an optimist with no better project for the afternoon than to try to bilk a farmer. Finding a car-owning optimist was harder, but Grandpa uncovered them like veins of mica in rocks. As he always had, he careened around the county, taking the curves on two wheels, looking for wealth. These days he had no money to buy vanadium rights, but sometimes his partner pro tem would put up the capital. After all, Bemont supplied the forms to sign. Thus it was that the rocks and bottles of acid continued to multiply on his table, along with his medications, which he now received as a ward of the county.

One evening, thinking he had hold of his eyedrops, he put several drops of nitric acid into each eye. I don't quite recall how the message reached us. My father was summoned to the hospital; some surgery was performed, but only to remove the damaged tissue. Bemont had blinded himself permanently, rendering himself unfit at last to serve as his wife's caretaker. Since my father had no means of preventing it, his parents were transferred to the county home for the indigent elderly — the poorhouse, as Carrie had relentlessly predicted. Bowed down by the disgrace, my father refused to let me accompany him on visits to this place. "I don't want you to see this," he said. "There are some things you just don't need to know." He went every day of the few weeks they lived. I don't know what was in his heart on the subject of his parents then; one morning as we drove to town, he said their death would be the end of a long punishment for him.

Carrie survived Bemont by one day. There was no funeral. We paid our last respects and said goodbye to them at the Missouri Pacific depot, as their coffins were loaded into the baggage car, bound for Goshen, Indiana. As a rule, Daddy said, a body may not travel alone, but he had somehow paid extra or made some arrangement so that he was not required to chaperone my grandparents on their journey to the only piece of property they had managed to hold on to. I intend one day to visit Goshen and see whether they actually were buried in the cemetery where my grandmother had owned plots for so many years, whether the old house is still standing, with its dark green paint and gingerbread trim, the house where Carrie Abbott read the history of England

and the *Odyssey* to her son and strove for respectability and fell ill, or whether it has been bulldozed for a parking lot. I want to see whether the undertaker, according to my father's instructions, really did erect the stone.

For years after moving to the farm, Mother and I spied on 122 Alamo sporadically, as if on some repository of atomic secrets. Since the new owners had no children, they removed the cherry-tree swing and the fence, causing us to shriek when we saw the desecration. The snowball bushes, the morning-glories, the wisteria, the spirea that had grown along the fence now had nothing to cling to, and the yard took on the haphazard look of my early childhood, when there'd been only dirt and weeds and you could drive a car right up to the front steps. The new owners stripped away the rose trellises, painted our neat green trim a hideous red, never cut the lawn.

"A wilderness. A crying shame!"

They even hung the windows with heavy curtains, so we could no longer see inside.

"Everybody to his own taste, but why smother those windows like that?"

"Pitiful! Imagine what it looks like inside! Look, that old biddy even took down the clothesline."

Sometimes we stopped to call on Thelma Miller and the girls, but soon they moved away, too. (Texaco took Mr. Miller off the delivery truck and made him an executive.) In any event, the Millers had no information about 122 Alamo, because the new people were unsociable. The lady had installed one of those new automatic clothes-drying machines, so she didn't talk over the fence. Nobody ever saw them out in the yard.

Hissing, whispering, Mother and I would drive past the house a third time to inspect each new atrocity, creeping along at ten miles per hour. If a face appeared at a window, we turned away,

pretended we were strangers, mere sightseers, eyes glued on the
back entrance to the Brown mansion, which never changed at all.
Finally we gave up spying, the way that people give up visiting a
relative in prison. I saw the house just one more time, and that
was after my father's death. It had taken on a frail, vacated look, a
ghostly, rickety old boneyard of a house with the wind whistling
through the cracks

$\mathcal{F}$ISH GOTTA SWIM

MY HIGH SCHOOL adventures in love were limited by my parents' circumstances as well as by the odd ideas I had absorbed from excess reading. I was a mermaid in search of a marble prince. I had considered several candidates, unsuccessfully, but when I was about sixteen, a boy called Tommy, tall and moderately handsome, seemed to qualify. Some two dozen boys in my class fell into the "cute" category, every one of them an athlete. (Never mind that our teams lost every game.) Girls were supposed to want these boys and scorn the tuba players in the band or kids who merely showed up for classes. The top two dozen girls already had them cornered, but not a girl in the whole high school refused to join the chase.

One of my classmates, a slow-witted, unkempt, obese girl named Myrtle, had been shunted along from grade to grade. But though she could not master arithmetic, Myrtle understood who the right boys were, and she used to stand grinning at their elbows and refuse to go away in the teeth of their insults. She tormented them with love notes, which they destroyed before her face. They called her a fat turd and other names, threatened to beat her up, stole her bookbag, pretended to befriend her and then wrote her lush love notes signed with somebody else's name.

She would hang her head and blush violently, but she never fought back, and nothing permanently extinguished her hope. The guidance counselor, Miss Telliard, a high school version of Miss Love without the wooden paddles, spent a lot of time drying Myrtle's tears and pleading with her to leave the boys alone, offering them sympathy but requiring mercy and forbearance in return, recruiting the coaching staff to back her up. In her rundown saddle oxfords and greasy blue jacket, Myrtle chased the football team along the hallways and up the stairs, an unconscious parody of every girl in the school.

Tommy ranked perhaps twenty-second in the top two dozen, not swaggeringly good-looking or a first-string halfback, but so much the better, I thought. I was determined to make him mine. I was relentlessly at the top of my class, the girl who always raised her hand, who knew the answer that stumped everyone else, who made 100 percent on the test and ruined the curve — definitely not the statue in any boy's garden. But in my dreams I offered the sea witch my tongue, my feet, my pride, my grade-point average, anything. Bunking parties as a girlish pastime had given way to other games, including one called TWIRP week: The Woman Is Requested to Pay. That week, girls asked boys for dates, provided the transportation, bought the gas and hamburgers. I didn't understand that the game was fixed. The boys just arranged everything with the girls beforehand. Steadies went with steadies. This was anything but open season on men. Nevertheless, I accosted Tommy in the hall and asked if he'd go to the dance with me the next Saturday. He said yes, and I can now imagine what he endured in the locker room that week, having been trapped by the valedictorian, a tall person with legs like a wading bird's and a streak of vulnerability that you could see from across the street.

I cast bright smiles at him whenever I saw him in the hallway, and he ducked his head and smiled back. It didn't bother me that he never sought me out, or asked what the plans were, or came and leaned on my locker door, the way other football players did with their girls, so tall, so massive, just sort of swinging on the door and — quick — pushing their heads inside for a kiss and a feel. Next week, I figured, after he'd spent an evening with me, he'd have overcome his natural shyness and his hesitation. Having sampled my company and my kisses, he'd be right there by my locker door, pushing my head inside for a fast but meaningful kiss, wanting me to wear his football jacket, offering me his class ring on a golden chain to wear around my neck, to bounce suggestively around my sweater front. Somehow, I knew, I was about to be forgiven for being too tall and too gangly and the only person out of two hundred in the junior class who genuinely liked Keats's odes. I would show him, and them, that it didn't matter. Meanwhile, I had an important occasion to prepare for, girlfriends to consult about which skirt, which sweater, were they wearing loafers and socks or flats and hose, would it be cold enough for a coat, did they think, or would my leather jacket do? I looked better in the jacket, less like somebody on the way to Sunday school. I arranged to spend the night with a girlfriend, who also had a date with a football player, her steady. We planned to pick the boys up in her car. She would drive. Tommy and I would be alone in the back seat. Friday afternoon, I managed to stop my man in the hallway long enough to tell him when to expect me. He was all grins and shyness, enough to melt my heart.

I spent the next afternoon at my girlfriend's house shampooing my hair, doing my nails. Not an inch of my body escaped my attention. I filed, brushed, polished, cleaned, clipped, plucked, curled, and groomed until I was perfect. I had bought a new lipstick, with a little mirror attached to the tube (two dollars extra). I took a bubble bath before I dressed. I put perfume on my pulse spots and promised myself to reapply it before leaving.

I used every trick magazines could suggest, and a few left over from *Gone With the Wind*, such as pinching my cheeks to make them rosy. I considered eating a large dinner so I wouldn't appear hungry at the dance, but that seemed silly. I measured my waist. A fat twenty-three. How had Scarlett gotten it down to sixteen? I sucked my stomach in brutally, considered and rejected the idea of wearing a panty girdle.

Standing in the bathroom with the door locked, half an hour before time to leave, I inspected the effect of Kleenex in the bra cups, wondering whether it was worth the risk. No, big breasts weren't even what men wanted, just think of Lauren Bacall, only I really was awfully small compared with most football players' girls, not to mention Grace Kelly. The phone rang, and I somehow knew it tolled for me. I stopped fidgeting with the Kleenex and the mirror and stood there. After a long time, my girlfriend knocked.

"Hey, I've got some news. Tommy isn't coming. He says he can't talk to you, but he told me to tell you he just can't make it. He said to tell you he was sorry." She sounded calm and noncommittal. Happens every day, nothing to get excited about. I knew that being stood up was a social catastrophe in the same category as being abandoned at the altar or left pregnant. A girl that could have this done to her wasn't worth much. She wasn't desirable enough, did not evoke enough masculine respect. Could not expect the rest of the male community to rally in her defense. Could not even expect her girlfriends to be indignant; only cool and slightly embarrassed. In each hand I held the folded Kleenex I had so recently removed from my brassiere. Each fingernail was perfectly manicured and polished bright pink. My tongue was as inoperative as if the sea witch had extracted it and fed it to the sharks. ,

"I can't call off my date," my friend continued through the door. "I know you wouldn't want me to. Mom and Dad are going to be here watching TV. They'd love to have you, they said. Honestly, I haven't got time to drive you home. I guess you could tag along to the dance with us, if you want to. Maybe that's what you should do. But I'm afraid Tommy might be there with somebody else."

I opened the bathroom door and saw the concern on her face. "No thanks, I guess I'll just stay here and watch TV." I wasn't angry with Tommy. I had reached womanhood: I internalized the event as neatly as Madame Bovary swallowed the poison. Forgiveness in my heart, I cast myself numbly into the sea foam. I should have known better, I should never have asked him. When at last I reached the privacy of my own bedroom, I believe I must have wept a good deal. I gave up eating. I spent long hours in silence, without moving. I refused to return to school for several days This was my first sustained experience with humiliation and grief. I'd no idea how to escape from this dark cave, where my own foolishness had chained me to the wall (it never occurred to me that Tommy had been foolish or cruel).

My parents never asked me exactly what happened, though my mother seemed to know without being told, for she kept muttering, in my general direction, "Stupid, rude boys. You're better off not to worry about them." She had been the belle of the county, with suitors swarming around the door by the time she was sixteen. One wrote her sonnets and threatened suicide. She had had six or seven proposals by the time she found my father. People still teased her about her boyfriends, and she in turn teased me about all the fathers I might have had but didn't.

My father was angry, though I couldn't tell at what. He had been opposed to the TWIRP dance anyway, a stupid idea, just a chance for young girls to get their feelings hurt and expose themselves to ridicule. So I could hardly describe my emotional bruises to him now, and in any case, I had defied him. How could I expect him to comfort me? He had, after all, spoken his mind about headstrong girls and drugstore cowboys who had football jackets now but would end up pumping gas for a living and why didn't I just forget it and translate fifty lines of Virgil for extra credit the way my Latin teacher had suggested, instead of going off to some dance? I didn't need to worry about men at my tender age, he thundered. His ranting was a kind of ultra-high-frequency message that no woman could live the life of the body in tandem with the life of the mind. You must choose — be the servant of men or an independent creature. But I was the person who had rewritten *Little Women* in order to marry Jo to Laurie. I still had no idea that Jo March, with her handsome suitor whom she oh-so-sensibly rejects and her eventual cozy marriage and gemütlich boys' school, was a fake. I was beginning to understand, however, why so few female names appeared on the spines of leather-bound volumes. How did you love men and have a brain at the same time? I had no answers, but my father's preaching suddenly alienated me and, more than anything else, gave me strength to show up for school once more.

Tommy and I never spoke to each other again or looked each other in the eye. I pretended he was in another dimension, and avoided the floor where his locker was. I had dreaded being the subject of gossip, but — final humiliation — no one except me seemed to care. I wondered at the gap between my stories and my life. I hardened into my role as class brain. I'd knock the curve so high those football players would all flunk.

In spite of my father — indeed, in spite of myself — I found other boys, with other lessons for me. One of them was also a football player, who seldom showed up for practice but somehow acquired the coveted jacket, probably by stealing it. Billy and I worked on the school yearbook together, which required frequent visits to the printing plant in a village nearby. He always drove his old Ford, which always broke down. I sat in the front seat while he tinkered with the carburetor, happy that although the car really wouldn't start, he wanted to kiss me. He was less reliable even than his Ford, and as marginal socially as I was. His grades were so hopeless that he didn't mind necking with the valedictorian. He didn't know what a valedictorian was. Grades, F's or A's, were without any significance to Billy. He never took me on a standard date, but he never demolished me either.

I didn't think of these encounters in the car as love, or of Billy as a lover. Lovers were tall and handsome, called for you at the door, gave you their class ring, sent you gardenias, gave your mother something to gossip with other mothers about. Other girls had lovers, steadies, and wore little pins on their sweaters. One night another girl's boyfriend, also called Tommy, cornered me in her kitchen and kissed me until my head swam with pleasure and desire and I had to hold on to him to stand up. "I wanted you to know what this was like," he explained, while I was still too dizzy to see. "I didn't know if anybody had ever kissed you." I was a charity case, but it was okay.

Love notes were part of adolescence then — secret, identical, spelled out in pencil on lined paper in the illiterate hand most high school boys wrote, having laid aside all that Miss Love and her colleagues had ever taught them. "You sure are one nice girl, and I hope we can see each other some time." "I sure do hope you like me as much as I like you. I'll never forget what happened Saturday night " "You sure are one sweet girl, and I like you." This Tommy began writing me such notes, and once showed up at my house, unannounced, driving a battered old car. His girlfriend either didn't know or didn't care, and whenever we managed to get in an hour's kissing, he made no promises and offered no trophies. Nevertheless, my wounds healed a little.

Another boy invited me to go driving, and without even asking if I'd first like a barbecue sandwich, he headed straight for the airport parking lot, deserted at night since the airport closed at 5 P M He was one of those unremarkable boys who just

showed up at school. He wanted more than kisses — not everything, just more than I had done before. I was terrified of preg-
nancy and convinced that one time was all it took; indeed, I
figured you could probably absorb those fearful little male cells
through your fingers — a comic but sensible enough attitude for
one not yearning to become a housewife at age seventeen. I was
deeply ashamed, however, of my own cowardice. Having been
raised on romantic fiction, I thought it was a disgrace to abstain
from sex, like going to the end of the diving board and not
jumping. Luckily for me, the young man was not a reader of
novels. He wanted to go to some big college in the East and
wasn't running any risks. He knew about rubbers but neither
trusted them nor had the courage to buy any. That didn't mean
you couldn't unbutton buttons and unzip zippers. Neither of us
swore that we loved each other, but the little quick places responded urgently, and he seemed to like mine fine, in spite of my
daunting grade-point average. For once I forgot about grades.

We spent many evenings that summer experimenting with
self-control in the airport parking lot. It was good exercise. It
made me happy, gave me courage. Emotionally and physically,
there was parity to what we did. You could do these things with a
boy and still be friends. No important vows or gametes were
exchanged, and nobody had to commit suicide. I hadn't yet
realized that sensuality between equals might be a better bargain
than romance, yet for the first time, in the crowded theater of my
mind, the marble prince and the mermaid got pushed temporarily off-stage. Casanova, my old friend, had tried to tell me that
love might be entirely dispensable but tenderness never could be.
Poor old rake, poor panting Casanova, disillusioned in every
encounter, restlessly seeking another. And a great deal easier to
have in one's arms than Tristan and Romeo and the love-death.
Still, in my youth and ignorance, I had no intention of renounc-
ing romance.

$\mathcal{L}$OVE STORY

I'VE LITTLE TO SAY here about my college years. Miss Telliard, the guidance counselor who tried to look after poor Myrtle, who couldn't learn, tried just as earnestly to look after me. Any number of famous colleges, she said, would be interested in admitting me and offering financial aid. In those days, colleges were not yet practicing affirmative action, but they were willing to consider bright kids from strange places such as Arkansas. Radcliffe College, among others, had responded to Miss Telliard's inquiries and was ready to make a deal. But when I brought this news home, half terrified myself, my father's face went pale. No, it was out of the question. I could not go. It didn't matter that they offered tuition and almost full expenses. He could not bear to send me away, he said, even if he could bear it, he could not afford the train fare. How would I like spending Christmas all by myself in my college room? I argued vigorously against him, but then my enthusiasm faded. The image of myself weeping in an empty college dining room on Christmas Eve (like the young Scrooge) was crushing. I could not picture myself in Cambridge, Massachusetts, among a covey of lawyers' and doctors' daughters.

Having settled this question, my father set out his requirements for a college, as follows: it must be nearby, cheap, and a women's college, preferably one at some distance from a men's college. Thus, by process of elimination, I enrolled at Texas State College for Women in Denton, Texas. I did well there, as always; in fact, my zeal for books was beginning to make even my father uneasy. My mother, wondering if I'd ever get married, sent me off with the exhortation to "find you a Texas millionaire," and she spent the summer stitching beautiful dresses and "dressmaker suits," as she called them, for me to wear to parties, dances, and football games in Dallas. After all, Texas A & M, a tough military school (safely two-hundred miles from the female campus), was the brother school of the college they had chosen for me. My mother imagined that handsome, uniformed Aggies would escort me to a succession of football games on various Texas campuses.

But the pretty dresses and suits stayed on their hangers. I attended one Aggie football game in Dallas with a uniformed escort who seemed more dead than alive. Custom demanded that every Aggie and his date stand upright throughout the entire afternoon, including half time — it was considered a small enough gesture toward the brave warriors on the playing field. Since chivalry mandated mercy toward female feet, my date rented a cushion for me to stand on, and I took off my high heels. We ate hot dogs afterward, since he couldn't afford a restaurant, and he kissed me cautiously in the car. Apart from that, I went through college almost without dating.

Surprisingly, my father's career as a bookmaker sputtered back into life from time to time. Sid McMath, the scourge of Hot Springs gambling, had gone on to the governorship, promising a new epoch of prosperity. But Earl Witt had been right about this handsome young reformer whose picture had been approvingly published in *Life* and every other national magazine. McMath had no program for a state that desperately needed a program (just anything would have done); his goal had been limited to self-advancement. His administration soon went down in a scandal over payoffs in the highway department, and McMath retired from politics.

Meanwhile, the old, crooked habits of Hot Springs reasserted themselves. The horse books reopened, on a small and precarious scale. Because my father had been Earl Witt's man and because affection for old times still lingered, and because he was known as a crackerjack, even among the younger men, he found work as a bookmaker occasionally and commuted from the farm. Having extracted obedience from me in the matter of choosing a college, he struggled all the harder for money. To pay my college tuition one year when he couldn't get a job at any of the downtown joints, he patched up his old quarrel with Johnny Strand (for who cared any longer who had or had not betrayed Mayor McLaughlin?), and the two of them set up their own illegal horse book in the Strand garage. They had two phones installed and got the racing results long distance. They laid off bets to establishments in Memphis and Little Rock. Their credit was good: they paid up, as gambling gentlemen always paid up.

Because Hat was smart and Johnny lucky, they usually had a profit after they filled their payoff envelopes, which they delivered surreptitiously to their customers. At sunset they would count up their cash like bandits and divide it. Cops and politicians got no rake-offs from clandestine shops like this; correspondingly, they offered no protection. Daddy and Johnny kept their ears peeled for the sound of a police car and were always ready to stash the sheets and flee into the woods behind the house.

Now and then Daddy would call me at college to tell me what their take had been, the bookmaker once more instead of the careworn farmer. He never sounded frightened. Indeed, the danger whetted his skills, and he loved the game of it. My zeal for knowledge intensified as I reflected that my father was risking the penitentiary for my benefit — a potentially deadly flirtation now that Earl Witt no longer sheltered him. Besides that, he paid no income tax. By that date, in the mid-1950s, all bookmakers were required by federal law to register as such and purchase a kind of license, a bookmaking "stamp," by which ruse the Internal Revenue Service kept track of them. Needless to say, Hat Abbott did not buy one.

Each summer I returned to pitch in on the farm or hold down some small job in Hot Springs. My last summer at home, a season in hell, I worked the soda fountain at Candle's Drugstore, one of a chain, a position brokered, as all things were, through connections. Jobs were scarce — why hire a college kid when you could get a family man to do the same work? But somebody had gotten my mother a job at one Candle store, and she asked Mr. Candle to give me a job at another one. My father, growing increasingly hopeless, did the farm chores that summer and watched Mother and me come and go, the three of us exhausted even at the breakfast table.

My high school cohorts had been absorbed into adult life as though wiped up by a sponge. Even Myrtle, who'd pursued the football team up and down the halls and failed everything, had married a fellow with a steady job and had a baby on the way. Others had married and gone to work at the telephone company or waiting tables at the Bluebell Café or typing invoices at radio station KTHS (Kum To Hot Springs). Some people had vanished without a forwarding address, searching for work in Kansas or Missouri, trying to start a business for themselves, learning to install wall-to-wall carpeting, working on a used car lot. Billy had been arrested in Missouri, though nobody knew for what. My partner of the airport parking lot had been unable to meet the academic demands of Yale and had suffered a nervous breakdown. I began to understand why my classmates had refused to memorize Keats or read *A Tale of Two Cities*. Books gave you no advantage.

The football queens and maids efficiently traded in their glamour for aprons and diapers. At three o'clock on a summer afternoon, they changed into clean shorts and peasant blouses, twined their locks around big pink curlers, put fresh sunsuits on their babies, and drove their Chevrolets to the Piggly Wiggly, where they congregated in the cool places beside the lettuce, feeding the babies animal crackers. Once in a while I'd hurtle past them on my way to buy a quart of milk, and they'd nod to me. If I paused to chat, they spoke only of the buff brick homes they intended to build any day now. Nobody used red brick anymore, only pale yellow. Their bathrooms would be paved with pink tiles, with toilets to match, in a shade called roseblush. Their refrigerators, matching their cooktops, would be avocado, with special little containers for the eggs and shelves in the door interiors.

These houses would have carports, dens, playrooms, and wonders unheard of by the lower middle class before this time. Some couples had already bought their lots, and the girls took strong positions on what section of town would be the "nicest." They used words like *equity*, spoke of contractors, septic tanks, and trips they'd made to Little Rock to view model homes, plan books, plumbing. I was racked with contempt for these women, as well as a passionate desire to be among them, arguing the merits of Kenmore versus Westinghouse. They were the pride of the city, beyond praise, beautiful young women ready to take the curlers out of their hair and get supper on the table by 5:30, founders of the next generation, what Life Was All About, the guests at Tupperware parties. They'd all be grandmothers before I even got my degree. I still possessed my virginity and had fewer prospects than ever of becoming a wife and mother. College had only made me weirder — a dingo among poodles.

Phil Candle, drugstore king, wore cheap clothes and drove

expensive automobiles — Packards, Cadillacs — trading for a new model every year, the way rich people were expected to do. His current wife, Gladys, drove a white Buick convertible. She had a simple, bottle-blond glamour. Gladys's job was to display herself, as part of Phil's affordables. She never put the top up, even in a rainstorm. Her platinum hair rode the wind like broom straws, jewels gleamed at her neck, and she handled the wheel by her palms, as if her plum-tipped nails would never be dry enough for any normal task. Her convertible and his sedan cruised the streets perpetually, pleasure yachts among rowboats, leaving a dark wake of envy behind them.

The Candle's I worked in stood on a bleak, sun-baked corner shared with a plate glass company, a drive-in liquor store, and a gas station. I worked eight hours a day seven days a week for twenty-five dollars cash and no overtime — an entirely illegal arrangement, since working women were supposed to have a day off, but Candle had evidently fixed the Labor Department. My mother cashiered at another Candle's store that summer, same hours. Her salary was thirty-five dollars, but since they took deductions out of her pay, my take-home, at age twenty, was actually larger than hers. The shifts ran from 7 A.M. to 3 one day and 3 P.M. to 11 at night the next. Candle reasoned that he was actually giving us every second day as a holiday: from 3 P.M. to 3 P.M. was a day, wasn't it? Daddy sneered at this reasoning and longed to report Candle to the authorities. However, we were desperate for the money. My father told me I should be grateful that I could save all my earnings for college instead of having to help support the family. Very true, O Socrates. But he also remarked, for the first time in my life, that women couldn't earn their way in the world. They needed a husband. "Now you tell me," I retorted. "Thanks a lot."

The work I did was clean and not backbreaking, but not even in school had I been so scrutinized. I stood behind the soda

fountain all day, except when venturing across the store to sell
lipstick or mosquito repellent or Kotex or Johnny Mops. At the
fountain I mostly made Cokes, squirting a little syrup on ice and
filling the glass with soda. The store had two tables, where
neighborhood boys settled and read comic books for free, sipping
a fifteen-cent Coke until the last sliver of ice had melted. I prayed
for a milkshake order, which entitled me to run the blender like a
real soda jerk and wash the container and the glass.

Candle's did not give lunch breaks. I ate my homemade sandwich standing up, and was told to keep track of any coffee I drank
so it could be deducted from my salary. Phil hired spies to check
up on the help. Were we loafing on the job? Shortchanging customers? Embezzling? Failing to push the specials? Eating free
ice cream cones? Anybody might turn out to be a Candle secret
agent. Reading on the job was strictly forbidden — "This ain't
the lieberry," Phil pointed out. His instructions were to look for
tasks when there weren't any. So my second week I took the soda
fountain apart and cleaned it, scraping away strata of sugary
grime embedded with dead insects and wads of chewing gum and
petrified bits of paper napkins pre-dating the Great Depression.
We had one huge keg of premium ice cream that we used for
cones, and another, compounded of waste lard, that we put in the
milkshakes. (It made a difference of three cents a shake, but I
always sneaked and used the good stuff.) By the time I finished
cleaning these ice cream kegs, I had been cured of my appetite for
ice cream and my belief in Louis Pasteur. If there had been such a
thing as filth-borne illness, the whole neighborhood would have
perished years before. After overhauling the fountain, I tidied up
the shelves around the store, which were equally lethal. Behind
the thin front line of relatively new merchandise, I discovered
little casks of makeup that must have been there before the Pure
Food and Drug Act was passed, jars with rusted lids, bottles of
liniment with prices ten years out of date. I carried box after box

to the trash. The dirt turned my hands and uniform black, but I was sorry to be finished, for then I had to go back to the soda fountain. Sitting down was against Candle's rules. "Grab a rag and dust something if you ain't got nothing better to do. A sittin'-down clerk keeps customers out." So I stood the whole eight hours, though I soon stopped worrying about the spies — you could spot their hangdog expression from across the street. You never knew, though, when Gladys might breeze past in the Buick, squinting toward our plate glass windows.

I was two-dimensionally thin, and my white seersucker uniform hung on me like a nightshirt. Terrified at what my life might turn out to be, depressed, I drank coffee constantly. From the first day my feet dominated my life, suffering feet that invaded my mind and denuded it of its powers. I wore sneakers, loafers, nurse's footgear, and Hushpuppies, spent my paycheck on Dr. Scholl's shoe pads, bought a rubber mat to stand on, but nothing helped. Mother said you finally got used to it, if you stood there long enough. My counterpart on the opposite shift, Olive, a divorced woman in her thirties, actually came to work in high heels and stood there for eight hours in them. I knew what the high heels meant: "Here I am, turn me on, I'm looking for a man." If Olive could find a man, she wouldn't have to work in the drugstore. My fantasies ran to beds, armchairs, hassocks, footstools, meadows, basins of cool water.

The store was sometimes busy, but few of the customers made small talk, let alone conversation. These were quaint times, in a quaint place, imbued with Baptist modesty and feminine nervousness. Just coming into a drugstore seemed to embarrass people, seemed always to expose some bodily function or shortcoming or physical need. I was charged with the sale of all sanitary pads and tampons — women asked for them in agonized whispers. (The occasional husband on a mission for his wife always approached the pharmacist. Most women thought it inconsiderate and downright slovenly to send their husbands out for *that*, and most husbands wouldn't do it.) Youths would circle the store ten times before entering and asking for condoms, an item that did not exist so far as I was concerned and that I certainly was not permitted to sell. A man appeared one day and asked quite audibly for a breast pump, an object so horrifying that people within earshot abruptly left the store. Prescription-buyers were ashamed of being ill; even magazine purchasers managed to look crestfallen. Seekers after birthday presents also seemed ashamed, no doubt because they hadn't made the trip to a department store and were settling for Candle's thousand-year-old dusting powder. I gave up on trying to make friends and fell back on women's magazines, which I read furtively behind the fountain.

My mother and I came and went like shadows, arriving home at midnight after the late shift, and at four the next day, with a twenty-two hour reprieve until it was time to leave at two the following afternoon. Besides sleeping, we spent much of that "day off" washing our uniforms and our hair and whitening our shoes, and Mother kept up with the housework — doing the laundry, taking care of the milk and eggs, churning the butter, making cottage cheese, cooking a big meal so there'd be left-overs, all the tasks that men could never learn to do. I helped when I could, but hypocritically allowed her to spare me. "You need your sleep," she'd say, as I arose shamefacedly at ten to find the washing already flapping on the line. How was I to escape the fate of women, the washtubs, the loneliness, the self-sacrifice? She spared my father, too. "I'd never trust your daddy with the churning," she said. "I couldn't do it to suit your mother," he reasoned.

My mind turned to a scrap-metal heap. I forgot about music. I forgot about reading at bedtime. I turned the light off and fell dead. The bookcase stood behind its door, untouched. When my father and I tried to talk to each other, it always ended in a disagreement, sometimes with both of us yelling and my mother pleading with us to pipe down. Among other issues, we had begun to argue over what he referred to as the Southern Way of Life, shouting angrily at each other about whether black people ought to work side by side with whites and earn the same wages, whether they ought to attend the same schools.

It was 1955, the year after the Supreme Court had ruled against segregated schools. I was disheartened, astonished to find my father, the Roosevelt supporter, the defender of the down-trodden poor, on the wrong side of these arguments. "Where do you get these radical notions?" he would demand. "What has turned you against your homeplace, against our way of life? Have you become a Communist?" And I would reply, scathingly, that my radical notions came from having actually read the U.S. Con-stitution, that he ought to read the Constitution sometime him-self. I would suggest that he reflect on his own background — how could a person like him line himself up with a lot of phony, rednecked, would-be Southern aristocrats? Shaking with wrath, he would shout that white people weren't meant to live with black people, that you couldn't force people to do what they refused to do, and that he and every right-thinking white parent would die in the streets before they saw their children in inte-grated schools. Mustering every rhetorical trick I knew, I'd re-spond with equal passion, higher decibels, and we'd continue until my mother cried out that she'd go crazy if we didn't stop and pleaded for an hour's peace in the house. My romance with my father was definitely over. Yet later I wondered if he hadn't sided with the conservatives to prepare himself for the coming rebellion in me. Never before had I seen him ally himself so solidly with the know-nothings.

After such encounters, I looked forward to going to work. Two pharmacists ran the store, but on different shifts from mine, so that in a given day I'd see both of them. The morning man was pale blond Albert, just out of pharmacy school, whose wife and baby belonged to the Piggly Wiggly crowd. Albert talked a lot about the buff brick ranch house that he secretly feared he would never acquire. Four years of college had failed to turn him into skilled labor. He gave in to every jobber, selecting exactly what the public would never buy, festooning the store with racks of shoe polish kits and bug traps that didn't work and sets of plastic dinnerware and iced tea glasses nobody wanted. But we'd run out of aspirin or Vaseline or Absorbine Junior or Ex-Lax or some other essential item. I assumed he knew how to fill prescriptions, as there were no known fatalities during his tenure. He disapproved of my reading, and made strict rules about how often the help (me) could use the toilet, an unutterably filthy hole at the back of the store. When he had nothing better to do, he would come and drink coffee with me and size me up.

"Fatten up a little. You're too bony to attract a man."

"Do you like that all-girl college you go to? You'd better transfer to some decent place, with men."

And he raced me for customers so his total would look better than mine.

Afternoons, Willie Flanders came in. A man of sixty or more, he lived in a garage apartment nearby, and his only ambition was to get to closing time without dying. Perched on a stool in the pharmacist's booth, he put away a daily pint of rye in judiciously spaced sips. He sent salesmen packing and refused to do the slightest thing to improve the sales record of the store. He laughed at my cleanup efforts. "Don't do the little twerp any favors. You want to make him richer than he is?"

Mr. Flanders's friends often came for private consultations at the booth, and several of them proved to have a vice I had never heard of — they were paregoric hounds. Respectable men — church deacons, Elks, Lions — apparently drank this stuff for kicks. They were always in a hurry. Mr. Flanders would slip his addicts a small brown bottle, and I'd supply large glasses of water as a chaser while they downed the dose. They'd shake and shudder as the stuff hit home. Dope fiends, I thought, but they went on back to being church deacons or Lions or whatever they pleased. I suspected that Mr. Flanders was pocketing extra money out of this, but I didn't mind, and he didn't mind how many magazines and books I read. After nine at night, when Gladys had cruised home, Mr. Flanders would lead me to a stool and command me to sit on it, and I'd read in the vacant neon glow while he finished his pint and the stoplight at the corner turned from red to green for nobody.

But one day in early July, another Mr. Flanders appeared, the old man's son. I'd been told that he was coming. "My boy, Will, just out of the navy," Mr. Flanders had said by way of explanation. "Kinda down on his luck at the moment. He's going to spend the summer with me, live with me at my apartment, kinda crowded, but I don't mind. Maybe look for work. Kinda needs a place to rest up before moving on to the next thing." That sounded dismal enough. But then the son came in and seated himself on a fountain stool.

"You're Shirley," he said. "Dad's had a lot to say about you. He thinks you're smart. I'm Will Flanders, Will James Flanders, the middle name's the way they tell the difference between my old man and me. I just got out of the navy. Would you mind if I sat and talked? I could buy you a Coke. It's nice and cool in here."

In his khakis and T-shirt, he was almost as skinny as I was, but his shoulders were broad and his arms lean and muscular, the way a sailor's were supposed to be. His black hair was mercilessly cropped, and his eyes were dark brown. He said he was a late-night reader, a habit he'd been unable to break ashore. He'd been through World War II on destroyers and mine sweepers and aircraft carriers and landing craft in the South Pacific, not primarily as a warrior but as a photographer. He'd been mustered out as chief photographer's mate, which sounded at least as impressive as rear admiral to me. Some of his pictures had appeared in *Life*, and many more in the newspapers. At my eager request, he brought me his album of prints and clips. A photographer, an artist! Famous — a *Life* photographer! He told me all this shyly, apologetically, as though I might ask why he hadn't spent his time torpedoing Japanese warships or ack-acking kamikazes or releasing depth charges or whatever men did on destroyers and mine sweepers and aircraft carriers. He also told me he was forty years old, having enlisted the year I was born. The huge gulf of years set me instantly at ease. Here was Odysseus. I knew how to play this role. (Though I have his letters and the photographs he gave me, I still wonder whether Will was not a daydream, fabricated in my own mind, as I always had fabricated love.)

We set up as friends at the soda fountain. "I'm a night owl," Will explained. "I read until almost sunup most days. Then I sleep till noon. Can I come and keep you company in the afternoons?" On days when I got off at three, Will would turn up about one, smelling of coffee and soap, his bristly crew cut still damp from the shower, his chin freshly shaved. On the days I arrived at three, he showed up about four. He'd break for supper, bringing back hamburgers for the two of us, or if the store was very busy he'd duck out for a walk or a movie. But if I was there on the evening shift, Will was there, too.

Mr. Flanders sat in the pharmacist's booth, drinking his pint and minding his own business. But the Albert days made me uneasy, for Albert hated Will, or feared he'd lead to trouble with Phil. He had no real right to order him out of the store — half the boys in the neighborhood just came and sat — but he did what he could to drive him off.

"Still living off the old man, huh?"

"Did you pay for that cuppa coffee, Will James?"

"Phil oughta charge you rent on that fountain stool."

"Now I know the meaning of drugstore cowboy."

These spitballs made me flinch, but Will was an old hand at ignoring insolent puppies. For my part, I tended vigorously to business when Will was there, rushed to aid customers before they could remember what they wanted, shined up the fountain and the showcases, gift-wrapped the perfumes and dusting powders in such cascades of curly bows that Albert grumbled about wasted supplies. Indeed, Phil Candle had never been so well served. I stopped worrying about Gladys. Will said she was nearsighted but too vain to wear glasses and couldn't have seen it if everybody in the store had been stark naked.

On my late days, the store would usually be empty by six or seven, and instead of aching feet and boredom, I had a storyteller. Voyages, wars. He'd been chief photographer aboard the aircraft carrier *Saratoga* and head of the photo lab at Admiral Nimitz's headquarters. As a combat photographer, he had flown, actually flown, in those tiny planes that shot off the deck and screamed through the skies with puffballs of explosives around them and somehow found the steel splinter and landed on it again.

"Didn't you feel free, doing that?" I begged. "Didn't you love being up in the sky that way? Wasn't it the most exciting thing you ever did?"

"God, no. The noise was earsplitting. It's a miracle I can hear anything right now. I was frightened out of my wits. We all were. You don't know what it's like to be frightened until somebody shoots at you, or you're running out of fuel and not sure you can make it home. I took pictures of people dying, planes being blown out of the sky. Please don't fall for the notion that war is glamorous. It's the ugliest, most boring thing there is. Where did you get the idea that fighter-bombers are so much more interesting than ice cream kegs? Being on shipboard is more boring than working at Candle's. You can't imagine how you count the hours. At least you can walk out of Candle's."

Will had been everywhere, whereas all my stories came out of my books. But he said that for his money, books were plenty good enough. He didn't know the history of English literature by heart, as I fancied I did, and he was far from literary. But he was a fast and avid reader and would take on anything. I ardently believed now in Good Literature, written chiefly by Englishmen (a notion my teachers had pounded into me) and no longer trusted my father's catholicism in books. But Will read everything — Kipling, Ernie Pyle, Somerset Maugham, James Michener, Pearl S. Buck, any chroniclers of Asia and the South Pacific. I'd already gone through most of Maugham, and we took on Michener together. I was in my most intense John Keats phase, and Will had never read Keats. He headed off to the library and appeared the next afternoon with several volumes in his hand, and we read together when the store cleared out. It drove Albert crazy to have Will at the soda fountain reciting Keats's odes — one irritating, incomprehensible ne'er-do-well contemplating another, and who knew what effect it might have on trade?

Emotionally I had journeyed from Cornel Wilde to Keats, this frail, racked youth, five feet tall at maturity and almost two centuries dead. His language spoke to my mind quite readily, stanzas embroidered with the conceits of Romanticism and the ornate locutions of the Augustan Age. Sovran shrines? Cloudy trophies? Melancholy fits? Will was no stranger to melancholy fits himself, or to temples of delight that you fail to recognize until the moment that joy breaks your heart, or to pleasure that turns to poison while the bee-mouth sips — or to any of the other delicate, erotic metaphors that delighted me so but that Will understood better than I. He told me his own romance, how he had chosen a wife in California and married her six months before

Pearl Harbor was bombed. They grew to hate each other; she was unfaithful. Late in the war, she sent him a note and told him it was over. She wanted a divorce. Not long afterward, Will was wounded. "I caught shrapnel in the head and shoulder," he told me, "but not so badly that I couldn't walk to the ship's dispensary. I remember walking down the long corridor as if I were watching myself, endless miles of passageway that led to where the doctor was, and I kept hearing funny little swishings behind me. It was a corpsman swabbing up my blood. I was convinced it was some other man leaving bloody footprints on the shiny deck. And that's the way it was when I got the note. I could not see that it was me bleeding. It had to be someone else."

Back in San Diego, after the war was over, he had gone to visit his wife's younger sister, a married woman and a new mother. I found this rather frightening, this real-life sharing of bedmates. Was this what grown-ups did? The romance had lasted several years, then she had to put an end to it. "I'll always love you," she promised. Will had gone from there to a full-scale breakdown, compounded, he thought, of battle shock, the lost wife, and the lost lover. He recovered, went back to active duty. But he was broken, he said, and finally took the medical discharge he was offered, and after divorcing himself from the navy, severed connections with his camera as well, and now had time to sit on a soda fountain stool and read poetry with me.

Having no romantic stories of my own to tell, I fell back on Keats's life, which Will knew nothing about, and explained how the poet constantly thought of his diseased lungs and how little time he had to live, which gave the poems their immediacy and passion, I thought, but Will said they were as close an account as any of what happens when you drink too much, or even when you read too much, and why some people get addicted to it, that falling through a trapdoor into a book, that snuffing out of consciousness, and the birdsong that obliterates reality like a drug. No one except my father had ever read poetry with me, or so willingly dallied in abstractions. No male acquaintance of mine had ever wished to speak of love. The gulf of years between us, that wide and reassuring moat, perceptibly narrowed.

He came every day that July and August. I began to set the clock by him. I knew that he would appear. I toyed with the idea that he wouldn't come. What if he didn't? Would I care? Of course not. And then one day he didn't. The clock hands clicked unproductively. Will did not come. I sagged against the edge of the soda fountain, fighting back tears, and waited on the customers in a dream. "Why are you so droopy?" my mother said when we drove home together that night. But I couldn't answer. Could not talk. Devastated by my own devastation, I wondered if I had begun to love this man, thin, with a crew cut, ridiculously old, divorced, burnt-out, awe-inspiringly experienced in sex, at least by comparison with me. Who knew how many women there had been in the port cities, in Yokohama, Macao, Hong Kong, Sydney, women he'd never even told me about?

The next morning, old Mr. Flanders, leery of his errand, wondering just how far things might have gone, scuttled in and out of the store, dodging Albert and bringing me the first of the many letters Will would write me that year. "My darling," he began. His darling. Wow. "Seems I've been sick. Nothing major, I think. Yesterday afternoon I slept through until too late to phone you at the store. I missed you terribly, even though asleep. I hope you missed me, too, but not enough to hurt. I'll be there today."

That afternoon I told him I was in love with him and I hoped he wouldn't be shocked. He spoke quite calmly. "I don't see anything shocking about two people loving one another. Please tell me why you expected me to be shocked? All I want is to love you, too."

"How do you mean?"

"I mean any way you choose. Sitting here on this stool reading poems, or talking about my life or yours, or walking down the street, or drinking too much coffee, or any other way you want to be with me. With strings or without."

Without was the way I chose. One evening, when I was certain he'd be alone, I finished my supper, showered, and put on a fresh dress, then borrowed my parents' car and drove to Will's address. Though I had never been there before, I knew the little side street where his father lived, in an apartment over a garage, with just enough space for two. I parked the car at a distance, in case Mr. Flanders somehow came home early, and made my way back along the shadowy street, lined with dark trees and full of summer crickets singing. Will waited at the top of the stairs, perhaps dreading the encounter more than I did (an inexperienced, headstrong girl, trouble). Men I met later would have their own ideas about seduction, that a woman needs to be tricked or coerced or trapped, but Will had seduced me already, or perhaps I had seduced myself.

On those rare mornings when my dreams are lucid and pure, just before I wake, Will still takes me in his arms and kisses me, and I still shake with fear — of violating all my parents' teachings, of losing my virginity to a man I had no intention of marrying, of having a baby, of having to live in Hot Springs the rest of my days. These qualms turned me frigid for what seemed a long time, but we proceeded. He trembled as much as I did, which reassured me. My terror soon gave way to a strong desire to appear passionate, which in turn gave way to what I assumed *was* passion. I was horrified when he produced that object of shame, a rubber. Frantically checking back through all the rubberless literary love scenes I could call to mind, I protested that rubbers weren't romantic, and besides, they didn't work. I wanted to quit and put my clothes on. But Will gently explained that I must listen to him in this matter. This was the only way, unless I happened to have a diaphragm, a word he then had to define.

I wonder if memories of this encounter with a nervous, cerebral schoolgirl ever awoke him from sleep, as they have sometimes pleasantly awakened me, as I dream of savoring him and discovering that he could savor me — my discovery of playfulness in what I had always assumed was a deadly solemn ritual. As though the event had been filmed, I recollect him naked and abed, his vulnerability, the sweat we sweated and the odd, embarrassing noises our bodies made as we sincerely strove to reach the heights in the swelter with not even an electric fan to cool us, his willingness to wait for me and teach me, the pleasure in his face and eyes and voice, as though I were the most accomplished partner a man ever had.

Will was too old for me. He had no future. A few days later I went back to school, without returning to his bed. He wrote to me almost every day that year, and I carelessly kept only a handful of his letters. He called me his duchess, which I liked even as I privately found it ludicrous, and he spoke of his love for me and the source of strength he said I had become for him. I had no other suitor that year, and was eager for the mail to arrive, though I scarcely knew how to handle the passion he expressed for me, this undemanding love. Because there were now several hundred miles between us, I responded with more eagerness than I felt. Rereading his letters, I see that I offered him reckless encouragement about himself, about me, that I flirted with him, teased him. He had told me that he had really wanted to go to medical school instead of joining the navy. With the arrogance of the young, I urged him to do that now. "You're wonderful to believe so much in me," he wrote in a letter dated September 18, shortly after I had returned to college. "You said that I'm free — at least free of the woman I was so unhappily married to — but you know the little niche I occupy now. I tried to believe I was free as I thundered down the flight deck with the roar of powerful engines all around. But that too was an illusion. If I could get into pre-med now, it would be ten years before I could see my first patient. It's not possible, dear girl. I am old enough to see my limits. But you need not see yours." He had gone to work by then as a laborer — a carpenter, a craft at which he told me he excelled.

I saw Will only once more. I never went to his apartment again, but on Christmas vacation I met him at Candle's, on Mr. Flanders's shift, and we spoke politely, jovially, like niece and uncle, never alluding to the love letters flying back and forth, much less to the evening in August. I explained that it was difficult for me to get away, that my parents and relatives took up all my vacation time, and of course I had papers to write. As always, the distance between farm and town was a problem — Will had no car. Though he tried to hide it, he looked unhappy. Still, he had promised that our love affair, such as it was, would be on my terms, not his.

Next spring, with thoughts on my mind of escaping Arkansas forever, I began to feel ashamed of him, of myself for encouraging him. I grew tired of his adoring letters, untied the ribbons from around them, and threw batches of the old ones in the trash. I wanted no obligations behind me when I fled, but cruelly refused to see the role he had played in giving me the will to go. I neglected to write to him, responding to his daily letters once a week and then not at all. In one of his final letters, he told me he was moving to a small town nearby, where a contractor had offered him a job. He would build kitchen cabinets in ranch houses, he said. And windowframes and doors — he would plane and sand them smooth, would give good value to his employer. (No doubt houses that he helped build are standing even now.) With no word of reproach or inquiry, he gradually stopped writing to me, and that was all.

$\mathscr{O}$N THE ROAD

"There is an aloneness which is common to us all. There are rooms in every heart where no one else can ever enter."

— A letter from my father, June 24, 1956

MY ESCAPE PLAN materialized nicely, as neatly as if I had tunneled out of jail. Having dreamed of New York throughout my college years, I had decided to settle there, though I had no money, and my parents certainly had none to give me, not for that purpose at least. But at the end of my senior year, I actually won a trip to New York in a contest for college girls sponsored by a woman's magazine. On June 1, I set off for a month as a guest editor for *Mademoiselle*, but then, according to the promise I had given my parents, I returned home. The magazine paid its guest editors a small salary and gave us airline tickets back to wherever we came from; I pocketed the salary, traded the plane ticket for round-trip train fare, and even had a little cash to spare. I went home only for a week, to collect a few possessions and say goodbye.

My parting with my father, when the moment came, took place at the train station — inevitable as the departure itself. Only three trains a week left Hot Springs now from the Missouri-

Pacific depot. (The service was canceled shortly afterward, and the old station fell into decay. People had to bid one another farewell at the Little Rock airport from then on.) It was a humid July evening, still over a hundred degrees at twilight, and the three of us trembled in the heat. The grime of the waiting room gave off the smell of tracks, gravel, and coal — the fragrance of travel when you come from a small town. I had my ticket, fifty dollars in cash, the promise of a place to stay — on Perry Street, just off Seventh Avenue — for a month when I got there, and a city map. I already knew how to get from Grand Central Station to Greenwich Village on the subway. I was not afraid.

I had spent the day not looking into my father's eyes, meticulously ironing every garment that was to be folded in my suitcase, polishing my shoes, taking an endless shower, doing all that I could do to make the hours go by. "You can't live in Greenwich Village," he had said. "I won't have it. It's full of dope fiends. You'll become a dope fiend too." But after a month's exposure, I was drunk on New York, and dizzily in love with it. Perhaps this was what my father was trying to combat, with every allegation he could think of.

Sometimes he argued from a statesmanlike stance. "I have a great deal to say to you as you start out in life, and I intend to do so," he had written to me just before I returned home. "Don't start to man your defenses, because I have no intention of trying to run your life. I love you and want you to be happy and successful, but how to attain that I surely do not know. If it is your firm desire to be a career girl in New York, you have a few qualities that might bring success. You have a great deal of natural ability. You have looks and poise (often quaking inwardly). You can bluff your way through a difficult situation, and you have a substantial reserve of the 'old con.' On the other side of the ledger you have no money, no wardrobe, no reserves. Lots of people are smarter and shrewder than you, and as you say your education has a lot of blind spots in it. And you belong here with your family. Your mother and I need you. Neither of us are well, and though we dread doing so, we may have to call on you sooner than we think."

But seeing that reason would not deter me, he descended to threats. "High prices." "White slavery." "Low wages." "Exorbitant rent." "Beatniks in beards." "You don't own a warm coat, and the temperature stays at zero for three months in the winter." "Nobody will marry a poor girl like you. Men marry to advance themselves." "New Yorkers are rude, rough folks." "The subways are dangerous. Will you promise me you'll never go into the subways?" "Who will look after my little girl if she gets sick?" Growing tired of his own barrage, he would subside into anger at one moment and grief the next.

I endured all this as best I could. My mother didn't want me to go, but at least admitted she knew very little about New York. I hadn't met any dope fiends yet, though the thought did make me anxious. But I was confident that there weren't any more of them south of Fourteenth Street than north. I knew the rents were high. I was frightened of hunting for a job. I'd no idea what I'd do when my month's sublet ran out. And I knew my father was right about the coat and the freezing winters. But I was leaving, drawing the line. I am my own creature, I said to myself. "Daughter" is not a lifelong assignment. I am not Athena, born from your head. Athena is not my goddess anymore. I will not aid the ladies in their spinning. I'll answer to myself. And my anger and terror would gnaw away at me like an impending nervous breakdown, until I too wept.

What would you say, I asked him silently, if I were leaving to be married, to become a wife? Would we dance our final waltz before you delivered me to my husband's arms, wrapped in white satin and tied with a bow? Would you have permitted me to leave in that manner, so that I at least belonged to another man, not to myself, and was not leaping into this maelstrom of independence and enterprise all on my own? No, you would be worse off than you are if I were getting married. This is what you designed me for, the mandate you gave me. How can I ride the top of the fast freight and serve as your caretaker at the same time? You fitted me out for this journey. And he replied, as silently as I, traitor, traitor, traitor. But the hour finally came, and we drove the long way to the station without speaking.

One shabby alcove was still marked COLORED, and the one dirty drinking fountain said WHITES. Such things were illegal now, but there were so few passengers that it hadn't seemed worth the trouble to remove the signs. The railroads were dying, Jim Crow was dying, gambling was dying, and it was a toss-up what to tear down first — the signs, the station, or the town.

"You'll be sorry," said my father for the hundredth time. "We always let you do what you wanted. You were a spoiled child. When we're dead and gone, you will wish you had stayed with us. No one will ever think as much of you as we do."

When had my father started saying "dead and gone"?

"Hat, hush. She's going. She deserves her chance. Can't we act like decent people?" My mother fanned herself with a newspaper, aiming small breezes in my direction when she could, smiling a crooked little smile, her face set, as on so many other occasions, with the effort of not weeping.

"At least," I said, indicating the WHITES sign, "I won't have to look at stuff like that anymore."

"Yeah, and niggers will be pushing you off the sidewalk."

"Don't say that word to me. Don't ever say that to me again." My anger kicked on as if by pilot light. We eyed each other with rage.

"You've got fifty dollars in your purse. That won't last long.

You must not expect us to finance this foolishness. We can't do it."

"I don't expect anything. I never intend to ask you for a dime."

"Please, please, hush, the both of you. You know we'll help you out if we can."

I turned my face toward the door, more than ready for the conductor's "All aboard." So many pilgrims had arrived here, often on stretchers, with every joint bent and aching, and then departed upright, or maybe never departed at all, throwing in their lot with this small society where the law of the land did not apply. I thought of the old gunfighters and con men who'd been unceremoniously ushered out of town, given their one-way ticket to Malvern on this very railroad. Now I was an outlaw, too. A ship-jumper. I ought to stay, I thought, and somehow go out on Central Avenue and do something constructive. But my home was no longer my home, and I could no longer comply with its demands. I had begun to see that what this society did to black people, it did to white women too, but requiring your full submission and collusion until you believed in Big Brother, until you became a collaborator and turned into a white male supremicist yourself.

The train had to back into the station from Little Rock, this being a branch line without any roundhouse. It clanged and puffed, this prehistoric beast, pulling its two musty day coaches, surely the last steam locomotive service. "Big choo-choo, all dark," I recollected myself saying years before. But this time my father wouldn't be waiting to collect me at the next junction. Only two other people were boarding that evening, and I was eager to join them, as panic overtook me and I wondered whether I'd be able to make the break. "Don't love me so much," I wanted to say to my mother. "I'm grown up now. You should have your own life. You should stop thinking about me." But I couldn't say it. A life at Candle's Drugstore? A life taking care of my father? If only they would say goodbye and leave, but they clung sweatily and desperately to each other and to me, mounting the steps with me, choosing the best seat for me, stowing my luggage on the rack. This ancient, straight-backed, day coach was grimier even than the waiting room. "Now you'll have quite a layover in Little Rock," my father was saying. "But I wouldn't go outside on the streets if I were you. Just stay in the station and have a cup of coffee. Be sure you check with the ticket agent. The train to St. Louis may be late. Be sure you check the track number."

I sat down, my knees weakening, and my parents perched briefly on the seat opposite. Images tumbled through my mind. The Tabu ad, that woman's fingers leaving the piano keyboard as she succumbed to the violinist's embrace. The red shoes, and the wicked old man in the tree, beckoning. Will Flanders wandering the corridors of an aircraft carrier with his bloodied head. I was by now convinced that this was happening to someone else. Out the filthy window, the small town beyond the station looked stripped, sacked by barbarians. An old hotel once teeming with traveling salesmen was now boarded up. The picture show had taken on a seedy look. The black community nearby showed every sign of decay. My God, was this what the South was doomed to?

My father's face suddenly flooded with tears, and he took my hands in his. "You mustn't do this to me, my darling. You mustn't leave me. You're all I've got. Who will I talk to now?"

"Stop, Daddy, don't." I put my arms around him. I felt deep sorrow for my mother. He could talk to her, if only he would ever try.

She began to cry, and I put my arms around her, too.

"I have to go. I'm going. That's all there is to it You have to let me go. I can't live here any longer. It has nothing to do with you. You mustn't carry on like this. Honest to God, I'll phone, I'll write. I'll come home every chance I get. You'll come and visit me. Mama, Daddy, I'll take care of myself. I won't get sick." And I babbled words of comfort to them, thinking, my father has led me to this moment; why does he tell me I cannot go?

The conductor called at last, and they kissed me and descended as the doors closed and the ancient locomotive clanged and screamed and began slowly rolling out of the station. I watched them go, my mother's arm around my father, and I loved them so much that I began to weep. In my purse, when I searched for a handkerchief, I found an envelope containing a hundred dollars. Which of them had put it there? The train rolled down through the ghetto, and bars lowered at the crossing, lights flashing like police cars in an emergency, and then we were out of town and gaining speed. Wet with tears and sweat, I wrestled the window open and thrust my head out into the oncoming breeze. The pain in my chest, the feeling of being stunned, the gathering migraine in my left temple, even the guilt, eased off in a few moments. The roadbed was ancient and the train rocked precariously, just coasting along until the track improved around Malvern. As we rounded the curves I could see the locomotive up ahead, its eye searching the darkening twilight. We lumbered past Malvern, where Daddy had come to claim me and take me home again eighteen years before, and the engineer opened up the whistle in the wind, loosened the throttle. We've got the right of way. Only some lingering sense of the ridiculous kept me from bursting into song, dancing in the vestibule, kissing my fellow passenger, a lady about my mother's age on her way to Little Rock. I wasn't riding the top of the train like my father, but I was free.

I didn't have to choose between self-ownership and death. I didn't even have to look for a job as a saleslady. I need not yearn for a proper young businessman to marry me and house me in a heavily mortgaged buff brick ranch. I could skip Sears, Roebuck and the washer-dryer. I need not wear my hair in a beehive! I alone have escaped alive to tell thee! I began to laugh, no matter what the lady thought. My father had forbidden me to go to New York, but so what? I was gone. I could live without my father's approval, maybe. The old pantheon had fallen down. If I broke Athena's bargain, as my father construed it, to love him and serve him forever, I at least had a chance to make good on the larger contract — to become some sort of bookmaker myself. And to stand on my feet and depend on no man, another segment of the bargain I made with him, for better or for worse.

$\mathscr{H}$OMEWARD THE PLOWMAN

And now they sin more and more,
  and make for themselves molten images .
Therefore they shall be like the morning mist
  or like the dew that goes early away,
like the chaff that swirls from the threshing floor
  or like smoke from a window.

— Hosea 13

BEFORE HE DIED, my father turned into a malevolent hornet
After I went to New York, he held a few more bookmaking jobs
downtown, in back-room operations. But one day my mother
came to pick him up in the car and found him standing dazed on
the sidewalk. "I don't know what happened to me today," he
explained "I was trying to figure the payoff on the fifth race, and I
couldn't handle the numbers I didn't know what they meant
I looked at all those figures on the scratch sheet, but I didn't know
what they meant " He wept at the supper table that night, promising her that it was only a fluke. But the next day the numbers
erupted from the scratch sheets once more, defying him to add
them, subtract them, combine them, or figure the payoff on a

ten-dollar show bet when the horse placed and paid seven to five.

Stunned by the failure of his wits, he collapsed behind the counter. The boss paid him off through Saturday, guided him onto the street, shook his hand, told him to come back when he felt better. He knew he was finished in the horse books, so he took one last job, this time in a new and promising Arkansas industry — a turkey processing plant. Here he had no odds to figure. His task was standing beside a conveyor belt, eviscerating turkeys and extricating their livers from the mess. His hands were drenched in blood all day. He said it taught him a lesson about just how high the cost of living could be. Shortly afterward he learned he was a diabetic, with complications that included hypertension, kidney disease, and arteriosclerosis. My mother sold off the last of the cattle and chickens and at length found a buyer for the farm. They moved once again, into a modest white stucco house just a few blocks from Alamo Street.

The old order was passing now, with almost indecent haste. Out of office, Judge Vern Ledgerwood still flourished, the only member of the former machine tough enough to have retained his health, good spirits, and the considerable fortune he had made as mastermind of an illegal and lucrative business. Leo McLaughlin, the man with the red carnation, Gentleman Jimmy, turned into a silent and embittered recluse. He never recovered from the drubbing he had taken — dragged into court, accused of crimes. Prescient of his approaching death and aware that his two elderly sisters, who kept house for him, could not long survive him, he turned his final thoughts to his horses, Scotch and Soda. In 1958, before he checked into the local hospital, he saw that the prancing pair were mercifully put to death.

After their brother was buried, the McLaughlin sisters vacated the mansion. Certain that Leo's money was hidden in the walls — for that had been the rumor all those years, that the mayor stuffed currency behind the plaster and inside his mattress every night —

vandals came in and brutally ransacked the old house, stripping the paper from the walls and knocking holes in the plaster. Leo's income off the rackets had certainly amounted to millions, and he had had no conspicuous pleasures except the horses and the women that his mother so heartily disapproved of. (Not that his women ever ended up with much, not even a bus ticket out of town.) But there was no money within the walls, not a dollar. So the ransackers proceeded to the cemetery and dug up Leo McLaughlin's corpse where it rested, next to his murdered sister, Irene. Not a thing was in the coffin except the corpse of Leo P. McLaughlin, and if a cache of currency ever existed, it has never been found. The sisters sold the mansion and grounds to the Safeway company, which plowed up the greensward and erected a supermarket where the house had stood.

Briefly, after Daddy was too far gone to care, gambling caught fire and flourished once more, in a frenetic upsurge that proved fatal. Indeed, it flourished so openly and wickedly that the United States Congress took notice and began an investigation. The local increase in crime may be credited partly to Orval Faubus, the Arkansas governor who in 1957 refused to obey the Supreme Court ruling on desegregation. Governor Faubus and a white mob blocked the integration of Central High School in Little Rock, thus earning international notoriety for the state. In the classic pattern of his predecessors, Faubus also collaborated with the Hot Springs gamblers, who took little interest in racial or educational questions but were glad to have their man in the statehouse. Flaunting their mob connections, Owney Madden and a group of investors opened Las Vegas–style casinos in the resort city, including one called the Vapors — a name that amused my literary-minded friends in New York. My hometown had become so flagrant, so raucous, that we could read about it almost weekly in the *New York Times*. The old Southern Club reopened, with dice tables, blackjack, roulette, and slot machines enlivening the old bookmaking parlor where my father had nursed so many migraines. The new marquee outside advertised name performers. In the supper club, people drank unlawful frozen daiquiris and devoured enormous slabs of sirloin while Mickey Rooney "did" Jimmy Stewart. On one visit I paid to the Southern, the name act consisted of three fat men in brown suits wisecracking about homosexuals. Women with multicolored hair pumped the one-armed bandits. The crowds didn't arrive in tailor-made suits anymore, didn't squint knowingly at the boards while savoring a good cigar, didn't know how blackjack was dealt, couldn't make their way through the racing form.

But it all was due to crash, along with Faubus, whom Arkansas replaced with a different kind of governor. Winthrop Rockefeller, an interloper from the North, refused to do business with Owney Madden and was far too rich to bother shaking down Hot Springs. Eventually the state police began raiding regularly, with no tip-off. In the end, they smashed the slot machines with rifle butts, made a bonfire of contraband gambling equipment, and buried the rubble with bulldozers. By the late 1960s, off-track betting and casino gambling in Hot Springs were finished. The death (from natural causes) and funeral of Owney Madden, in 1965, was a suitable marker for the end of the era. Owen Vincent Madden, Prohibition whiskey baron, nightspot owner, killer, and gray eminence in our community for so many years, was laid to rest in a handsome casket, as his obituary noted, amid a profusion of flowers. The local politician who spoke the eulogy recalled that "this community's prosperity and welfare were uppermost in the heart of this man, who for thirty years has given his all to Hot Springs. We know not and care not what they said about him in New York, Chicago, or Washington." Mourners in snappy clothing appeared from all over the nation, and his pallbearers, as was only fitting, included such respected local citizens as the chief of police

In the 1880s, after the Flynn-Doran battle, the town had exiled the riverboat gamblers and gunfighters; the politicians and deal-makers then began their long reign, with the connivance of the underworld. Now the politicians and the gangsters, too, were out of a job. Proposals to legalize casino gambling and off-track betting have appeared on the ballot since then, only to be rejected by an electorate that has had all it wants of Las Vegas nights. Horse-players amuse themselves at the racetrack only, which is carefully regulated by the state.

At age fifty-nine or so, settling under the roof of his last dwelling, Daddy instantly became an old man, ravaged by diabetes, undermined by the failure of his kidneys and by evil little strokes that slowed his speech and wiped out his remaining ability to deal with numbers. He grew thin — his ice cream suits and the pinstripes would have swallowed him, even if they were not sadly out of style, even if Mother had not ripped up the tailor-made shirts for cleaning rags. Now he wore polyester blends. He'd always had bad teeth, and few of them. Now he had none, except his ill-fitting set of false ones, which, to my mother's outrage, he refused to wear, so that though he was only sixty, his cheeks sank in like an old man's. His eyes turned innocent as a child's, the rage and intelligence quenched — Carrie Abbott's eyes, patient, placid, beyond suffering. Sometimes he picked up his blue-and-gold copy of Gibbon, but imperial Roman history now induced slumber. He had kept this volume on his nightstand for thirty years, opening it almost daily; now he returned it to the bookcase to gather dust beside its fellows. His magazine subscriptions expired. He had stopped reading.

Television was more to his taste: Lawrence Welk, fingering his accordion, his grin fixed as though in plaster. His lead singer, called the Sparkling Little Champagne Lady, oozed her ballads, and the Pretty Little Lennon Sisters (all females on the show were "little") trilled and crooned — entertainment for nursing homes, for the spent, the worn-out. Hat Abbott, too, sat entranced. The doctor had ordered mild exercise, a prescription Daddy followed by walking a block to the grocery store, buying a sack of candy, and slyly devouring it as he walked home, though Mother always spotted the wrappers in the trash. He kept a glass of sweet, cold coffee on the kitchen counter, another source of forbidden sugar, which he sucked at intermittently all day. God help anybody who poured it down the sink before he was done with it. Mother liked a pristine kitchen, and leftover coffee on her otherwise aseptic Formica disgusted her. Coffee was for breakfast, hot. Contrary to doctor's orders, Daddy continued to smoke two packs of Lucky Strikes a day, and the house stank murderously of smoke and ashes. I came to visit as often as I could pay the plane fare, finding him sicker and more dispirited each time I came, his mind as slack as his skin. O Telemachus, my father! At night I sometimes had to hide under the bedcovers and pile the pillows on my head so no one would hear me weeping.

Mother had a job now in a local hospital for arthritics, giving massages, teaching her patients to exercise their swollen joints, wading into hot pools of water with those who could no longer walk, holding them in her arms while they rehearsed the skills of locomotion. It was hard labor at low pay, but her lunches in the cafeteria were free and the workweek ended at noon Saturdays, as she gratefully pointed out. She liked her patients, among whom were many arthritic children. They always asked for her to be their therapist when they returned from year to year. The mail brought postcards and thank-you letters daily. Her bureau drawers were crammed with boxed handkerchiefs and colognes and leather wallets and other gifts. Sometimes patients actually gave her money, which she saved toward plane tickets to New York.

Every day at 4:30, she came into the kitchen from the carport, changed quickly from her white uniform to a housedress, and went straight to the stove. Nothing she cooked suited my father. He'd sit at the table muttering, "She never roasts a turkey anymore" or "She can't be bothered to make a decent pan of cornbread." Then, toothless, he would begin to eat. If Mother was half an hour late, he'd fret about a possible car accident — what would happen to him, he'd demand, if she was laid up in the hospital? When she fell ill, as she frequently did these days, he would grumble about his probable fate if she died and he was left to what he contemptuously called "Shirley's tender mercies." I couldn't look at him, refused to admit that this dreadful coot was my father. My father was the cynical, good-looking chap with a watch chain looping across his vest. This hateful, sick old bastard who abused my mother was somebody else.

The tears I shed by night turned into hatred by day, sweet, keen hatred. Because we had no words for each other now (books having been essential to our discourse). Because he seemed to hate me, too — I who had been the apple of his eye, the rationale for his life, as he had been given to saying. Because his wretchedness rebuked and undid my own accomplishments. Because, where I was concerned, he had become a prating, agonizing bore.

I was living in Greenwich Village, just the way I had said I would — in a succession of cramped, slanty-floored, cockroach-ridden apartments: Perry Street, Jane Street, Hudson Street; I reveled in the very names. Having worked a year in a low-level publishing job, I won a scholarship for a year in France, and another for a year of graduate work at Columbia University. I was then hired as a junior editor at *Horizon* magazine, a beautiful new bimonthly of history and the arts. I had friends. Could afford theater tickets. Went to museums. Heard *Don Giovanni* at the Metropolitan Opera, saw the Bolshoi Ballet on its first American visit. Spent hours in the New York Public Library daily, as part of my job. Shook hands with John F. Kennedy as he campaigned on

Madison Avenue. Worked, in minor capacities, for the civil rights movement in New York.

Finally, as though to put an end to all my father's croaking about the bad end I would surely come to, I went through a succession of dates, acquaintances, and romantic disasters until the man I loved and was least likely to be happy with, asked me to marry him, and I accepted. Though we both deeply doubted the wisdom of what we were doing, we did indeed marry — in a historic Episcopal church on lower Fifth Avenue whose assistant rector I had met at a beach party. Wearing a chic knee-length white satin dress, I almost fainted from terror when the organist began the processional. But my best friend and the assistant rector held me up and insisted that I walk to the altar. My groom was paler than I was, but we said "I will."

Yet nothing I did evoked praise from my father. Rather than rejoicing in the scholarship that took me to France, he begged me not to go and then urged me in almost every letter to return home immediately. "Maybe this will satisfy your wanderlust once and for all," he wrote, "and you'll come back to your home and your parents. We need you." When I entered graduate school instead, he tartly reminded me that he couldn't and wouldn't contribute a dollar toward my expenses (I had not asked for money). When I found the magazine job soon after finishing my studies, he told me *Horizon* was too highbrow and predicted it would fail. Furthermore, they were underpaying me, he felt, and exploiting the ambitions of a foolish young girl. Too ill to attend my wedding, he said only that now I was lost to him forever He made no attempt to get acquainted, even at a distance, with my husband.

In a frenzy of newly married pride, I expunged my own and my father's surname from my bank account, my social security number, my driver's license. If an *A* had been monogrammed on any of my towels, I'd have picked the stitches out. During the first year of my marriage I determined to obliterate my identity, to become an ideal wife, to cook, to clean, to serve leftovers appealingly, to watch eagerly for a shirt collar to fray or a button to fall off so that I could whip out my mending basket. I prepared nourishing meals, complete with old-fashioned desserts, until my husband pleaded with me to reduce the calories. I conducted all my correspondence on writing paper printed with "Mrs." at the top, followed by my husband's full name. I had gone to Tiffany's to have the stuff engraved. In my letters home, I referred to myself only in the first-person plural. My father simply ignored all this. To avoid using my married name, he insisted that Mother henceforth address all envelopes to me. But little time was left to squabble over such details.

The night my father died, I stayed at the hospital with him, like the dutiful daughter I had ceased to be. My mother had telephoned me three days earlier. "Daddy's awfully bad. But don't come yet. We've got him in the hospital. He's feeling a little better today. You never can tell with this old diabetes. I think he's had a small stroke." Mother thought I ought not to leave my husband, my job. So I telegraphed a plant, and when she urgently summoned me and I finally arrived, exhausted and ten hours late because of canceled flights and other problems, this plant, an azalea pink as spring, sat on the table beside his bed, the only flowers he had. I bent over him, squeezed his hands, patted his pallid cheeks, stroked his head until his eyes opened. He said nothing but gestured weakly toward the azalea and smiled.

Local etiquette, indeed ethics, requires that no family member be left alone in a hospital room for so much as a minute. A blood relation or spouse must sit round the clock with the sick and the dying; a uniformed professional at a nurse's station is no substitute. Since my mother had already sat up for two nights, I persuaded her to go home and allow me to keep the vigil that

night. She agreed, feeling encouraged by my arrival and his
smile, and by his having willingly swallowed a glass of water and
some ice cream that afternoon. Cautioning me to offer nourish-
ment frequently and not to allow him to pull out his catheter,
which he had done several times already, she departed.

Scarcely had the door closed behind her when an orderly came
into the room with a suctioning machine. I did not yet believe
my father was dying, although he hadn't spoken for two days and
was having breathing difficulties. "Here we go, Pop," the orderly
said, wielding the brutal mechanism like a vacuum cleaner.
I turned to the young man (younger than I was) in astonishment.
Nobody in all my father's life had ever called him Pop. "This man
is Mr. Abbott. You ought to call him Mr. Abbott." But the
orderly did not reply.

I offered my father water through a straw, pleaded with him to
take a little ice cream off his supper tray, but he shut his eyes.
I wondered suddenly if his first wife was still alive, and whether
her letters still caused havoc. Imogene no doubt remembered my
father as I saw him, perversely, even now: six feet tall, slender, his
feet planted defiantly on the front steps of his parents' house, as
in the old photograph I used to study, the one in Grandma's candy
box. As I watched him breathe, I summoned — and quickly cast
aside — certain memories that surged forward. I'd never seen
him handsome, blond, and slender. He was gray-haired by the
time I was born, overweight until misfortune had wasted him.
And yet he danced before my eyes like the prince in a ballet. He
certainly had fooled me about his looks.

The month was April, and it rained all night. Because he
seemed so peacefully asleep, I stationed myself in the easy chair,
mercifully provided, where I dozed and woke and the rain still
fell, washing down the walls of the hospital, running in rivers,
sheets, so that it was impossible to see the streetlights outside
I visited my father's bedside, offering water, murmuring ques-

tions about his state of health. I knew the circumstances called for
tears, but my serenity was unshakable, my eyes were dry. I tried
to make a mental movie of my father taking care of me, but no
movie rolled, only the sound of the copious rain, as though the
dark sky were equipped with faucets. "What will you miss most
about your father?" some voice queried as I dozed. "I'll miss that
azalea," I replied, pointing to the plant. "I intend to set out that
azalea in my mother's yard," I added illogically. "Next spring it
will bloom, so beautiful, azaleas." And finally I fell deeply asleep.

I awoke about dawn — the rain had not let up — to find him
looking at me. I went to his bedside. "Daddy." I bent toward his
ear. "Do you want anything?" I saw that the sheet was off him.
He was quite naked. During the night he had ripped the catheter
from his penis, the act of disobedience my mother had begged me
to prevent, and now he had done this thing in the night while I
slept. The tears came to my eyes at last. How painful it must have
been, that cruel tube with the tiny balloon at its upper end! Had
he cried out while I slept? (Some terrible association leapt into my
mind, crushing me with guilt: oh yes, the disciples snoring while
Jesus prepared to die!) Poor limp, dark penis. Out of this had
sprung the molecules that made me. Thou shalt not look upon
thy father's nakedness. I covered him gently with the sheet.
I would give him water through the little plastic straw, and I
poured it into a glass. I'd get the nurse to replace the catheter.
Then, when I touched his cheek, I saw that he was dead. I went
out of the room, shut the door, and leaned against it.

After a time the night nurse discovered me, went briefly
inside, and returned to lead me away. "You sit down here, honey.
What's Velma's phone number? Let me make that call for you.
We need to get her back up here. Which mortuary you want me
to call, Gross or Carruthers? We have to do it now, baby, it can't
be helped. That's what we have to do. Don't you fret, they'll take
good care of him " She telephoned my mother and told her the

story: "I'd come on back up here if I was you, Miz Abbott. I think
he may be getting a little worse."

Later that day, Mother and I went to the funeral home to make
the arrangements. I had read the recent best-selling book by
Jessica Mitford about the wiles of undertakers and the foolishness
of Americans when it came to death and burial, and I was spoil-
ing for a fight, but when we went to inspect caskets in the
showroom, with twenty open boxes like new cars, it was hard to
pick the cheapest. Mother was accustomed to picking the cheapest, though, and needed no help from me to resist the sales talk on
costly containers that were guaranteed waterproof. She wrote the
check and made arrangements to buy two plots, and then we
hurried home. By now the phone was ringing, and the women
surged into the house, setting things to rights, vacuuming and
dusting, changing the bed linen, receiving dishes of food that
were delivered to the door, with the name of the donor taped
considerately to the bottom so that the dish could be returned.
Soon a huge coffee urn arrived and was set in action; soon every
available surface was covered with baked hams, plates of fried
chicken, vegetables of every description, cakes, pies, salads.
"Stay and eat," the women admonished, as families arrived on
condolence calls. And my mother greeted each arrival at the door,
weeping briefly on people's shoulders as they hugged and kissed
her, exclaiming over the three-bean salads and the heavenly hash,
or the sponge cakes, or the pound cans of coffee. Flowers arrived,
too, stiff arrangements of chrysanthemums, gladiolas, thrifty
kinds of flowers that last for two weeks. Soon the table lamps had
to be set on the floor to make room for them. Their bitter
fragrance competed with the perking coffee. All was quickly in
place: callers occupying every available chair, balancing huge
plates of food and coffee cups as they spoke of nothing in particular (for it is not good manners to speak of the dead at such

gatherings), the women washing dishes at the sink (for not so much as a coffee cup may be left for the bereaved to deal with) — a gathering of plenty and good will that blotted out death, a ritual that must take place whether the widow and orphans are upright and smiling or unconscious with grief in the next room.

The funeral food, the ritual partaking of each dish, the soft voices talking recipes or the weather or the price of groceries, the square womanly hands in the hot suds at the sink, the arms extended, the gentleness of those who had come to watch over us so that despair was kept at bay outside the door and grief would descend by slow degrees — these offerings had the force and beauty of a sacrament. I could not discount these gestures or tell these kindly, well-meaning souls to go away. But among them I was my father's only friend, an alien as he had been. I thought of a hungry young man leaping from a boxcar near Laramie, Wyoming, of him and Mike reciting poetry in the Chicago streets, of the ragged cabbie who'd had fourteen different jobs already by the time he was twenty-five, of his hands loosening Imogene's red hair, young bodies limb to limb in long and rapturous bliss, as Oscar Wilde so decorously put it, of a bootlegger rounding the curves of a lonely road on two wheels with the cops not far behind him, of a child who called himself by the names of Greek heroes driving a milk cart through the streets of Goshen, Indiana, at dawn. In the bookcase, now wedged into a corner of the tiny living room, the worn copies of the *Iliad* and the *Odyssey*, the matched volumes of Edward Gibbon lined up like English gentlemen in a club, the Oscar Wilde, the Casanova that had taught me the motions of love, the volumes elegantly inscribed from Mike, all these emblems of learning, these foreign voices — these rooms in my father's heart that only I had tried to enter — silently mocked this pious enterprise. I became so vividly aware of my father's outcast state that I could not bite into the fried chicken or the seven-layer coconut cake or even swallow the coffee. I was dizzy, ill. I yearned for a shot of whiskey, the good fiery whiskey that he used to down each morning on his way to work. But no whiskey was offered at this wake.

At some point that day, we all went down to the funeral home for the viewing. Choosing my father's shroud that morning, I had searched in vain for a shirt and suit from the old days, but Mother said she didn't want him dressed in those old-timey things and insisted on laying him out in the beige polyester leisure suit she had bought at Penney's last Christmas. He had never worn it, had stowed it at the bottom of his bureau drawer. When she packed it in a paper bag, she also included his false teeth, wrapped in Kleenex. The workers in the embalming room put plenty of makeup on him, and glued the dentures firmly in place. Dead to all feeling by then, I took part in the viewing — this strange body laid out in the coffin, looking nothing like my father, the mourners gathered around with their hankies pressed to their cheeks, assuring Mother and me that he looked real natural, just like himself. I did not mind their saying this. Confronted with this waxen body on a satin cushion, what else could they say? Anyway, the embalmers were friends of my mother's, working the same hours she did for about the same pay. A favorite verse of my father's swam into my head, something about "the short and simple annals of the poor." Something about twilight falling. What could it be? Gray's "Elegy" surfaced in my mind:

> The curfew tolls the knell of parting day,
> The lowing herd wind slowly o'er the lea,
> The plowman homeward plods his weary way,
> And leaves the world to darkness and to me

Except that for some reason, when he recited it he always said, "Homeward the plowman," even though I told him it was the other way around. I considered asking the preacher to read it at the funeral next day, but knew it would never do.

The bookmaker was laid to rest by a Baptist preacher, who spoke of him only as a sick old man; "This our Christian brother, who returned to the Lord in his last days, and we shall see him in paradise." As the soprano sang in her sweet, clear voice, "Just as I am, without one plea, O Lamb of God I come," I imagined Daddy presenting himself to this lamb, and uncharacteristically began to pray. "Oh God, I've got one plea, even if he hasn't, and that is for Christ's sake not to put this man in your Baptist heaven. It won't work out. Find him space with the Buddhists, where he can sit cross-legged in the lotus position, exuding light. Ask him to write the formula for the unified field theory or compose the longest periodic sentence in the universe. Or lend him to your Shinto colleagues and let him live in a tree." Then the baritone chimed in, "Rock of Ages, cleft for me, let me hide myself in thee," and I felt a killing stab of anguish, and wanted to destroy the world. Ten presidents had ruled the nation since he was born. Thousands of legislators had been elected and served. Had any of them cared about the waste? For in fact, given the chance, he could have done any job on earth requiring brains. Intelligence is not listed on the commodity futures exchange in the United States. Kids with brains are born every day. Then they go to work in the turkey factory or on the milk cart, or driving bootleg whiskey or pushing drugs in the streets. Why, Contriver of the universe, do you so squander your treasure? Maybe it isn't brains you love.

At some funerals, the mourners are content. It is possible to cite the good deeds, the offices held, the churches tithed to, the children begotten and raised, the grandchildren now making their way in the world, the kindnesses remembered from a life completed. (A good story, with an ending, even if shot with falsehoods.) And there are the other funerals, the kind that make ghosts. This particular horse race was over, and there was no purse. We put him in the cemetery lot that we had paid for the previous day, and laid his pall — a blanket of red carnations my mother had selected — over the raw earth. The mourners, few in number, were Mother's relatives and friends, or the parents of high school friends of mine who had known him through me. Not one bookie or gambler or con artist or crooked politician remembered Hat that day. Perhaps they too were dead.

"In the beginning was the Word, and the Word was God, and the Word was with God." I had asked the preacher to read that at the graveside, and he did; an odd selection, people must have thought, and hardly funereal. Escorting my mother to the undertaker's black limousine, I felt only relief as the service ended and the gravedigger arrived to fill in the hole and finish the job.

For the next few days, Mother busied herself with the tasks of death, which seemed numerous and pressing that first morning, as though we should never finish them, but were in fact quite simple. We visited the social security office, and she wept in gratitude to the U.S. government upon discovering that a death benefit was due. She applied for the death certificate and located the life insurance policy and the will. She addressed the envelopes for the thank-you cards the funeral home had given us — "Your kind expression of sympathy in our sorrow was deeply appreciated," printed in a curlicue script that rivaled Miss Love's penmanship. She washed the casserole dishes the funeral food had been brought in, and I drove her from house to house to return each dish. She went down to the hospital and settled the bill in person. Together we packed up my father's clothes and called the Salvation Army. The truck came the next day and took every last shirt, jacket, and sock away. I impulsively ransacked his bureau one last time, searching fruitlessly for Imogene — an old envelope, a telephone number, an address from this phantom who had ignited my parents' rage and my fantasies for so many years.

I wanted to tell her that Hat Abbott was dead. Actually, I wanted to go visit her — and Gray, and Abigail, and Henry. But a call to Chicago information, which I made while my mother was out of the house, yielded no information at all.

We went together to the tombstone man, and Mother wisely selected the very plainest, smallest bronze plaque, and had an inscription cast under his name: "Our Daddy." "Our Daddy?" I inquired, momentarily aroused. He was *my* daddy, not her daddy. "My child," I thought sardonically, might better have described his relationship to her lately. But perhaps she meant to say that he had belonged to her as much as to me, in spite of the way we shut her out, he and I, back when we did our dance of father and daughter, reading poems aloud to one another in the reign of the Antonines. I suddenly lost all interest in what she put on his tombstone. "Whatever you want, Mama. I think 'Our Daddy' would be nice." The battle was over. Amnesia was the best solution. I was happy he was gone.

My mother's mourning was quickly completed: she voiced no fears of living alone, and insisted I get back to my job right away. Returning for a visit a few months after my father's death, I was surprised to see that the house had fallen prey to mildew and dust and had taken on the musty fragrance of neglect. Like a person miraculously cured who throws out all her pill bottles, she had quit her housewifely habits. Surfaces that she had waxed and polished once a week for thirty years now gathered dust. The ironing collected on the ironing board. Instead of leftover roast beef, neatly packaged portions of vegetable soup, and the remains of lemon meringue pies, the refrigerator contained an empty bread wrapper and a crusty jar of strawberry jam. My mother told me she ate supper with her girlfriends every night, following the specials from one motel dining room or steak joint to another.

When I brought up the subject of my father, she said only, "What a sweet man. So good to his daughter and his wife.

Worked so hard, and every Saturday brought the money home,"
as if speaking of strangers. ("This is a C-note. It comes from
Latin. The Roman numeral for one hundred. You don't know
about the Romans, but I'll teach you.") As it happened, my
mother had less than two years to live. On a bitter January
afternoon less than eighteen months hence, I would be choosing
the inscription for her bronze plaque. But now, as though I were
the adult and she the child, I was shocked to see her relishing
widowhood — this season with other women who ate hilarious
suppers at Pizza Hut and Sizzlin' and the Ramada Inn, slept alone
in their double beds, gulped a cup of instant coffee and departed
the next morning, oblivious to yellowing curtains and the dust
thickening on the end tables. So far as I know, my mother never
fried another chicken or made another pie, and I am glad.

She told me she intended to have the Salvation Army come and
collect the bookcase — "your Grandma Abbott's old bookcase."
She yearned to be rid of a lot of this clutter, she said. Had no use
for it. Did I want any of my father's books? So I packed the books
in vodka boxes and hired a moving van for the bookcase, over my
mother's protests. "You must be crazy, honey. You don't want that
old thing in your home." But I insisted on having it crated up and
dispatched on an interstate moving van. Thus it was that this last
material witness to my grandparents' long-ago prosperity in
Goshen, Indiana, was delivered to a small apartment in Manhat-
tan. It wouldn't fit the space I'd imagined it in and looked
grotesquely out of scale in the low-ceilinged living room. The
glass doors had somehow survived the move, but the back panels
proved to be pasteboard and crumbled when I tried to clean
them. My husband said the bookcase was hideous. Transporting
it had been money wasted, pure sentimentality on my part, he
said — pardonable, to be sure, understandable, but foolish. He
wanted Danish modern. So did I. He helped me carry the de-
crepit thing to the sidewalk, and next morning it was gone,

whether carted off by the Sanitation Department or claimed by some thrifty and shelfless person I never knew. Since I was now shelfless myself, I had to keep my father's books in their cartons for a year or two. Having no furnishings was fashionable in our circle, a badge of youth and high spirits, though suddenly everyone began buying sofas, wing chairs, and innerspring mattresses and worrying about finding a two-bedroom apartment when and if the baby arrived.

Now my father's grave is old, the best kind of grave, to be visited in serenity on a lovely fall or spring afternoon. I never took my daughters to that cemetery as children, but now that they are adults, or nearly, I have taken them once or twice to stand with me at my parents' grave. "Our Daddy." "Beloved wife and mother." I go often to Hot Springs, and whether I arrive in some low-flying two-engine plane from Little Rock, barely clearing the mountaintops, or by highway, rolling up Malvern Avenue past where the old McLaughlin mansion stood, I am propelled by a deep and ineradicable sense of home, though in fact I own nothing here and have nowhere in particular to hang my toothbrush. The sight of the bluish hills curving amply like old women sleeping on their daybeds, as I conceived them to be in my childhood, gladdens and heartens me. I am a stranger here, but this place is mine.

The streets have been altered; indeed, the city I walked as a schoolgirl exists largely in my head. The high school is no longer the high school. The hospital my father died in is no longer a hospital. The bathhouses, except for one, no longer offer baths. One of the elegant old structures has been restored as a museum. The Southern Club is no longer a gambling den but Josephine Tussaud's Wax Museum. On the treads of the staircase that I once climbed wearing my Shirley Temple dress and with my hair in corkscrews stand so-real-they-talk images of Clark Gable, Mae

West, and Sophia Loren, among others. In fact they are garish
and unreal, in spite of the surrounding hoopla about the "wax-
makers' art." At the top of the stairs is a waxen replica of the Last
Supper, and above it, in the archway framing the once grand
entrance to the gaming room, hangs the slick white body of the
crucified Christ: no blood, no sweat, and no genitals under the
modest loincloth, of course. Leering companionably from a
corner, however, is a life-size Al Capone, chewing a fat cigar.
Nearby, the voice of Franklin D. Roosevelt emerges from a 1940s
radio, ceaselessly, inexplicably announcing the bombing of Pearl
Harbor. Owney Madden has not made it into the waxworks,
unfortunately, nor Earl Witt, nor Leo P. McLaughlin. Investigat-
ing this place recently, I glanced upward and was overjoyed to see
that the ancient domed ceiling with its great chandelier is still in
place. Downstairs, in the Southern Grill, where vicious criminals
once convivially downed their oysters and lighted their cigars
with ten-dollar bills, is the wax museum ticket booth and sou-
venir shop, which, in the spirit of the good old days, nicks you a
pretty penny for a leaflet and a T-shirt.

The auction houses are still in business, with the same gilt
statuary and the auctioneers still yodeling in the twilight about
their works of art. The Arlington Hotel, carefully restored and
maintained but otherwise exactly as I remember it, presides over
the city in turreted, verandahed grandeur, its facade turned toward the racetrack, which attracts hundreds of thousands of
customers now and even stays open Sundays, Baptists or no
Baptists. (So far as I know, Hot Springs makes its living these
days out of tourists and the annual race meet. The splendid
climate and low cost of living have also made it a popular place to
retire.) In the park and along the avenue, our ancient magnolia
trees bloom and shed their velvet petals, and the willows waft
their foliage like delicate arms in the summer breeze. By its very
existence, this place deconstructs and demolishes the American

dream of virtue and hard work crowned by success, as well as all platitudes and cant about the democratic process and small-town American life. After an upbringing here, New York City politics, or Watergate, or even the savings and loan scandal, could hardly come as a surprise.

In the tales that constituted his legacy to me, my father's favorite character was himself — Hat, the adventurer caught in misfortune's web, the misfit, the man of intellect, the reader among illiterates, the outsider. He too was an unraveler of myths, even as he furiously knitted them, ensnaring me in the mythologies he based his life on. Yet he also taught me that fathers are not all-powerful — a useful concept for the times I grew to maturity in. He taught me that a flawed patriarch such as himself may actually prefer a daughter to a son. ("I never wanted a boy, I wanted you" has brought me through many a trial.) For some of us, as my father so ardently believed, true salvation can be found only on the printed page — as in the books he read and the books he surely would have written had he been a bookmaker of another kind.

Convention, "the majority however composed, ultimately give the law."[18] The problem, of course, is that the majority may have force but not justice on its side. Madison insisted on both. Majority rule is a necessary but not sufficient condition of free government. A government independent of the will of the society is unrepublican and illegitimate, but so too is a majority that has power but not right on its side.[19] Fully aware of the long historical list of injustices associated with popular government, Madison nonetheless was adamant that the ultimate and only legitimate solution to the problem of governmental and majority tyranny is the cultivation of the just sense of the community.

When the assertions in *Federalist* 51 are attended to in the context of the two preceding *Federalist Papers*, a nascent idea beats in the ear of Publius's audience. It is reason, not passion, that ought to prevail over legislative decisions. Specifically, it is the reason *of the public* that ought to control the government.[20] In the Party Press Essay "Spirit of Governments," Madison pounded the republican drum to a rolling cadence. Contrasted with the imposter republican government advanced by some, which is actuated by private interest and avidity and pretends to operate by the liberty of the many, but in fact is supported by the domination of the few, Madison set forth the true republican model:

A government, deriving its energy from the will of the society, and operating by the reason of its measures, on the understanding and interest of the society.

This "is the government for which philosophy has been searching, and humanity sighing, from the most remote ages," we recall. This is the kind of "republican government" America invented and that is its "unrivalled happiness to possess."[21] In the same vein of thought that runs through *Federalist* 49, 50, and 51, "Spirit of Governments" reinforces and intensifies the claims of Publius. The spirit of republicanism, Madison emphatically pronounced, requires that the will of the government be dependent on, "or rather the same with," the will of the society, and that the will of the society be subject to "the reason of the society."[22] The process of subjecting the public will to the precepts of reason directs popular government toward the ends of justice and the general good. In turn, the resulting laws inform

---

[18] Madison to Edmund Randolph, January 10, 1788, *PJM* 10:355.
[19] *Federalist* 51:292–93; cf. "Vices of the Political System of the United States," *PJM* 9:350, 355.
[20] *Federalist* 50:287; *Federalist* 49:285.
[21] "Spirit of Governments," *PJM* 14:234.
[22] "Universal Peace," *PJM* 14:207.

the citizens' understanding and influence their perception of the public interest. This has been the ambitious quest of philosophy and the ardent longing of humanity from time immemorial, Madison declared. America has answered humanity's call, and upon its soil the greatest political aspirations are to be realized.

"The great desideratum" in government, Madison wrote in preparation for the work at Philadelphia in 1787, is the establishment of a "disinterested & dispassionate umpire" that renders impartial judgments between the different passions and interests of the society.[23] The achievement of reasonableness and impartiality in republican government, he believed, hinges on a "modification of the Sovereignty." Prior to the Constitutional Convention, Madison conceived of this just umpire determining national policy as well as officiating over state legislation and exercising the power of veto in the case of unconstitutional or unjust local legislation. After the Convention's rejection of his proposed constitutional negative on state laws, Madison continued to seek the establishment of an impartial referee that would sit in judgment on national concerns.[24] The great problem in popular government, he argued in the 10th *Federalist*, is that the parties to the case must themselves also be the judges.[25]

Scholars have often interpreted Madison's notion of a "disinterested & dispassionate umpire" to mean the national legislature of the United States, the members of which hail from large legislative districts and are more likely to be fit choices than those who come from the assembly districts of Rhode Island or even Virginia or Massachusetts.[26] Of course Madison noted the

[23] Madison to Washington, April 16, 1787, *PJM* 9:384; cf. "Vices of the Political System of the United States," 9:357; Madison to Jefferson, October 24, 1787, *PJM* 10:214.

[24] Madison to Jefferson, October 24, 1787, *PJM* 10:214. Cf. "Notes on Government," *PJM* 14:158. A fuller discussion of Madison's negative on state laws is included in my forthcoming work, *Madison's Voyage to the World of the Classics*.

[25] *Federalist* 10:48.

[26] For example, Gordon Wood claims that Madison meant by this the national legislature, elected from large districts and composed of an aristocratic set of statesmen whose elite and independent judgment would answer the ends sought ("Interests and Disinterestedness in the Making of the Constitution," in Richard Beeman, Stephen Botein, and Edward C. Carter, eds., *Beyond Confederation: Origins of the Constitution and American National Identity* [Chapel Hill: University of North Carolina Press, 1987], 92; *The Creation of the American Republic, 1776–1787* [Chapel Hill: University of North Carolina Press, 1969], 562). Alan Gibson claims that the Madisonian remedy of an impartial umpire consists in the formation of just majorities in Congress, made possible by (1) the inclusion of a multiplicity of interests in a large territory with a diverse population, which obstructs the communication of factious views and leaves representatives fairly independent in the exercise of their trust, and (2) large electoral districts from which impartial representatives are more likely to be chosen. For Madison, public opinion "was simply a public consciousness formed from the

benefit of representatives from large electoral districts; he did not, however, look to representation as the panacea for popular injustice or conceive of minority government as the cure for majority faction.[27] Indeed, time and again he made clear the fundamental principle that informed his understanding of republican government: "[T]he majority ... alone have the right of decision."[28] In his concluding discussion of the cure for the diseases most

aggregate of individual sentiments." Moreover, Gibson argues – and in this he is in agreement with Wood – that Madison's goal was not to reform the citizens of an unjust majority or to educate and form civic character (Gibson, "Ancients, Moderns, and Americans: The Republicanism–Liberalism Debate Revisited," *History of Political Thought*, 21:2 [2002], 287, 282; "Impartial Representation and the Extended Republic: Towards a Comprehensive and Balanced Reading of the Tenth Federalist Paper," *History of Political Thought* 12:2 [1991], 285, 300–1; Wood, "Interests and Disinterestedness," 81).

While I do not disagree that Madison hoped that the national representatives would be enlightened and virtuous, I reject the view that a reliance on the "better sorts" of men constituted Madison's "great desideratum" for the achievement of impartial justice in republican government. Lance Banning's analysis of the issue, I think, is much closer to the mark. According to Banning, Madison was "adamant that once the proper checks had been imposed and passing passions had been cooled, the will of the majority must rule." Banning does not, however, follow Madison's thought to the next step, which involves the politics of deliberative communication at both the governmental level and throughout the society, thereby refining and, to the extent possible, uniting and settling public opinion, resulting in a rightful authority that government must obey. Instead, he argues that in order for Madison's republican theory to work, representatives in Congress must reflect the diverse views of their constituents (*Sacred Fire of Liberty*, 372, 209).

As a result, Banning opens himself up to the kind of criticism that Gibson makes of his argument. Gibson claims that by failing to account for the achievement of impartiality in public decision making, Banning ultimately succumbs to the pluralist model he tries to avoid ("Impartial Representation and the Extended Republic," 267–68). Conversely, Banning argues that Gibson does not take account of the importance of the practicable extent of territory and the role it plays in maintaining the rulers' responsibility to the people in Madison's theory. "Madison *never* argued that the national legislators would be capable of acting as impartial referees over clashing interests at the national level," Banning declares (*Sacred Fire of Liberty*, 212, n. 61; 470, n. 54). I would add that Gibson's combination model does not solve the difficulty of preventing the communication and spread of factious views among the national representatives, who meet in person in the capital city and have open, easy lines of communication and ample opportunity for the formation of factions, which could well prove an overmatch for contrived institutional rivalries. Cf. Woody Holton, "'Divide et Impera': *Federalist* 10 in a Wider Sphere," *William and Mary Quarterly* 62:2 (2005), 339–82.Contrary to the generally agreed-upon importance of large legislative districts to Madison's political theory, Holton argues that Madison was a "relative moderate" on the question of the size of legislative districts.

[27] Alan Gibson disagrees; he argues that Madison's (and the original Federalists') schema of government "risked tyranny created by independent acts of public officials in order to control tyranny created by the influence of popular majorities" (Gibson, *Understanding the Founding: The Crucial Question* [Lawrence: University Press of Kansas, 2007], 228).

[28] Madison to Washington, April 16, 1787, *PJM* 9:384; cf. "Vices of the Political System of the United States," *PJM* 9:357.

incident to popular government, he declared that "a coalition of *a majority of the whole society* would seldom take place on any other principles than those of justice and the general good." Note that Madison does not say that a coalition of *a majority of the legislature* would rarely take place on any other basis than justice and the general good. His remedy of a "disinterested & dispassionate umpire" for the problem of popular injustice is not contingent on gathering a few good men at the seat of government. It is, rather, a more complex and genuinely republican solution to the chief problem that has plagued popular governments throughout history.

As Madison made clear in "Vices of the Political Systems of the United States," *The Federalist*, the "Notes on Government," and the Party Press Essays, in devising a solution to the leading problem of majority faction in popular government, the institution of the principle of representation is auxiliary to the establishment of an extensive territory. But the size of the nation and the multiplicity of economic interests and religious sects that it encompasses are not the culmination of Madison's republican theory either. When the components of territorial size and representation are viewed as part of a more comprehensive Madisonian design informed by an overarching theory of public opinion, they fit together to form a coherent vision of republican self-government. Madison grounded his theory of public opinion in a new conception of the politics of communication. He envisioned a commerce of ideas in the extended republic that would not only refine the will of the majority *in the legislature* but, to the extent possible, would also modify and enlarge the will and views *of the majority (or society) itself.* His aim was to honor the republican principle that identifies power with right; even more importantly, his goal was to place popular power on the side of right, thereby forming a sovereign public genuinely worthy of republican esteem.

Although Madison sought to check the communication of factious views via the enlargement of the orbit, representation, separation of powers, and checks and balances, it was not his design to stymie the communication of all opinions throughout the society. At each of three levels of political interaction – that is, within the government, between the representatives and their constituents, and among the citizenry themselves – political communication is a double-edged sword. It is both part of the political problem Madison identifies and an integral part of the republican solution he presents. Communication is the means by which minority and majority factions form and unite, but it is also the vehicle necessary to collect, form, and refine the will of the society. Communication makes possible a public check on governmental tyranny *and* the formation of a positive agency that directs governmental measures.

"Public Opinion," Madison declared, "sets bounds to every government, and is the real sovereign in every free one."[29] In all governments, public opinion operates as a force that limits the power of government. In all free governments public opinion is the ground of all legitimate authority; it functions as both a defensive power that controls government and an active agency that influences the will of the government. As the embodiment of the highest expression of public opinion, the Constitution provides a standard to which officials and citizens can appeal to limit the power of government, as well as a source of instruction concerning individual rights and responsibilities. The latter is what Madison meant by the beneficial effects of a bill of rights over time, as it is sanctified and incorporated into public opinion.[30] In addition to its manifestation in the Constitution, public opinion has three other modes of expression: as the censor of governmental acts, as the constitutional majority on which positive acts of government depend, and as the general spirit that permeates the nation (and perhaps beyond). The censorship of governmental acts by public opinion is a defensive measure that finds expression via state political organs and by educated men through the print media.[31] The appeal may be to the people of the states or even directly to the people as a collectivity. However, public opinion in these cases does not carry the force of law, though it may well "lead to a change in the legislative expression" of the public will or even to a change in judicial opinion.[32] The affirmative force of public opinion manifests itself through frequent elections and responsible representation, by which "the will of the largest political body may be concentered and its force directed to any object which the public good requires."[33] In the expression of public opinion by the constitutional majority the people's agency is not direct, but it is nonetheless their will, and not a government insulated from the actual views of the people, that guides public measures. Finally, public opinion in its broadest sense consists of the settled views and general convictions of the people. Its potential power is prodigious: it can preserve or alter public morality; it can support or scorn the laws. The formation of constitutional majorities occurs within a sphere permeated by an overarching and ubiquitous public opinion. When settled, the opinion of the constitutional majority

---

[29] "Public Opinion," *PJM* 14:170; cf. "Notes on Government," *PJM* 14:161–62.

[30] "Notes on Government," *PJM* 14:162–63; "Public Opinion," *PJM* 14:170; Meyers, *Mind of the Founder*, 169.

[31] James Madison to Thomas Jefferson, October 24, 1787, *PJM* 10:214; *Federalist* 44 and 46; Meyers, *Mind of the Founder*, 262–64.

[32] Meyers, *Mind of the Founder*, 270.

[33] *Federalist* 14:68–69.

is absorbed by this more general and pervasive public opinion, contributing to the ongoing modification and enlargement of the sense of the community in a republic.[34]

Madison discovered a republican remedy to the age-old problem of majority faction – that is, a cure that preserves and vindicates the ultimate right of the majority to rule – via an analysis of the politics of communication in an extensive republic. On the one hand, a nation should be large enough to include a multiplicity of interests and sects, thereby neutralizing the effects of interest or passion by effectually denying any one interest or sect majority status. The extensive size of the territory makes it less likely that a majority activated by a common passion or interest will be able to communicate effectively and unite for unjust ends. On the other hand, the territory must not be so large that it precludes the communication of ideas within the society. Madison repeatedly insisted on limiting the size of the territory to a practicable sphere – in both the 1780s and the 1790s – because it was a critical component in creating a political environment in which the citizens are able to communicate their honorably motivated sentiments and views and form a public opinion grounded in the principles of justice and the general good. The practicable limit on territorial size thus contributes to the positive political role of a national majority united by a common opinion. The communication of opinions in a large but practicable sphere results in a *modification* of the views of a latent majority. The modified opinion of the majority is achieved through established constitutional processes in a practicably large, representative, federal government, which provides the arena in which to collect, temper, and refine the public views.

Accordingly, Madison did not conceive of the multiplicity of interests and parties in a large republic as an end in itself.[35] The purpose of the

---

[34] "Vices of the Political System of the United States," *PJM* 9:355.

[35] In *Republics Ancient and Modern*, 3 vols. (Chapel Hill: University of North Carolina Press, 1994), Paul Rahe claims that Madison's chief purpose in arguing for the extension of the territory is to achieve a "multiplication of factions" within the society (3:47–48, 55). His scheme "deliberately subverted *homónoia* by promoting in the citizenry a diversity in interests, passions, and even opinions" that was limited only by the "veneration" of citizens for their Constitution (63). Nevertheless, Rahe claims that Madison "recognized all along" that the "consolidation of public sentiment was, in fact, the glue binding the Union together" and that "he never for a moment doubted the need for a measure of unanimity regarding fundamental political principles." The problem, however, is that his arguments in *The Federalist* were "seriously inadequate" and even "flawed" – which Madison came to see in 1791 (182 and n. 158). I appreciate Rahe's acknowledgment that Madison recognized "all along" the need to form a common opinion among the citizenry, particularly on fundamental principles. However, to my knowledge, Madison *never* promoted a multiplicity of *factions*, nor did he encourage a multiplicity of opinions per se (Martin Diamond makes these errors

theory of the 10th *Federalist* is to place obstacles in the path of those groups that are actuated by partial interests and harmful passions, and that themselves impede the discovery of the "comprehensive interests" of the society.[36] Having demonstrated the negative effects of the extensive territory on communication in *Federalist* 10, Madison can then show in the 14th *Federalist* how representation in a large territory encourages communicative activity in the nation. In *Federalist* 14 Publius shifts his focus from the divisive effects of a large territory to the things that unite Americans across the broad swath of republican land. Americans have mingled and shed their blood in defense of freedom and the sacred rights of humanity, he reminded his citizen-readers. They are "knit together... by so many cords of affection," forming one family that has built and inhabits a great and respectable empire. They have a shared past and triumph in governing themselves: they are "mutual guardians of their mutual happiness." In a word, they have consecrated their union.

Madison returned to the subject of forming a common opinion in a large but practicable territory three years later in the Party Press Essay "Public Opinion." In this essay he explained how the proper size and structure of the territory affect the formation of public opinion and contribute to achieving its appropriate degree of influence on government. Contrary to the predominant interpretation of his theory, Madison does not employ the factors of territorial size and governmental structure for the sole purpose of preventing the formation of a factious majority. He also utilizes them to establish the conditions in which *a certain kind of majority* can feasibly form.[37] When public opinion is fixed, Madison taught, it must be obeyed

---

as well; see "Ethics and Politics," 87–90). Moreover, both as Publius and in his letter to Jefferson of October 24, 1787, Madison acknowledged that his discussion in *The Federalist* was incomplete and that a more thorough discussion of republicanism was needed; he did not, however, say or imply (then or later) that his argument was flawed (see *Federalist* 51: 288–89; *PJM* 10:205–20; see also "Notes on Government," *PJM* 14:159, and "Parties," *PJM* 14:198).

[36] *Federalist* 62:347. In the 51st *Federalist* Madison asserts that if a majority is united by a common interest, the rights of the minority will be insecure. Nonetheless, in the 14th, 46th, 52nd, and 58th *Federalists* he argues *for* the discovery of common interest in the society. See *Federalist* 14:67, 46:265, 52:295, and 58:325.

[37] See the excellent article by Tiffany Jones Miller, "James Madison's Republic of 'Mean Extent' Theory: Avoiding the Scylla and Charybdis of Republican Government," *Polity* 39:4 (October 2007), 545–69. Contrary to Miller's suggestion (549), however, she and I actually agree that Madison's aim in promoting the practicable sphere was to achieve the dual objective of thwarting the formation of majority factions *and* achieving due governmental dependence on the people, or public opinion. See, for example, my essay, "The Commerce of Ideas and Cultivation of Character in Madison's Republic," in Bradley C. Watson, ed., *Civic*

by the government. When not settled, it may be influenced by those in government. The extensive size of the territory and the large population make it difficult for a faction to "counterfeit" the opinion of the public; the limitation imposed by the practicable sphere enables the "real" opinion of the public to form and carry effect.[38] Madison argued in both *The Federalist* and the Party Press Essays that the practicable boundaries of a republic can be stretched without sacrificing the formation of the public voice if conditions that ease communication among the citizens are present. These conditions include good transportation routes, improvements in interior navigation, the free circulation of newspapers, and representatives traveling to and from the capital city, all of which act as equivalents to a contraction of the territorial size.[39]

Thus, unlike Rousseau, who opposed the principle of representation and believed that the communication of views is detrimental to achieving the general will, Madison envisioned utilizing a scheme of representation to facilitate the general communication of sentiments and views. Although he was acutely aware of the aggravating effects of seductive rhetoric within legislative chambers, he also claimed that there is an "advantage enjoyed by public bodies struck out by the collision of arguments." We know from the 10th *Federalist* that Madison considered the principle of representation part of the republican solution to the problem of majority faction. We also know that politicians cannot be depended on to exercise reason and restraint. In order to derive the benefit of the "full effect" of representation, Madison tells us in *Federalist* 63, it must be combined with an extensive territory.[40] The will of the society is manifested in government through the constitutionally prescribed processes, which give to the legislature preeminence in public policymaking. A frequently elected legislature is more closely aligned with the will of the people than are the other branches of government. In a large republic, it is less likely to be the pawn of a majority faction than in a small one.

Those who argue that the ancients were unaware of or did not incorporate the idea of representation in classical polities are mistaken, according

Education and Culture (Wilmington, Del.: ISI Books, 2006), 49–72, in which I argue that "the purpose of limiting the territory to a practicable sphere is to keep the representatives dependent on the will of the society"; also see Sheehan, "Public Opinion and the Formation of Civic Character in Madison's Republican Theory," *The Review of Politics*, 67:1 (Winter 2005), 43–44.

[38] "Public Opinion," *PJM* 14:170.

[39] *Federalist* 14:70–71; "Public Opinion," *PJM* 14:170; "Notes on Government," *PJM* 14:161.

[40] *Federalist* 63:355.

to Madison. In *Federalist* 63 Madison offered a number of examples of the institution of popularly elected representative assemblies and councils in classical Greece and Rome. What the ancients failed to do was (1) exclude the people from direct participation in government and (2) combine the principle of representation with territorial extension. The establishment of representation in a small polity does not sufficiently distance the representatives from popular passions and partial interests; even with the existence of a senate to check the representative assemblies of the people, the will of the latter tends to be an irresistible force that ultimately reigns alone in a small territory.[41] Conversely, the extension of the territory considered by itself achieves the inclusion of a multiplicity of interests and sects within the society, thereby making factious combinations of the majority improbable, but it lacks a vehicle for the political formation and expression of the society's will.

In Madison's schema, "the great principle of representation" denies the people a direct agency in lawmaking, but it also functions as the "great mechanical power in government" by which the will of the society converges at a common center and directs the government to the common good.[42] Representation is thus a vehicle for the collection and modification of society's will. In contrast to a nation that is too small and where a majority faction easily arises, or to one that is too large and the public voice cannot be collected, Madison taught that a territory of practicable extent provides the conditions for the communication of ideas, the proper formation of public opinion, and its proper degree of influence on the representatives. Under these circumstances, the representatives are effectively distanced from the influence of the ephemeral passions and partial interests of the diverse factions within their districts while simultaneously being kept dependent on the will of the society.

While separation of powers is generally considered a contrivance to prevent governmental tyranny, Madison sought to use this prudential device to maintain governmental dependence on the people as well. Separation of powers contributes to the "chain of dependence" that binds the will of the government to the will of the public.[43] The "great principle of responsibility" is jeopardized when the powers of government are not effectively divided, Madison argued, and it is sacrificed when the powers are improperly

---

[41] *Federalist* 63:353–57.
[42] *Federalist* 14:68–69.
[43] See "Removal Power of the President," *PJM* 12:256; 12:236–37.

mixed.[44] In the first Congress of the United States, Madison spent considerable time on the floor of the House of Representatives arguing against the proposal to combine the Senate with the executive in the power of removal of officials from the executive branch. Such a mixture of the powers of government violates the principle of separation of powers, he said, for it invites influence and corruption and negates the intended effect of providing for responsibility to the community. Separation of powers assists in promoting a due "responsibility" of government officials to the community, however, in a republic that allows for the effective formation and influence of public opinion.

Madison's goal, then, is not properly understood when it is reduced to the distillation of the people's will by representatives in Congress. To the degree that he sought to distill the popular will through the establishment of "an equilibrium in the interests & passions of the Society," it was for the purpose of creating the conditions necessary to refine and enlarge the opinion of the society.[45] Madison's insight into how territorial size contributes to the achievement of the just majority involves more than a technical dependence on the people via their representatives in Congress. It also entails, to the extent possible, the tempering of factious impulses and the elevation of opinion within the society by means of a dynamic "commerce of ideas" at the level of government and throughout "the entire body of the people."[46] Madison's "modification of the sovereignty" is not merely the alteration of individual state interests and popular views by the national legislature. It is also the modification of public opinion itself.

"In the extent *and proper structure* of the union," Madison wrote in the conclusion to *Federalist* 10, "we behold a republican remedy to the diseases most incident to republican government."[47] In the climactic conclusion of the 51st essay he restates the importance of size *and structure*: "And happily for the *republican cause,* the practicable sphere may be carried to a very great extent by a judicious modification and mixture of the *federal principle.*"[48] The federal structure of the union is an essential component of Madison's theory of the extended republic. In a nation that is too large or lacks such prudential equivalents to territorial limits, the public voice is effectually "silenced." To counteract this, a large nation must incorporate the federal principle, which provides a means to form and collect the public

[44] Ibid., *PJM* 12:237.
[45] "Notes on Government," *PJM* 14:158–59.
[46] Ibid., *PJM* 14:168; "Public Opinion," *PJM* 14:170.
[47] *Federalist* 10:52, emphasis added.
[48] *Federalist* 51:293.

voice. Indeed, without a due degree of power at the state (or what he often called "local") level of government, the extent of the territory would make it impossible for the people to communicate effectively and form a united voice by which to control and direct the measures of government.[49] Conversely, wherever "public opinion is fixed," even "the most arbitrary government is controuled."[50] In a large territory, federalism helps to promote governmental responsibility to the people; it contributes to making the environment conducive to the communication of ideas and the mobilization and expression of public opinion in a nation that would otherwise be too large for republican government.[51] Given the importance of federalism to Madison's republican theory, it is not surprising that when he perceived a Federalist threat to the rightful constitutional authority of the states, he exhorted citizens to support the federal nature of the union and to maintain power within its proper boundaries.[52] In 1792 Madison called upon Americans to dedicate themselves, "with a holy zeal," to their constitutional "scriptures." As social compacts, constitutions are superior to all other forms of political obligations. They are in fact "sacred" trusts, "bound on the conscience by the religious sanctions of an oath."[53] Deriving their moral force from "the only earthly source of authority," they represent the most fundamental expression of the sovereignty of the people and of public opinion. "As metes and bounds of government, they transcend all other land-marks, because every public usurpation is an encroachment on the private right, not of one, but of all."

Madison believed that the authority of public opinion is limited *by* the act of consent to a constitution. But he rejected the idea that it is limited *to* the act of constitutional consent or that it is merely an intermittent expression of authority at times of elections.[54] While the authority of the Constitution is

---

[49] "Consolidation," *PJM* 14:138. Cf. *Federalist* 46; *PJM* 17:247.

[50] *PJM* 14:192.

[51] See the Party Press Essay "Consolidation," *PJM* 14:138–39. Cf. the precursor of the arguments in this essay in *Federalist* 44 and 46. Cf. *PJM* 10:68.

[52] "Charters," *PJM* 14:192.

[53] "Ibid., *PJM* 14:191.

[54] Gary Rosen is correct that for Madison the Constitution is the manifestation of the sovereign "sense of the community" (*American Compact: James Madison and the Problem of Founding* [Lawrence: University Press of Kansas, 1999], 165). However, his insistence that "Madison's solution was a kind of constitutional passion, an unthinking attachment to the Constitution as an end in itself" (127), neglects Madison's concern for public enlightenment and fails to take into account his conception of the dynamic character of public opinion and its continuous operation and influence in the everyday life of the polity. Roger Sharp also gives Madison's conception of public opinion a static quality, arguing that although Madison called for dependence on an enlightened and watchful public, in the early 1790s

fixed and its provisions are unalterable except through the modes of amendment prescribed in the document itself, there are myriad political decisions
that do not involve constitutional questions. In these instances, the government ought to be informed by the considered views of the community. "In
no case," Madison declared, "ought the eyes of the people to be shut... nor
their tongues tied." If left uncontrolled by the people, government "ever
will be administered by passions more than by reason."[55] Contrary to the
notion that Madison wanted the people's involvement limited to voting – or
as Richard K. Matthews puts it, to kicking the bums out of office when

he did not suggest how public opinion would be collected and articulated, regarding it as "a
fixed entity that was supportive of republicanism but essentially inert" (*American Politics in
the Early Republic: The New Nation in Crisis* [New Haven, Conn.: Yale University Press,
1993], 45).

55 "Political Reflections," *PJM* 17:238–39; cf. "Who Are the Best Keepers of the People's
Liberties?" *PJM* 14:426–27; *Federalist* 49:285; *Federalist* 50:287. See also James Madison,
Virginia Ratifying Convention, June 20, 1788, *PJM* 11:163.

"I have observed," Madison said, "that gentlemen suppose, that the general legislature
will do every mischief they possibly can, and that they will omit to do every thing good
which they are authorised [sic] to do. If this were a reasonable supposition, their objections
would be good. I consider it reasonable to conclude, that they will as readily do their
duty, as deviate from it: Nor do I go on the grounds mentioned by gentlemen on the other
side – that we are to place unlimited confidence in them, and expect nothing but the most
exalted integrity and sublime virtue. But I go on this great republican principle, that the
people will have virtue and intelligence to select men of virtue and wisdom. Is there no
virtue among us? If there be not, we are in a wretched situation. No theoretical checks –
no form of government can render us secure. To suppose that any form of government will
secure liberty or happiness without any virtue in the people, is a chimerical idea. If there
be sufficient virtue and intelligence in the community, it will be exercised in the selection of
these men. So that we do not depend on their virtue, or put confidence in our rulers, but in
the people who are to choose them."

This passage is sometimes cited to demonstrate that Madison limited the role of the
people to electing the better sorts of men to public office. But Madison does not in fact
make this argument here. Rather, he says that, as a republican, he believes the people will
have sufficient virtue and intelligence to make a good choice in the election of political
leaders. He does not say that their responsibility is limited to voting good men into office,
nor does he say that a sufficient amount of popular virtue and intelligence guarantees that
those placed in office will possess the requisite virtue and wisdom. He does not say that
once the people cast their votes, they can rest easy in the assurance that their rulers will
exercise moral and intellectual virtue. Instead, Madison argues that once they are elected,
the people should not expect all their representatives to be knaves, nor should they expect
from them "the most exalted integrity and sublime virtue" or place "unlimited confidence"
in them. Madison believed that it is on the people's character and judgment that we must
place ultimate dependence in republican government; since some degree of caution or lack of
trust is appropriate in respect to the rulers, it is logical that the people's judgment should not
sleep between elections, but rather remain actively exercised. Thus, as he argues in "Who
Are the Best Keepers of the People's Liberties?" the antirepublicans believe:

they got out of line – Madison explicitly argued the reverse.[56] The doctrine that has "so ardently been propagated by many, that in a republic the people ought to consider the whole of their political duty as discharged when they have chosen their representatives" and "that the people ought at all times to place an unlimited confidence in rulers" they have chosen, is false, he protested. Just as he had indicated in *The Federalist* a decade earlier, in "Political Reflections" Madison insisted that the people are the primary control on the government, that they have a real and ongoing role in the political life of their country, and that the manifestation of the reason of the public results from their active political participation and the communication of ideas.

The advent of circulating newspapers significantly increased communication among the people and contributed to the power of public opinion in the eighteenth century, a phenomenon clearly grasped by Madison and many of his contemporaries abroad.[57] The rise of the mass media also made communication over a large territory possible for the first time in history. It was now possible to found a nation large enough to impede the formation of a majority faction and at the same time establish the circumstances that make possible a genuine "commerce of ideas" throughout an extensive territory. To my knowledge, this original, momentous insight belongs to James Madison. Madison envisioned newspapers serving as vehicles for circulating the ideas of the literati to the people of the extensive American

> The people are stupid, suspicious, licentious. They cannot safely trust themselves. When they have established government they should think of nothing but obedience, leaving the care of their liberties to their wiser rulers.

In contrast, Republicans believe:

> Although all men are born free, and all nations might be so, yet too true it is, that slavery has been the general lot of the human race. Ignorant – they have been cheated; asleep – they have been surprized; divided – the yoke has been forced upon them. But what is the lesson? That because the people *may* betray themselves, they ought to give themselves up, blindfold, to those who have an interest in betraying them? Rather conclude that the people ought to be enlightened, to be awakened, to be united, that after establishing a government they should watch over it, as well as obey it.

[56] See Richard K. Matthews, *If Men Were Angels: James Madison & the Heartless Empire of Reason* (Lawrence: University Press of Kansas, 1995), 159; cf. 162–63. See also Thomas Pangle, *The Spirit of Modern Republicanism* (Chicago: University of Chicago Press, 1988), 44, 96–98.

[57] For a discussion of the relationship between newspapers and the influence of Democratic-Republican societies in America in the 1790s, see Albrecht Koschnik, "The Democratic Societies of Philadelphia and the Limits of the American Public Sphere, circa 1793–1795," *William and Mary Quarterly* 58:3 (July 2001), 615–36.

republic, resulting in the refinement and enlargement of the public views and the emergence of an enlightened public opinion.

Indeed, Madison assigned a free press and the literati a critically important role in republican government. "If we are to take for the criterion of truth the majority of suffrages," Madison wrote in early 1790, "they ought to be gathered from those philosophic and patriotic citizens who cultivate their reason, apart from the scenes which distract its operations, and expose it to the influence of the passions."[58] Moreover, "it is the duty . . . of intelligent and faithful citizens to discuss and promulgate [political information and ideas] freely" in order to control government by the "censorship of public opinion" and "according to the rules of the Constitution."[59] Circulating print media serve to communicate the ideas of the educated and patriotic members of society to the people at large. The literati are thus charged with the role of civic educators in Madison's republic, and their contribution to the common benefit of the community is no less necessary than that of the husbandman or the manufacturer. The "literati," Madison declared,

are the cultivators of the human mind – the manufacturers of useful knowledge – the agents of the commerce of ideas – the censors of public manners – the teachers of the arts of life and the means of happiness.[60]

Madison's use of the language of agriculture and manufacturing in his description of the highest aims of the new republic was clearly no accident. He intentionally meant to contrast his vision of the American commercial republic and its hero, the merchant of ideas and mores, with the narrower Hamiltonian emphasis on commerce as material exchange and profit. Madison's choice of wording in this Party Press Essay reminds one of a passing comment by David Hume in one of his essays. Perhaps Madison meant to remind his colleague Hamilton of the broader and more elevated views of the Scotsman whom he admired. According to Christopher J. Finlay, Hume saw the role of the men of letters as that of "moderating opinion through dialogue" and contributing to "a *commerce* of ideas" within society.[61] "The Materials of this Commerce must chiefly be furnish'd by Conversation and

---

[58] Madison to Benjamin Rush, March 7, 1790, *PJM* 13:93.
[59] Meyers, *Mind of the Founder*, 264.
[60] "Notes on Government," *PJM* 14:168.
[61] Christopher J. Finlay, "Hume's Theory of Civil Society," *European Journal of Political Theory* 3:4 (2004), 384.

common Life," Hume wrote. "The manufacturing of them alone belongs to Learning."[62]

The indispensable role Madison assigned the enlightened citizens of a republic demonstrates that he was no adherent of the notion that the clash of rival interests is an acceptable substitute for "better opinions" in a republican society.[63] In fact, he looked to the most thoughtful and virtuous citizens to keep the people informed about political activity at the seat of government; to prompt them, when necessary, to censure governmental measures; and, in general, to instruct the citizenry in the morals and manners of republicanism. Their influence on public opinion serves to anchor a republican citizenry in the moral principles of free government.

Madison's advocacy of the commerce of ideas and politics of public opinion was his sustained attempt to solve the problem of majority opinion in a manner fully consistent with the form *and spirit* of popular government. The spirit of free government cannot be attained by achieving the people's consent and then dissociating them from the acts of government. The spirit of republicanism is present only when it is embodied in the minds and mores of the citizens and sustained by the activity of political participation and communication throughout the land. The construction of public opinion involves a process of instructive dialogue and deliberation that permeates the whole society, from the influence of the literati, the statesmen, and the laws on the mores and views of the citizens, to the communication of ideas throughout the great body of the people, to the influence of the settled opinion of the community on the representatives in government. Accordingly, public opinion is both acted upon and is itself an active political agent upon which government depends for its direction. The process of forming public opinion is a time-consuming and complex one, much like the process of establishing precedents in courts of law or, better yet, the challenge of education in a free society. Majority opinion in a republican polity is constantly in the process of constructing itself within an intellectual, moral, and psychological milieu larger than itself. This architectonic influence over the minds and morals of the public influences the decisions of government and the laws of the land, which in turn operate on the understanding and interest of the public. This is Madison's solution to the difficult challenge he set himself when preparing for the Federal Convention, that is, how to

---

[62] David Hume, "Of Essay Writing," in David Hume, *Essays: Moral, Political, and Literary*, Eugene F. Miller, ed. (Indianapolis: Liberty Classics, 1985), 535.

[63] See Diamond, "Ethics and Politics: The American Way," 93.

achieve a "modification of the Sovereignty."[64] Public opinion is the sovereign authority in a genuine republic whose mild voice of reason is capable of transforming the will of a nation. It is no surprise, then, how often Madison put pen to paper in the public press, or that he urged his fellow citizens, despite all artificial and circumstantial distinctions, to come together as one people under the mantle of the "Empire of reason."

[64] "Vices of the Political System of the United States," *PJM* 9:357.

5

The Politics of Public Opinion

Throughout the 1790s, Madison worked to prevent measures that he believed were contrary to the sovereign authority of the people as expressed in the Constitution. He also sought to establish and secure a political system dependent on the ongoing sovereignty of public opinion. These modes of authority informed Madison's stances on policy questions during the 1790s. To show as clearly as possible how Madison's republican theory informed his political practice in this period, the issues of the Washington administration will be treated thematically rather than chronologically in this chapter. We begin with those measures that raised the issue of the relationship between public opinion and constitutional meaning, that is, the adoption of a bill of rights, the establishment of a national bank, and governmental support of manufactures, and then proceed to the policy issues that impacted the ongoing politics of public opinion, viz., the national debt, foreign policy, and commercial discrimination.[1] In the next chapter the Alien and Sedition Acts and the Kentucky and Virginia Resolutions will be examined, as well as the main philosophic points of agreement and disagreement between the two leading Republicans, Madison and Jefferson.

---

[1] Early in the first Washington administration Madison took an active role on issues concerning the Revolutionary War debt, including an attempt to distinguish between original and present holders of the debt certificates and the effort to stymie Hamilton's plan for the national assumption of states debts as they presently stood, i.e., after some states had complied with the old Congress's request for payment and others had not.

Debt discrimination and assumption were clearly important issues for Madison; they involved the application of equal justice to individuals and citizens of states. As important as they were, however, he also understood that they were issues that were not clear-cut or of enduring significance to the republican character of the nation.

When Madison introduced the Bill of Rights in the first Congress in 1789, he did so with some reluctance. His concern was that the specification of certain rights in the Constitution might be erroneously construed to disparage other rights not listed in the document. He insisted many times over that the United States Constitution was one in which the people gave to government certain enumerated powers, not one in which government gave to the people certain rights. Still, the opponents of the new Constitution had expressed serious reservations about whether the proposed plan would effectually limit the powers of government. In 1788, Madison pledged his support for a bill of rights. His support was a tactical move to win ratification of the Constitution without calling a second convention. But he also had another reason: A bill of rights, like maxims that preceded the constitutions of old, could have the effect of educating public opinion on the fundamental principles of the polity.[2] As respect for these rights becomes incorporated into public opinion, public opinion defines and limits the demands of the majority. Over time, a bill of rights acts as a kind of republican schoolmaster, serving as a civic lexicon by which the people teach themselves the grammar and meaning of freedom. The more ancient the lineage of the constitutional declaration, the more influence it exerts on the views and sentiments of the people. As an expression of the political principles and moral sentiments of the society, a bill of rights is a manifestation of how ethical motives can and do influence the formation of majority opinion.

Thus, even before the formation of the new government (and before Hamilton unveiled any part of his program and prior to Jefferson's return to the United States), Madison applied his theory of public opinion to political practice. He grounded his ultimate support for a bill of rights on the benefit of incorporating "political truths" into the fabric of "national sentiment" and worked to establish the practice of making "an appeal to the sense of the community" on certain critical constitutional questions.[3] Shortly after taking his seat in the First Congress he repeated his reasons for advocating a declaration of rights, adding that the act would help to consolidate the opinion of the community in support of the new Constitution.[4] It would

---

[2] For an in-depth discussion of Madison's position on a bill of rights, see Edward J. Erler, "James Madison and the Framing of the Bill of Rights: Reality and Rhetoric in the New Constitutionalism," *Political Communications* 9 (1992), 213–29.

[3] Madison to Jefferson, October 17, 1788, *PJM* 11:298–99.

[4] Ibid.; "Amendments to the Constitution," June 8, 1789, *PJM* 12:204–9. See also Madison to Jefferson, December 8, 1788, *PJM* 11:382–83; "Notes on Government," *PJM* 14:162–63.

contribute to establishing the principles of free government not merely on paper, but in the minds and hearts of the American citizens. "In proportion as government is influenced by opinion," Madison wrote, "it must be so, by whatever influences opinion. This decides the question concerning a Constitutional Declaration of Rights, which requires an influence on government, by becoming part of the public opinion."[5]

In the debate over the bank bill in early 1791 Madison again appealed to public opinion, claiming that the establishment of a national bank was contrary to the sense in which the Constitution had been understood and adopted.[6] "[T]he enlightened opinion and affection of the people," he argued, "[are] the only solid basis for the support of this government."[7] If those congressmen who have suggested an "appeal to the public opinion" are sincere, then "we ought to let our constituents have an opportunity to form an opinion on the subject."[8] In the months following this controversy, he and Jefferson began working actively to foster the agency of public opinion and establish its authoritative role in the politics of the new nation.

Madison's central argument against the institution of a national bank was that it violated the Constitution, as understood by the people who ratified and adopted it.[9] He viewed Hamilton's proposal to establish the bank as an attempt to use unconstitutional means to accomplish legitimate ends. Hamilton's "Report on Manufactures" went even further: it proposed the national exercise of power to achieve *ends* not mandated by

---

[5] "Public Opinion," *PJM* 14:170. See also "Notes on Government," *PJM* 14:162–63; Marvin Meyers, *The Mind of the Founder: Sources of Political Thought of James Madison* (Hanover, N.H.: Brandeis University Press, 1981), 169.

[6] "The Bank Bill," February 2, 1791, *PJM* 13:381.

[7] Ibid., February 8, 1791, *PJM* 13:386–87.

[8] Ibid., *PJM* 13:387. See also "The Bank Bill," February 2, 1791, *PJM* 13:381. Madison later defended his change of position on the constitutionality of the national bank on the grounds that the issue had been determined by established precedents and settled public opinion. He denied the charge of inconsistency by demonstrating that in both cases he had appealed to the same standard of public opinion. By 1816, not only had the national bank been sanctioned by successive legislatures and by local authorities, it had received the "acquiescence ... of the nation at large" and there was little if any prospect for "any change in the public opinion." Under such circumstances, Madison concluded, an executive veto "would have been a defiance of all obligations *derived from a course of precedents amounting to the requisite evidence of the national judgment and intention*" (Meyers, *Mind of the Founder*, 393, emphasis added).

[9] "The Bank Bill," February 2, 1791, *PJM* 13:372–382; "The Bank Bill," February 8, 1791, *PJM* 13:383–387; "Draft Veto of the Bank Bill," *PJM* 13:395–96; Max Farrand, ed., *The Records of the Federal Convention of 1787*, rev. ed., 4 vols. (New Haven, Conn.: Yale University Press, 1937), 3:533–34.

the Constitution.[10] Madison viewed the Constitution of the United States as the embodiment of the highest expression of the opinion of the public. No expression of the public, however widespread and popular, is superior to the voice of the people expressed in its most sovereign capacity in this document. Only the extraconstitutional invocation of the right of revolution can claim moral superiority. The American idea of constitutionalism is derivative of the principle of popular sovereignty, which forms the democratic basis for the doctrine of originalism. No one took this doctrine more seriously than Madison. Indeed, as Jack Rakove argues, Madison was the founding father of originalism, or the original originalist.[11] Madison viewed Hamilton's construction of the Constitution as more than a point of legal debate. It struck at the central philosophical tenets of republican government. The idea of consent of the governed means that something was consented to – understood and agreed to – by the people in their most sovereign capacity. The people are "the only earthly source of authority," Madison wrote. The charters authenticated by their seal in the solemn act of founding constitute the most sacred trusts. Constitutions are, in essence, the holy writs of this world, the "political scriptures" of faithful citizens. "They are bound on the conscience by the religious sanction of an oath . . . , [transcending] all other land-marks, because every public usurpation is an encroachment on the private right, not of one, but of all."[12] Hamilton's loose interpretation of the Constitution effectively removed the limitations on the power of government placed there by the authority of the people, undermining the very principle of popular sovereignty.

It has been argued that Madison's altered position on the national bank during his presidency represents an abandonment of the doctrine of constitutional supremacy since, in this instance, he trumped the authority of the Constitution with the power of ordinary public opinion and legislative precedent.[13] I believe this is an erroneous reading of the explanation Madison provided for his change of view. Madison was not arguing that ordinary public opinion – even when settled over a course of many years and informing established precedents – is ever superior to the Constitution. His argument

---

[10] Madison to Henry Lee, January 1, 1792, *PJM* 14:180; Madison to Henry Lee, January 21, 1792, *PJM* 14:193.

[11] See Jack N. Rakove's Pulitzer Prize–winning book *Original Meanings: Politics and Ideas in the Making of the Constitution* (New York: First Vintage Books, 1996), ch. XI. I would disagree with Rakove, however, that Madison's originalism was the result of a conversion to the doctrine in the mid-1790s.

[12] "Charters," *PJM* 14:191.

[13] Meyers, *Mind of the Founder*, 389–90; Gary Rosen, *America Compact: James Madison and the Problem of Founding* (Lawrence: University Press of Kansas, 1999), 140.

was that for over twenty years public opinion had acquiesced in the decision to establish a national bank, demonstrating that *the generation that ratified the Constitution* was in fact *not* adverse to it and did not understand it to be contrary to the Constitution – even if Madison himself, in "his solitary opinion," had.[14] Accordingly, the bank was not *nor ever had been* unconstitutional. Madison is not here confessing to any weakening of his dedication to the Constitution as the supreme authority in all cases, nor is he admitting to any inconsistency of principle. Rather, he is conceding that he had misread public opinion on the issue in the early 1790s. The establishment of a national bank was not, as he had earlier thought, contrary to the Constitution, as understood by the public who ratified it. Thus, as president, he could respect legislative precedent because the institution of the bank was not an unconstitutional exercise of power, but only an ordinary, legitimate legislative act. His action as president did not represent an exception to the idea of the fundamental authority of the Constitution, and indeed he was, without fail, committed to the doctrine of constitutionalism throughout his life. "A Constitution being derived from a superior authority," he said in 1831, "is to be expounded and obeyed, *not controlled or varied*, by the subordinate authority of a Legislature."[15] Accordingly, Madison did change his mind on the issue of the constitutionality of a national bank – as he openly conceded – but he did so in order to remain consistent with his fundamental principles.

Whereas Madison's original position on the national bank and the "Report on Manufactures" stemmed from his perception that such exercises of power were contrary to the constitutional voice of the public, his opposition to the perpetuation of the public debt resulted from the effect it would have on the ongoing sovereignty of public opinion. Hamilton was correct to think that he had Madison's general support for funding the public debt, and indeed Madison argued on the floor of the House of Representatives in early 1790 that the debt incurred in the war for independence must be funded. However, Madison's general view was that although funding was at times necessary in the life of a nation, it was nonetheless an evil.[16] While he assented to those measures necessary to reestablish public credit and retire the debt, he was adamantly opposed to a perpetuation of it and, in fact, had been so for many years.[17] The extension of the debt would only increase the

---

[14] Meyers, *Mind of the Founder*, 390–93.
[15] Ibid., 391, emphasis added.
[16] "Assumption of State Debts," *PJM* 13:75.
[17] Madison to Edmund Randolph, March 14, 1790, *PJM* 13:106, "Address of the House of Representatives to the President," *PJM* 13:317; cf. "Discrimination between Present and

distance between the national government and the interests of the people. Public debt generally results from the costs of running a war and outfitting an army, all of which tend to increase executive discretionary power, corruption in government, and governmental independence of the popular will, he argued in the Party Press Essay "Universal Peace."[18] Such has been the ploy used by governments to extend and perpetuate arbitrary power throughout human history. The cure for this, Madison declared, is to make the will of the government "subordinate to, or rather the same with, the will of the community."[19] Furthermore, to the extent possible, each generation should bear the financial burden of debts it has taken on, thereby prompting "avarice . . . to calculate the expences of ambition" and "in the equipoise of these passions, [leaving] reason . . . free to decide for the public good."[20] By "permanent and constitutional maxims of conduct" the executive temptation to go to war must be moderated by the legislative representatives' willingness for war, contingent on the opinion of their constituents. The people's temptation to wage war is controlled by "subjecting the will of the society to the reason of the society."[21]

A few years later, in the exchange with Hamilton writing as Pacificus, Madison as Helvidius insisted on the legislative nature of the power to declare war and make treaties, as delineated in the Constitution. "Under colour of vindicating an important public act," Helvidius wrote in his first installment, Pacificus "advanced [principles] which strike at the vitals of [the nation's] constitution, as well as at its honor and true interest."[22] The violation of the principle of separation of powers manifested in the president's Proclamation of Neutrality in 1793 was a travesty in respect to "the simple, the received, and the fundamental doctrine of the constitution, that the power to declare war[,] including the power of judging of the causes of war[,] is *fully* and *exclusively* vested in the legislature."[23] The arguments of the Helvidius essays encompass both a question of constitutional meaning and the issue of governmental dependence on the will of the people. In respect to the former, Madison declared the proclamation unconstitutional based

Original Holders of the Public Debt," *PJM* 13:37; "Notes on Debates," February 21, 1783, *PJM* 6:272; "Notes on Debates," February 27, 1783, *PJM* 6:298.

[18] "Universal Peace," *PJM* 14:206–9, "The Union: Who Are Its Real Friends?" *PJM* 14:274–75; Madison to Jefferson, February 15, 1795, *PJM* 15:474; "Political Observations," *PJM* 15:518.

[19] "Universal Peace," *PJM* 14:207.

[20] Ibid., *PJM* 14:208.

[21] Ibid., *PJM* 14:207.

[22] "Helvidius Number 1," *PJM* 15:66.

[23] "Helvidius Number 4," *PJM* 15:108.

on original intent, that is, on the "simple" meaning of the Constitution and the manner in which it was "received" or understood by the Framers and the ratifying public. In his second claim, we see how he combined the "doctrine" of American constitutionalism with the principle of the ongoing sovereignty of public opinion. In essence, Madison argued that Pacificus's defense of the Neutrality Proclamation is contrary to the republican principles that inform the Constitution. Specifically, it is grounded in an interpretation of the prerogative power that is inconsistent with the doctrine of popular sovereignty. Madison would later employ a similar twofold argument in his case against the Sedition Act. In the present case, however, he did not have a constitutional provision to demonstrate decisively the "simple" and "received" meaning of the Constitution, nor, given the increasingly imprudent antics of the French minister Genet, was it at all clear that public opinion endorsed his viewpoint. He was thus compelled to focus on the much more theoretical and complex argument regarding the republican doctrine at the foundation of the United States Constitution and, when his efforts proved ineffective, to adopt a more quarrelsome approach and tone. When all was said and done, Madison was disappointed in his own performance as Helvidius. His frustration stemmed from the resulting "polemical" character of the essays and his failure to do justice to the complex constitutional and practical issues involved in the controversy over the war and treaty powers.[24]

Helvidius's case for governmental dependence on the will of the people continued the argument Madison presented in "Universal Peace." "War is in fact the true nurse of executive aggrandizement," Helvidius wrote.[25] Quoting one of Hamilton's contributions to *The Federalist*, Helvidius argued that a "hereditary monarch . . . [is] often the oppressor of his people," though generally he has too much personally at stake in his government to be corrupted by a foreign power.[26] An elective magistrate, on the other hand, may

---

[24] See "Detached Memoranda" in Jack N. Rakove, ed., *James Madison: Writings* (New York: Library of America, 1999), 770. Later in his life (ca. 1819?), Madison wrote about his Helvidius essays: "I ought not perhaps to acknowle[d]ge my having written this polemic tract, without acknowle[d]ging at the same time my consciousness & regret, that it breathes a spirit which was of no advantage either to the subject, or to the Author. If an apology for this, & for other faults can be made it must be furnished by the circumstances, of the pamphlet being written in much haste, during an intense heat of the weather, and under an excitement stimulated by friends, agst a publication breathing not only the intemperance of party, but giving as was believed a perverted view of President Washington's proclamation of neutrality, and calculated to put a dangerous gloss on the Constitution of the U.S." Cf. Curtis A. Bradley and Martin S. Flaherty, "Executive Power Essentialism and Foreign Affairs," *Michigan Law Review* 102 (2004), 684–88.

[25] "Helvidius Number 4," *PJM* 15:108.

[26] Ibid., *PJM* 15:109.

be tempted by avarice to sacrifice the interests of his fellow citizens and by ambition to betray his country. Madison feared that Pacificus's construction of the American Constitution would destroy the rudimentary constitutional conditions necessary to the achievement of an impartial umpire in republican government. The advantage of absolute monarchy, he argued, is that the king is sufficiently neutral toward the different interests and parties of his country, whereas in a republic the will of the majority may sacrifice the interests of the minority.[27] Conversely, the advantage of republics is that the sovereign will is sufficiently restrained from making decisions contrary to the interests of the society; in monarchy it is not, and the king may sacrifice the interests and happiness of his subjects to his own personal ambition and gain. The arbitrariness of republican government is remedied by enlarging the sphere, thwarting the formation of a majority faction, and providing adequate conditions for the refinement of public views. This remedy, however, is contingent on maintaining the beneficial effects of republican government: the will of the government must be dependent on the will of the whole society and prevented from setting up an interest adverse to it. The United States Constitution lodges the question of war and peace with the legislature, not with the president, Helvidius asserted, and gives the latter only a partial and not the sole power to make treaties, precisely to weaken the executive temptation to betray the interest of the nation and to ensure that the will of the government is dependent on and responsible to the people.

Madison understood that political neutrality and commercial nondiscrimination toward the British were critical to the success of Hamilton's domestic economic program. He viewed Hamilton's willingness to allow the continuance of American economic subordination to the British as a sacrifice of national honor and interest in order to advance short-term economic gains. In the long run, Madison believed, the economic, political, and moral strength of the United States were tied to achieving a nonsubservient economic position. (Hamilton had claimed just the opposite result from his policies, that is, some short-term disadvantages but long-term economic and political benefits.) Prior to and at the very outset of the First Congress, and time and time again throughout the 1790s and in subsequent years, Madison argued that the establishment of a beneficial or at least more equitable commercial policy with the British would take fully into account American preeminence in agriculture and Great Britain's dependence on American produce. While England depended on the United States for the

---

[27] "Vices of the Political System of the United States," *PJM* 9:357; Madison to Washington, April 16, 1787, *PJM* 9:384.

raw materials used in its manufacturing industry, its West Indian colonies – from which it drew an immense income – depended on the United States for the necessities of life. In Madison's judgment, there was no good reason to adopt Hamilton's servile response to British commercial dominance and allow it to treat the United States as if it were still a British colony. Commercial retaliation against the British would force a change in trade policy; other markets, particularly France, could substitute for losses in Anglo-American commerce.

Throughout Madison's political career the British commercial monopoly was a stinging thorn in his side, which perhaps explains his unrealistic assessment that America could bring the world's most advanced economic nation to its knees.[28] Nevertheless, he pursued a policy based on this train of thought for decades. In the Washington administration he viewed the Hamilton-inspired Neutrality Proclamation of 1793 and the Jay Treaty of 1795 as continuing demonstrations of shameful deference to the empire that America had fought and defeated in order to end political oppression and economic subjugation. During his tenure as secretary of state under President Jefferson, the United States finally demanded a fairer trade policy from the British and, in the effort to force Great Britain to comply, passed the Embargo Act of 1807. The retaliatory policy had little effect on Great Britain but was economically disastrous for the United States, the very result Hamilton had predicted during the Washington administration. By 1812 America was embroiled in war with the British, which was derisively tagged by some "Mr. Madison's War." Hamilton was no longer around to say, "I told you so," but many of his Federalist cohorts were.

During the war between England and France in the 1790s, Madison attempted to counteract the "Anglican Party" and the false appearance that public opinion endorsed its prejudices for England and against France. He and James Monroe produced a model resolution to be distributed at country meetings, the object of which was to provide a means to mobilize, collect, and manifest "the genuine sense" and "real sentiments of the people" – that is, "the agricultural" and "commanding part of the society" – and to negate the counterfeiting of public opinion coming from the nation's commercial centers.[29] He believed that the Federalists' domestic political and economic policies, like their foreign commercial policy, catered to the wealthy few

---

[28] See Stanley Elkins and Eric McKitrick, *The Age of Fedealism: The Early Republic, 1788–1800* (New York: Oxford University Press, 1984), 130–31, 376–77.

[29] Madison to Jefferson, September 2, 1793, *PJM* 15:92–93; cf. Lance Banning, *The Sacred Fire of Liberty: James Madison & the Founding of the Federal Republic* (Ithaca, N.Y.: Cornell University Press, 1995), 377–78.

and ignored the opinion of the majority of the people who resided outside the capital and the urban financial centers of New York and Philadelphia. Hamilton's plan to perpetuate the national debt undercut the republican principle of governmental responsibility to the will of the people. The establishment of a national bank and governmental support of manufacturers exacerbated this, further creating a two-tiered class system with wealthy urban financial speculators favored at the expense of the opinions and interests of the majority of rural farmers who worked for a living and produced the real wealth of the nation.

In both the international and national arenas, Madison advocated a system of free trade grounded in the property rights of individuals (versus the artificial notion of the wealth of nations, which served as the excuse for commercial discrimination policies). In the first month of the first session of the First Congress, before Jefferson's return from France and before Hamilton had been offered the position of secretary of the treasury, Madison declared on the floor of the House:

> I own myself the friend to a very free system of commerce, and hold it as a truth, that commercial shackles are generally unjust, oppressive and impolitic – it is also a truth, that if industry and labour are left to take their own course, they will generally be directed to those objects which are the most productive, and this in a more certain and direct manner than the wisdom of the most enlightened legislature could point out.[30]

If the general principle that "commerce ought to be free, and labour and industry left at large to find its proper object" is a good one, Madison said, the only question remaining is to discover the exceptions to this rule that must be considered because of particular circumstances.

Speaking directly to the representatives of the northern states, whose interest it was to promote the manufacturing industry, he said: "The states that are most advanced in population and ripe for manufactures, ought to have their particular interest attended to *in some degree.*"[31] Though manufactures may arise without any encouragement from government, as has happened in some of the states, in other states import duties and regulations have advanced the industry, and these manufactures ought not to go out of business because of the establishment of a new general government. To neglect those industries already established and turn their labor into other channels would be cruel, for the shift from one employment to another is neither easy for men nor without injury to them. It is therefore prudent for

[30] "Import and Tonnage Duties," *PJM* 12:71.
[31] Ibid., *PJM* 12:70 (emphasis added).

government to offer a fostering hand to some of those existing manufactures that would otherwise fail.[32]

However, Madison contended, it was also proper for the members of the legislature to consider the means to encourage agriculture, which is justly considered "the great staple of America." The agricultural industry cultivates the spontaneous productions of nature and has "manifest preference . . . over every other object of emolument in this country." Furthermore, America is unrivaled in the world in agricultural resources and potential productivity, and this is not the case with manufactures. The establishment of a beneficial or at least more equitable commercial policy with other countries, particularly Great Britain, would take fully into account American preeminence in agriculture and other nations' dependence on its produce. In Madison's view, agriculture was the most beneficial object of human employment for the United States and the industry most productive of real wealth in a nation. Governmental encouragement of manufactures artificially diverts human industry from a more to a less beneficial course and therefore ought to be limited to prudential considerations regarding existing establishments that would otherwise perish.[33]

A nation whose citizens depend for their livelihood on the manufactured production of superfluities and the whims of fashion and fancy, Madison claimed, is one in which one class of citizens lives in servile dependence on another. "In proportion as a nation consists of that description of citizens, and depends on external commerce, it is dependent on the consumption and caprice of other nations."[34] Madison did not share Hamilton's dream that America become an industrial prodigy. The way of life of the husbandman, he argued in 1792, is "the most truly independent and happy."[35] A nation predominant in agriculture is most favorable to the health, virtue, intelligence, competency, liberty, and safety of the greatest number of individuals. A manufacturing nation, by contrast, courts the dangers of wantonness and waste, inviting into its environs the wretchedness of the Bridewells and Bedlams.[36] As population increases, a proportion of the inhabitants of a

[32] Ibid., *PJM* 12:72.

[33] Ibid., *PJM* 12:70–72.

[34] "Fashion," *PJM* 14:258; cf. "Notes on Government," *PJM* 14:164–65; "Dependent Territories," *PJM* 17:559–60.

[35] "Republican Distribution of Citizens," *PJM* 14:246. For an extensive and excellent treatment of Madison's ideas on political economy see Drew R. McCoy, *The Elusive Republic: Political Economy and the American Revolution* (Chapel Hill: University of North Carolina Press, 1992).

[36] "Republican Distribution of Citizens," *PJM* 14:244–46; "Fashion," *PJM* 14:257–59.

nation will gradually and naturally shift their employment from agriculture to the manufacturing, mechanical, and commercial industries, but this diversion ought not to be artificially encouraged. Rather, "it ought to be seen with regret as long as occupations more friendly to human happiness lie vacant." Domestic manufactures would develop naturally, he said, at the stage when "hands [are] not called for by agriculture."[37]

The idea of jump-starting the manufacturing and mechanical industry in order to encompass within the extended republic a greater number and variety of interests and enhanced rivalry of parties was not part of Madison's vision in the 10th or any other *Federalist* essay.[38] It is in fact contrary to his anticipations in that work. There was no reason for him to believe that, when writing essays for *The Federalist*, anything but the natural course of economic development would affect the choice of occupations of American citizens or the commercial character of the republic. Domestic manufactures would develop naturally, he contended, at the stage when agricultural labor reaches a surplus.[39]

In the Party Press Essay "Parties" Madison argued against governmental measures that encourage further divisiveness in society, claiming that such a policy is not consistent with republicanism. In "Property" he added to this discussion the claim that such measures violate both the rights of property and the rights of persons. Property is not secure, he asserted, when unequal taxes burden one kind of property and reward another; nor is it protected when part of the citizenry is denied the free exercise of their faculties and the free choice of their occupations. Building on *Federalist* 10's claim that the rights of property originate in men's free exercise of their diverse faculties, he argued that the individual's free use of his faculties and choice of occupation not only constitute his property in the common meaning of the word, but are the "means of acquiring property strictly so called."[40] When understood in this context, it is not difficult to comprehend Madison's alarm when Hamilton unveiled his "Report on Manufactures." The protection of these different faculties, Madison had written in *The Federalist*, "is the first object of government."[41]

---

[37] *Federalist* 41:230.
[38] See Alan Gibson, "The Commercial Republic & the Pluralist Critique of Marxism: An Analysis of Martin Diamond's Interpretation of *Federalist* 10," *Polity* 25:4 (Summer 1993), 497–528, especially 506–9, 513.
[39] *Federalist* 41.
[40] "Property," *PJM* 14:267.
[41] *Federalist* 10:46.

Stemming from the free exercise of his faculties, man has a property "in his opinions and in the free communication of them."[42] When the power of government is excessive and unjustly interventionist, no man is secure in his opinions or in the effective communication of them. This is a particular danger in a large republic, since the size of a nation has the effect of making communication and the discovery of a united purpose more difficult. If public opinion is to exert adequate and proper control on the government, it must have sufficient channels through which it can be expressed, formed, and enlightened. The work of collecting, coalescing, and shaping public opinion is accomplished by a variety of conditions and processes, including state and local governmental bodies, educational institutions and the learned professions, the circulation of newspapers throughout the nation, the exchange of views between representatives and their constituents, and deliberation among the representatives at the seat of government.

From Madison's perspective, the sum total of the Federalist initiatives of the 1790s constituted an agenda clearly intended to undermine republican principles and practices. Inspired by Hamilton's vision of economic and political greatness for America, the Federalists supported a slavish dependence on the British commercial empire and the creation of a system that promoted inequality of property by governmental fiat and tied the interests of the favored opulent class to the national government. Madison believed that this clever scheme would have the effect of strengthening and consolidating the powers of the national government and undermining the constitutional and practical limitations placed on its authority. The concentration of power at the national level would diminish the power of the state governments. Since a single national legislature is not competent to regulate all the objects of government over so large a territory, the power of the national executive would unduly grow; this would open the way for legislative corruption and render less effectual the voice of the people and their control on the legislature.[43] This would have the eventual effect of transforming the executive office into one of "unlimited discretion," in opposition "to the will and subversive of the authority of the people."[44] By the close of the 1790s, with the passage of the Alien and Sedition Acts, Republicans saw only too vividly what they had vaguely feared earlier in the decade: if successful, Federalist measures would produce a "universal silence," leaving the national

---

[42] "Notes on Government," *PJM* 14:166.
[43] "Consolidation," *PJM* 14:138.
[44] "The Union: Who Are Its Real Friends?" *PJM* 14:274.

government to act independently of the will of the society and free to pursue a *"self directed course."*[45]

Madison's opposition to the Hamiltonian-led Federalist agenda was not the result of inconsistency, nor was Jefferson responsible for the political estrangement between the two leading Publii. As noted earlier, in the case of the influence of a bill of rights on the formation of public opinion as well as Madison's advocacy of commercial discrimination against the British, he had formulated and publicly expressed his views on these matters before Jefferson's return from France and prior to Hamilton's stint as secretary of the treasury. Madison did not, as some scholars contend, seek to insulate national politics from public opinion in the 1780s and then develop "a new feeling for the legitimacy of majorities" and embark on a "new course of theorizing" in the 1790s.[46] Rather, in his writings subsequent to *The Federalist* period he continued to work through the problem of majority faction and to build upon, further formulate, and hone his conception of the politics of public opinion, ultimately placing it at center stage.

Madison had as little confidence that enlightened statesmen would always be at the helm as he had that a simple or aggregate majority of the community would always and only demand those things consistent with natural and political right.[47] Majority faction is the greatest threat and requires the most intense theoretical scrutiny in all polities in which majority opinion actually does reign supreme. In the 1780s, Madison focused his mental energies more on solving the problem of majority faction than minority faction because he was committed to the principle of majority rule *and he envisioned the majority as ultimately determining the law in America.* He did not change his mind about this in the 1790s. In the battle with Hamilton and the Federalists, he fought against minority schemes that he believed would undermine the formation and force of the public voice and substitute an independent

[45] "Consolidation," *PJM* 14:138.

[46] Jack N. Rakove, *James Madison and the Creation of the American Republic* (Glenview, Ill.: Scott Foresman/Little, Brown Higher Education, 1990), 100; Elkins and McKitrick, *The Age of Federalism*, 266; Alan Gibson, "Veneration and Vigilance: James Madison and Public Opinion," *Review of Politics* 67:1 (2005), 5–35.

[47] For the view that Madison relied on enlightened leadership, or the "better sort" of men, see Robert A. Dahl, *A Preface to Democratic Theory* (Chicago: University of Chicago Press, 1956), 1–33; James Roger Sharp, *American Politics in the Early Republic: The New Nation in Crisis* (New Haven, Conn.: Yale University Press, 1993), 2; Garry Wills, *Explaining America: The Federalist* (Garden City, N.Y.: Doubleday, 1981), 179–264; Gordon Wood, "Interests and Disinterestedness in the Making of the Constitution," in Richard Beeman, Stephen Botein, and Edward C. Carter, eds., *Beyond Confederation: Origins of the Constitution and American National Identity* (Chapel Hill: University of North Carolina Press, 1987), 91–93.

governmental will. And he fought to establish in practice what he had conceived at his writing desk. I doubt that he was as surprised about the political realities of the new administration with men such as Hamilton and Adams in power as is often thought. He knew a fair amount about their views, though he did not know for certain how their ideas would play out vis-à-vis the decisions that had been made at Philadelphia and endorsed by the people. Once he saw that the Federalists were bent on ignoring the understanding of those who adopted the Constitution and intent on severing the government from the will of the people, he reacted to their agenda. At the same time, he remained committed to achieving and vindicating majority rule, the architectonic challenge that marked his vocation as the leading philosophic mind of the American Founding.

The philosophic divergence between Madison and Hamilton did not originate in the 1790s, though their prior differences were clearly exacerbated by political events in the formative years under the new Constitution.[48] Certainly, the decisions made in Philadelphia in 1787 and ratified by the people influenced Madison's understanding of the American political system, but this is fully in accord with his unerring commitment to the idea of the Constitution as the encapsulation of the sovereign voice of the people.[49] The accusation of inconsistency would in fact be warranted if he had taken the reverse tack, that is, if he had *not* heeded the authoritative intent of the people, who he believed alone infused the Constitution with life and validity. From Madison's perspective, Hamilton's lack of respect for the authoritative opinion that informed the Constitution and his determination to substitute his own economic and political vision despite the decree of the sovereign public constituted the crux of their political division.

The disagreement between Madison and the Federalists, and in particular with Hamilton, was a battle over the very character of republican

---

[48] See Madison to Jefferson, August 11, 1788, *PJM* 11:227. Regarding the joint authorship of *The Federalist,* Madison told Jefferson that "Though carried in concert the writers are not mutually answerable for all the ideas of each other there being seldom time for even a perusal of the pieces by any but the writer before they were wanted at the press and sometimes hardly by the writer himself." In the "Detached Memoranda," Madison wrote that although at the outset he and Hamilton had sent their essays to each other before they went to press, they soon abandoned this because of the "shortness of time" and also because "it was found most agreeable to each, not to give a positive sanction to all the doctrines and sentiments of the other, there being a known difference in the general complexion of their political theories" (Rakove, *James Madison: Writings*, 769). Cf. Lance Banning, "The Hamiltonian Madison: A Reconsideration," *Virginia Magazine of History and Biography* 92 (1984), 3–28.

[49] See Banning, *Sacred Fire of Liberty*, 171, 191.

government and the extent to which the people are capable of governing themselves. Hamilton did not think Madison's solution of the extended republic and representation went far enough to prevent the problem of majority tyranny. Madison thought Hamilton's measures substituted private interest for public good and undermined the sovereign authority of public opinion. Interestingly, scholars have generally attributed the vision of a modern commercial republic composed of diverse and rival economic interests actuated by the untutored passion of acquisitiveness to James Madison. But this was not, nor ever had been, Madison's vision of republicanism. It is closer to Hamilton's.[50] In fact, Hamilton fits better the description that has traditionally been reserved for Madison, while Madison was a more unhesitating democrat than is generally believed. Hamilton is the chief American theorist of the modern commercial republic, Madison the philosophic architect of the politics of public participation and republican self-government in America.

---

[50] For example, Martin Diamond attributes to Madison the theory that a large republic supplies the remedy for faction only if it is also a *commercial* republic ("Ethics and Politics: The American Way" in Robert H. Horwitz, ed., *The Moral Foundations of the American Republic*, 3rd ed. [Charlottesville: University Press of Virginia, 1986], 54–55; "The Federalist," in Leo Strauss and Joseph Cropsey, eds., *History of Political Philosophy* [Chicago: Rand McNally, 1972], 648). However, I would argue that Diamond's presentation of the commercial republic theory is actually a much more apt interpretation of Hamilton's political and economic thought. According to Diamond's interpretation, Madison's scheme replaces the historical battle between the haves and have-nots with a new factional struggle based on the diversity of economic interests. This required magnifying the operation of interest (and taming or devitalizing passion and opinion) so that citizens would divide themselves on the basis of narrow and particularized economic interests, thereby allowing the society to evade the fatal kind of factionalism caused by opinion and class interest in the past. Rejecting any attempt to refine and improve the citizens' opinions of the advantageous and just, Madison instead accepted as "irredeemably dominant" the self-interested passions sown in human nature. In light of this, he sought to channel the powerful passions and interests of the society by way of shrewd institutional arrangements rather than engage in the futile attempt to form the character of the citizenry. While the theory of the commercial republic presented by Diamond and attributed to Madison actually describes much of Hamilton's thought, it does not aptly characterize Hamilton's vision in one important respect. Hamilton's theory of the commercial republic did not merely rest on a multiplicity of rival interests to produce the common good, nor did it advance the notion of a multiplicity of factions. At the New York Ratifying Convention, Hamilton proclaimed that the objective was "to abolish factions, and to unite all parties for the general welfare" ("New York Ratifying Convention: First Speech of June 25 [Francis Child's version]," *PAH* V:85). Like Necker, Hamilton sought to achieve public confidence and unity of national sentiment via the effects of a good administration. Cf. Gibson, "The Commercial Republic & the Pluralist Critique of Marxism"; Banning, *Sacred Fire of Liberty*, 261, 62–63, 368, 471, n. 66; Charles R. Kesler, "*Federalist* 10 and American Republicanism," in *Saving the Revolution: The Federalist Papers and the American Founding* (New York: Free Press, 1987), 14–18.

Madison did not differ with Hamilton, Adams, Ames, Sedgwick, or any of the other Federalists about the need to filter the interests, passions, and opinions of the citizens or about the need to achieve a reasonable, impartial, and durable will in government, but he very much disagreed with them about who or what legitimately gives voice to this will and whether the process involves modifying the actual views of the citizens. Hamilton and Adams attempted to solve the problems of the predominance of partial interests, the contagion of passion, and the danger of demagoguery in the legislature by establishing a system of institutional counterbalances within government. Hamilton added to this the beneficial effects of a diversified, commercial, and industrial nation. The Federalists sought to achieve a reasonable and permanent will via an independent and energetic executive whose administration would advance the interest of the nation and inspire in the people an opinion of confidence and a habit of obedience. By contrast, Madison's solution was to call the representatives to stand before the bar of public opinion. He sought to establish an equilibrium of passions and interests in the society in order to reduce the likelihood of majority faction, as well as to shape an environment conducive to the formation of a public will tempered and modified by the commerce of ideas.

Hamilton relied on the people to pursue their own material advantage and to support a government that benefits them economically. Neither he nor Adams saw wisdom in encouraging political hyperactivity among the citizenry, which only invites demagoguery and civil unrest, as the French example too perfectly illustrated. For Madison, the citizens' political duties were substantial and ongoing. They did not end at choosing the better sorts of men to represent them; their guardianship over public affairs was not an intermittent responsibility. Both the Federalists and Madison relied significantly on an educated elite to accomplish their ends. However, in the one case, it was a type of statesmanship that sought to inspire in the citizenry respect for and confidence in the government more than it sought to teach them their rights and responsibilities. In the other case, it was a kind of civic leadership that aspired to cultivate civic understanding, refine mores and manners, and educate the people for their indispensable role in a free and self-governing republic.

6

Madison and Jefferson

An Appeal to the People

On March 28, 1797, James and Dolley Madison began the journey from the United States capital at Philadelphia to the Madison family home at Montpelier, Virginia. Three and a half weeks earlier, on March 4, Thomas Jefferson had taken the oath of office for vice president of the United States. Though Jefferson originally contemplated not traveling from Monticello to Philadelphia for the inauguration ceremonies, perhaps because he thought the office as "insignificant" as Adams had, he ultimately decided to make the trip out of respect for the public, as well as to dismiss reports that he considered the second station beneath him. Jefferson and Madison were now trading places. Madison had remained on the scene of national politics and at the helm of the Republican Party throughout the Washington administration, while Jefferson had resigned his post as secretary of state in the second term and resettled in Virginia. Now it was Madison's turn to return home. Finally, he could devote his attentions to the woman he adored, his wife of only three years. Adding color and vivacity to his life, Dolley Payne Todd Madison had changed her husband from a reticent bachelor to a man at ease with domestic life. Gone were the late nights poring over ancient musty texts in a rented room more than 200 miles from home. Gone was a life dedicated almost exclusively to philosophy and politics.

Despite his elevation to the second highest office in the nation, Jefferson too expected extensive periods of domestic quiet. Since the vice presidency would require only nominal duties, he thought he would likely spend most of his time "above the storms" at Monticello.[1] Jefferson's anticipation of a calm and easy tenure of office had much to do with his confidence in John

---

[1] Compare Jefferson to Adams of December 28, 1796, in *PTJ* 29:235, in which he describes politics as "riding in the storm," and Jefferson to Maria Cosway, of October 12, 1786, in

Adams's ability to lead the nation in the right direction. In general, he still associated Adams with the spirit of '76 and anticipated good working relations with his old revolutionary friend and ally. He was, admittedly, anxious about the monarchical influence in America, and particularly about the Federalists' attachment to Great Britain and animosity toward France, but he believed that the new president would be able to avoid war with France and restore "general harmony" to the nation. With Adams, he hoped the American vessel would be put back on its republican tack and the nation would return to the path of "regular liberty, order, and a sacrosanct adherence to the Constitution."[2] In early 1797, Jefferson even began strategizing Republican support to give Adams another presidential election victory in 1800. If Adams could be induced "to administer the government on it's [*sic*] true principles, & to relinquish his bias to an English constitution," he wrote Madison, it might be in the public interest "to come to a good understanding with him as to his future elections." This might be the only sure way to prevent "Hamilton's getting in."[3]

The very first thing Jefferson did when he arrived at the nation's capital was to call upon Adams. Adams returned the visit the following day, March 3. Their discussion centered on America's relations with France and the choice of ministers to send there. In addition to Charles Cotesworth Pinckney and Elbridge Gerry, Adams wanted Madison for the special mission. Jefferson doubted Madison would accept, but out of politeness to Adams agreed to broach the subject with him. At a dinner party hosted by former President Washington, Adams and Jefferson met again a few days later. At the close of festivities, they took their leave together and Jefferson

---

PTJ 10:447, in which Monticello is Jefferson's edenic retreat, situated high on a hilltop and "above the storms."

[2] Jefferson to James Sullivan, February 9, 1797, *PTJ* 29:290.

[3] Jefferson to James Madison, January 1, 1797, *PJM* 16:440. In this letter Jefferson enclosed a letter he had written to John Adams of December 28, 1796, but had not yet sent. It contained a warning about machinations to "cheat" Adams out of his succession by his "arch-friend of New York," i.e., Hamilton. He requested Madison to have it delivered to Adams or to return it to him if for any reason he thought it should not be sent. In his reply of January 15, 1797, Madison offered a number of reasons why the letter ought not be delivered, including that, given Adams's "ticklish" temperament, he might misconstrue Jefferson's intent and the probability that the course of the Adams administration would "force an opposition from the Republican quarter" (*PJM* 16:455–57). According to Nicholas P. Trist, a protégé of Madison (and who, incidentally, studied law under Jefferson and married his granddaughter Virginia Jefferson Randolph), he and Madison together read Jefferson's letter of January 1, 1797, when he was visiting Montpelier in December 1827. When they came to the end of the first paragraph, in which Jefferson talked about supporting Adams's reelection to the presidency as a "barrier against Hamilton's getting in," Madison "stopt, shook his head, and said 'Hamilton *never* could have got in'" (*PJM* 16:441, n. 3).

spoke of Madison's unwillingness to go to France. In embarrassment, Adams responded that certain objections had been raised to Madison's nomination for the mission. According to both the president and vice president, this event, only a few days into the new administration, marked the beginning of a breach between them and foreshadowed the resumption of partisan wrangling in the late 1790s.

At this juncture, Jefferson remained in Philadelphia for only ten days. When he returned to the capital on May 11, 1797, for a special session of Congress, the relative general goodwill of the past March had been disrupted. Before he left Monticello, an alleged copy of a letter he had written to Philip Mazzei more than a year prior appeared in the *Minerva*, Noah Webster's New York paper. The copy, though inexact, had a partisan tone and reawakened the enmity many Federalists felt toward Jefferson and his republican ideas. In the spring of 1797, Jefferson acknowledged an "uneasiness" in his relationship with President Adams that, he suspected, resulted from the machinations of the monarchical faction led by Hamilton. The president's address to Congress on May 16, which Jefferson interpreted as increasing the possibility of war with France, deflated his former confidence in Adams. He concluded, probably unfairly, that Adams had changed his stance and was now encamped with the "ultras." According to Dumas Malone, if Jefferson "had not already turned decisively against Adams he now did so."[4] At any rate, by the summer of 1797, a rift between the two was unmistakably evident. Historian John Murray Allison describes their relationship at this time thus:

The younger man now looked upon the older one as so much under the influence of chauvinists and warmongers as to render most improbable any lengthy extension of peace with honor. The older man, if he still believed in Jefferson's integrity, now thought of him more than ever as one whose talents were spurred and directed by a relentless and potentially dangerous ambition.[5]

Neither man was immune to gossip, whether on the giving or the receiving end, and surely the propensity of the younger to speak openly in "private" communications and the tendency of the elder to feel acutely the sting of wounded pride had something to do with the rupture of 1797. Just as certainly, the mounting effects of party politics lent to the deterioration of trust and the rise of suspicion between them.

[4] Dumas Malone, *Jefferson and the Ordeal of Liberty* (Boston: Little, Brown, 1962), 316.
[5] John Murray Allison, *Adams and Jefferson* (Norman: University of Oklahoma Press, 1966), 178.

With Madison now gone from Philadelphia, the burden of Republican leadership fell on Jefferson. In the early 1790s, after his return from France, Jefferson became the symbolic leader of the Republican Party, but it was Madison who led the philosophic and political cause.[6] In the summer of 1797 Jefferson assumed leadership of the Republicans, and from this point on the party gradually took on a somewhat different tone and a more active partisan mission. Throughout the remainder of the Adams administration, Jefferson directed events much like a conductor leads an orchestra. Situated at center stage, his position as vice president afforded him a better view of the position and needs of the party than was available to any other Republican. He saw his job as organizing and preparing the ensemble for its future performance; if he had done his work properly, his task on concert night would be for the most part pro forma. Jefferson's style was to allow a great deal of autonomy to the various Republican forces throughout the nation, though he provided a general directive influence that would be evident only at a later date when all the parts came together to produce a successful performance. On the eve of the election of 1800, he could be seen standing before his party, baton in hand, directing the finale and anxiously awaiting the public's reaction to the republican concert he had orchestrated.

In contrast to Madison's leadership of the Republican Party, Jefferson's style was more indirect and, at the same time, more politically savvy. Madison had spent much of his time in the early 1790s in careful study and preparation, on which he relied to deliver well-honed speeches on the floor of the House of Representatives and to pen terse but powerful opinion tracts for the newspapers. His victories frequently resulted from the respect that others naturally gave to the best researched and most reasoned argument. Jefferson, by contrast, tended to study in fits and starts, often losing concentration partway through the task at hand. While Madison occasionally met socially with colleagues to hammer out political bargains, Jefferson was the master of the political dinner party and tended to operate almost exclusively behind the scenes. Jefferson's work offstage, as it were, was executed with the panache of someone born for backroom politics. His strong suit was people. He had one of those personalities that engages others and draws them in with a magnetic allure. He was at once polished and natural, urbane yet casual, captivating others at the same time that he put them perfectly at their ease. I do not think his charm was manufactured; he was a good listener and

[6] See Noble E. Cunningham's excellent study on the origins of the Republican Party in *The Jeffersonian Republicans: The Formation of Party Organization, 1789–1800* (Chapel Hill: University of North Carolina Press, 1957).

naturally genial and sociable, finding pleasure in company and amusement in the ways of the world, which goes a long way toward explaining why he and Franklin – though not Adams – were such hits on the Parisian circuit. Given his desire for amiability and dislike of personal discord, though, he was not always frank with others.

As second in command to Adams, Jefferson vowed that he had no intention of using his official position to influence executive decisions, and in this he was as good as his word. In his official capacity he had little to do but to preside over the forms of the Senate with impartiality. This suited Jefferson just fine. He also understood the first of his official duties to be the preservation of the Constitution that secured the union of the states. This left him free to criticize the administration and, if need be, to guide and mobilize opposition to it – in an even more energetic way than he might have done while in the appointed position of secretary of state. Given the independent election of the first and second offices of the executive in the 1790s, that is, prior to the establishment of the party *system* in America and the ratification of the Twelfth Amendment, Jefferson believed he was at liberty to use his position to influence the nation at large and to lead the public in any way not inconsistent with the Constitution.

Jefferson's actions from 1797 to 1800 were essentially those of an opposition leader. Such a use of the vice presidency had not before been seen, nor has it occurred since in American politics. In 1796 Fisher Ames predicted Jefferson's performance in the office:

In a Senate that will bring him into no scrapes, as he will have no casting votes to give, responsible for no measures, acting in none that are public, he may go on affecting zeal for the people; combining the *antis*, and standing at their head, he will balance the power of the chief magistrate by his own. Two Presidents, like two suns in the meridian, would meet and jostle for four years, and then Vice would be first.[7]

Ames's prophecy of "Two Presidents" during the Adams administration was uncannily close to the mark.

Prior to Jefferson's return to political life, the disagreement between Federalists and Republicans had become increasingly acute as a result of the fight over the Jay Treaty, though this conflict was largely confined to the halls of Congress. The Republican "Party" was not a systematic and orderly structure, but rather a loose arrangement distinguished by its general opposition to policies of the Federalist administration. The arrangement essentially

---

[7] Fisher Ames to Christopher Gore, December 17, 1796, in William B. Allen, ed., *Works of Fisher Ames*, as Published by Seth Ames, 2 vols. (Indianapolis: Liberty Classics, 1983), 2:1208.

consisted of a small group of men, with Madison and Albert Gallatin in the House of Representatives forming the center, joined by a few key figures from other states. They were supported by a handful of partisan newspapers and, to a degree, by local political clubs (or "democratic-republican societies"), which Washington and other Federalists associated with the Republicans. There was as yet no mechanism for the nomination of candidates for office; "candidates" were chosen through informal agreements of key local leaders, though in the strict sense candidacy was not avowed.[8]

In 1797, with Madison now absent from the seat of government, Albert Gallatin assumed the Republican leadership in the House of Representatives. Given Gallatin and Jefferson's alliance in principle and policy, there was little the latter needed to do to direct the able Republican congressman. Instead, Jefferson spent much of his time during these years energetically pursuing the self-appointed task of Republican reporter to prominent men of the Republican persuasion throughout the country, including, of course, James Madison. Often he returned from Congress and hastily recorded the latest political events to his correspondents, thereby providing them with the most updated information that could be gained through an infrequent post. In his letters sent round the country, Jefferson clearly sought to influence moderates he considered hopeful allies and to reassure solid Republican affiliates. He was training his forces and building a national coalition.

If any one event can be said to mark the beginning of the transition from the Madisonian to the Jeffersonian Republican Party and to a new organizational emphasis, it was the letter Jefferson sent Aaron Burr in June 1797.[9] Though an alliance with Burr had previously been initiated, it was not strong and may in fact have ceased. Jefferson recognized the importance of Burr and New York if the Republican Party was to succeed in the nation as a whole. He called upon Burr to help restore the equilibrium that had been disrupted by executive encroachments and to take part in reviving the "spirit of 1776." Burr responded by setting up a meeting with Jefferson,

---

[8] Malone, *Jefferson and the Ordeal of Liberty*, 273.

[9] Stanley Elkins and Eric McKitrick claim that in the 1790s Madison and Jefferson intended to establish a two-party system in the United States (*The Age of Federalism: The Early Republic, 1788–1800* [New York: Oxford University Press, 1993], 296). James Roger Sharp argues that the Federalists and Republicans were in fact "proto-parties," each of which aimed to vanquish the other (*American Politics in the Early Republic: The New Nation in Crisis* [New Haven, Conn.: Yale University Press, 1993], 7–9). Sharp's view more accurately describes the way in which Madison, Jefferson, and Hamilton conceived of their respective party's mission during this era. Nonetheless, during his vice presidency, Jefferson built a party apparatus and used it to win the election of 1800, setting the pattern for party politics in America from then on.

Monroe, and Gallatin in Philadelphia within a week's time. Except for the absence of Madison, "the inner Republican circle had been re-formed."[10] Jefferson, however, became the galvanizing center of this circle in a way that the unassuming Madison had never been.

The period from 1797 until the last year of the Adams administration was beset by the break in Franco-American relations, the XYZ affair, the passage of the Alien and Sedition Acts, and the publication of the Kentucky and Virginia Resolutions. During these years the Federalist Party attained and held the dominant position in government. In Jefferson's view, the dominance of the Federalists was unnatural, for they were not representative of the opinions of the majority of American citizens. Writing to John Taylor in June 1798, he counseled "patience till luck turns." Rule by the minority party is only temporary; the people will in time recover from the spell cast by the Federalists, and the true principles of government will be restored.[11] "This is a game," Jefferson declared, "where principles are at stake."

With the passage of the Alien and Sedition Acts Jefferson's patience had run out. Both his official and private civic duties required him to oppose such gross violations of the Constitution vigorously, yet he considered open protest by the vice president inexpedient. As in the Cabell incident of 1797,[12] Jefferson's chosen mode of opposition was via the state legislatures. He drafted the Kentucky Resolutions, and he called upon Madison to pick up his pen once again in service of the rights and liberties of the American people. In response, Madison drafted the Virginia Resolutions. The Kentucky Resolutions, however, went far beyond the vocal criticism and dissent expressed in the Virginia Resolutions. Jefferson's resolutions boldly proclaimed the Alien and Seditions Acts "unauthoritative, void, and of no force." His reasoning was:

[T]o this compact each State acceded as a State, and is an integral party, its co-States forming, as to itself, the other party[;] . . . as in all other cases of compact among

---

[10] Malone, *Jefferson and the Ordeal of Liberty*, 324.
[11] Jefferson to John Taylor, June 4, 1798, *PTJ* 30:389.
[12] In the spring of 1797 Samuel Jordan Cabell, a Republican representative from Virginia who had publicly and vehemently attacked the Adams administration, was "presented" by the grand jury of the federal circuit court of Richmond for endeavoring to disseminate ungrounded calumnies against the federal government during a time of public danger. In response, Jefferson submitted a petition to the Virginia state legislature condemning the presentment and requesting legislative redress. The House of Delegates passed a resolution declaring the presentment "a violation of the fundamental principles of representation . . . an usurpation of power . . . and a subjection of a natural right of speaking and writing freely." See Adrienne Koch, *Jefferson and Madison: The Great Collaboration* (New York: Oxford University Press, 1964), 182–84.

powers having no common judge, each party has an equal right to judge for itself, as well of infractions as of the mode and measure of redress.[13]

The Kentucky Resolutions assured the other states that Kentucky remained sincerely anxious for the preservation of the union of the states, but that it would not submit to the exercise of undelegated and unlimited power by the national government. Since the members of the national government are chosen by the people, "a change by the people would be the constitutional remedy," Jefferson wrote. But when unauthorized powers are assumed, "a nullification of the act is the rightful remedy," for "every State has a natural right in cases not within the compact." Nonetheless, out of respect for the other states, Kentucky wished to communicate with the other parties to the compact, who were "solely authorized to judge in the last resort of the powers exercised under it." Rebuking the Federalist mantra of the need for public confidence in government, Jefferson proclaimed, "free government is founded in jealousy, and not in confidence." It is jealousy, not confidence, that sets constitutional limitations on the exercise of power. In the United States, the Constitution has prescribed "the limits to which, and no further, our confidence may go." The intensity of Jefferson's reaction to the Sedition Act was due to at least three factors. First, he was committed to states' rights and loathed what he viewed as the unconstitutional usurpation of power by the national government. Second, the Sedition Act's negation of the fundamental right of free speech – the bedrock of a free republic – left him in a political panic. Third, Jefferson had in mind the long-term detrimental effects the act would have in respect to the improvement of the human mind and the progress of the human condition. "What is once acquired of real knowle[d]ge can never be lost," Jefferson wrote to his friend William G. Munford in 1799. "To preserve the freedom of the human mind then & freedom of the press, every spirit should be ready to devote itself to martyrdom; for as long as we may think as we will, & speak as we think, the condition of man will proceed in improvement."[14]

[13] "Resolution Adopted by the Kentucky General Assembly," November 10, 1798, *PTJ* 30:550. Cf. "Jefferson's Draft of the Kentucky Resolutions of 1798" [before October 4, 1798], *PTJ* 30:536; "Jefferson's Fair Copy of the Kentucky Resolutions of 1798" [before October 4, 1798], *PTJ* 30:544.

[14] Jefferson to William G. Munford, June 18, 1799, *PTJ* 31:126–30. Cf. Koch, *Jefferson and Madison*, 180–81. According to Koch, Jefferson viewed the Sedition Act as a "denial of one of the philosophic principles he held most sacred. Knowledge and freedom of inquiry – the submission of man-made truths to man-made confirmations or disproofs – were valued by him not only as a means but also as a noble human end." For Jefferson, these beliefs were connected with a "faith in scientific methods of establishing hypotheses and in supporting

In the Virginia Resolutions, Madison deliberately refrained from declaring acts of the national government null and void. Nonetheless, the Virginia Resolutions do represent the radical boundary of Madison's constitutional thought, manifesting an anxiety for free government that could, if pushed too far, result in a declaration of the right of revolution. By August of the next year desperation had enveloped Jefferson, who made explicit a threat of disunion; in response, the arguments in Madison's Virginia Report of 1800 were very carefully set forth, making crystal clear a sincere attachment to and cultivation of the union of the American states.[15] Whatever alarm for republicanism Madison may have felt two years prior, he was not buying into Jefferson's heightened panic or menacing tone, nor did he endorse Jefferson's arguments. Neither the Virginia Resolutions nor the Virginia Report claim sovereign authority for a state or the states, the anachronistic account that attributes a Calhounian view of states' rights to Madison notwithstanding.[16] That the people had, by their sovereign authority, established a partition between the national and state governments was sufficient to insist on respect for the constitutional limitations on power. But Madison had an additional reason to stress the importance of the federal character of the American republic: he considered the state (or "local") governments essential to the collection and articulation of the public voice. Without a due degree of power at the state level of government, the extent of the territory would make it impossible for the people to communicate effectively and convey a united voice by which to control government. Conversely, "the most arbitrary government is controuled where the public opinion is fixed."[17] As Madison had written in *The Federalist*, in cases of unconstitutional

---

them by firm clusters of 'facts.'" Cf. T. V. Smith, "Thomas Jefferson and the Perfectibility of Mankind," *Ethics* 53:4 (1943), 293–310.

[15] Koch, *Jefferson and Madison*, 194–211.

[16] Adrienne Koch and Harry Ammon, "Virginia and Kentucky Resolutions: An Episode in Jefferson's and Madison's Defense of Civil Liberties," *William and Mary Quarterly* 5:2 (1948), 145–76; cf. *PJM* 17:247. For a different perspective on the controversy, see John Patrick Diggins, *John Adams* (New York: Henry Holt, 2002), 110–19. Diggins claims that Madison's and Jefferson's opposition to the Sedition Act stemmed less from the concern for freedom of speech and the press and more from a defense of states' rights. He agrees with David McCullough – and with Adams himself – that the Alien and Sedition Acts should be seen as "war measures" in a time "of fear and insecurity." Moreover, Diggins argues, the entire episode can be viewed as "an embarrassment to Madison," who had taken "the exact opposite position" in 1787. Jefferson too flip-flopped on the sovereignty issue, originally a vehement defender of it, but as president more than willing to execute the Louisiana Purchase and impose the embargo. "But in the heated controversies surrounding the Adams administration, theoretical consistency succumbs to party politics without so much as a blush."

[17] *PJM* 14:192.

usurpation by the central government, the state legislatures may "sound the alarm to the people, and ... exert their local influence in effecting a change of federal representatives," thereby "annul[ling] the acts of the usurpers."[18]

Madison applied the theory of the importance of the states in marshaling public opinion to practice in his battle to overturn the Alien and Sedition Acts. Both the Alien Act and the Sedition Act, he declared, constitute clear violations of the United States Constitution; in the one case the national government assumed a power not granted by the Constitution, and in the other it exercised a power expressly forbidden by the First Amendment. What is particularly interesting in his discussion of the Sedition Act is that over and above his charge of unconstitutionality – which he believed must decide the matter – he also provided an explanation of the reasoning that informs the American Constitution in this matter. In free governments, he argued, "it is the duty as well as right of intelligent and faithful citizens, to discuss and promulgate [the proceeding of government] freely, as well to control them by the censorship of the public opinion, as to promote a remedy according to the rules of the constitution."[19] In a large republic in which the central government possesses extensive powers and where the great body of the people is far removed from the seat of government, the state governments serve as "intermediate" bodies. The purpose of the Virginia Resolutions, he explained, was to utilize the states as vehicles to excite public reflection and mobilize public opinion.[20] Furthermore, the difficulty of circulating knowledge about governmental proceedings throughout the large nation and of maintaining responsibility to the people by public officials requires a particularly high degree of liberty of the press.[21] He believed the Federalists' measure restricting freedom of the press was based on a different and nonrepublican political model, yet another manifestation of their proclivity to imitate the British. Driven by a desire to "extend the ground of public confidence," the Federalists would place a censorial power in the government over the people.[22] Madison's concern was that the government demonstrate responsibility to the people; in "republican government ... the censorial power is in the people over the government, and not in the government over the people."[23] A free press "alone can give efficacy to [the

---

[18] *Federalist* 44:254; cf. *Federalist* 46:266.
[19] *PJM* 17:342.
[20] *PJM* 17:348.
[21] *PJM* 17:341.
[22] *PJM* 17:346.
[23] *PJM* 15:391; cf. 11:163; James H. Read, *Power versus Liberty: Madison, Hamilton, Wilson, and Jefferson* (Charlottesville: University Press of Virginia, 2000), 69–70.

national government's] responsibility to its constituents," he wrote. It is the means for freely examining public characters and public measures, and for the free communication of opinions, that is "the only effectual guardian of every other right" in a free society.[24]

Both the Kentucky and Virginia Resolutions represent attempts to remedy the problem of usurped constitutional power via an extraconstitutional appeal to the people of the several states, though the Kentucky Resolutions were fitted with a hair trigger that Jefferson came dangerously close to releasing. Invoking the right of the citizens *of a particular state* to declare an act of the general government null, void, and of no force, Jefferson set forth a constitutional doctrine that could undermine the republican union Madison had worked for over a decade to explicate and cement. Jefferson's doctrine must have been as much of a political nightmare for Madison as Hamilton's and Adams's antirepublicanism. Like Jefferson, Madison was an adherent of the right of revolution, and in fact the reader of the Virginia Resolutions can sense just how much he was struggling to find a constitutional ground short of revolutionary politics. Still, he did not invoke the right of revolution or in any way imply that the people of a single state retained any sovereign standing inherent in the theory of constitutional government. In later years, when the idea of perpetual union was under attack from John C. Calhoun, he explained in no uncertain terms what he did not say quite as candidly when Jefferson was living, at least not in any extant letters or memoranda of private conversation.[25] There is no reversion to the parties of the compact to decide constitutional questions, he declared; there is only the constitutional processes or, barring the success of these processes, the right of revolution. Once ratified, the Constitution represents the supreme authority of the sovereign people; whether that be the people of the nation or the several states, it does not matter, since both are a legitimate authority in accord with the republican principle of consent of the governed.

The subject of an appeal to the people to remedy usurpations of constitutional power or to make effectual the ongoing sovereignty of the people was hardly a new subject of discussion or concern for Jefferson and Madison in 1798–99. It had occupied Jefferson's attention in the *Notes on the State of Virginia* and in the draft constitution for Virginia, which he appended to

---

[24] *PJM* 17:189–90, 345. Cf. Robert W. T. Martin, *The Free and Open Press: The Founding of American Democratic Press Liberty, 1640–1800* (New York: New York University Press, 2001).

[25] See Madison, "Notes on Nullification," 1835–36, in Marvin Meyers, *The Mind of the Founder: Sources of Political Thought of James Madison* (Hanover, N.H.: Brandeis University Press, 1981), 418–42.

the *Notes* and which had attracted Madison's attention at least since 1788 (and probably before), when he responded to Jefferson's draft constitution in *Federalist* 49. A convention to rewrite a new constitution is necessary to correct the defects of the present one, Jefferson argued in the *Notes*. It should include laws that "bind up the several branches of government," which, when overstepped, "become nullities," thereby rendering "unnecessary an appeal to the people."[26] By an "appeal to the people" in Query 13 of the *Notes*, Jefferson explicitly stated that he meant a "rebellion." His primary concerns were that the current state constitution was not authorized by delegates chosen by the people to represent them in their sovereign capacity and that it lacked sufficient barriers among the several departments of government, leaving the legislature, on which the executive and judicial branches were dependent, with a clear path to assume unlimited power. "Must the people rise in rebellion," he asked, "on every unauthoritative exercise of power by the legislature?" – "[O]r their silence be construed into a surrender of that power to them?" No, he answered, in republican government there is no presumption of any intention to surrender the people's rights on every infraction of those rights.[27]

In his 1783 Draught Constitution for Virginia, Jefferson proposed not only constitutional barriers among the departments of power, but also that a convention should be called whenever two-thirds of any two of the three branches deemed it necessary to alter the Constitution or correct breaches of it. This provision represented the attempt to avoid extraconstitutional appeals to the right of revolution by setting in place a regular method to correct usurpations of power. It was aimed particularly at the legislature, whose predominant authority in republican government would be controlled by the extraordinary authority of the people's delegates assembled in convention. Six years later, Jefferson mentioned to Madison that in the draft constitution he "had once a thought of proposing," he had "endeavored to reach all the great objects of public liberty." He also admitted that the plan was probably "imperfectly executed."[28] He had not intended to include in it a bill of rights, he said, but this deficiency would have been corrected by other provisions. At the federal level under the new Constitution, a bill of rights is indispensable for limiting the acts of the general government, and especially for controlling the formidable power of the legislative branch, "the principal object of my jealousy."

---

[26] Notes on Virginia, Query 13, *WTJ* 2:178.
[27] Ibid., *WTJ* 2:171.
[28] Jefferson to Madison, March 15, 1789, *PJM* 12:14.

A few months later, in September 1789, Jefferson took up a related issue in his correspondence with Madison. Written during his tenure as minister to France and influenced by his experiences there, this letter has since become one of his more famous scribblings, generally referred to as the "Earth Belongs to the Living" letter. Madison did not read this letter right away. In fact, he did not read it for almost five months, because Jefferson kept it, rewrote it, and only finally sent it early the next year, after he had returned to the United States. The uncommon hesitation on Jefferson's part resulted, I believe, from two concerns. One was the fundamental importance of the topic to the politics of self-government, and the other was Jefferson's awareness of the keenness of Madison's mind. Jefferson wanted to get the logic right. He anticipated that his thoughtful and philosophically careful friend might not be fully persuaded of the generational theory of sovereignty he was proposing. He was right.

In this celebrated letter Jefferson argued that "the earth belongs always to the living generation." He applied this idea to property rights, public debts, laws, and constitutions. The dead have no right to bind the living generation, he argued, nor can the living burden posterity with the public debt they incur. Moreover, each generation has the right to make its own constitution and laws, an idea that Condorcet also incorporated into his political theory.[29] Jefferson grounded his reasoning in higher law principles, arguing that the living majority is morally answerable not to past generations, but only to the laws of nature and of nature's God. He intended this theory to have a practical result: the establishment of the actual and ongoing sovereignty of the people. Calculating a new generation to emerge about every nineteen years, Jefferson argued that every constitution and every law would naturally expire at the end of each generational period. If "the will of the majority could always be obtained fairly & without impediment," he claimed, this would not be necessary. But even with the various checks on government, the people's representatives in the legislative councils are too often influenced by personal interest, bribery, and factious views. The power of repeal is not

[29] Whether the theory of generational sovereignty was originally Jefferson's brainchild or he learned it from either Richard Gem or Condorcet is a matter of some dispute. Iain McLean, for example, argues that Jefferson derived "both its formulae and its modes of reasoning from Condorcet, not (as the editors of the *Jefferson Papers* believed – Boyd et al 1950 –, 15: 390ff) [from] Richard Gem" ("Thomas Jefferson, John Adams, and the Déclaration des Droits de l'Homme et du Citoyen," in Robert Fatton, Jr., and R. K. Ramazani, eds., *The Future of Liberal Democracy: Thomas Jefferson and the Contemporary World* [New York: Palgrave Macmillan, 2004], 17). See also Iain McLean and A. B. Urken, "Did Jefferson or Madison Understand Condorcet's Theory of Social Choice?" *Public Choice* 73:4 (1992), 445–57.

a sufficient equivalent, he contended, for every act of government and every constitution that binds the will of the living to the decrees of the dead is an act of force and not of right. Whereas in the draft constitution of 1783 Jefferson presented the case for ad hoc constitutional conventions to correct unlawful assumptions of power by governmental officials, in 1789 he presented the more radical call for the periodic dissolution of constitutional charters, and presumably the periodic reconstitution of new governments via convention.

Madison's criticisms of Jefferson's proposals are contained in *Federalist* 49 and in his February 4, 1790, response to his friend's letter. In the *Federalist* essay Madison began by praising his friend's "original, comprehensive, and accurate" turn of thinking and his "fervent attachment to republican government and . . . enlightened view of the dangerous propensities against which it ought to be guarded."[30] In essence, Madison argued, the dangers Jefferson feared are correct, but the specific provision he proposed to remedy them is defective. Madison disagreed with Jefferson's advocacy of frequent appeals to the people through constitutional conventions for a number of reasons, including his belief in the impracticality of the idea of generational conventions, the danger of interregnum, the loss of veneration for government, and the encouragement of factions that would result from frequent conventions. In sum, the ad hoc appeals Jefferson proposed would simply not provide the remedy Jefferson sought, and they would create vast new problems of their own.

Interestingly, in *Federalist* 49 Madison's use of the phrase "an appeal to the people" is synonymous with constitutional conventions. But it also reminds the reader of the identical wording used by Jefferson not in the draught constitution but in the main text of *Notes on the State of Virginia*. As we have seen, in the *Notes* Jefferson does not mean by "an appeal to the people" a constitutional remedy to governmental usurpation but rather "a rebellion." Madison's choice of words in *The Federalist* indicates the propinquity of constitutional conventions and revolutions. Constitutional conventions cannot be limited to specific objects of alteration because, according to the argument of *Federalist* 40, "in all great changes of established governments, forms ought to give way to substance." Publius's argument is this:

[A] rigid adherence in such cases to the former, would render nominal and nugatory the transcendent and precious right of the people to "abolish or alter their governments as to them shall seem most likely to effect their safety and happiness. . . . "[31]

---

[30] *Federalist* 49:281.
[31] *Federalist* 40:220–21.

In theory, Madison believed, constitutional conventions cannot be limited in their objects; they are tantamount to refoundings, the most extraordinary and perilous of all lawful political acts. In practice they are often irregular events that, like rebellion or revolution, shake the foundations of a nation. Such experiments are consequently "of too ticklish a nature to be unnecessarily multiplied" and should be reserved for "great and extraordinary occasions." The charge of keeping the various departments of government within their constitutional boundaries – the subject of *Federalist* essays 49 and 50 – ought generally to be treated as a routine rather than an extraordinary political task.

In *Federalist* 50 Madison made the case against periodic submission of the Constitution to the people's delegates assembled in convention for the purpose of correcting abuses of governmental power. In his 1790 reply to Jefferson's letter regarding generational sovereignty, he argued against periodic constitutional expiration and refounding. As he had in *Federalist* 49, in this letter he tactfully but soundly criticized Jefferson's failure to temper theoretic reasoning with the lessons of experience. If carried to its logical conclusion, Madison said, the theory of a new convention every nineteen years would result in a continuous constitutional convention. Moreover, "the *improvements* made by the dead form a debt against the living," who derive benefit from them. Nonetheless, he claimed, he did not mean "to impeach either the utility of the principle in some particular cases; or the general importance of it in the eye of the philosophical Legislator." The principle should be "always kept in view as a salutary restraint on living generations from unjust and unnecessary burdens on their successors."[32] Madison was not simply flattering his older and more distinguished colleague. In 1792, for example, he applied this principle to the idea of national debt in his Party Press Essay "Universal Peace." Still, this was a "particular case," and as we shall discuss, Madison's criticisms constituted a civil but certain warning against the spirit of philosophic speculation.

The diverse perspectives of Madison and Jefferson on generational sovereignty and the calling of constitutional conventions to correct governmental abuses or revert to first principles have often been cited by scholars as evidence of the temperamental differences between the two men, with Jefferson the more impetuous and Madison the decidedly more cautious and careful thinker. For many scholars, these issues also reveal a fundamental philosophic disagreement between the two friends, with Jefferson's faith in the common man juxtaposed against Madison's less democratic – perhaps

---

[32] Madison to Jefferson, February 4, 1790, *PJM* 13:21.

undemocratic – mind and temperament, at least in the 1780s and prior to
Jefferson's return from France and alleged influence over him.[33] The case for
Jefferson's optimism in the capacity of the people for self-government and
Madison's lack of democratic faith can be summarized as follows: Jefferson
favored frequent appeals to the people; Madison staunchly opposed such
appeals, except in the most extraordinary circumstances. Jefferson wanted
government to obey the will of the majority; Madison wanted the people to venerate the government. Jefferson believed the people were capable of enlightened reasoning and was sanguine about their ability to control government and govern themselves; Madison relied on institutional
arrangements to control government and believed that to expect enlightened reason from the people was folly. Instead, he argued, "the most
rational government" will seek to enlist the people's "prejudices . . . on its
side."[34]

This interpretation neglects Madison's explicit expression of agreement
with the philosophic principles Jefferson set forth. In the draught constitution for Virginia and the "Earth Belongs to the Living" letter, the central idea
upon which Jefferson grounded his arguments was that the fundamental and
ongoing sovereign authority in the American republic remains always with

---

[33] According to Robert Wiebe (*The Opening of American Society: From the Adoption of the
Constitution to the Eve of Disunion* [New York: Alfred A. Knopf, 1984], 38–39), Madison's appeal to "the reason of the public" in the 49th *Federalist* was actually a way for
the gentry to free themselves of their "sovereigns." His notion of public reason and public
opinion was the equivalent of "community values," not of an actual power in political
life (38–40). For Garry Wills, Alan Gibson, and Gary Rosen, the argument of *Federalist* 49 demonstrates the passivity of Madison's concept of public opinion. Wills contends
that Madison encouraged "an almost abject trust [in] governmental power" (*Explaining
America: The Federalist* [Garden City, N.Y.: Doubleday, 1978], 27). Gibson claims that
this essay demonstrates Madison's advocacy of civic veneration of government, as opposed
to the civic watchfulness and vigilance he came to endorse in the 1790s ("Veneration and
Vigilance: James Madison and Public Opinion," *Review of Politics* 67:1 [2005], 5–35).
"Madison's solution," Rosen argues, "was a kind of constitutional passion, an unthinking attachment to the Constitution as an end in itself" (*American Compact: James Madison and the Problem of Founding* [Lawrence: University Press of Kansas, 1999], 137).
Indeed, Madison's "safe expression of consent . . . lacked the grandeur of the political right
of nature, defended by Jefferson in all its breadth," but it was consistent and practical.
It prevented "temporary *governing* majorities" from mistakenly thinking of themselves as
the "*sovereign* majority of the social compact" (136–37). Like Gibson, James Roger Sharp
claims that the importance Madison placed on the role of public opinion in the 1790s is
a change from the stance he took in The Federalist, though even in the 1790s, Madison's
conception of public opinion possesses a static quality – it is "a fixed entity that was supportive of republicanism but essentially inert" (*American Politics in the Early Republic*,
45).
[34] *Federalist* 49:283.

the people.[35] Madison was no less committed to the principle and practice of popular sovereignty than Jefferson; indeed, the same central idea informs the Virginia Resolutions and his responses to Jefferson in *The Federalist* and in personal correspondence. The disagreement between the two men was not over the principle of popular sovereignty or the importance of the active participation of the people in republican politics. It was not over what constitutes the rightful authority to rule in free governments. On this they were in complete agreement.[36] "The basis of our government being the opinion of the people," Jefferson maintained, "the very first object should be to keep that right." Indeed, he declared, "Public opinion" is the "lord of the universe."[37] "In a Government of opinion, like ours," Madison asserted, "the only effectual guard must be found in the soundness and stability of the general opinion." It is the "only real sovereign."[38] What Madison and Jefferson disagreed about was not whether public opinion is sovereign, but *how* the sovereign authority of public opinion is best gathered and actively expressed in republican government. Jefferson called for an appeal to the people through the politics of constitutional conventions. Madison believed such measures ought to be reserved for extraordinary occasions and instead emphasized the importance of appealing to the people through the ordinary and ongoing politics of public opinion. Whereas Jefferson sought to establish a recurrent constitutional road to the decisions of the people, Madison sought to establish a political practice in which the settled decisions of the people would control and direct government. Madison's cure was not to pit the extraordinary authority of the people against the ordinary deliberative processes of majority decision making, but to hold the government dependent on and answerable to the sovereign public.

Madison rejected Jefferson's reliance on convention politics not because he opposed the active participation of the citizenry in political decision making, but because he believed that constitutional conventions would seldom cure the problem of governmental tyranny that Jefferson hoped they would – that in fact, they would tend to be composed of the very legislative

---

[35] The arguments of the Kentucky Resolutions are inconsistent in this regard. On the one hand, Jefferson argues that the people are sovereign and that in the case of an unconstitutional exercise of power by the national government they have constitutional recourse via the election process. On the other hand, he empowers the citizens of one state (i.e., a minority) with the authority to void acts of the official representatives of the constitutional majority.

[36] See Lance Banning's insightful study of the two Virginians and their ideas in *Jefferson and Madison: Three Conversations from the Founding* (Madison, Wis.: Madison House Publishers, 1995).

[37] Jefferson to Edward Carrington, January 16, 1787, *PTJ* 11:49; Jefferson to William Short, April, 13, 1820, *WTJ* 15:246.

[38] Madison to Edward Livingston, July 10, 1822, *WJM* 9:101.

members whose tyrannical conduct was often the issue. In any case, convention politics would "inevitably be connected with the spirit of pre-existing parties, or of parties springing out of the question itself," and "the *passions*, therefore, not the *reason*, of the public would sit in judgment." In the original act of establishing the Constitution of the United States, as in any future constitutional conventions that might be called, the process of decision making consists of a relatively simple two-step procedure of proposal and ratification. Although supermajorities are required in each of the two phases of the amendment process, the procedure itself is not encumbered with multiple layers of deliberative activity, as the passage of ordinary legislation is. Under such circumstances, opinions are too often driven by passion and may easily give way to jealousy and party spirit. Despite the wide berth of territory, in such a situation the nation tends to divide into two major camps; in the case of a question of overstepping constitutional limits, the very leaders involved in the action will probably compose the leadership of one of the vying parties. In essence, calm reflection and deliberate choice are not the usual accompaniments to the act of founding or refounding. Given the ultimate and unchecked sovereign authority of the people in framing and ratifying amendments – in other words, the theoretical and practical impossibility of imposing limits on the alterations that may be instituted – one ought not to be sanguine about such constitutional roads to the decisions of the people. The relatively unencumbered process is an invitation to decisions made on the basis of party passions and partial interests.[39]

---

[39] According to James Roger Sharp, Madison's deliberate and repeated appeals to the people in the 1790s were inconsistent with his criticism of frequent appeals to the people in the 49th *Federalist* essay (*American Politics in the Early Republic*, 45). In *Federalist* 49 he warned against frequent appeals to the people on constitutional matters because this would deprive the government of "veneration" and "stability." Although Madison's argument in this essay was about constitutional and not legislative issues, in the first administration legislative issues ultimately depended on how one interpreted the Constitution, Sharp argues. I read Madison's argument in *Federalist* 49 differently. Madison is discussing constitutional questions in this essay, but his point is not whether the issue being addressed is a constitutional or legislative one, but whether the remedy sought in such cases should involve a *constitutional appeal to the people*, that is, an appeal to the people in their constitutional capacity via constitutional conventions. Madison rejected frequent constitutional appeals of this sort to enforce the prescribed boundaries of governmental power. He did not, however, reject the idea of appealing to the people for their opinion on legislative or constitutional questions. This is an entirely different matter. See also the provocative, but I think fundamentally erroneous, interpretation of Troy E. Smith, in "Divided *Publius*: Democracy, Federalism, and the Cultivation of Public Sentiment," *The Review of Politics* 69 (2007), 568–98. Smith makes the same mistake Sharp does in his reading of *Federalist* 49, confusing Madison's warning about too frequently relying on constitutional conventions with the influence of public opinion on constitutional and policy decisions. As a result, Smith essentially limits the public's check on governmental abuse of power to elections (585) and ignores Madison's

It is as important to see that Madison reserved a constitutional path to the decision of the people as it is to understand why he severely restricted it. Madison supported the right of the people to alter their constitution because he agreed with Jefferson that the absence of such provision would make the government "one of force and not of right."[40] He agreed with Jefferson's general philosophy that "no society can make a perpetual constitution, or even a perpetual law." He further agreed that "the earth belongs always to the living generation" and that no generation should slough off its debts on its children and grandchildren, but neither should a people forget what they owe to past generations who have sacrificed for their well-being. Because all human beings are created equal, consent of the governed is necessary to found government and establish constitutional law. Prudence teaches, however, that in the absence of explicit revocation of the constitution, tacit consent must be inferred. Otherwise, no person upon reaching his maturity could, without his express consent, be bound by the decisions of the majority. By establishing a constitution via convention, the people have in their most sovereign capacity prescribed laws by which they solemnly agree to abide. They may change their constitution, but only by means of the constitutional prescriptions to which they have consented.

Madison reminded Jefferson that majority rule is not a principle of natural law, but rather one that results "from compact founded on utility." In essence, he told Jefferson, your theory is built on the false premise that the equality of human beings and the principle of majority rule are equally simple deductions of the law of nature. But this cannot be true if, on the basis of the law of nature, there are some rights that are inalienable and for the defense of which the right of revolution can be rightfully invoked. Indeed, it is a contradiction of the idea of human equality to equate the will of the majority with the precepts of the law of nature, thereby allowing power to act as a substitute for right. The living majority is the sovereign authority of the nation, but its sovereignty is derived from a constitutional compact or pledge that has created a "moral person," and this moral person is as answerable to the laws of nature as each individual.[41]

repeated arguments and emphasis on the influence of public opinion in the ordinary course of republican politics. Had Smith paid more attention to Madison's arguments in *Federalist* 51 and the Party Press Essays (regarding the primary dependence on the people and the primary importance of public opinion), he would likely not have concluded that Hamilton favored an appeal to the public on constitutional and disputed policy questions and Madison did not – or did only as a last resort.

40 Madison to Jefferson, February 4, 1790, *PTJ* 16:150.

41 "James Madison, "Notes on the Social Compact," *The James Madison Papers*, The Library of Congress American Memory, Series 1: General Correspondence and Related Items, Image 1188. http://memory.loc.gov/ammem/collections/madison_papers/mjmser1.html.

Jefferson's "confusion" in the "Earth Belongs to the Living" letter educed from Madison a firm demonstration of the locus of his error, though it did not elicit a lengthy lecture or any suggestion of moral condemnation. Madison knew of Jefferson's propensity to evolve theories in his mind, sometimes working them out less rather than more. He also knew that Jefferson himself had clearly set forth the principles of right in the Declaration of Independence, and better than any other man in America could probably have done. It would have been impertinent to have said more or to have said it any more bluntly than he did in his response letter. If he had, it may have led to embarrassment and awkwardness on Jefferson's part that might never be wholly forgotten and that might have changed the course of their friendship. To avoid this, Madison consciously exercised gentlemanly restraint in the face of Jefferson's philosophic errors and excesses. Had the latter been more of a philosopher – had he been more ruled by the head and less by the heart – Madison might have been more outspoken and aggressive in his argument. But he knew his friend's temperament as well as anyone, and while he might gently chide him for his speculative spirit, he did not test his pride or quarrel with his intentions or general principles.

Madison's gentle exposure of the contradictions and problems in Jefferson's theory of generational sovereignty did not end the latter's commitment to it, which he pursued up to the last years of his life.[42] His lack of concern about the dangers Madison pointed out stemmed from two particular philosophic perspectives that he endorsed and that Madison did not. These were the extreme version of the "moral sense" philosophy prominent among some eighteenth-century Scottish thinkers, and the ideas of "progress" and "perfectibility" introduced by Rousseau and developed by various French theorists, most notably Condorcet. In regard to the moral sense, Jefferson believed that

justice is instinct and innate, [and] that the moral sense is as much a part of our constitution as that of feeling, seeing, or hearing; as a wise Creator must have seen to be necessary in an animal destined to live in society.[43]

To his favorite nephew, Peter Carr, he explained that while the moral sense is somewhat susceptible to the guidance of reason, on the whole it is an innate and independent faculty. It is "a small stock" of reason that is needed

[42] See, for example, Jefferson to Washington, May 14,1794, *PTJ* 28:74–75; Jefferson to Samuel Kercheval, July 12, 1816, in Merrill D. Peterson, ed., *The Portable Thomas Jefferson* (New York: Viking Press, 1975), 552–61; Jefferson to Thomas Earler, September 28, 1821, *WTJ* 15:470–71.

[43] Jefferson to Adams, October 14, 1816, *WTJ* 15:76.

for the operation of the moral sense, he argued, "and even less for Common sense." "State a moral case to a ploughman and a professor. The former will decide it as well, and often better than the latter, because he has not been led astray by artificial rules."[44] Despite these kinds of statements, Jefferson also believed deeply in the importance of education. Moreover, according to Jean Yarbrough, he did not believe that the moral sense "spontaneously result[s] in virtuous actions" but rather requires "a long process of development and habituation before [it] produce[s] the steady inclination to virtue that is called character."[45] Unlike some of his French compatriots, he did not think that theoretic and scientific knowledge necessarily brought in their wake moral understanding. Still, there were occasions when he seems to have flirted with the idea, and it should come as no surprise that the flirtation can be directly traced to the time he spent in France.

Two years before Jefferson traveled to France to take up the post of American minister to the court of Louis XVI his beloved wife died in childbirth, leaving him doleful and despondent. In time, France mended his sorrow and renewed his spirit. Maria Cosway won his heart; French philosophy captured his mind. Like Franklin before him, Jefferson became a regular in Parisian social and philosophic circles, exchanging ideas with the leading French aristocrats and intellectuals of the time, including Lafayette, Condorcet, La Rochefoucauld, and Brissot de Warville. Indeed, the American minister from Monticello joined members of the French revolutionary circle as they worked out their ideas for the new government. Jefferson's theory of generational sovereignty was inspired by "the course of reflection"

---

[44] Jefferson to Peter Carr, August 10, 1787, *PTJ* 12:15.

[45] Jean Yarbrough, "Jefferson and Property Rights," in Ellen Frankel Paul and Howard Dickman, eds., *Liberty, Property, and the Foundations of the American Constitution* (Albany: SUNY Press, 1989), 65–83. On Jefferson's moral sense philosophy, see Adrienne Koch, *Philosophy of Thomas Jefferson* (New York: Columbia University Press, 1943), and compare Koch's discussion of Jefferson's conception of the moral sense to Garry Wills's in *Inventing America: Jefferson's Declaration of Independence* (Garden City, N.Y.: Doubleday, 1978). See also Ronald Hamowy, "Jefferson and the Scottish Enlightenment: A Critique of Garry Wills's Inventing America: The Declaration of Independence," *William and Mary Quarterly* 36:4 (1979), 503–23. On the importance of education to Jefferson, see, for example, Jefferson to William C. Jarvis, September 28, 1820, in Willson Whitman, ed., *Jefferson's Letters* (Eau Claire, Wis.: E. M. Hale and Company, 1940), 338–39; Gilbert Chinard, "Jefferson Among the Philosophers," *Ethics* 53:4 (July 1943), 255–68. Chinard argues, erroneously I think, that despite the personal friendships Jefferson formed with various Frenchmen during his time in France, there is "no strong evidence... that he received much from them besides... invaluable mental stimulation, or even that he was eager to become thoroughly acquainted with their theories" (261).

on the fundamental principles of politics and society in which he and his French friends routinely immersed themselves.[46] One of these fundamental principles concerned the idea of progress and the effect that this has, or ought to have, on constitutions and the institutions of government. "Laws and institutions," Jefferson wrote in 1816,

> must go hand in hand with the progress of the human mind. As that becomes more developed, more enlightened, as new discoveries are made, new truths disclosed and manners and opinions change with the change of circumstances, institutions must advance also and keep pace with the times."[47]

Jefferson likened his conception of progress and the perfectibility of the human mind to the ideas of Condorcet, who had set forth his theory on the subject in *Esquisse d'un tableau historique des progrès de l'esprit humain* (*Sketch for a Historical Picture of the Progress of the Human Mind*). "I am among those who think well of the human character generally," Jefferson wrote, and "I believe also, with Condorcet . . . that [the human] mind is perfectible to a degree of which we cannot as yet form any conception."[48] In fact, Jefferson believed that this was one of the central issues that separated the first political parties in America. "One of the questions . . . on which our parties took different sides was on the improvability of the human mind in science, in ethics, in government, etc.," he wrote in 1813. One side held that there are no known limits to that progress, while the other side denied that improvement over the principles and institutions of our ancestors was likely or even possible. But we "possess . . . too much science not to see how much is still ahead of [us], unexplained and unexplored. [Our] own consciousness must place [us] as far before our ancestors as in the rear of our posterity," Jefferson explained to Adams, whom he knew would wince at such ideas.[49]

Jefferson's agreement with Condorcet's views on progress and perfectibility places him in the most progressive and radical school of thought at the time. While there were many who believed that progress in scientific understanding is possible, and indeed that they lived in a time in which they were witnessing the accumulation of an amazing store of scientific knowledge, Condorcet and Jefferson also believed that humanity itself can be improved over time, both intellectually and morally. Moreover, Jefferson argued at

---

[46] Jefferson to Madison, September 6, 1789, *PJM* 12:382.

[47] Jefferson to Samuel Kercheval, July 12, 1816, in Peterson, ed., *The Portable Thomas Jefferson,* 559.

[48] Jefferson to William G. Munford, June 18, 1799, *PTJ* 31:127.

[49] Jefferson to Adams, June, 15, 1813, in Whitman, ed., *Jefferson's Letters,* 286.

one point, improvements in science can have the effect of inculcating virtue and improving the morals of men. In speaking before the Congress of the United States in 1821 to protest the book tax, Jefferson said:

> The value of science to a republican people, the security it gives to liberty by enlightening the minds of its citizens, ... [and] in short, its identification with power, morals, order and happiness ... are considerations [that should] always [be] present and [bear] with their just weight.[50]

But whatever influence Jefferson believed science may have on the progress of morality, he did not claim that "the rules of our moral conduct [are] a matter of science."[51] God would have been a "pitiful bungler" had he designed things this way, because "for one man of science, there are thousands who are not." Instead, God endowed us with a moral sense of right and wrong that we may live together in society.

While it may be difficult to fathom the seemingly effortless mixing of French rationalism and Scottish moral sense philosophy in Jefferson's mind,[52] in the eighteenth century there were some who did not think there

---

[50] Jefferson, "Memorial on the Book Duty," November 30, 1821, in Merrill D. Peterson, ed., *Public Papers of Thomas Jefferson* (New York: Library of America, 1984), 476.

[51] Jefferson to Peter Carr, August 10, 1787, in Paul Leicester Ford, ed., *The Works of Thomas Jefferson*, 12 vols. (New York: G. P. Putnam's Sons, 1904), 5:324–27.

[52] According to Gordon Wood, "the importance of this domesticated modern virtue [of the moral sense] to Jefferson's thinking, can scarcely be exaggerated." Jefferson's "faith" in democracy and the common man was part of his "optimistic" and "rosy temperament," even perhaps his "Pollyanna" innocence (see *Revolutionary Characters: What Made the Founders Different* [New York: Penguin Press, 2006], 106–7, 114–15). While this assessment is not inaccurate – throughout most of his life Jefferson was the eternal optimist – it does represent a tendency among scholars to attribute Jefferson's ideas to his native sanguinity and to some extent to neglect the philosophic perspectives he endorsed. For a more nuanced treatment of Jefferson's philosophic vision, see Darren Staloff, *Hamilton, Adams, Jefferson: The Politics of Enlightenment and the American Founding* (New York: Hill and Wang, 2005), especially ch. 4; cf. Andrew Burstein, *The Inner Jefferson: Portrait of a Grieving Optimist* (Charlottesville: University Press of Virginia, 1995). One of the reasons for such different treatments of Jefferson's thought is that his views are often not consistent, and sometimes they are blatantly contradictory. Moreover, he often seems breezily unaware of any incongruence in his theory or at least not particularly concerned about it. Jefferson's adoption of both the moral sense doctrine and the theory of progress and perfectibility would seem to be an example of this, representing the embrace of two mutually exclusive strands of Enlightenment thought, as Gertrude Himmelfarb describes these diverse "roads to modernity" in her recent work on the "Enlightenments." The Scottish moral sense school was grounded in a teaching about social virtue and moderation, she argues, while the French theory of perfectibility was rooted in a kind of rationalism and romantic idealism that led to the Terror (*The Roads to Modernity: The British, French, and American Enlightenments* [New York: Alfred A. Knopf, 1994], passim). Despite Jefferson's incorporation of aspects of both of these streams of thought, however, Himmelfarb discusses only the Lockean and

was a necessary contradiction between the two doctrines. Rousseau was the leading voice in this regard, arguing both for the existence of an instinctive moral sense and for a theory of progress and perfectibility.[53] Another was Condorcet. Condorcet seems to have adopted Adam Smith's theory of moral sentiments, viewing them as the foundation of virtue and rights.[54] His wife, Sophie de Grouchy, published a translation and commentary on Smith's *Theory of Moral Sentiments* in 1798 in which she interpreted "Smith through the lens of Rousseau" and read "Scottish moral philosophy through the prism of French political experience."[55]

Condorcet agreed with the Scottish moral philosophers' criticism of the egoistic philosophy of the seventeenth and eighteenth centuries. He took particular aim at his fellow Frenchman, Helvétius, who reduced the motives of men to self-interest. "I am not of the opinion of Helvétius," he wrote, "because I admit, in man, a sentiment whose force and influence he does not seem . . . to have suspected. . . ."[56] Condorcet's acceptance of the existence of a natural sentiment of compassion in man was not, however, a full-fledged endorsement of the Scottish moral sense school. The Scots erroneously attributed "to the human soul a new faculty, distinct from those of sensation and reason, tho' at the same time combining itself with them" rather than looking to an analysis of "our actual faculties," which provide morality with "a basis sufficiently solid and pure."[57] In contrast to the notion of a separate moral faculty or sixth sense, Condorcet (and his wife as well) pursued Rousseau's analysis of the faculty of experiencing pain and pleasure, concluding that the origin of morality and the foundation of justice are "deduced from the nature of our feeling," which "may not improperly

Scottish influences on Jefferson and neglects the influence of Condorcet and the French philosophers on him (200–1).

[53] For Rousseau's notion of perfectibility see *Discourse on the Origin of Inequality*, in *The Social Contract and Discourse on Inequality*, Lester G. Crocker, ed. (New York: Washington Square Press, 1967), passim; for Rousseau's adherence to an innate, instinctual moral sense see *Emile, or On Education*, Allan Bloom, trans. (New York: Basic Books, 1979), 286–90. Rousseau argues that acts of morality result from the combination of conscience and imagination. Conscience is the "instinct" of the soul; it is "innate" and "independent of reason." Just as passions are the "voice of the body," conscience is "the voice of the soul."

[54] Emma Rothschild, *Economic Sentiments: Adam Smith, Condorcet, and the Enlightenment* (Cambridge, Mass.: Harvard University Press, 2001), 211.

[55] Evelyn L. Forget, "Cultivating Sympathy: Sophie Condorcet's Letters on Sympathy," http://society.cpm.ehimeu.ac.jp/shet/kenkyukai/claeys&forget/forget2.doc.

[56] Quoted in Emma Rothschild, "Condorcet and the Conflict of Values," *The Historical Journal* 39:3 (1996), 682.

[57] Marie-Jean-Antoine-Nicolas Caritat, Marquis de Condorcet, *Outlines of an Historical View of the Progress of the Human Mind* (Liberty Fund, Inc.: The Online Library of Liberty, 2008), 83–84. http://olldownload.libertyfund.org/EBooks/Condorcet_0878.pdf.

be called our moral constitution." It is only through reason and the development and progress of civil society, however, that this instinct becomes virtue, that is, "an active compassion which interests itself in all the afflictions of the human race."[58]

In his examination of the historical development of the human mind, Condorcet claimed to have discovered that all errors in morals and politics are grounded in "philosophical mistakes, which, themselves, are connected with physical errors," or in other words, ignorance of the laws of nature. Accordingly, Condorcet believed in the possibility of developing a science of politics and morality, which, along the same lines as the physical sciences, cannot be disturbed by human passions and interests. Improvements in the precision of language will overcome errors of reasoning, which will spur men to reflect upon their conduct and lead to advances in moral practice "not less than that of science itself." In subjecting human conduct to conscience and reason, Condorcet argued, virtually every human being may possess the "principles of a strict and unsullied justice, those habitual propensities of an active and enlightened benevolence, of a delicate and generous sensibility, of which nature has implanted the seeds in our hearts, and which wait only for the genial influence of knowledge of liberty to expand and to fructify."[59] The false philosophy of pride and selfishness set forth by Helvétius and others, Condorcet claimed, was finally exposed and shattered by the truth of "the infinite perfectibility of the human mind."

Jefferson spent many an evening at the salon of the Condorcets during his time in Paris. Like his French *amis*, and perhaps influenced by their views, he saw no inconsistency in blending together Scottish moral sense philosophy and the theory of progress and human perfectibility. Like Condorcet, Jefferson attacked Helvétius's reduction of human motivation to self-interest. By "interest" Helvétius meant not only economic interest, but all that may bring us pleasure or remove pain. Jefferson agreed with him that "good acts give us pleasure," but he believed that Helvétius "fell one step short of the ultimate question." How does it happen that such acts give us pleasure, he asked? "Because nature hath implanted in our breasts a love of others, a sense of duty to them, a moral instinct, in short, which prompts us irresistibly to feel and to succor their distresses."[60]

---

[58] Ibid., 7.

[59] Ibid., 101, 118; cf. 122 regarding Condorcet's advocacy of a "universal language."

[60] Jefferson to Thomas Law, June 13, 1814, *WTJ*, 14:141. On the one hand, Jefferson claimed that the moral sense has been impressed on our hearts so that our moral precepts "shall not be effaced by the subtleties of our brain" (Jefferson to James Fishback, September 27, 1809, *WTJ* 12:315). Further, he declared that "morals were too essential to the happiness of man,

Jefferson sought to remove the obstacles that hinder the exercise of man's moral constitution and impede the path of human progress and perfectibility. To this end, he called strenuously for the elimination of all religious shackles, the abolition of primogeniture, the eradication of all hereditary class distinctions, the establishment of universal free trade, and the implementation of generational sovereignty via periodic constitutional conventions (all of which Condorcet advocated as well). His goal was to unshackle the mind from the chains of ignorance that enslave it and to release the benevolence of human nature. The core of Jefferson's philosophy of freedom is set forth in the Virginia Statute for Religious Liberty, whose opening lines capture the essence of his view of what it means to be human. In language his atheist friend Condorcet would not have endorsed, Jefferson wrote: "Well aware that Almighty God hath created the mind free." He continued: "The plan of the Holy author, who being Lord of both body and mind, yet chose not to propagate [religion] by coercions on either, as was in his Almighty power to do." In Jefferson's original draft, which was modified by the Virginia assembly, he also argued that although God did not propagate religion by coercion on body and mind, He did choose "to extend it by its influence on reason alone." This argument follows another in the draft of the Virginia Statute that was dropped in the final version, viz., "that the opinions and belief of men depend not on their own will, but follow involuntarily the evidence proposed to their minds." Jefferson believed that human freedom is located not in the unrestrained will, but in the will that conforms to the dictates of the moral sense as well as to the precepts of the natural law.

The idea of the law of nature is the rule of reason, which the Creator implanted in the nature of man. According to natural law tradition, God did not bargain with human beings, saying, I will give you freedom if you will

to be risked on the uncertain combinations of the head. . . . [Nature] laid their foundation, therefore, in sentiment, not in science" (Jefferson to Maria Cosway, October 12, 1786, *PTJ* 10:450). On the other hand, he offered a great many tributes to the power of reason and its predominant role in republican self-government. "No experiment can be more interesting than that we are now trying, and which we trust will end in establishing the fact, that man may be governed by reason and truth" (Jefferson to John Tyler, June 28, 1804, in Whitman, ed., *Jefferson's Letters*, 222; see also Jefferson to George Mason, February 4, 1791, *PTJ* 19:241). Moreover, the reason that God gave man constitutes "the umpire of truth" (Jefferson to Miles King, September 26, 1814, *WTJ* 14:197). On at least one occasion, he seemed to view the head and the heart as equals: "The true fountains of evidence [are] the head and heart of every rational and honest man. It is there nature has written her moral laws, and where every man may read them for himself" (Jefferson, "Opinion on the Treaties with France," April 28, 1793, *PTJ* 25:609). Whether Jefferson's views are merely inconsistent or there is a fuller explanation that would resolve the seeming contradictions in his thought deserves a fuller explanation than I am able to offer in these pages.

give me obedience. He simply gave human beings freedom of the mind out-right. This extraordinary gift was not in the form of a contract or transaction, though by the very nature of the gift a moral debt accrued to human beings, making them accountable for the way in which they use their freedom.[61] Human beings have the capacity for moral liberty and self-government as well as the duty to exercise their freedom in accordance with their reason and conscience. This debt of moral accountability applies to societies of men as well as to individuals.

In his first inaugural address, Jefferson celebrated the "sacred principle" that the "will of the majority is in all cases to prevail," reminding his fellow citizens, however, that in order for their "will to be rightful," it "must be reasonable." Violations of the rights of others are acts of oppression that result from those "who feel power and forget right." Jefferson thus makes two fundamental claims in his inaugural address: that the will of the people is sovereign and that the sovereignty of their will is conditional and depends upon its subordination to natural law. These two claims do not always coincide, but they are nonetheless both required if the standard of moral freedom set by the Virginia Statute is to be met. Similarly, both are required to meet the standard of the Declaration of Independence, which is encapsulated in the idea that "all men are created equal." Jefferson's inaugural message is in fact a continuation of the teaching of these two documents, reminding the sovereign people of America that their right to power is legitimate only if it is grounded in reason and the recognition of their moral duty to protect the equal rights of all human beings. This is why it is not merely the right but also the duty of the people to alter or abolish a government whose design is to reduce humanity under the force of despotism.

Madison and Jefferson were as much in agreement about the moral basis of majority rule and popular sovereignty as they were in disagreement about the nature of the moral sense and the doctrine of human perfectibility. Unlike Jefferson, Madison rejected the notion of inevitable progress toward universal human knowledge and perfectibility. In contrast to Condorcet, he did not believe that language can perfectly express ideas, that *évidence* has the power to conquer human passions and interests, or that all human beings

---

[61] This idea undergirds Jefferson's famous lines in the *Notes on the State of Virginia*: "God who gave us life gave us liberty. Can the liberties of a nation be secure when we have removed a conviction that these liberties are the gift of God?" Jefferson's question in this famous passage is clearly made for public consumption. I have no doubt that Jefferson believed that liberty was the gift of God; he did not, however, believe that there is a personal God who takes an active stance on the justices and injustices of this world.

can become philosophers.[62] Madison's warning in *Federalist* 49 against expectations of a race of philosophic kings, and his plea to recognize that patriotic prejudice and salutary opinion are the most that can be expected from many citizens, were directed at those overly optimistic souls enamored of the dream of historical progress. It should be emphasized, as well, that Madison's warning is given in the *Federalist* essay that is organized around a critique of Jefferson's views on the efficacy of "an appeal to the people" to remedy oppressive acts of the government. For Madison, passion and interest are as much a part of man's nature as the capacity to reason, and they are all too often resilient to the power of conscience or evidence. Madison's philosophic realism did not, however, translate into pessimism regarding the capacity of mankind for self-government. It is as important to recognize that he rejected the atomism and materialism of his time and that he strenuously disagreed with what he considered the utopian notions of Saint-Pierre, Rousseau, and the Marquis de Condorcet. His goal was not the vain anticipation of universal philosophic wisdom or universal peace but the more tempered one of enlightened and salutary opinion. His invocation of "the reason . . . of the public" that should sit in judgment in republican government is just such an enlightened opinion, akin to Montesquieu's notion of "impure reason" or the *esprit* that results from a complex set of phenomena in a given society. While enlightened opinion lacks the intellectual rigor of philosophical wisdom, it may have a similar effect in producing stability, order, and relations of justice in political life.

Like Jefferson, Madison believed that it is the right of the majority to rule, but that the procedural right to rule is conditional upon its accord with the substantive moral precepts of natural law. They were in full agreement about the fundamental problem of force and right (or what Madison tended to term "power and right") in republican government. The difference is

---

[62] In *Federalist* 37 Madison explained the unavoidable inaccuracies associated with language as the vehicle for the expression of ideas: "The use of words is to express ideas. Perspicuity, therefore, requires not only that the ideas should be distinctly formed, but that they should be expressed by words distinctly and exclusively appropriate to them. But no language is so copious as to supply words and phrases for every complex idea, or so correct as not to include many equivocally denoting different ideas. Hence it must happen that however accurately objects may be discriminated in themselves, and however accurately the discrimination may be considered, the definition of them may be rendered inaccurate by the inaccuracy of the terms in which it is delivered. And this unavoidable inaccuracy must be greater or less, according to the complexity and novelty of the objects defined. When the Almighty himself condescends to address mankind in their own language, his meaning, luminous as it must be, is rendered dim and doubtful by the cloudy medium through which it is communicated."

that Madison sometimes emphasized the case of an unjust majority in his theoretic analysis and at other times underscored that of a just majority whose voice is not sufficiently heeded by government, while Jefferson almost exclusively highlighted the latter problem. This makes perfect sense given their diverse views on the nature of man and what is or is not needed to moderate the force of the ignoble passions and selfish interests. In Madison's view, the power of passion and interest, as well as the power of opinion, are sown in the nature of man. Thus, the problem of placing power and right on the same side in popular government is not solved simply by removing the unjust societal practices that skew the moral sense and obstruct the mind's freedom. History is no panacea for the causes of injustice. Instead, historical progress depends on the difficult and eternal human challenges that can be met only by free and conscious moral choice. In free societies, improvements depend on the constant forming and reforming of public morality and public opinion in an environment conducive to the conditions of freedom.

Madison too believed in the existence of the conscience, but he did not make the leap to the notion that it was instinctual and in little, if any, need of reason. For him, conscience was neither a sixth sense nor a kind of premoral instinctual, animalistic aversion to pain, tantamount to the sentiment of compassion. Instead, he adopted the more moderate conception of conscience associated with traditional natural law teaching. In "Memorial and Remonstrance" he associated the freedom of conscience with the moral duties such freedom imposes upon human beings, following his teacher, John Witherspoon, in this regard. The obligation of every human being to God is higher than his duty to his country, he asserted. Freedom of conscience is an inalienable right because "what is here a right towards men, is a duty towards the Creator." Before human beings are members of civil society, they are subjects of the "Governor of the Universe," and not even a majority in society has the legitimate right to interfere with a man's allegiance to divine authority. Madison's claim for religious and moral liberty is thus an aspect of his understanding of the hierarchy of obligations and responsibilities of human beings. "A just government," Madison wrote, will protect "every citizen in the enjoyment of his Religion with the same equal hand which protects his person and his property."[63]

The best encapsulation of Madison's understanding of the fundamental moral responsibility in human and political life is to be found in his short

---

[63] See the thoughtful essay by Peter Augustine Lawler, "Religion, Philosophy, and the American Founding," in Thomas S. Engerman and Michael P. Zuckert, eds., *Protestantism and the American Founding* (Notre Dame, Ind.: University of Notre Dame Press, 2004), 180–81.

essay entitled "Property," published in the *National Gazette* in 1792. This essay captures Madison's conception of the dependence of the Constitution on the natural law principles of the Declaration of Independence. In this article he argued that there are two senses of the word "property." In regular usage, "a man's land, or merchandize, or money is called his property." In another and even more fundamental sense, "a man has a property in his opinions and the free communication of them. . . . [A]s a man is said to have a right to his property, he may be equally said to have a property in his rights." "Conscience is the most sacred of all property," Madison declared; it is "a natural and inalienable right." He continued:

To guard a man's house as his castle, to pay public and enforce private debts with the most exact faith, can give no title to invade a man's conscience which is more sacred than his castle, or to withhold from it that debt of protection, for which the public faith is pledged, by the very nature and original conditions of the social pact.

"Every good citizen," he declared, must be "a centinel over the rights of the people." The public trespass on private right by a majority is in fact an encroachment on the rights of all. Every member of a republican society owes "a debt of protection" to the rights of every other member, which is required "by the very nature and original conditions of the social pact" to which "the public faith is pledged." Accordingly, "the very nature" of the American Constitution imposes on every citizen a positive obligation to recognize and respect the rights of others.

Madison's argument in "Property" reveals the moral debt that is at the basis of his compact theory of government. This debt results from the first principles of natural law and the idea that all human beings are created equal; it imposes on members of a constitutional society the obligation to protect other human beings in their equal rights to life, liberty, and self-government. The "debt of protection" of which he speaks is the moral debt of humanity that results from the original gift of freedom. It simultaneously dictates the right of a people to govern themselves and their moral obligation to govern according to a standard of right higher than mere human will. Madison looked upon the great experiment in constitutional government that originated in the United States as a "revolution" no less great than that for which Americans fought and died at Concord and Lexington, at King's Mountain and Bennington, and at Brandywine and Saratoga. Marking a new and triumphant epoch in the political practice of the world, it established "the legitimate authority of the people" as the only just basis of government. As the expression of sovereign authority, Madison taught that public opinion is bound by the fundamental principles of right that justify its power.[64] Its authority derives from a sacred trust that imparts to the majority not only the right to govern, but the obligation to govern according to the moral principles that legitimate its rule.[65]

For over five decades Thomas Jefferson and James Madison worked together to establish the principles and practices of freedom and self-government firmly on American soil. Their legacy to Americans is encapsulated in the Declaration of Independence and the United States Constitution. In their twilight years, after each had served two terms as president and was resettled in Virginia, they could be seen riding the roadway between their two homes, anticipating the genial companionship and lively conversation that always marked their hours together. The road between Monticello and Montpelier is today called "Constitution Way," which perfectly captures the connection that binds the two men and their greatest efforts. The road leads from the principles of the Declaration of Independence to the provisions of the Constitution, linking them together in an unbroken chain of ideas.

Madison understood his work at the Constitutional Convention of 1787, in the ratification debates, and in the 1790s to be in the service of establishing and vindicating the cause of popular government in America. His commitment to the experiment in self-government was not merely self-proclaimed, however; it was the way in which the author of the Declaration of Independence also understood Madison's life work. Toward the close of his life, the eighty-two-year-old Jefferson wrote to Madison, then a young seventy-five:

The friendship which has subsisted between us, now half a century, and the harmony of our political principles and pursuits, have been sources of constant happiness to me through that long period. . . . It has also been a great solace to me, to believe that you are engaged in vindicating to posterity the course we have pursued for preserving to them, in all their purity, the blessings of self-government. . . .[66]

In response, Madison also reflected on the many years of close friendship and joint political labors:

You cannot look back to the long period of our private friendship & political harmony, with more affecting recollections than I do. If they are a source of pleasure to you, what ought they not to be to me? We cannot be deprived of the happy consciousness of the pure devotion to the public good with which we discharged the

---

[64] See "Charters," *PJM* 14:192. Theoretically, the majority relinquishes its moral and constitutional authority if it exercises its power licentiously.

[65] Meyers, *Mind of the Founder*, 395–96.

[66] Jefferson to Madison, February 17, 1826, in Adrienne Koch and William Peden, eds., *The Life and Selected Writings of Thomas Jefferson* (New York: Modern Library, 1972), 728.

trusts committed to us. And I indulge a confidence that sufficient evidence will find its way to another generation, to ensure, after we are gone, whatever of justice may be withheld whilst we are here. The political horizon is already yielding in your case at least, the surest auguries of it. Wishing & hoping that you may yet live to increase the debt which our Country owes you, and to witness the increasing gratitude, which alone can pay it.... [67]

The bond that more than any other united Madison and Jefferson in friendship was their mutual dedication and labor to secure the blessings of liberty and self-government to their countrymen. Acknowledging the debt his fellow citizens owed Jefferson, Madison knew that his friend had devoted himself to his country without any expectation of a return. He had done precisely the same. They understood that the legacy of the Founders is a debt that can be repaid only by a citizenry whose gratitude is manifested in their faithfulness to the principles of self-government. Such a debt is never really repaid, however, for as long as the principles of the Declaration of Independence live in the spirit of the American Constitution, they call on each new generation to rededicate itself to the moral terms of the original compact. So it is that the more the debt of the American Founding is paid, the more it is due.

[67] Madison to Jefferson, February 24, 1826, in James Morton Smith, ed., *The Republic of Letters: The Correspondence between Thomas Jefferson and James Madison 1776–1826*, 3 vols. (New York: W. W. Norton, 1995), 3:1968.

7

The Spirit of Republican Government

In the March 13, 1791, note Jefferson sent Madison asking him to join him for "a wade in the country," he also invited Madison to stay at his larger and more comfortable residence in Philadelphia. Jefferson had transported a large shipment of books to Philadelphia and was renovating space in his new lodgings to house them. His library would soon be open, he told Madison, and "you will often find a convenience in being close at hand to it."[1] Madison declined Jefferson's offer, having just settled into his "harness for compleating the little task" he had allotted himself. "My papers and books are all assorted, around me," he said. "A change of position would necessarily give some interruption – & some trouble on my side whatever it might do on yours."[2] Clearly, Madison had chatted earlier with his friend about his planned undertaking. Jefferson understood that it was a fairly extensive research project and that Madison would need to consult some volumes from his collection. I believe Madison's "little task" was not the correction of the Convention Notes, as has generally been assumed – which would not require access to Jefferson's library or, in fact, the use of any books at all – but the much broader scholarly task he undertook in the "Notes on Government."

Madison's inquiry in the "Notes on Government" led him on a journey far afield from Philadelphia and America, to the world of the classics as depicted in the great books of Western civilization. In the "Notes" Madison cited a plethora of classical works in political philosophy and history, including Xenophon, Plato, Aristotle, Thucydides, Strabo, Dionysius Halicarnassus, Livy, and Plutarch. The "Notes" also include references to modern authors

[1] Jefferson to Madison, March 13, 1791, *PTJ* 19:551.
[2] Madison to Jefferson, March 13, 1791, *PJM* 13:405.

such as Montesquieu, Gibbon, Robertson, Pownall, Moyle, Franklin, contributors to the *Encyclopédie méthodique*, Publius, and Madison himself (including his Party Press Essays of 1791–92, a citation he apparently added to his "Notes" at a later date). The vast majority of references, however, are to Jean Jacques Barthélemy's *Voyage du jeune Anacharsis en Grèce dans le Milieu du Quatrième Siècle avant l'ère vulgaire* (Paris, 1788), an erudite multivolume work that took Barthélemy over thirty years to write. Jefferson sent Barthélemy's work to Madison in 1789, and Madison included the volumes in the booklist he made up in August 1790 for shipment to his new residence in Philadelphia.[3] Sometime prior to the fall of 1791, probably in the spring of that year, Madison engaged in a close reading (or perhaps a more methodical rereading) of Barthélemy's work, taking extensive notes on the texts and incorporating his comments and citations into an outline on the subject of government.[4]

Madison's study of Barthélemy's opus was clearly a time-consuming intellectual task. One can imagine him burning the midnight oil for the better part of a month or two during the recess that followed the adjournment of the First Congress. This is a rather remarkable undertaking for Madison at this time, given the very practical political concerns of a man whose life during this period was dominated by public service. Nonetheless, the de facto leader of the new House of Representatives of the United States donned

---

3 In 1789 Jefferson remarked to a friend that Barthélemy's work was one of "the most remarkable publications we have had in France, for a year or two." It is "a very elegant digest of whatever is known of the Greeks," he continued, though "unuseful . . . to him who has read the original authors, but very proper for one who reads modern languages only" (Jefferson to Joseph Willard Paris, March 24, 1789, *PTJ* 14:697). Like Jefferson (who purchased a set of Barthélemy's work for himself as well), Madison also read Greek. Nonetheless, Madison found Barthélemy's *Voyage* to be of great assistance in his study of Hellenic thought and culture, utilizing both the author's keen insights into classical political philosophy and his references to primary materials.

4 According to the editors of *The Papers of James Madison*, Madison composed the "Notes on Government" (or what they refer to as "Notes for the *National Gazette* Essays") between approximately December 19, 1791, and March 3, 1792 (*PJM* 14:157). Given the considerable research and specific references that characterize the "Notes," I believe that Madison likely worked on the project for several weeks. Besides the late winter/early spring of 1791, the only other periods when Madison was in Philadelphia and had access to his (and Jefferson's) books, and when he would have had time for the project, were between August 23 and September 2, 1791, and after October 22, 1791. In his brief return to Philadelphia in the summer, however, his friends were keen to spend time in his company and conversation, and there is no reason to believe he did not oblige them (see Jefferson to Madison, August 18, 1791, *PJM* 14:71). Upon his return to the capital in the fall of 1791, his time was immediately taken up with public responsibilities (see Madison's letter to his father, James Madison, Sr., October 30, 1791, *PJM* 14:90).

his scholarly togs and immersed himself in the literature of the classics. He surely must have had a compelling reason to pursue such an intellectual project at this particular stage of his career.

If I am correct in dating his composition of the "Notes on Government" to the late winter/early spring of 1791, Madison's concentrated period of scholarly activity immediately followed his vigorous opposition to Hamilton's bank bill, his mounting anxiety about the Federalists' attempt to mimic the British economic and political system, and his concern that the government was turning a deaf ear to public opinion in America. It also followed on the heels of Adams's serial publication of the *Discourses on Davila* (the fourth volume of *A Defence of the Constitutions of Government of the United States of America*) in Fenno's *Gazette of the United States*. Four years after the publication of his first volume of the *Defence*, Adams was still harping on the fatal consequences to any political order that concentrates power in one center instead of dividing sovereign authority in a tripartite and balanced system of government that incorporates the rival interests of society into its constitutional structure. Only a third party could supply the disinterestedness of an "umpire" or "impartial mediator," Adams argued. "A simple sovereignty in one, a few, or many, has no balance, and therefore no laws."[5] Although Madison had not yet reached the state of alarm that would seize him about a year later, he was at this juncture sufficiently concerned about the influence of Adams's aristocratic ideas on public opinion and Hamilton's flawed and dangerous conception of republicanism to set for himself the "little task" of making a "more thorough investigation" into the workings of republican government than he had previously done.[6]

While Madison's 1791 studies were in part motivated by a desire to refute Adams's one-dimensional treatment of ancient and modern republicanism in the *Defence*, his immersion in the classical texts of political history and political philosophy was also due to his serious scholarly temperament. His goal was to investigate the causes that preserve or destroy the various forms of government, particularly republican government, as well as to provide a sketch of the well-constituted republican order. In Barthélemy's work, Anacharsis's long and arduous voyage through ancient Greece had brought him face to face with the permanent political questions identified by the great Hellenic oracles of political wisdom. In the spring of 1791, Madison became a fellow traveler with Anacharsis on his voyage to the classical world.

---

[5] Adams, *Davila*, *Defence*, vol. IV, *WJA* 6:323, 396, 431.
[6] "Notes on Government," *PJM* 14:159.

Upon its release, the Abbé Barthélemy's work became an overnight international success. In Paris, leading socialites hosted fashionable parties built around the Anacharsis theme, with guests arriving draped in Greek garb and met by a display of fare fit for the classical *citoyen*, including the sumptuous cuisine of the Mediterranean as well as a selection of thin and no doubt unappetizing Lacedemonian broth. A number of children were even christened with the name "Anacharsis," among them the famous revolutionary Anacharsis Cloots and the third son of Jefferson's friend and Madison's acquaintance, the Brissot de Warville (born in 1791). Although Barthélemy presented *The Voyage of Anacharsis* in the fictional narrative style popular in the eighteenth century, his work was not meant simply to entertain; it contains more than 2000 references to primary classical texts intended for the benefit of men of letters. According to the Chevalier de Boufflers, whose oration formally marked Barthélemy's induction into the Académie française in 1789, *Anacharsis* made Greece live once again. He captured the ideas, the wonder, and the splendor of a civilization that knew no rival in the annals of humanity, and in his portrait he showed his countrymen the way to freedom. In the abbé's work, the chevalier wistfully continued, one senses that the principles of the Greeks are his principles, that their knowledge lives in his spirit, and that their virtues reside in his heart.

The *Voyage of Anacharsis* tells the story of a Scythian (whose mother was Greek, and from whom he learned her native tongue) who journeyed to the Hellas prior to the birth of Alexander. From his residence in Athens, Anacharsis traveled extensively throughout the Greek republics and colonies for twenty-six years, finally quitting the Hellenic world upon its enslavement by Philip of Macedon, at which time he returned to Scythia and wrote an account of his travels. During his lengthy sojourn, Anacharsis studied the history, literature, art, music, mathematics, religions, economics, philosophy, ethics, and politics of the Greeks and engaged in discussions with the leading minds of the time, including Xenophon, Plato, Aristotle, and Demosthenes. Barthélemy choose this era for his *voyage imaginaire* for two reasons: it marked the apex of Hellenic civilization and the age in which the political face of Greece was forever altered.[7] Between the time of Pericles and that of Alexander, Anacharsis witnessed the flourishing of Greek art and culture and the simultaneous loss of Greek freedom. The elation Anacharsis felt upon first setting foot in Thebes and the wonder and edification that filled his mind during these years are, in the end, exchanged for sadness and resignation. The Scythian's dream of the golden age of Greece was Barthélemy's

---

7 *Voyage* 1:xiv.

dream for a republican France. But Barthélemy learned from Aristotle that there is a fundamental paradox in political life and that the golden age could not last. While civilization can make a home in large states, freedom cannot. Conversely, small states, in which freedom and civilization can coexist, are forever at the mercy of large military empires. Although the virtue of the citizen-soldiers of the free Greek republics triumphed over the powerful Persian Empire in the early battles, in the final analysis, Alexander's victory over the Persian Empire led to the death of Greek liberty.[8]

If Anacharsis emerged from his travels to the classical world dispirited by the fragility of free government, Madison emerged from his journey reinvigorated and inspired with a new hope for republicanism. Instead of conceiving of the republican polity and the empire in mutually exclusive terms, Madison envisioned combining the strengths of each into a new model of free government. Unlike anyone who had gone before him, he envisioned the possibility, and the desirability, of a *republican empire*. This, more than anything else, is Madison's stunning contribution to the science of politics. He rejected the views of those who employed the language of republicanism but were willing to give up the freedom and participation of the citizen. He refused to settle for some version of mixed government (and the diminution of republicanism) to ensure constitutional liberty in large modern nations. He believed instead that the authority of public opinion, which Aristotle had identified as the central source of freedom and stability in the classical polity, must be reclaimed and reconfigured to fit the realities of the modern world. He was convinced that he had discovered a way to achieve both the liberty of the constitution and the liberty of the citizen in a large territory. Rather than modifying the meaning of freedom to fit a new version of republicanism, he modified the size of the territory, making it *even larger*, to accommodate an older version of republicanism and to reclaim its core principles. With the volumes of Anacharsis spread about him in his little room at Fifth and Market, Madison found new inspiration for the grand old quest of republican self-government.

Madison's "Notes on Government" are recorded in a bound notebook of ninety-nine numbered pages, prefaced by a table of contents containing thirteen headings or chapters.[9] Eight of these chapter headings concern

---

[8] See Leo Strauss, Lectures on Aristotle's *Politics*, Lecture XI:13–14, University of Chicago, autumn 1967, unpublished. I am grateful to Joseph Cropsey for granting me permission to cite Professor Strauss's lectures.

[9] These are designated "Notes for the *National Gazette* Essays" by the editors of *PJM*; see *PJM* 14:157–69. Many of the pages of the notebook are blank, ostensibly because Madison originally intended to work more on this project than he was able to do, at least at the current

the various "influence(s)... on Government," including the influence of the size of the nation, public opinion, education, religion, and slavery. This section of the "Notes" is followed by four chapters that examine the structure of government, including attention to separation of powers, governmental checks, and federalism, and a final chapter that provides a kind of model plan for a free and healthy republic. The central argument of the "Notes" is contained in the fourth chapter, the "Influence of Public Opinion on Government." Public opinion is the pivotal element in Madison's schema, the central locus at which the other influences on government interact to produce the republican desideratum that Madison is seeking. As we have seen, in the Party Press Essay "British Government," which is based on chapter 4 of the "Notes," Madison argued for the predominant influence of public opinion (over and above the separation and balancing of powers) in achieving stability and maintaining free government. In the outline "Notes" he carried his investigation beyond its application to the British model and situated it within the broad context of classical political philosophy and the problem of regime preservation, consulting in particular the analysis of Aristotle in Book V of the *Politics*.

"Theoretical writers" such as Plato contend that there is a natural rotation in government from monarchy to aristocracy to democracy and then back again to monarchy.[10] In modern times "more practical" writers such as Jonathan Swift have adopted Plato's view.[11] In *Politics* Book V, chapter 12, however, Aristotle took issue with Plato's rather rudimentary claim. "It appears from Aristotle that under the influence of public opinion, the rotation was very different in some of the States of Greece," Madison wrote. Viewed within the context of the thematic primacy of public opinion that Madison developed in the "Notes on Government," this commentary on Aristotle is quite staggering, at least to the generations of students who have assimilated the traditional interpretation of Madisonian political theory. First, Madison's insightful observation demonstrates that his study of Aristotle's *Politics* was anything but cursory. Second, and most significantly, Madison's appeal to Aristotle's analysis of the force of public opinion to

---

juncture. The portion of the notebook filled by Madison equals approximately eleven typeset pages.

[10] *PJM* 14:162.

[11] Aristotle's criticisms of Plato's theory of the cycle of regimes refer to Plato's account in Book VIII of the *Republic*. For Jonathan Swift's thoughts on the rotation of governments, see *A Discourse of the Contests and Dissentions Between the Nobles and Commons in Athens and Rome* (Oxford: Clarendon Press, 1967). Whether Swift's arguments are serious or satirical is a point of dispute.

help explain his own views on the subject is a matter of considerable consequence, and it has never been explored. Third, Madison's remark indicates that he disagreed with contemporary writers (for example, Jacques Peuchet in the *Encyclopédie méthodique*) who claimed that public opinion was a new political force in the modern era. Finally, Madison's interpretation of Aristotle is diametrically opposed to that of John Adams's commentary in the first volume of the *Defence* (which he had brought with him to Philadelphia and which, I believe, he consciously sought to refute in the "Notes").

According to Adams, there is a natural cycle of regime types, as attested to by such thinkers as Plato and Jonathan Swift.[12] What the classical analysis proved, Adams asserted, was the necessity of mixed and balanced government. Adams acknowledged that some of the classical philosophers placed primary reliance on the education of citizens and the formation of character to reduce factional conflict and prevent degeneracy of the political order. He further admitted that Pythagoras and Socrates had "no idea of three independent branches in the legislature" and believed the laws could be effective only if "mankind were habituated, by education and discipline, to regard the great duties of life, and to consider a reverence of themselves, and the esteem of their fellow-citizens, as the principal source of their enjoyment." This might be effective in small communities, Adams argued, "but the education of a great nation can never accomplish so great an end." In a nation of millions, "no principles, no sentiments derived from education, can restrain [them] from trampling on the laws." The only security is to establish "orders of men, watching and balancing each other...; power must be opposed to power, and interest to interest."[13]

To counteract the problem of political instability and governmental degeneration to the extent possible, Plato and most leading thinkers throughout the ages recognized "the necessity of permanent laws, to restrain the passions and vices of men... and the necessity of different orders of men, with various and opposing powers, prerogatives, and privileges, to watch over

---

[12] Adams, *Defence*, vol. 1, WJA 4:383–89, 462–63.

[13] Ibid., WJA 4:557. Adams found the clearest illustration of the classical solution to the problem of the degeneration of governments in passages of Polybius, which he noted were published at the end of Edward Spelman's translation of Dionysius Halicarnassus' work, *Roman Antiquities* (also cited by Madison in the "Notes"). To the extent that some of the classical republics were able to preserve themselves for any period of time, this was due to the attention given to a balance in the orders of society. To demonstrate the truth of this, Adams examined the constitutions of various republics of antiquity, including Sparta, Carthage, Crete, Athens, Corinth, Locris, and Rome.

one another, to balance each other, and to compel each other at all times to be real guardians of the laws."[14] Citing Aristotle's critique of the eighth book of Plato's *Republic* at *Politics* V:12, Adams wrote in the *Defence*:

Whether these observations of Aristotle upon Plato be all just or not, they only serve to strengthen our argument, by showing the mutability of simple governments in a fuller light. Not denying any of the charges stated by Plato, he [Aristotle] only enumerates a multitude of other changes to which such governments are liable; and therefore, shows the greater necessity of mixtures of different orders and decisive balances to preserve mankind from those horrible calamities which revolutions always bring with them.[15]

In the "Notes on Government" Madison implicitly took aim at Adams's flawed reading of classical political thought, and particularly with what he regarded as his superficial treatment of Aristotle. In the passage at *Politics* V:12 Aristotle argued that, contrary to Socrates' assertion in the *Republic*, there is no simple theory or fixed pattern of regime rotation. There are many causes of stasis in government, just as there are numerous factors that tend toward the preservation of a political order. For example, although tyrannies tend to be of short duration, some have endured longer than others due to the influence of public opinion. The tyrannies at Sicyon, Corinth, Athens, and Syracuse are examples of this. Rather than aiming at the three things generally sought by tyrannies, that is, that the ruled have modest thoughts, distrust each other, and are incapable of action, the successful tyrants of these cities sought "popularity with the many" and thus were able to extend their rule.[16] Aristotle further illustrated the power of public opinion to preserve regimes in his discussion of other types of government. For example, at *Politics* II:11 and VI:5 he explained that although the constitution of Carthage deviates from the best form of government in a number of respects, it is nonetheless a "well-organized regime"; at Carthage "the people voluntarily acquiesce in the arrangement of the regime" and there is no significant "factional conflict." In a word, "the Carthaginians have acquired the friendship of the people."[17] In this regard, Aristotle argued, Carthage resembles Sparta, despite the fact that they are different types of regimes.[18]

---

[14] Adams, *Defence*, vol. 1, *WJA* 4:462.
[15] Ibid., *WJA* 4:508–9.
[16] Aristotle, *Politics*, Carnes Lord, trans. (Chicago: University of Chicago Press, 1984), V:11, 175; 178–81 (1314a15–29; 1315b11–1316b25).
[17] Ibid., VI:5, 190 (1320b5–6); cf. 2:11, 81 (1272b29–32).
[18] Ibid., II:11, 80–81 (1272b24–33). Cf. Montesquieu, *SOL* 1:123 and *PJM* 10:278.

Madison believed that Adams had fundamentally misunderstood the classical solution to the problem of regime degeneration, which had led to a critical error in his analysis of republican government. While Adams promoted a scheme that pits factionalized orders and interests against each other and achieves stability by balancing these groups within the government – which he claimed was also the solution proffered by the classical republican philosophers – Madison believed the formation of a genuine community of citizens to be the preeminent classical concern. This cannot be achieved in a political system that substitutes mechanical arrangements for civic education and its indispensable role in shaping public opinion. If left uncountered, Madison feared that Adams's superficial reading of the classics and analysis of republican government would influence others to adopt the same misconceptions and undermine the American experiment in self-government.

In the *Voyage of Anacharsis* Madison discovered or confirmed his analysis of Aristotle's understanding of the power of public opinion. "The most absolute authority becomes lawful if the subjects consent to establish or support it," Barthélemy wrote in his commentary on Aristotle.[19] By gaining the "confidence of their people," Aristotle demonstrated in *Politics* V:12 that even some tyrannies subsisted for a longer time than is usually the case because the rulers were able to obtain "the esteem or the confidence of the people."[20] This was the case because of the fundamental political fact that "the part of the city that wants the regime to continue must be superior to the part not wanting it."[21] The "unanimous decision" of all of the Greek philosophers and lawgivers, Barthélemy argued, was that "the solid foundations of the tranquility and happiness of states" are to be found in "the institutions which form the citizens, and give activity to their minds" and in "the public voice when it makes an exact distribution of contempt and esteem." Without the force of public morality and public opinion, the laws are powerless to maintain the constitution. It is owing to "the *moeurs* of a people," Barthélemy declared, that constitutions are destroyed or their defects corrected, for *moeurs* "restrain the citizen by the fear of the public opinion."[22]

Barthélemy's emphasis on the importance of institutions that form the manners and opinions of the citizens is directly derived from the central thesis of Aristotle's *Politics*. "The greatest of all the things that have been

[19] *Voyage* 5:62, 225.
[20] Ibid., 5:62, 233.
[21] Aristotle, *Politics* IV:12, 136 (1296b16).
[22] *Voyage* 5:277.

mentioned with a view to making regimes lasting... is education relative to the regimes," Aristotle argued.[23] "For there is no benefit in the most beneficial laws, even when these have been approved by all those engaging in politics, if they are not going to be habituated and educated in the regime." By education and habituation in the regime Aristotle meant education and habituation in the *principle* of the regime, which he did not conceive of solely or even primarily in abstract theoretical terms. Rather, civic education was for Aristotle a practice that actively engages the minds and mores of the citizens in the fundamental principle or idea that informs their polity. In the practical science of politics, just as in biological science, the principle of the body politic (like that of the human body) is made known through its manifestation in actual movement or activity. The unmoving principle and the activity (or ethos) of the polity, however, are not directly linked. The former is the final but not the efficient cause of the active way of life of a given people. As Leo Strauss has argued, between the principle and the ethos there is a connecting link or bridge that Aristotle identified, which may be termed the "spirit" of the regime. [24] In other words, the effectiveness of the principle, and of the laws based upon it, depends on the spirit of the constitution, which infuses the thinking and moral habits of the people and gives the regime its particular ethos or character. In and of themselves, the laws do not rule, for every government is constituted by human beings who make the laws and who do so based on a particular view or principle of justice. The spirit of the regime makes the principle an *operative principle*, which in turn results in the specific character of a given polity. The preservation or destruction of the constitution depends on the maintenance and renewal of the spirit of the regime and the concomitant civic habits of mind and heart. This is what A. D. Lindsay meant when he argued that the principal concern for the classical political philosophers, and indeed for anyone who wishes to understand politics and government, is not the laws per se, but the ideals or principles that are operative in the minds of the citizens and that make them support and maintain their form of government or resist and destroy it.[25] And this is precisely what John Adams rejected. According

---

[23] Aristotle, *Politics* V:9, 167 (1310b12–14).

[24] See Aristotle, *Politics* VIII:1, 229 (1337a12–17); cf. Strauss, "Lectures on Aristotle's *Politics*," XVI:7–8.

[25] A. D. Lindsay, *The Modern Democratic State* (New York: Oxford University Press, 1962), 37. See also Paul A. Rahe's perceptive and beautifully written account of the importance to the ancients of cultivating a common way of life in "Between Trust and Distrust: *The Federalist* and the Emergence of Modern Republican Constitutionalism," in Kevin L. Cope, ed., *1650–1850: Ideas, Aesthetics, and Inquiries in the Early Modern Era*, 14 vols. (New

to one leading scholar of Adams's thought, he categorically rejected "the 'spirit' or *arche* that animated many of [the classical] regimes, and he had nothing but contempt for the ancient view of citizenship and virtue."[26]

Following the central line of inquiry marked out by Aristotle, and not satisfied by Montesquieu's treatment of the issue, Barthélemy sought "to penetrate to the spirit of the laws, and to follow them in their effects." In "Spirit of Governments" Madison too reclaimed the primary place for the spirit of governments within the science of politics. Like Barthélemy, he appreciated Montesquieu's contribution to the recovery of a way to think about politics that was more than the mechanical legalism of Hobbes and that acknowledged the force of human mores and opinion in political life.[27] But, again like Barthélemy, he believed that Montesquieu had stopped short in his analysis and ultimately abandoned the core teaching of the classics. Montesquieu had learned from Aristotle the significance of the principle and the spirit of the laws in governments in general, as well as the predominance of the principle and the spirit of liberty in republics. However, given the seemingly impossible project of reconciling the active participatory liberty of the citizens with stability and moderation, he relinquished the classical republican task of educating the citizens in the spirit of the constitution. Instead, he made liberty the *end* of modern republicanism and abandoned it as the *operative principle* of republican government.[28] Hence he was able to defend and advance the idea of constitutional liberty without relying on the classical idea of the liberty of the citizen and the cultivation of civic character. Madison believed that he had discovered a way to get past the obstacles that seemed insurmountable to Montesquieu. He was persuaded that it was not necessary to sacrifice the (real) liberty of the citizen to achieve the liberty of the constitution or vice versa.[29] Publius described this dual objective thus: "To secure the public good and private rights against the

York: AMS Press, 2005), 11:375–406. The *trópoi* or "ways" that constitute the peculiar ethos of the Athenians was for them of greater importance than the laws or institutions; the character of the citizens, not the institutions of government, constituted "the city's soul" (378–80). Rahe's overemphasis on institutions and underemphasis on political communication, public deliberation, and the means to shape and refine the opinions and manners of the citizens, at least in the thought of Madison, leads him to qualify more than is necessary the extent to which the American republic was designed to promote a civic *paideia* similar in purpose (though not necessarily in all means) to that of the classical republicans (401).

[26] C. Bradley Thompson, *John Adams and the Spirit of Liberty* (Lawrence: University Press of Kansas, 2002), 192.

[27] See Montesquieu, *SOL*, especially Book 19.

[28] See ibid., 11:5, 156.

[29] In his provocative and subtle translation and commentary of Montesquieu's *Spirit of Laws* (forthcoming), William B. Allen argues that Montesquieu actually rejected the corporate

danger of such a faction, and at the same time to preserve *the spirit and the form* of popular government, is then the great object to which our inquiries are directed."³⁰ This was the "great desideratum" to which the sage of Montpelier directed his inquiries in *The Federalist* and continued to direct his intellectual energy in the "Notes on Government."

In 1791 Madison responded directly to Aristotle's analysis of the force of public opinion in supporting and renewing the spirit of popular government. He also responded explicitly to Montesquieu's reformulated theory of the spirit of governments. On this particular and fundamental point, he accepted Aristotle's categories and rejected Montesquieu's, though he adopted Montesquieu's doctrine of separation of powers as a partial response to the problems of republican government that Aristotle had delineated. He believed, however, that neither Aristotle nor Montesquieu had fully met the challenge they had marked out. In classical times the means of communication within society were essentially limited to the spoken word, thereby confining the operation of public opinion in a republic to a small territory. As a result, the ease of communication made the problem of stasis or faction an ever-present danger. Aristotle's response to the problem lacked the institutional precautions Montesquieu would recommend; Montesquieu's solution failed to attend adequately to the fact that there is always a prevailing opinion in free societies that cannot be controlled merely by resort to political mechanics. It is in the interstice between these two theories that Madison developed his own unique contribution to the theory of republican government. He employed Montesquieu's method for preserving the liberty of the constitution and at the same time reclaimed the Aristotelian political task that took seriously the liberty of the citizen and the need for civic education in the spirit of the regime.³¹ He accomplished this, he believed, by rethinking the question of the size of the territory in a new age of communication.

As was always understood, it is more difficult for a people to communicate their views in a large territory or empire. This, combined with separation of powers and checks and balances, is favorable to the prevention of majority faction. It is, however, unfavorable to liberty. Madison followed up on this problem and took the argument to the next step. The advent of new means of communication, he argued, made possible the circulation and commerce

conflict model of government in favor of the liberty of the citizen, thus giving the advantage to justice.

³⁰ *Federalist* 10: 48.
³¹ See Montesquieu, *SOL*, Books 11 and 12.

of ideas throughout an extensive nation. These avenues of communication act as equivalents to a contraction of the territorial limits and favor liberty in a large republic.[32] Still, the task of forming a majority or public opinion in a large republic is much more difficult than in a small one. It requires significant time and energy and necessarily involves a process of deliberation to which the representatives' and the citizens' views are subjected. Madison used the factor of territorial size to control the problem of faction, and, in conjunction with modern means of communication, he employed this same factor of territorial size to promote the formation of a deliberative and reasonable public opinion in order to achieve self-government in a republican polity.

In contrast to the classical thinkers, and to modern authors such as Montesquieu, William Robertson, and Edward Gibbon, who are referenced in the "Notes," Madison did not believe that empires necessarily are, or degenerate into, despotisms. Rather, he offered the strikingly bold conclusion that a republican empire can solve the problems associated with republicanism on the one hand and empire on the other. With Montesquieu, Robertson, and Gibbon he supported the idea of a federation of states, but he rejected their model of an alliance of *sovereign* states. Such an alliance is sustained by a balance of power in the international arena in much the same way that the domestic balance of power achieves stability and the peaceful coexistence among the different and conflicting classes and interests within a given society. In contrast to this, Madison envisioned a sharing of sovereign or constitutional authority between the states and the central government. In the most fundamental sense of sovereignty, however, Madison did not believe it is the province of either the states or the federal government, but that it resides with the people themselves and is expressed in the ongoing will and opinion of the society. The sovereignty of public opinion was not for Madison a mere abstraction or a pseudodemocratic sleight of hand. It was the active expression of the fundamental authority of popular government and the process by which the spirit of republicanism renews itself through civic activity. Contemporary scholars who insist on defining the challenge Madison posed in narrow, analytically sterile terms miss the fundamentally human and dynamically political character of his political thought. For Madison, the "great desideratum" was not to depoliticize and anesthetize the opinions and mores of the citizens and replace the expression of different views of justice with shrewd mechanical arrangements, but to provide

---

[32] "Public Opinion," *PJM* 14:170.

an environment in which the various views of justice can be expressed, enhanced, and, to the extent possible, harmonized.[33]

Madison's response to the classical dilemma of polity versus empire and the modern problem of despotic empire was to promote the founding of a federal republican "empire of reason." He distinguished this from the "overgrown empires" of Persia, Macedonia, and Rome, in which there were insufficient local organs of government to collect and convey public opinion. Consolidated government in a large territory does degenerate into despotism. A federal republican union, grounded in the sovereignty and ongoing politics of public opinion, however, simultaneously derives support from the liberty of the citizens that one finds in the polis and the external strength associated with empire. It provides for the communication and combination of the citizens' sentiments and views, the prevention of governmental oppression, and the maintenance of governmental dependence on the will of the society.

In the long and rich "digression" to Jefferson in his October 24, 1787, letter, which he refers to in the "Notes," we recall that Madison called for a modification of the sovereignty to achieve the "great desideratum of Government."[34] It has often been noted that the task of modifying the sovereignty in order to achieve impartial government (of which Madison also spoke in "Vices of the Political System of the United States" and in his letter of April 16, 1787, to Washington) refers to the change from confederalism and state sovereignty to union and federal supremacy under the terms of the new Constitution. Madison certainly intended this, but he also meant to accomplish much more than a structural shift of power in the new nation. He did not mean simply a shifting of the locus of authority from the states to the national legislature, thereby placing his confidence in representatives of larger electoral districts who, in all probability, would be less local in spirit, better educated, and of a more, or at least broader, reputable character. He meant also, and fundamentally, the modification of the sovereign opinion of the public, on which he insisted the representatives of republican government must continually depend for their political authority.

The extension of the territory, representation, separation of powers, checks and balances, and federalism are essential parts of Madisonian republicanism, but they are leitmotifs to his grand narrative of self-government. The success of the experiment in self-government requires the establishment of a dynamic communicative process throughout the society that both

---

[33] See, for example, "A Candid State of Parties," *PJM* 14:371–72.
[34] *PJM* 10:209.

favors liberty and promotes self-control. The environment most conducive to this, Madison believed, is a vast land filled with intelligent, sturdy yeoman-farmers of independent means and virtuous character. No less essential to a well-ordered republic are literate and enlightened private citizens, whose contribution to the health of the citizens' minds and souls places them in a rank above the manufacturer or merchant or sailor. To this indispensable class of "cultivators of the human mind" and "manufacturers of useful knowledge," who act as "the agents of the commerce of ideas" and "the censors of public manners," Madison added the philosopher and the divine. In fact, he placed the latter at the apex of the distribution of occupations and vocations in a republic. They are no less necessary to the new republic than to the old, though in the new world they are without special privilege or official place. The philosopher and the divine have the most difficult but also most important commission of all, for they are tasked with teaching their fellow citizens "the arts of life and the means of happiness."[35]

Drew McCoy has remarked that Madison's analysis of the well-ordered republic in the "Notes on Government" and Party Press Essays reflects classical republican assumptions, particularly evident in his praise of the way of life of the virtuous, independent yeoman-farmer and his negative opinion of industrialization, urbanization, wage labor, and wide disparities of wealth. Madison's description of the occupations of the citizens of a republic is in fact strikingly similar to a blending of Aristotle's (and Barthélemy's) description of the citizens in the best sort of democracy with that of the middling element in the best practicable polity.[36] Despite the classical flavor of Madison's description of republican citizens, McCoy argues that Madison was also in favor of free trade and commerce and thus was "caught between the claims of classical republicanism and modern commercial society."[37] McCoy's assessment forms part of a decades-long debate concerning the character of the political thought of the American Founders. Were they classical republicans or modern liberals? Were they allied more with the ancients or the moderns in the battle of ideas between the two conflicting philosophies? Or did they achieve a synthesis of both, however witting or unwitting, however coherent or contradictory such an amalgamation of ideas might be?

Reams of paper have been devoted to this debate by numerous scholars. Many have concluded that the synthesis theory must prevail, and some have

---

[35] "Notes on Government," *PJM* 14:168.
[36] Aristotle, *Politics* VI:4, 186–87 (1318b6–1319a19); *Voyage* 5:62, 257.
[37] Drew R. McCoy, *The Elusive Republic: Political Economy and the American Revolution* (Chapel Hill: University of North Carolina Press, 1992), 134.

determined that the debate has been exhausted. But as Alan Gibson has shown in his fine study and exposition of this contemporary debate, "even if this [amalgam theory] approach is superior to an either/or formulation, it raises as many questions as it dissolves."[38] Among the issues that remain are whether the contemporary categories of analysis have clarified and improved our understanding of the Founding and whether, in some instances, a more thorough and careful exploration of the individual thought of central figures of the Founding generation is needed.

A study of Madison's ideas in the "Notes on Government" contributes to advancing the latter project and helps us to situate his thought within categories of inquiry that he himself employed. There is no doubt that in practical politics and in all of his major theoretical endeavors throughout his life, including the "Notes on Government," Madison's dedication to republican government included the commitment to natural human equality, popular sovereignty, and the rights and liberties of mankind. There is little disagreement among contemporary scholars regarding the modern character of these ideas, though it should be pointed out that in some analyses of classical thought, including Barthélemy's, the ideas of popular sovereignty, equality, and liberty are purportedly found in Aristotle's discussion of the democrats' perspective and are not simply dismissed by the Stagarite philosopher.[39]

In part, the contemporary controversy concerns how Madison intended to secure political liberty and implement the principles of republicanism in America. Did he believe that mechanistic governmental arrangements that channel passions and self-interest are a substitute for the traditional methods of quelling faction, making enlightened statesmen and the formation of civic character unnecessary to achieving the ends of political life? Was the political task he envisioned characterized by a lowering of the ends of political life? Or does his analysis of popular government reveal a dependence on the formation of an active citizenry capable of self-government and, at least at critical moments, the presence of enlightened statesmen, thereby reflecting a substantive classical republican component in his political thought? While the synthesis theory historians and political scientists now generally accept is that Madison was part of a Founding tradition that embodied both the need for modern defensive political mechanisms and the traditional emphasis on statesmanship, which of these influences was ascendant remains a point of

---

[38] Alan Gibson, "Ancients, Moderns and Americans: The Republicanism–Liberalism Debate Revisited," *History of Political Thought* 21:2 (2002), 265.

[39] See Martin Ostwald's excellent treatment of the classical notion of popular sovereignty in *From Popular Sovereignty to the Sovereignty of Law: Law, Society, and Politics in Fifth-Century Athens* (Berkeley: University of California Press, 1986).

significant controversy. Those whom Gibson labels the "Neo-Lockeans," for example, have abandoned an earlier emphasis on the selfish, atomistic individualism of an earlier generation of scholars and accepted that liberalism itself has some need for "virtue, community and the common good." Still, they contend, modern liberalism was the most prevalent influence. Scholars who in the past vigorously advanced the classical republican interpretation now generally maintain "that they had never meant to suggest that republicanism and liberalism were rival and mutually exclusive traditions of political thought."[40] What is generally lacking still, however, is a serious discussion of the component of Madison's thought that calls for the active role of an enlightened citizenry in republican self-government.

In one sense, the shifting and broadening positions of scholars on this issue have added a much-needed recognition of the complexity and nuance that characterize the thought of the Founders. In another sense, however, the "neither/both" synthesis obscures critical distinctions in the history of political ideas. The difficulty stems in part from a definition of liberalism that is exclusively the product of modern philosophy. If we are willing to shed our contemporary parochialism and to think beyond the definitions that are prevalent today, we may be able to gain a perspective on the matter that is perhaps more consonant with Madison's. In "The Dialogic Community: Education, Leadership, and Participation in James Madison's Thought," Bradley Kent Carter and Joseph F. Kobylka argue that we must be especially on guard against employing an anachronistic account of the political problem when judging the character of the Founders' thought.[41] For example, if we insist on direct participation in a small polis and sumptuary laws as necessary conditions for determining Madison's seriousness about participatory republicanism and the formation of civic character, then, of course, we must conclude that his brand of republicanism does not reflect the classical spirit. I would add that such insistence is also a rejection of the approach of classical political philosophy in favor of modern abstract political theory; the former begins with the actual conditions of political life, with which the latter is unconcerned. According to Carter and Kobylka,

Madison puts the problem of community in perspective: a large republic must use representative political institutions, and its citizens will perforce aggregate to make their voice heard. Neither tendency, by itself, leads to loss of community and participation,

---

[40] Gibson, "Ancients, Moderns and Americans," 280–81.
[41] Joseph F. Kobylka, "The Dialogic Community: Education, Leadership, and Participation in James Madison's Thought," *The Review of Politics* 52 (Winter 1990), 32–63.

but it does lead to a redefinition of both. A continental commonwealth cannot be a Greek *polis*; the assembly of all must give way to representative bodies. Face-to-face forensic discussion must yield to pen, press, and petition; the public interest must form and unite across the miles.[42]

Envisioning new means for the education of the citizenry in the extended republic, Madison "believed public opinion set the bounds of government and [public] debate, written or spoken, informed and elevated." He envisioned, in short, "a dialogical community," based not on possessive individualism or market liberalism, but on "a marketplace of ideas operating in a system premised on shared principles."[43]

In addition to avoiding the temptation to conceptualize liberalism in exclusively modern terms, we should avoid adopting a definition of republicanism that is trapped in history. Republicanism and liberalism were not always thought of as mutually exclusive categories. Consider the distinction between classical and modern republics, on the one hand, and classical and modern liberalism, on the other.[44] As Harvey C. Mansfield has argued, "republicanism... is not a continuous tradition from ancient to modern times," though some contemporary scholars have applied the term "classical republican" to political orders that in their essence constitute a rejection of the substantive principles of classical republicanism.[45] In fact, classical republicanism was in its essence liberal (in the classical sense of the word), and modern republics might retain a place for the principles of classical liberalism.[46]

Madison and the other Founders did not make a distinction between republicanism and liberalism. Rather, the distinction that Madison often employed was that between ancient and modern, as in ancient and modern republics or ancient and modern confederacies. Usually, he employed these terms to denote historical eras. In contemporary scholarship, Montesquieu's theory of the British constitution is usually described as modern republicanism, and for good reason, since Montesquieu himself identified Great Britain as a republic, albeit one that was based on a new conception of the republican form.[47] Madison, however, denied the name of republic to

---

[42] Ibid., 38–39.

[43] Ibid., 47, 59.

[44] See Leo Strauss, *Liberalism Ancient and Modern* (Ithaca, N.Y.: Cornell University Press, 1968), 26–64, and passim.

[45] Harvey C. Mansfield, *Machiavelli's Virtue* (Chicago: University of Chicago Press, 1996), 293.

[46] Strauss, *Liberalism Ancient and Modern*, 15.

[47] See Montesquieu, *SOL* 5:19, 70; cf. 11:6.

the British constitutional model. He did not accept that the republican form of government was so protean an idea that it could be rent from its fundamental principle of liberty understood as active popular sovereignty. He was fully aware that Montesquieu and other balanced government theorists were attempting to redefine the meaning of republicanism, and he explicitly and soundly rejected their project.

Madison did not deny the significant contributions made by those who analyzed the mechanics of governmental arrangements, but like the "practical" author Jonathan Swift, he refused to accede to the idea that such balances and weights could serve as substitutes for the formation of a republican citizenry whose opinion is fundamentally determinative of the nation's ethos. As a reader of Swift's works, Madison was familiar with the essential distinction between ancient and modern political philosophy. In this sense, he recognized the categories of ancient and modern as substantively and not merely historically grounded. It is important to note, however, that Swift's description of the quarrel between the ancients and the moderns rejects the modern redefinition of the ends of republicanism. Rather, the categorization illuminates the differing conceptions of the ends of political life and the distinct approaches employed to achieve those ends. In the case of ancient political philosophy, the ends of political life are not synonymous with the *summum bonum*, but they are conducive to the most honorable and noble human aspirations. In the work of modern political philosophers, there is a conscious lowering of the ends of politics. For example, Hobbes adopted the deductive method of modern natural science, which severs politics from ethics and makes it a science in its own right. This move opened up the prospect of constructing a theory of the modern impersonal state that denies the substantive nature of opinions about justice that so occupied the classical political philosophers.[48]

Montesquieu's new definition of republicanism is part of this attempt to construct a political order that is based on the impersonal rule of law in such a manner that its impartiality does not depend on the existence of a dominant, substantive view of justice in the society. To a significant extent, but without the Frenchman's nuance, Adams adopted Montesquieu's perspective; Madison feared that others in America might settle for it as well. Madison did not reject their aim to establish an equilibrium or balance in the powers of government, thereby providing greater security to individuals against the concentration of power and governmental oppression. He accepted this uniquely modern view of liberty. What is decisive, however,

[48] See Mansfield, *Machiavelli's Virtue*, 293.

is that he did not intend this conception of liberty as individual security to replace the broader and richer view of republican liberty that he discovered in the literature of the classics. The need to form an active citizenry whose ongoing participation in the life of the polity and responsibility for its destiny was no less part of Madison's republican vision than the doctrine of separation of powers and checks and balances. It was, in fact, the more overarching concern for him. The modification of public opinion and the formation of the character of a republican citizenry is the crux of his political theory; it is the reason that he concentrated so much of his efforts on constructing a political environment that would encourage the commerce of ideas. Madison did not abandon the classical project.[49] Instead, he consciously understood himself to be engaged in constructing the political order for which "philosophy has been searching... from the most remote ages." This was, for him, still the most vital quest of humanity and the architectonic political charge. Indeed, it is the timeless quest of the political philosopher and the humane legislator – the former to construct in the mind and the latter to erect in practice a republic that, as much as possible, answers the call of the human spirit.

In Madison's republic, public opinion is the means by which the spirit of the nation is released and its energy communicated to others. It is, in Sayers's formulation, a "social power" that works to "bring all minds into its own unity." Public morality and law constantly reshape themselves within the boundaries set by public opinion; majority opinion is ever in the process of reconstructing itself within its perimeters. Public opinion is the social power that can revitalize the republican idea within the minds and souls of the citizens and fortify the nerve that links together the ethos and the aspirations of republican self-government.

---

[49] See Marvin Meyers's discussion of this issue in "The Least Imperfect Government: On Martin Diamond's 'Ethics and Politics,'" *Interpretation: A Journal of Political Philosophy* 8:3 (1980), 5–15. According to Meyers, the Founders did not consider themselves as part of a "great campaign" against the ancients, though most of them did oppose the modern notion of republicanism that attempted to blend "remnants of the canon and feudal law"; the latter included John Adams and others who held up the corrupt British monarchy as the model for America.

Epilogue

The Philosopher's Stone and the Poet's Reprise

When John F. Kennedy stood on the Capitol steps and took the oath of office as the thirty-fifth president of the United States on that hoary January day, America had only fifteen years before defeated the greatest external threat to freedom the Western world had yet known. By 1961, with the advances in military technology and the increasing threats associated with the Cold War, the world had become a different and a more dangerous place since America's birth in 1776. "Yet," Kennedy said, paraphrasing the words of Jefferson, "the same revolutionary beliefs for which our forebears fought are still at issue around the globe – the belief that the rights of man come not from the generosity of the state, but from the hand of God. We dare not forget today that we are the heirs of that first revolution." And "let every nation know," Kennedy continued, "that we shall pay any price, bear any burden, meet any hardship, support any friend, oppose any foe, in order to assure the survival and the success of liberty."[1]

Almost a half-century later, with technology keeping stride with the passage of time, our world is now an even more dangerous place. The Cold War may be over, but the threats to freedom and the burden that must be borne by its defenders have not lessened. Following the terrorist attack on the United States on September 11, 2001, President George W. Bush remarked in his second inaugural address that the American "response came like a single hand over a single heart." "Freedom is the permanent hope of mankind, the hunger in dark places, the longing of the soul," he said. The hope of our Founders, of Union soldiers, and of the citizens who,

---

[1] Richard D. Heffner, *A Documentary History of the United States*, 7th ed. (New York: New American Library, 2002), 387.

still today, marched "under the banner 'Freedom Now'" were acting on the basis of this "ancient hope."

On what will America's success or failure against the enemies of freedom depend? Do we have what is required to sustain freedom in our age? Terrorism is one of the threats to freedom in our world today, but it is not the only one. Every political order has a way of life that is ever in the process of growing stronger or becoming weaker. Like individuals, it has a particular ethos or character, a kind of unique identification print; unlike the DNA print of a human being, however, the print of a nation can become clearer and sharper over time, embedding itself in the land, or it can become blurred and distorted, and perhaps expunged. A nation can be destroyed by either outside forces or inner deterioration, but it can be preserved only by strength from within, by a citizenry conscious of its own purpose and commitments. A land that is able to maintain itself must have the courage and strength to fight against that which would destroy it, and even more importantly, it must know what is worth fighting *for*.

If the people of the United States today find common agreement in their commitment to human freedom, it is not because they all mean the same thing by the same words. In fact, on some issues that Americans believe are of fundamental importance, there is a marked difference of views, or at least a lack of consensus and settled opinion within the country. This is the case with economic and foreign policy, as it is with many social and moral issues confronting our nation today. Although the same words and phrases are often invoked in contemporary debates over these same concerns, the American citizenry is essentially divided into two groups with opposing principles. The plea for toleration does not and cannot settle these disagreements. This is a lesson we need to learn. The toleration of one version of freedom too often means the destruction of another. America is, now as much as ever, in need of a good and substantive definition of freedom. But in this, public opinion in the nation does not speak with a single voice, and there are many hands placed over many hearts that do not love the same things.

Madison would not have advocated toleration as the remedy for our current civic difficulties. He was not a pluralist or a moral relativist; he never considered toleration a principle of free government. He did not think that a mere aggregation of interests could justly solve the problems of disagreement and conflict within democratic nations, and he never valued toleration in and of itself. In regard to the most fundamental human rights and duties, he looked upon the appeal to toleration as a show of condescension. The duty of free citizens, he believed, is to consult their consciences and to form a "common cause" on the basis of republican principles in spite of their many and differing interests and sentiments. This common cause is encapsulated in public opinion, the sovereign authority in all free governments. The issue of the respect due to public opinion was at the core of Madison's ideas and actions during the Founding era. Indeed, it was the central issue in the dispute between the Republicans and the Federalists in the 1790s. It stamped their divergent views of the expectations for the new constitutional order they helped to frame and the new nation they were working to build. The disagreement shook the foundations of the nascent political order and gave definition to the challenge of self-rule in America.

The concerns, insights, and analyses of Madison and the Founders regarding public opinion are no less relevant to contemporary American citizens than they were to citizens of the early republic. The respect due to public opinion is a perennial issue of American politics and a critical question of contemporary democratic theory. With extraordinary advances in communications technology over the past few decades, the potential power of public opinion in the United States is in fact today at its historic height. Yet, as Daniel Yankelovich has perceptively noted, in our age little attention is given to how we might identify and enhance the *quality* of public opinion. There is an essential difference between "mass opinion" and "public judgment," he argues, and while we "have learned a great deal about how to measure public opinion (and how to manipulate it) [we] . . . have almost nothing to say about how to improve it."[2] Accordingly, Yankelovich and other "deliberationist" theorists have been working to remedy the lack of attention to the qualitative aspect of public opinion in contemporary studies. The respect due to public opinion depends on whether the processes and conditions of political communications produce an informed and reasonable public opinion, they argue; the formation of public opinion through "collective deliberation is essential to the realization of democratic ideals."[3] Madison would have agreed. Indeed, he was the first democratic theorist in America to make explicit the central importance of public opinion to free government and the conditions that are needed for its proper formation and articulation. Ironically, however, Madison's theory of public opinion is either neglected by the deliberationist theorists or he is ascribed virtually the opposite view on the subject than the one he actually held. The Founders, including Madison, "tended to take the idea of deliberation in an elitist

---

[2] Daniel Yankelovich, *Coming to Public Judgment: Making Democracy Work in a Complex World* (Syracuse, N.Y.: Syracuse University Press, 1991), 15–23, 1, xi–xii.

[3] Benjamin I. Page and Robert Y. Shapiro, *The Rational Public: Fifty Years of Trends in Americans' Policy Preferences* (Chicago: University of Chicago Press, 1992), 363.

direction, disdaining public opinion and attempting to insulate leaders from it," Page and Shapiro contend.[4]

Yankelovich, Shapiro, Page, and others have sparked a renewed concern over the quality of civic understanding and the content of democracy in America. At the same time, however, they have divorced the idea of a rational public from one of Madison's primary concerns, that is, the substantive moral content of public judgment. While Yankelovich claims to consider the ethical as well as the cognitive dimensions of public opinion, a moral standard by which to measure the quality of public opinion is conspicuously lacking in his discussion. Rather, he defines the quality of public opinion by its degree of firmness and consistency and the public's willingness to take responsibility for the consequences of its views.[5] Page and Shapiro justify their claim that collective public opinion is "'reasonable,' 'responsible,' and 'rational'" on the basis of its "general stability, differentiation, and coherent patterning of collective policy preferences, and . . . responsiveness to new situations and new information."[6] They concede, however, that even if public opinion is stable and predictable, this does not "dispose of the Founders' concern that majority opinion might be dangerous to 'rights'" or that some demands of the majority might be "improper or wicked."[7] Nonetheless, they argue that "in our secular times, skeptical of absolutes and sensitive to trade-offs, it is not easy to specify rights that deserve complete protection against majority rule." The unwillingness of many contemporary political theorists to make a substantive moral distinction between just and tyrannical public opinion undermines the conditions for popular government set forth by Madison, leaving the majority with no greater claim to rule than the most oppressive despot.

In contrast to contemporary democratic theorists, Madison consciously sought to overcome the problem of majority tyranny and to anchor public opinion in the moral principles of republicanism. In attempting to preserve not only the form but also the spirit of republicanism, Madison's remedy harkened back to the classical concern for forming the minds and characters of the citizens. This separated him from other Founders who believed that the new science of politics allowed modern thinkers to end the futile quest for the Holy Grail of politics. "We may preach till we are tired of the theme," Hamilton wrote, the classical fervor for virtue and "disinterestedness in

---

[4] Ibid., 363; cf. Lawrence R. Jacobs and Robert Y. Shapiro, *Politicians Don't Pander: Political Manipulation and the Loss of Democratic Responsiveness* (Chicago: University of Chicago Press, 2000), 299.

[5] Yankelovich, *Coming to Public Judgment*, 5, 24.

[6] Page and Shapiro, *The Rational Public*, 388.

[7] Ibid., 438.

republics, without making a single proselyte." The dissimilarity between the ancients and the moderns in the circumstances and manners of society is total, Hamilton argued, and "it is as ridiculous to seek for models in the simple ages of Greece and Rome, as it would be to go in quest of them among the Hottentots and Laplanders."[8] Madison too believed that there were important differences in the circumstances of ancient and modern civil society, one of which was the great strides made in commerce in the modern era, enabling not only the commerce of goods but the commerce of ideas over a vast territorial distance. However, this did not mean for him that the difficult task of forming the character of republican citizens should now be abandoned. It meant just the opposite: that the republican order for which "philosophy has been searching, and humanity has been sighing, from the most remote ages" is not a futile quest at all, but is now, in the modern world, a genuine possibility.[9]

Madison never meant to imply that he had discovered anything like the Philosopher's Stone. He understood that the difficulties and dangers of republican government are sown in and spring from the very nature of man. There is, as it were, no formulaic solution or easy fix to the form of political community grounded in the complex nature of humanity and the freedom of mind and will that demands, in every age and for every people, the trial of self-government. This demand is not premised on a guarantee; it is built on an aspiration.

Alexis de Tocqueville's warning about the problem of the tyranny of the majority in *Democracy in America* has often alarmed readers and prompted a search for a model of government that can resist the omnipotence of public opinion.[10] Certainly, Tocqueville was right that public opinion is an unparalleled force in the modern world, a power that cannot be ignored or neglected by those who would attempt to found or perpetuate a decent political order. But Tocqueville's warning about the power of public opinion is just as much the advice of a cautious but nonetheless hopeful observer about the prospects of democracy in the modern world as it is the counsel of prudence about the conditions of freedom in future ages. Like Aristotle and Madison, Tocqueville understood as well as anyone that there is no panacea that will catapult us into the golden age. To attempt to devise a system that rids us of the aspiration, however, is no less tyrannical than one

---

[8] The Continentalist, No. 6, July 4, 1782, *PAH* III:103.
[9] "Spirit of Governments," *PJM* 14:234.
[10] Alexis de Tocqueville, *Democracy in America*, J. P. Mayer, ed. (New York: Harper Perennial, 1969), 246–61.

that guarantees its attainment. In politics, the golden age is better thought of as a quest of which each of us is a part and that adds up to something we call a "community." The journey of the community depends, finally, on the journey of each individual soul.

This is the challenge and the paradox of the search for the Philosopher's Stone. The quest for knowledge is one that requires the greatest of efforts. In some respects, the effort – which is nothing short of the work of making moral choices – is even more important than the knowledge gained. As Shakespeare's Portia taught, to do is often more difficult than to know what to do: if chapels had been churches, poor men's cottages would be princes' palaces. The truth at the core of the Philosopher's Stone has been uncovered in our time by the young philosopher Harry Potter, and by a noted philosopher or two in times before him. Neither magic nor modern science and technology can produce the prized possession. They cannot solve the mysteries of human life and the universe because the very nature of our being does not admit of such "solutions." The Sorting Hat put Harry Potter in Gryffindor, not Slytherin, not because Harry was without resourcefulness and a certain amount of unscrupulousness in the way he disregarded the rules, but because he "asked not to go in Slytherin." You now understand, Dumbledore told Harry, what makes you different from Voldemort. "It is our choices, Harry, that show what we truly are, far more than our abilities."[11]

When Robert Frost realized that he would be unable to read the poem "Dedication" at Kennedy's inauguration, he remarked to the audience, "I think I'll say, this was to be a preface to the poem I can say to you without seeing it."[12] The poem he could recite without text was "The Gift Outright." Thus, according to Frost, "Dedication" is the preface to "The Gift Outright." But "dedication" to what? Frost meant, of course, to offer the new poem to mark the dedication ceremony of John F. Kennedy's ascension to the presidency. But the poem itself reveals, not surprisingly, that there was more in Frost's mind than merely the commemoration of the moment. He meant especially to pay tribute to the principles of the American Founding. Frost's "Dedication" is a dedication to remember and to act upon the understanding of the deed of gift, the gift of freedom, that has been bestowed on humanity. This is what it means, he tells us in "The Gift Outright," to belong to the land we call America. America's creed is not only for its citizens, but

---

[11] See Alan Jacobs, "Harry Potter's Magic," *First Things* 99 (2000), 35–38.
[12] Quoted in Lawrance Thompson and R. H. Winnick, *Robert Frost: The Later Years, 1938–1963* (New York: Holt, Rinehart and Winston, 1976), 281.

applies to all human beings and calls all to its standard. In being the first people to adopt by constitutional decree the "new order of the ages," Americans made their nation a harbinger to the rest of world and, as such, are for the time being the caretakers and teachers of the creed. Our task, Frost tells us, is to teach others "*how* Democracy is meant." The new order of the ages is "A democratic form of right divine/To rule first answerable to high design."

In 1956 Frost delivered a talk to the graduating class of Sarah Lawrence College, choosing as his themes freedom and self-government. I have never particularly valued the freedom that's conferred on me, he remarked. "I value myself on the liberties I take, and I have learned to appreciate the word 'unscrupulous.'"[13] There is a certain measure of unscrupulousness in bending a story one is telling, for example – in not being a "sticker at trifles." I do not mean, Frost said, you should lie – that is corruption – but you should leave out what you don't want to say. It's like Toynbee, he said, "when he writes about the history of the world – you know, he leaves Vermont out – unscrupulous."

Frost believed that we should be unscrupulous especially in our thinking. Too much following the rules for its own sake is numb dependence; it is just fretful uncertainty and timidity. There are some questions that we pick up in college, or along the way, that are worth picking up again and again the rest of our lives. We should treat them like knitting that is kept to be picked up at odd moments. We should pick them up not in a spirit of uncertainty and diffidence, but to knit our brows over, "to have ideas about." I don't mean just to opinionate about, Frost said. "Opinion is just a pro and con, having your nose counted." No, I mean things that you form ideas about. "That's something more." One of the things I have been knitting about lately, Frost mused, is this thing called "the dream." It gets thrown in my face every now and again, and always by someone who doesn't believe it has come true. When I pick it up,

"I wonder what the dream is, or why. And the next time I pick it up, I wonder who dreamed it. Did Tom Paine dream it? Did Thomas Jefferson dream it: did George Washington dream it? Gouverneur Morris?

"Lately I've decided," Frost told his audience, that "the best dreamer of it was Madison." I've been reading *The Federalist Papers*, he said, and I wonder if Madison's dream is a dream for us today, and for future generations,

---

[13] Robert Frost, "A Talk for Students" (New York: Fund for the Republic, 1956). The original version of Frost's commencement address, overscored with revisions by the Fund for the Republic, can be found at Princeton University Library.

or has it gone by? "Can we treat the Constitution as if it were something gone by? Can we interpret it out of existence?" Does it mean something different every day until it wouldn't mean anything at all to Madison?

In the course of his address at Sarah Lawrence College, Frost recited two of his favorite poems, "The Gift Outright" and "Birches." He implied that the two poems are intrinsically linked, though he left it to his audience to draw the connection. "I should prefer to have some boy bend" the birches and ride them down and take the stiffness out, Frost wrote in "Birches" – a boy,

> who learned all there was
> To learn about not launching out too soon
> And so not carrying the tree away
> Clear to the ground. He always kept his poise
> To the top branches, climbing carefully
> With the same pains you use to fill a cup
> Up to the brim, and even above the brim.
> Then he flung outward, feet first, with a swish,
> Kicking his way down through the air to the ground.

"So was I once myself a swinger of birches," Frost admitted. "And so I dream of going back to be." I think of "climbing black branches up a snow-white trunk toward heaven, till the tree could bear no more, but dipped its top and set me down again."

The boy who swung on birches knew just how far he could bend the tree until it could bear no more. He was spirited in his climb up. But he also knew the measure. He knew not to launch out too soon and bring the tree to its knees, but to let it dip and set him down gently.

Madison's dream, like the New England boy's, was a dream of ascent to freedom. It was a dream not so much of liberty conferred but rather of liberties to be taken. Madison challenged Americans to climb to the top with poise and then to launch outward, feet first, with a swish. He encouraged us to use our freedom to form ideas, not just to voice opinions pro or con, but to craft our opinions into ideas and knit them into the broadcloth of the public mind. Frost knew that he himself was a bit of a rebel, perhaps even an unscrupulous democrat. But he always respected the measure.

"Measure always reassures me," Frost said. "Now I know, I think I know, as of today – what Madison's dream was. It was just a dream of a new land to fulfill with people in self-control. In self-control. That is all through his thinking." Madison's "dream was to occupy the land with character – that is another way to put it – to occupy a new land with character." Frost admired the boy who climbed the white birch as high as he could, but knew not to launch out too soon or to bring the tree to its knees – like filling a cup to the brim, and even just above the brim, without letting it spill over. Frost offers these vignettes to show us the point of conjunction between freedom and self-control. In these homely illustrations he teaches us the meaning of self-government in a land of seemingly unlimited horizons. Self-government is the idea that makes the land we call America something more than the land. It is the spirit that makes us who we are and it is the measure of what we can become.

Bibliography

Allen, William B., ed. *Works of Fisher Ames*, as Published by Seth Ames, 2 vols. Indianapolis: Liberty Classics, 1983.

"Justice and the General Good: *Federalist* 51." In *Saving the Revolution: The Federalist Papers and the American Founding*, edited by Charles R. Kesler, 131–49. New York: Free Press, 1987.

"The Constitution to End All Constitutions: The Descent of the American Founding into the Twentieth Century, or The Perfect State Is Not Ideal." Michigan State University. http://www.msu.edu/~allenwi/presentations/Constitution_to_End_all_Constitutions.

Allen, William B. with Kevin A. Cloonan. *The Federalist: A Commentary*. New York: Peter Lang, 2000.

Allison, John Murray. *Adams and Jefferson*. Norman: University of Oklahoma Press, 1966.

Aquinas, St. Thomas. *Summa Theologica*. In *Aquinas Ethicas: Or, the Moral Teaching of St. Thomas*, Vol. II. Edited and translated by Joseph Rickaby Thomas. New York: Benziger Bros., 1896.

Aristotle. *Nichomachean Ethics*. Translated by Martin Ostwald. New York: Macmillan, 1962.

Politics. Translated by Carnes Lord. Chicago: University of Chicago Press, 1984.

Austen, Jane. *The Complete Novels of Jane Austen*, 2 vols. New York: Modern Library, 1992.

Baines, Paul and Edward Burns, eds. *Five Romantic Plays, 1768–1821*. Oxford: Oxford University Press, 2000.

Baker, Keith Michael. *Condorcet: From Natural Philosophy to Social Mathematics*. Chicago: University of Chicago Press, 1975.

Inventing the French Revolution: Essays on French Political Culture in the Eighteenth Century. Cambridge: Cambridge University Press, 1990.

Banning, Lance. *The Jeffersonian Persuasion*. Ithaca, N.Y.: Cornell University Press, 1978.

"The Hamiltonian Madison: A Reconsideration." *Virginia Magazine of History and Biography* 92 (1984): 3–28.

The Sacred Fire of Liberty: James Madison & the Founding of the Federal Republic. Ithaca, N.Y.: Cornell University Press, 1995.

Jefferson and Madison: Three Conversations from the Founding. Madison, Wis.: Madison House Publishers, 1995.

Conceived in Liberty: The Struggle to Define the New Republic, 1789–1993. Lanham, Md.: Rowman & Littlefield, 2004.

Barthelémy, Jean Jacques. *Travels of Anacharsis the Younger in Greece during the middle of the fourth century before the Christian aera*, 4th ed., 8 vols. London, 1806.

Beard, Charles A. *An Economic Interpretation of the Constitution of the United States.* New York: Free Press, [1913] 1986.

Bertrand, Louis. *La Fin du Classicisme et le Retour a l'Antique.* New York: Burt Franklin, 1897.

Des droits et des devoirs du citoyen. Edited by Jean-Loius Lecercle. Paris, 1972.

Bradley, Curtis A. and Martin S. Flaherty. "Executive Power Essentialism and Foreign Affairs." *Michigan Law Review* 102 (2004): 545–688.

Brissot de Warville, Jacques Pierre. "Discours sur l'humanité des juges dans l'administration de la justice criminelle." In *Bibliothèque philosophique du législateur.* Berlin, 1782–1785.

Brookhiser, Richard. *Alexander Hamilton: American.* New York: Free Press, 1999.

Brown, Robert E. *Charles Beard and the Constitution: A Critical Analysis of "An Economic Interpretation of the Constitution."* Princeton, N.J.: Princeton University Press, 1956.

Burnard, Léonard. *Necker et l'Opinion Publique.* Paris: Honoré Champion, Éditeur, 2004.

Burstein, Andrew. *The Inner Jefferson: Portrait of a Grieving Optimist.* Charlottesville: University Press of Virginia, 1995.

Carter, Bradley Kent and Joseph F. Kobylka. "The Dialogic Community: Education, Leadership, and Participation in James Madison's Thought." *The Review of Politics* 52, no. 1 (1990): 32–63.

Chan, Michael D. *Aristotle and Hamilton: On Commerce and Statesmanship.* Columbia: University of Missouri Press, 2006.

Chernow, Ron. *Alexander Hamilton.* New York: Penguin Books, 2004.

Chinard, Gilbert. "Jefferson Among the Philosophers." *Ethics* 53, no. 4 (July 1943): 255–68.

Chisick, Harvey. "Public Opinion and Political Culture in France During the Second Half of the Eighteenth Century." *English Historical Review* 117 (2002): 48–77.

Chojnowski, Peter. "A Sense of Honor: Justice and Our Moral Debt." *Angelus*, XXII. 1999.

Condorcet, Marie Jean Antoine Nicolas de Caritat. *Outlines of an Historical View of the Progress of the Human Mind.* Liberty Fund, Inc.: The Online Library of Liberty, 1795. http://olldownload.libertyfund.org/EBooks/Condorcet_0878.pdf.

Cornell, Saul. *The Other Founders: Anti-Federalism & the Dissenting Tradition in America, 1788–1828.* Chapel Hill: University of North Carolina Press, 1999.

Corwin, Edward S. *American Constitutional History.* New York: Harper and Row, 1954.

Cunningham, Noble E. *The Jeffersonian Republicans: The Formation of Party Organization, 1789–1800*. Chapel Hill: University of North Carolina Press, 1957.

Dahl, Robert A. *A Preface to Democratic Theory*. Chicago: University of Chicago Press, 1956.

DeLolme, Jean Louis. *The Constitution of England; or, An Account of the English Government*. Edited by William Hughes. London, [1771] 1834.

Diamond, Martin. "The Federalist." In *History of Political Philosophy*, edited by Leo Strauss and Joseph Cropsey, 659–79. Chicago: Rand McNally, 1972.

"Ethics and Politics: The American Way." In *The Moral Foundations of the American Republic*, 3rd ed., edited by Robert H. Horwitz, 75–108. Charlottesville: University Press of Virginia, 1986.

Diggins, John Patrick. *The Lost Soul of American Politics: Virtue, Self-Interest, and the Foundations of Liberalism*. New York: Basic Books, 1984.

John Adams. New York: Henry Holt, 2002.

Elkins, Stanley and Eric McKitrick. *The Age of Federalism: The Early Republic, 1788–1800*. New York: Oxford University Press, 1993.

Epstein, David E. *The Political Theory of The Federalist*. Chicago: University of Chicago Press, 1984.

Erler, Edward J. "James Madison and the Framing of the Bill of Rights: Reality and Rhetoric in the New Constitutionalism," *Political Communications* 9 (1992): 213–29.

Estes, Todd. "Shaping the Politics of Public Opinion: Federalists and the Jay Treaty." *Journal of the Early Republic* 20, no. 3 (2000): 393–423.

The Jay Treaty Debate, Public Opinion, and the Evolution of Early American Culture. Amherst: University of Massachusetts Press, 2006.

Faggen, Robert. *Robert Frost and the Challenge of Darwinism*. Ann Arbor: University of Michigan Press, 2001.

Farrand, Max, ed. *The Records of the Federal Convention of 1787*, rev. ed., 4 vols. New Haven, Conn.: Yale University Press, 1937.

Fayyaz, Sam. "Participation without Communication: Rousseau's Conception of Deliberation and Habermas' Challenge," unpublished. The University of Maryland. http://www.bsos.umd.edu/gvpt/Theory/Fayyaz.pdf.

Ferguson, Robert. "The American Enlightenment, 1750–1820." In *Cambridge History of American Literature*, edited by Sacvan Bercovitch, 345–538. Cambridge: Cambridge University Press, 1994.

Finlay, Christopher J. "Hume's Theory of Civil Society." *European Journal of Political Theory* 3, no. 4 (2004): 369–91.

Flaumenhaft, Harvey. *The Effective Republic: Administration and Constitution in the Thought of Alexander Hamilton*. Durham, N.C.: Duke University Press, 1992.

Ford, Paul Leicester, ed. *The Works of Thomas Jefferson*, 12 vols. New York: G. P. Putnam's Sons, 1904.

Forget, Evelyn L. "Cultivating Sympathy: Sophie Condorcet's Letters on Sympathy." http://society.cpm.ehime-u.ac.jp/shet/kenkyukai/claeys&forget/forget2.doc.

Frank, Joseph. *Cromwell's Press Agent: A Critical Biography of Marchamont Nedham, 1620–1678*. Lanham, Md.: University Press of America, 1980.

Frost, Robert. "A Talk for Students." New York: Fund for the Republic, 1956.

Garner, Bryan A., ed. *Black's Law Dictionary*. St. Paul, Minn.: West Group, 1999.

Gibson, Alan. "Impartial Representation and the Extended Republic: Towards a Comprehensive and Balanced Reading of the Tenth Federalist Paper." *History of Political Thought* 12, no. 2 (1991): 263–304.

"The Commercial Republic & the Pluralist Critique of Marxism: An Analysis of Martin Diamond's Interpretation of *Federalist* 10." *Polity* 25, no. 4 (Summer 1993): 497–528.

"Ancients, Moderns and Americans: The Republicanism–Liberalism Debate Revisited." *History of Political Thought* 21, no. 2 (2002): 261–307.

"The Madisonian Madison and the Question of Consistency: The Consistency and Challenge of Recent Research." *The Review of Politics* 64, no. 2 (2002): 311–38.

"Veneration and Vigilance: James Madison and Public Opinion." *Review of Politics* 67, no. 1 (2005): 5–35.

Interpreting the American Founding: Guide to the Enduring Debates over the Origins and Foundations of the American Republic. Lawrence: University Press of Kansas, 2006.

Understanding the Founding: The Crucial Questions. Lawrence: University Press of Kansas, 2007.

Gordon, Daniel. *Citizens without Sovereignty: Equality and Sociability in French Thought, 1670–1789*. Princeton, N.J.: Princeton University Press, 1994.

Gunn, J. A. W. *Queen of the World: Opinion in the Public Life of France from the Renaissance to the Revolution*. Oxford: Voltaire Foundation, 1995.

Habermas, Jürgen. *The Structural Transformation of the Public Sphere*. Translated by Thomas Burger. Cambridge, Mass.: MIT Press, 1989.

Hamowy, Ronald. "Jefferson and the Scottish Enlightenment: A Critique of Garry Wills's *Inventing America: Jefferson's Declaration of Independence*." *William and Mary Quarterly* 36, no. 4 (1979): 503–23.

Haraszti, Zoltán. *John Adams and the Prophets of Progress*. Cambridge, Mass.: Harvard University Press, 1952.

Harper, John Lamberton. *American Machiavelli: Alexander Hamilton and the Origins of U.S. Foreign Policy*. Cambridge: Cambridge University Press, 2004.

Heffner, Richard D. *A Documentary History of the United States*, 7th ed. New York: New American Library, 2002.

Himmelfarb, Gertrude. *The Roads to Modernity: The British, French, and American Enlightenments*. New York: Alfred A. Knopf, 1994.

Holton, Woody. "'Divide et Impera': *Federalist* 10 in a Wider Sphere." *William and Mary Quarterly* 62, no. 2 (2005): 339–82.

Hume, David. *Essays: Moral, Political, and Literary*. Edited by Eugene F. Miller. Indianapolis: Liberty Classics, 1985.

Jacobs, Alan. "Harry Potter's Magic." *First Things* 99 (2000): 35–38.

Jacobs, Lawrence R. and Robert Y. Shapiro. *Politicians Don't Pander: Political Manipulation and the Loss of Democratic Responsiveness*. Chicago: University of Chicago Press, 2000.

Jaenicke, Douglas W. "Madison v. Madison: The Party Press Essays v. The Federalist Papers." In *Reflections on the Constitution: The American Constitution after Two Hundred Years*, edited by Richard Maidment and John Zvesper, 116–35. New York: Manchester University Press, 1989.

Kaiser, Thomas E. "The Abbé de Saint-Pierre, Public Opinion, and the Reconstitution of the French Monarchy." *The Journal of Modern History* 55, no. 4 (1983): 618–43.

Kesler, Charles R., ed. *Saving the Revolution: The Federalist Papers and the American Founding*. New York: Free Press, 1987.

Knickbocker, K. L. and H. Willard Reninger, eds. *Preliminaries to Literary Judgment: Interpreting Literature*, 5th ed. New York: Holt Rinehart and Winston, Inc., 1974.

Knott, Stephen F. *Alexander Hamilton and the Persistence of Myth*. Lawrence: University Press of Kansas, 2002.

Koch, Adrienne. *Philosophy of Thomas Jefferson*. New York: Columbia University Press, 1943.

Jefferson and Madison: The Great Collaboration. New York: Oxford University Press, 1964.

ed. *James Madison's Notes of Debates in the Federal Convention of 1787*. Athens: Ohio University Press, 1966.

Koch, Adrienne and Harry Ammon. "Virginia and Kentucky Resolutions: An Episode in Jefferson's and Madison's Defense of Civil Liberties." *William and Mary Quarterly* 5, no. 2 (1948): 145–76.

Koch, Adrienne and William Peden, eds. *The Life and Selected Writings of Thomas Jefferson*. New York: Modern Library, 1972.

Koschnik, Albrecht. "The Democratic Societies of Philadelphia and the Limits of the American Public Sphere, circa 1793–1795." *William and Mary Quarterly* 58, no. 3 (2001): 615–36.

Kramer, Larry D. *The People Themselves: Popular Constitutionalism and Judicial Review*. Oxford: Oxford University Press, 2004.

"The Interest of the Man: James Madison, Popular Constitutionalism, and the Theory of Deliberative Democracy." *Valparaiso University Law Review* 41, no. 2 (2007): 697–754.

La Vopa, Anthony J. "The Birth of Public Opinion." *Wilson Quarterly* 15 (1991): 46–55.

Lawler, Peter Augustine. "Religion, Philosophy, and the American Founding." In *Protestantism and the American Founding*, edited by Thomas S. Engeman and Michael P. Zuckert, 165–85. Notre Dame, Ind.: University of Notre Dame, 2004.

Leibiger, Stuart. *Founding Friendship*. Charlottesville: University of Virginia Press, 2001.

Lerner, Ralph. "Commerce and Character: The Anglo-American as New-Model Man." *William and Mary Quarterly* 36, no. 1 (1979): 3–26.

Le Trosne, Guillaume François. *De l'administration provinciale et de la réforme de l'impôt*. Basel, 1779.

Lewis, C. S. *The Abolition of Man*. New York: HarperCollins, 2001.

Lieberman, David. "The Mixed Constitution and the Common Law." In *The Cambridge History of Eighteenth-Century Political Thought*, edited by Mark Goldie and Robert Wokler, 317–46. Cambridge: Cambridge University Press, 2006.

Lindsay, A. D. *The Modern Democratic State*. New York: Oxford University Press, 1962.

Lutz, Donald. "The Relative Influence of European Writers on Late Eighteenth-Century American Political Thought." *American Political Science Review* 78, no. 1 (1984): 189–97.

Mably, Gabriel Bonnot de. *Doutes proposés aux philosophes économistes, sur l'Ordre naturel et essentiel des sociétés politiques*. The Hague: Durand, 1767.

Des droits et des devoirs du citoyen. Edited by Jean-Louis Lecercle. Paris: Didier, 1972.

Madison, James. "James Madison. Notes on the Social Compact." *The James Madison Papers*, The Library of Congress American Memory, Series 1: General Correspondence and Related Items, Image 1188. http://memory.loc.gov/ammem/collections/madison_papers/mjmser1.html.

Malone, Dumas. *Jefferson and the Ordeal of Liberty*. Boston: Little, Brown, 1962.

Manin, Bernard. "On Legitimacy and Political Deliberation." Translated by Elly Stein and Jane Mansbridge. *Political Theory* 15, no. 3 (1987): 345–48.

"Montesquieu." In *A Critical Dictionary of the French Revolution*, edited by François Furet and Mona Ozouf, 728–31. Cambridge, Mass.: Harvard University Press, 1989.

Mansfield, Harvey C. *Machiavelli's Virtue*. Chicago: University of Chicago Press, 1996.

Martin, Robert W. T. *The Free and Open Press: The Founding of American Democratic Press Liberty, 1640–1800*. New York: New York University Press, 2001.

"Reforming Republicanism: Alexander Hamilton's Theory of Republican Citizenship and Press Liberty." In *The Many Faces of Alexander Hamilton: The Life and Legacy of America's Most Elusive Founding Father*, edited by Douglas Ambrose and Robert W. T. Martin, 109–33. New York: New York University Press, 2006.

Matthews, Richard K. *If Men Were Angels: James Madison & the Heartless Empire of Reason*. Lawrence: University Press of Kansas, 1995.

McCoy, Drew R. "James Madison and Visions of American Nationality in the Confederation Period: A Regional Perspective." In *Beyond Confederation: Origins of the Constitution and American National Identity*, edited by Richard Beeman, Stephen Botein, and Edward C. Carter II, 226–60. Chapel Hill: University of North Carolina Press, 1987.

The Elusive Republic: Political Economy and the American Revolution. Chapel Hill: University of North Carolina Press, 1992.

McDonald, Forrest. *We the People: The Economic Origins of the Constitution*. Chicago: University of Chicago Press, 1958.

The Presidency of George Washington. New York: W. W. Norton, 1974.

Review of *The Papers of Alexander Hamilton*, Vols. XX–XXII. *William and Mary Quarterly* 33, no. 4 (1976): 677–80.

Alexander Hamilton. New York: W. W. Norton, 1979.

Novus Ordo Seclorum. Lawrence: University Press of Kansas, 1985.

McLean, Iain. "Thomas Jefferson, John Adams, and the Déclaration des Droits de l'Homme et du Citoyen." In *The Future of Liberal Democracy: Thomas Jefferson and the Contemporary World*, edited by Robert Fatton, Jr., and R. K. Ramazani, 13–30. New York: Palgrave Macmillan, 2004.

McLean, Iain and A. B. Urken. "Did Jefferson or Madison Understand Condorcet's Theory of Social Choice?" *Public Choice* 73, no. 4 (1992): 445–57.

Mercier, Louis-Sébastien. *Tableau de Paris: Nouvelle édition*, 12 vols. Amsterdam, 1782–88.

Meyers, Marvin. "The Least Imperfect Government: On Martin Diamond's 'Ethics and Politics.'" *Interpretation: A Journal of Political Philosophy* 8, no. 3 (1980): 5–15.

The Mind of the Founder: Sources of Political Thought of James Madison. Hanover, N.H.: Brandeis University Press, 1981.

Millar, John. *An Historical View of the English Government*, 4 vols. Edited by Mark Salber Phillips and Dale R. Smith. Indianapolis: Liberty Fund, 2006.

Miller, John C. *Alexander Hamilton & the Growth of the New Nation.* New York: Transaction Publishers, 2003.

Miller, Joshua. "The Ghostly Body Politic: The Federalist Papers and Popular Sovereignty." *Political Theory* 16, no. 1 (1988): 99–119.

Miller, Tiffany Jones. "James Madison's Republic of 'Mean Extent' Theory: Avoiding the Scylla and Charybdis of Republican Government." *Polity* 39, no. 4 (2007): 545–69.

Montesquieu, Charle-Louis de Secondat, Baron de La Brède et de. *De l'esprit des lois* (1748). Available at http://classiques.uqac.ca/classiques/montesquieu/de_esprit_des_lois/partie_6/esprit_des_lois_Livre_6.pdf.

The Spirit of Laws. Forthcoming. Translated by William B. Allen.

Necker, Jacques. *A Treatise on the Administration of the Finances of France*, 3 vols. Translated by Thomas Mortimer. London: J. Walter, 1785.

Nedelski, Jennifer. *Private Property and the Limits of American Constitutionalism: The Madisonian Framework and Its Legacy.* Chicago: University of Chicago Press, 1990.

Noelle-Neumann, Elisabeth. *The Spiral of Silence: Our Social Skin.* Chicago: University of Chicago Press, 1993.

O'Brien, Karen. "Robertson's Place in the Development of Eighteenth Century Narrative History." In *William Robertson and the Expansion of Empire*, edited by Stewart J. Brown, 74–91. Cambridge: Cambridge University Press, 1997.

Ostwald, Martin. *From Popular Sovereignty to the Sovereignty of Law: Law, Society, and Politics in Fifth-Century Athens.* Berkeley: University of California Press, 1986.

Ozouf, Mona. "'Public Opinion' at the End of the Old Regime." Translated by Lydia C. Cochrane. *The Journal of Modern History* 60 Supplement (1988): S1–S21.

Page, Benjamin I. and Robert Y. Shapiro. *The Rational Public: Fifty Years of Trends in Americans' Policy Preferences.* Chicago: University of Chicago Press, 1992.

Paley, William. *Principles of Moral and Political Philosophy.* In *Works of William Paley*, 4 vols., edited by Edmund Paley, 475–514. London: [1785] 1838.

Palmer, Paul A. "The Concept of Public Opinion in Political Theory." In *Essays in History and Political Theory, in Honor of C. H. McIlwain*. Edited by Carl Wittke, 230–57. Cambridge, Mass.: Harvard University Press, 1936.

Pangle, Thomas. *The Spirit of Modern Republicanism*. Chicago: University of Chicago Press, 1988.

Parini, Jay. *Robert Frost: A Life*. New York: Henry Holt, 1999.

Peach, W. Bernard and D. O. Thomas, eds. *The Correspondence of Richard Price*, 3 vols. Durham, N.C.: Duke University Press, 1991.

Peirce, Charles. *A Meteorological Account of the Weather in Philadelphia: From January 1, 1790, to January 1, 1847*. Philadelphia: Lindsay & Blakiston, 1847.

Peterson, Merrill D., ed. *The Portable Thomas Jefferson*. New York: Viking Press, 1975.

——— ed. *Public Papers of Thomas Jefferson*. New York: Library of America, 1984.

Peuchet, Jacques. "Discours préliminaire." In *Encyclopédie méthodique: Jurisprudence*, vol. 9, *Police et municipalités*. Paris, 1789.

Price, Richard. *Observations on the Importance of the American Revolution, and the Means of Making It a Benefit to the World*. Dublin, 1785.

——— *Observations on the Nature of Civil Liberty*. In *Political Writings*, edited by D. O. Thomas, 20–100. Cambridge: Cambridge University Press, [1776] 1991.

Quesnay, François. "*Évidence*." In *Encyclopédie*, vol. 6, edited by Denis Diderot, Jean Le Rand d'Alembert, et al. Paris: Briasson, 1756.

Rahe, Paul A. *Republics Ancient and Modern: Classical Republicanism and the American Revolution*. Chapel Hill: University of North Carolina Press, 1992.

——— *Republics Ancient and Modern*, 3 vols. Chapel Hill: University of North Carolina Press, 1994.

——— "Forms of Government: Structure, Principle, Object, and Aim." In *Montesquieu's Science of Politics: Essays on The Spirit of Laws*, 69–108. Lanham, Md.: Rowman & Littlefield, 2001.

——— "Between Trust and Distrust: The Federalist and the Emergency of Modern Republican Constitutionalism." In *1650–1850: Ideas, Aesthetics, and Inquiries in the Early Modern Era*, 14 vols., edited by Kevin L. Cope, 11: 375–406. New York: AMS Press, 2005.

——— "Machiavelli in the English Revolution." In *Machiavelli's Liberal Republican Legacy*, ed. Paul A. Rahe, 1–35. Cambridge: Cambridge University Press, 2006.

——— *Soft Despotism, Democracy's Drift*. New Haven, Conn.: Yale University Press, 2008.

Rakove, Jack N. *James Madison and the Creation of the American Republic*. Glenview, Ill.: Scott, Foresman/Little, Brown Higher Education, 1990.

——— *Original Meanings: Politics and Ideas in the Making of the Constitution*. New York: First Vintage Books, 1996.

——— ed. *James Madison: Writings*. New York: Library of America, 1999.

Raynal, Guillaume Thomas François. *Histoire philosophique et politique des établissemens . . . dans les deux Indes*. Amsterdam, 1770.

Read, James H. *Power versus Liberty: Madison, Hamilton, Wilson, and Jefferson*. Charlottesville: University Press of Virginia, 2000.

Rosanvallon, Pierre. "Political Rationalism and Democracy in France in the 18th and 19th Centuries." *Philosophy & Social Criticism* 28, no. 6 (2002): 687–701.

Rosen, Gary. *American Compact: James Madison and the Problem of Founding.* Lawrence: University Press of Kansas, 1999.

Rothschild, Emma. "Condorcet and the Conflict of Values." *The Historical Journal* 39, no. 3 (1996): 677–701.

Economic Sentiments: Adam Smith, Condorcet, and the Enlightenment. Cambridge, Mass.: Harvard University Press, 2001.

Rousseau, Jean-Jacques. *The Social Contract and Discourse on the Origin of Inequality.* Edited by Lester G. Crocker. New York: Washington Square Press, 1967.

Emile: On Education. Translated by Allan Bloom. New York: Basic Books, 1979.

Sayers, Dorothy L. *The Mind of the Maker.* San Francisco: HarperCollins, 1941.

Schambra, William A., ed. *As Far as Republican Principles Will Admit: Essays by Martin Diamond.* Washington, D.C.: AEI Press, 1992.

Schwarz, Michael. "The Great Divergence Reconsidered: Hamilton, Madison, and U.S.-British Relations, 1783–89." *Journal of the Early Republic* 27, no. 3 (2007): 407–36.

Sharp, James Roger. *American Politics in the Early Republic: The New Nation in Crisis.* New Haven, Conn.: Yale University Press, 1993.

Sheehan, Colleen A. "Public Opinion and the Formation of Civic Character in Madison's Republican Theory." *The Review of Politics* 67, no. 1 (Winter 2005): 43–44.

"The Commerce of Ideas and Cultivation of Character in Madison's Republic." In *Civic Education and Culture,* edited by Bradley C. Watson, 49–72. Wilmington, Del.: ISI Books, 2006.

In press. *Madison's Voyage to the World of the Classics.*

Smith, James Morton. "Alexander Hamilton, the Alien Law, and Seditious Libels." *Review of Politics* 16, no. 3 (1954): 305–33.

ed. *The Republic of Letters: The Correspondence between Thomas Jefferson and James Madison 1776–1826,* 3 vols. New York: W. W. Norton, 1995.

Smith, Steven D. *The Constitution and the Pride of Reason.* New York: Oxford University Press, 1998.

Smith, Troy E. "Divided *Publius*: Democracy, Federalism, and the Cultivation of Public Sentiment." *The Review of Politics* 69 (2007): 568–98.

Smith, T. V. "Thomas Jefferson and the Perfectibility of Mankind." *Ethics* 53, no. 4 (1943): 293–310.

The Society of American Archivists. "A Guide to Deeds of Gifts." http://www.archivists.org/publications/deed_of_gift.asp.

Staloff, Darren. *Hamilton, Adams, Jefferson: The Politics of Enlightenment and the American Founding.* New York: Hill and Wang, 2005.

Stourzh, Gerald. *Alexander Hamilton and the Idea of Republican Government.* Stanford, Calif.: Stanford University Press, 1970.

Strauss, Leo. *What Is Political Philosophy?* Westport, Conn.: Greenwood Press, 1959.

Lectures on Aristotle's *Politics,* Lecture XI:13–14. University of Chicago, autumn 1967, unpublished.

Liberalism Ancient and Modern. Ithaca, N.Y.: Cornell University Press, 1968.

Swift, Jonathan. *A Discourse of the Contests and Dissentions Between the Nobles and Commons in Athens and Rome.* Oxford: Clarendon Press, 1967.

Thompson, C. Bradley. *John Adams and the Spirit of Liberty*. Lawrence: University Press of Kansas, 2002.

Thompson, Lawrance. *Robert Frost*, 3 vols. New York: Holt, Rinehart & Winston, 1966–76.

Thompson, Lawrance and R. H. Winnick. *Robert Frost: The Later Years, 1938–1963*. New York: Holt, Rinehart & Winston, 1976.

Tocqueville, Alexis de. *Democracy in America*. Edited by J. P. Mayer. New York: Harper Perennial, 1969.

Toriccelli, Robert G. and Andrew Carroll, eds. *In Our Own Words: Extraordinary Speeches of the American Century*. New York: Kodansha International, 1999.

Trees, Andrew S. *The Founding Fathers and the Politics of Character*. Princeton, N.J.: Princeton University Press, 2003.

Van Doren, Mark. "The American Poet." *Atlantic Monthly* 187 (1951): 32–34.

Wade, Ira O. *The Structure and Form of the French Enlightenment*, 2 vols. Princeton, N.J.: Princeton University Press, 1977.

Walling, Karl-Frederich. *Republican Empire: Alexander Hamilton on War and Free Government*. Lawrence: University Press of Kansas, 1999.

Webking, Robert. *The American Revolution and the Politics of Liberty*. Baton Rouge: Louisiana State University Press, 1988.

White, Morton. *Philosophy, The Federalist, and the Constitution*. Oxford: Oxford University Press, 1987.

Whitman, Willson, ed. *Jefferson's Letters*. Eau Claire, Wis.: E. M. Hale and Company, 1940.

Wiebe, Robert. *The Opening of American Society: From the Adoption of the Constitution to the Eve of Disunion*. New York: Alfred A. Knopf, 1984.

Willert, P. F. *Mirabeau*. London: Macmillan & Co., 1923.

Wills, Garry. *Inventing America: Jefferson's Declaration of Independence*. Garden City, N.Y.: Doubleday, 1978.

——— . *Explaining America: The Federalist*. Garden City, N.Y.: Doubleday, 1981.

Wood, Gordon. *The Creation of the American Republic, 1776–1787*. Chapel Hill: University of North Carolina Press, 1969.

——— . "Interests and Disinterestedness in the Making of the Constitution." In *Beyond Confederation: Origins of the Constitution and American National Identity*, edited by Richard Beeman, Stephen Botein, and Edward C. Carter, 69–112. Chapel Hill: University of North Carolina Press, 1987.

——— . *Revolutionary Characters: What Made the Founders Different*. New York: Penguin Press, 2006.

Wootton, David. "Liberty, Metaphor, and Mechanism: The Origins of Modern Constitutionalism." In *Liberty and American Experience in the Eighteenth Century*, edited by D. Womersley, 209–74. Indianapolis: Liberty Fund, 2006.

Worden, Blair. "Marchamont Nedham and the Beginnings of English Republicanism, 1649–1656." In *Republicanism, Liberty, and Commercial Society, 1649–1776*, edited by David Wootton, 45–81. Stanford, Calif.: Stanford University Press, 1994.

——— . "'Wit in a Roundhead': The Dilemma of Marchamont Nedham." In *Political Culture and Cultural Politics in Early Modern England: Essays Presented to*

David Underdown, edited by Susan D. Amussen and Mark A. Kishlansky, 301–37. Manchester, U.K.: Manchester University Press, 1995.

Worden, Blair and Joad Raymond, "The Cracking of the Republican Spokes." *Prose Studies* 19 (1996): 255–74.

Wright, Johnson Kent. *A Classical Republican in Eighteenth-Century France: The Political Thought of Mably*. Stanford, Calif.: Stanford University Press, 1997.

Yankelovich, Daniel. *Coming to Public Judgment: Making Democracy Work in a Complex World*. Syracuse, N.Y.: Syracuse University Press, 1991.

Yarbrough, Jean. "Jefferson and Property Rights." In *Liberty, Property, and the Foundations of the American Constitution*, edited by Ellen Frankel Paul and Howard Dickman, 65–84. Albany: State University of New York Press, 1989.

Zuckert, Michael P. *The Natural Rights Republic: Studies in the Foundation of the American Political Tradition*. Notre Dame, Ind.: University of Notre Dame Press, 1996.

Zvesper, John. *Political Philosophy and Rhetoric: A Study of the Origins of American Political Parties*. Cambridge: Cambridge University Press, 1977.

"The Madisonian Systems." *The Western Political Quarterly* 37, no. 2 (1984): 236–56.

Index